Welcome to

Introduction to Educational Research
with Research Navigator™

This text contains some special features designed to aid you in the research process and in writing research papers. As you read this textbook, you will see special Research Navigator™ (RN) icons cueing you to visit the Research Navigator™ Web site to research important concepts of the text.

> To gain access to Research Navigator™, go to **www.researchnavigator.com** and login using the passcode you'll find on the inside front cover of your text.

Research Navigator™ includes three databases of dependable source material to get your research process started.

■ **EBSCO's ContentSelect Academic Journal Database**   EBSCO's ContentSelect Academic Journal Database contains scholarly, peer-reviewed journals. These published articles provide you with specialized knowledge and information about your research topic. Academic journal articles adhere to strict scientific guidelines for methodology and theoretical grounding. The information obtained in these individual articles is more scientific than information you would find in a popular magazine, in a newspaper article, or on a Web page.

■ **The New York Times Search by Subject Archive**™   Newspapers are considered periodicals because they are issued in regular installments (i.e., daily, weekly, or monthly) and provide contemporary information. Information in periodicals—journals, magazines, and newspapers—may be useful, or even critical, for finding up-to-date material or information to support specific aspects of your topic. Research Navigator™ gives you access to a one-year, "search by subject" archive of articles from one of the world's leading newspapers—*The New York Times*.

■ **"Best of the Web" Link Library**   Link Library, the third database included on Research Navigator™, is a collection of Web links organized by academic subject and key terms. Searching on your key terms will provide you with a list of five to seven editorially reviewed Web sites that offer educationally relevant and reliable content. The Web links in Link Library are monitored and updated each week, reducing your incidence of finding "dead" links.

In addition, Research Navigator™ includes extensive online content detailing the steps in the research process, including:

■ Starting the research process

■ Finding and evaluating sources

■ Citing sources

■ Internet research

■ Using your library

■ Starting to write

For more information on how to use Research Navigator™ go to
www.ablongman.com/aboutrn.com.

Introduction to Educational Research

FIFTH EDITION

Introduction to Educational Research

Craig A. Mertler
Bowling Green State University

C. M. Charles
Emeritus, San Diego State University

PEARSON

Boston ■ New York ■ San Francisco
Mexico City ■ Montreal ■ Toronto ■ London ■ Madrid ■ Munich ■ Paris
Hong Kong ■ Singapore ■ Tokyo ■ Cape Town ■ Sydney

Senior Editor: *Arnis E. Burvikovs*
Editorial Assistant: *Megan Smallidge*
Marketing Manager: *Tara Whorf*
Production Administrator: *Michael Granger*
Editorial-Production Service: *Omegatype Typography, Inc.*
Composition Buyer: *Linda Cox*
Manufacturing Buyer: *Andrew Turso*
Cover Administrator: *Joel Gendron*
Electronic Composition: *Omegatype Typography, Inc.*

For related titles and support materials, visit our online catalog at www.ablongman.com.

Between the time Website information is gathered and then published, it is not unusual for some sites to have closed. Also, the transcription of URLs can result in typographical errors. The publisher would appreciate notification where these errors occur so that they may be corrected in subsequent editions.

Many of the designations used by manufacturers and sellers to distinguish their products are claimed as trademarks. Where those designations appear in this book, and Allyn and Bacon was aware of a trademark claim, the designations have been printed in initial or all caps.

Library of Congress Cataloging-in-Publication Data

Mertler, Craig A.
   Introduction to educational research / Craig A. Mertler, C. M. Charles. — 5th ed.
     p. cm.
   Charles's name appears first on the earlier edition.
   Includes bibliographical references and indexes.
   ISBN 0-205-41412-5
    1. Education—Research. I. Charles, C. M. II. Title.

LB1028.C515 2005
370'.7'2—dc22

                        2004043670

Printed in the United States of America
10   9   8   7   6   5   4   3   2   1   09   08   07   06   05   04

In memory
of my father, Chuck . . .
for helping me to understand why it's important
to always take pride in my work!

~C.A.M.

CONTENTS

Preface   xix

Using Research Navigator™   xxv

PART ONE   Orientation to Educational Research   1

1   Educational Research: Its Nature and Rules
of Operation   1

Preview   1

Targeted Learnings   1

Chapter Information Organizers   2

New Questions about Elmwood's Schools   3

Seeking Answers to Questions   3

The Scientific Method   5

Research and the Scientific Method   6

The Meaning of Research   6

The Process of Educational Research   7

Research and Educational Research   9

Rules of Operation in Educational Research   9

Legal Principles   10

Ethical Principles   11

■ APPLYING TECHNOLOGY   Human Subjects Research Approval   12

Philosophical Principles   15

Procedural Principles   16

Educators as Researchers   19

■ APPLYING TECHNOLOGY   Ethics and Standards of Research   20

■ DEVELOPMENTAL ACTIVITY   Guiding Principles of Research   21

Chapter Summary   22

List of Important Terms   23

Your Current Status   23

Activities for Thought and Discussion   23

Answers to Chapter Exercises   24

References and Recommended Readings   24

2   **Types of Educational Research and Corresponding
Sources of Data   25**

   Preview   25

   Targeted Learnings   26

   Variables and Educational Research   26

      Continuous, Discrete, and Dichotomous Variables   26

      Independent and Dependent Variables   28

   Types of Educational Research   28

      Types of Research Categorized by Practicality   28

      Types of Research Differentiated by Methodology   29

      Types of Research Defined by Questions Addressed   30

   Primary and Secondary Sources of Research Data   35

   Specific Sources of Research Data   36

   Procedures Used in Collecting Data   37

   Qualities Required in Research Data   39

      Authenticity and Believability   39

      Validity and Reliability   40

   Treatment and Presentation of Data   41

      ■ **APPLYING TECHNOLOGY**   More about Variables and Questions   42

   Additional Terminology Related to Data   42

      Participants, Samples, and Populations   43

      ■ **DEVELOPMENTAL ACTIVITY**   Type of Research   43

   Chapter Summary   44

   List of Important Terms   45

   Your Current Status   45

   Activities for Thought and Discussion   45

   Answers to Chapter Exercises   46

   References and Recommended Readings   46

P A R T   T W O   **Preliminary Skills Needed
for Conducting Research   47**

3   **Selecting, Refining, and Proposing a
Topic for Research   47**

   Preview   47

   Targeted Learnings   47

   Where to Find Good Research Topics   49

Topics for Teachers   49

Topics for Administrators   50

Topics for Other Educators   51

Preliminary Considerations in Selecting Topics   51

■ **APPLYING TECHNOLOGY**   Sources for Research Topics   52

Refining the Research Topic   54

Some Necessary Terminology   55

Regulating the Size of Research Topics   60

Foreseeing the Research Report Format   61

The Value of Conventional Procedures and Reports   62

Refining the Topic: An Illustrative Case   63

Jan's Concern about Students' Entry Age to Kindergarten   63

Preparing a Research Proposal   65

■ **DEVELOPMENTAL ACTIVITY**   Research Topic Refinement   67

Chapter Summary   68

List of Important Terms   69

Your Current Status   69

Activities for Thought and Discussion   69

Answers to Chapter Exercises   70

References and Recommended Readings   70

4   **Locating Published Research   71**

Preview   71

Targeted Learnings   71

Using the Research Library   72

Secondary Sources in the Library   73

Locating Secondary Sources   76

Primary Sources in the Library   76

Specific Directories of Primary References   77

Locating Primary Sources   79

■ **APPLYING TECHNOLOGY**   Electronic Journals   82

■ **APPLYING TECHNOLOGY**   Searching ERIC Online   83

A Purposeful Visit to the Library   87

**Not Just for Conducting Research—Valuable Sources
for Professional Development   88**

■ **DEVELOPMENTAL ACTIVITY**   Locating Published Research   88

Chapter Summary   89

List of Important Terms   90

Your Current Status   90

Activities for Thought and Discussion   90
Answers to Chapter Exercises   91
References and Recommended Readings   91

5   Interpreting and Summarizing
Published Research   92

Preview   92
Targeted Learnings   92
Reading Research Reports   93
    Skimming the Information   93
    Summarizing the Reports   95
Interpreting the Statistical Information You Encounter   98
    ■ APPLYING TECHNOLOGY   Writing a Review of Literature   99
    Status Reports   100
    Review of Terminology Used in Status Reports   103
    Comparison Reports   103
    Review of Terminology Used in Comparison Reports   106
    Correlational Reports   106
    Review of Terminology Used in Correlational Reports   107
The Concept of Significance   108
    ■ DEVELOPMENTAL ACTIVITY   Reviewing Published Research   110
Chapter Summary   111
List of Important Terms   112
Your Current Status   112
Activities for Thought and Discussion   112
Answers to Chapter Exercises   113
References and Recommended Readings   113

PART THREE   Conducting Your Own Research Project   114

6   Designing a Research Project   114

Preview   114
Targeted Learnings   114
How Planning Should Be Done   115
The Approach to Planning Advocated in This Book   116
Tasks to Be Accomplished When Planning Research   116

Task 1. State the Topic, Problem, and Questions and/or Hypotheses   117

Task 2. Outline the Library Search for Related Information   122

Task 3. Identify Needed Data and Sources   124

Task 4. List the Steps You Will Need to Carry Out to Complete the Study   126

Task 5. Specify the Procedures and Tools You Will Employ in Collecting Data   127

Task 6. Foresee How Data Can Best Be Analyzed and Interpreted   128

Task 7. Anticipate the Appropriate Report Format for Your Research   129

■ **APPLYING TECHNOLOGY**   More Guidelines for Reports   130

Illustrative Example of Planning a Research Project   131

Topic and Problem   131

Examination of the Literature   132

Required Data and Data Sources   132

Appraisal of Holly's Plan   133

■ **DEVELOPMENTAL ACTIVITY**   Planning for Your Research   134

Chapter Summary   135

List of Important Terms   135

Your Current Status   136

Activities for Thought and Discussion   136

References and Recommended Readings   136

7   Procedures and Tools for Gathering Data   137

Preview   137

Targeted Learnings   137

Types of Research and Their Typical Foci   139

Types of Data Needed   140

Sources of Data for Various Types of Research   140

Samples and Their Selection   141

Are Samples Necessary in Research?   141

Can Small Samples Represent Large Populations?   142

Probability Sampling   142

Nonprobability Sampling   143

■ **APPLYING TECHNOLOGY**   Probability and Nonprobability Sampling   145

Size of Samples   146

Relationships among Research Focus, Data, Source, and Sample   148

Validity and Reliability in Data Collection   148

Validity of Data   148

Determining Validity of Test Data   148

Determining Validity of Non-Test Data   149

Reliability of Data   150

Determining Reliability of Test Data   150

Determining Reliability of Non-Test Data   151

Relationship between Validity and Reliability   151

Procedures in Data Collection   151

Notation   152

Description   152

Analysis   153

Questioning   154

Testing   157

■ **APPLYING TECHNOLOGY**   Survey Construction   158

■ **APPLYING TECHNOLOGY**   Searchable Online Test Locators   159

Measurement   160

Relationships between Types of Research and Data Collection   161

A Composite of Research Types and Data Collection Procedures   163

Data Collection Profiles   163

■ **DEVELOPMENTAL ACTIVITY**   Data Collection Decisions   163

Chapter Summary   165

List of Important Terms   166

Your Current Status   166

Activities for Thought and Discussion   166

Answers to Chapter Exercises   167

References and Recommended Readings   167

8   Analyzing Research Data and Presenting Findings   168

Preview   168

Targeted Learnings   169

Qualitative Data and Quantitative Data   170

An Example of Qualitative Analysis   171

An Example of Quantitative Analysis   172

Analyzing Ethnographic Data   173

Cautions and Reminders in Qualitative Data Analysis   175

Analyzing Quantitative Data   176

Populations and Parameters; Samples and Statistics   176

What Statistics Are Used For   177

Descriptive Statistics and Inferential Statistics   179

■ **APPLYING TECHNOLOGY**   More about Statistics   182

■ **APPLYING TECHNOLOGY**   Interactive Statistical Calculations
Using StatCrunch   183

Cautions in Using Statistics   187

■ **APPLYING TECHNOLOGY**   Selecting an Appropriate Statistical Test   188

Presenting Your Findings   188

■ **DEVELOPMENTAL ACTIVITY**   Statistical Analysis Decisions   189

Chapter Summary   191

List of Important Terms   191

Your Current Status   191

Activities for Thought and Discussion   192

Answers to Chapter Exercises   192

References and Recommended Readings   192

9   Preparing a Research Report   193

Preview   193

Targeted Learnings   193

Conventions in Research and Reporting   194

Conventions of Style   195

Title   195

Person and Voice   195

Tense   196

Tentative versus Definitive Statements   196

Simplicity of Language   197

Consistency   197

Conventions of Format   198

Introduction   198

Review of Related Literature   199

Procedures or Method   201

Findings or Results   201

Conclusions or Discussion   204

Front and Back Material   205

Style Guides   205

A Composite Outline of Format Conventions   206

■ **APPLYING TECHNOLOGY**   Organizing Research Papers
with TakeNote!   207

Sample Pages   208

For Research Papers and Journal Articles   208

For Masters' Theses   211

For a Thesis That Reports Action Research   211

Thesis Format for Other Types of Research   218

■ DEVELOPMENTAL ACTIVITY   Preparing to Write Your Report   221

Chapter Summary   222

List of Important Terms   222

Your Current Status   223

Activities for Thought and Discussion   223

Answers to Chapter Exercises   223

PART FOUR   **Procedures and Exemplars in Eight Types of Research   224**

10   Ethnographic Research   224

Preview   224

Targeted Learnings   224

The Nature of Ethnographic Research   225

Topics in Ethnographic Research   226

Procedures in Ethnographic Research   226

The Richness of Ethnographic Research   228

Strengths and Concerns in Ethnographic Research   229

An Example of Ethnographic Research: "Teachers in Bars: From Professional to Personal Self"   229

Organizing for Ethnographic Research   239

■ Additional Examples of Published Ethnographic Studies   240

■ APPLYING TECHNOLOGY   More about Qualitative Research   241

Chapter Summary   242

List of Important Terms   243

Activities for Thought and Discussion   243

Answers to Chapter Exercises   244

References and Recommended Readings   244

11   Action Research and Evaluation Research   245

Preview   245

Targeted Learnings   245

Action Research   247

The Importance of Action Research   247

Characteristics of Action Research   248

An Example   250

The Action Research Process   252

A Published Example of Action Research: "Designing an
Authentic Assessment"   253

Review of Action Research   257

Organizing for Action Research   257

■ Additional Examples of Published Action Research Studies   258

Strengths and Cautions in Action Research   260

Evaluation Research   260

Evaluating Methods, Materials, and Programs   261

An Example of Evaluation Research: "Class Size Does Make a Difference"   262

Organizing for Evaluation Research   267

■ Additional Examples of Published Evaluation Research Studies   268

■ **APPLYING TECHNOLOGY**   More About Action
and Evaluation Research   270

Chapter Summary   272

Activities for Thought and Discussion   272

Answers to Chapter Exercises   273

References and Recommended Readings   274

12   Descriptive Research and Historical Research   275

Preview   275

Targeted Learnings   275

The Nature of Descriptive Research and Historical Research   277

Purpose and Topics   277

Hypotheses and Questions   277

Data Sources and Collection   277

Tools for Obtaining Data   279

Treatment and Analysis of Data   281

**An Example of Descriptive Research: "Urban Teachers
Who Quit: Why They Leave and What They Do"   281**

■ Additional Examples of Published Descriptive Studies   285

**An Example of Historical Research: "An A Is Not an A
Is Not an A: A History of Grading"   285**

■ Additional Examples of Published Historical Studies   289

Organizing for Descriptive Research and Historical Research   290

Case Study   291

Purposes of a Case Study   291

■ **APPLYING TECHNOLOGY**   More about Descriptive
and Historical Research   291

Organizing and Conducting the Case Study   292

Chapter Summary   **293**

Activities for Thought and Discussion   **294**

Answers to Chapter Exercises   **294**

References and Recommended Readings   **294**

13   **Correlational Research**   **295**

Preview   **295**

Targeted Learnings   **295**

Weather and the Process of Education   **296**

Correlations   **297**

The Nature of Correlational Research   **298**

Cautions Concerning Cause and Effect   **298**

Topics for Correlational Research   **299**

Hypotheses and Questions in Correlational Research   **299**

Correlational Research Design   **300**

Data Sources and Collection   **301**

What Can Be Correlated and How   **301**

   Product-Moment Correlation   301

   Biserial Correlation and Point-Biserial Correlation   302

   Phi Correlation and Tetrachoric Correlation   302

   Correlations from Rankings   302

Multivariate Correlations   **302**

   Partial Correlation   302

   Multiple Regression   303

   Discriminant Analysis   303

   Factor Analysis   303

An Example of Correlational Research: "Relationship of Computer Science Aptitude with Selected Achievement Measures among Junior High Students"   **303**

Organizing for Correlational Research   **306**

   ■ Additional Examples of Published Correlational Studies   307

   Selecting the Variables   308

   Stating Questions or Hypotheses   309

   Assessing and Quantifying the Variables   309

   Selecting a Sample   310

   Collecting Data   310

   Analyzing the Data   310

   ■ Applying Technology   More about Correlational Research   311

Chapter Summary   **312**

List of Important Terms   **313**

Activities for Thought and Discussion   313

Answers to Chapter Exercises   313

References and Recommended Readings   314

14   Experimental, Quasi-Experimental, and Causal-Comparative Research   315

Preview   315

Targeted Learnings   315

The Search for Causation   317

Experimental Research   317

Quasi-Experimental Research   318

Causal-Comparative Research   318

Fundamentals of Experimental and Quasi-Experimental Research   319

Cause and Effect   319
Random Selection and Assignment   319
Use of Experimental Research   319
Experimental Designs   320
Quasi-Experimental Designs   323

The Commonality of Experimental and Quasi-Experimental Designs   324

Threats to Internal and External Validity   325

An Example of Experimental Research: "The Development of a Positive Self-Concept in Preservice Teachers"   326

■ Additional Examples of Published Experimental Studies   332

Causal-Comparative Research   333

The Nature of Causal-Comparative Research   333
Conducting Causal-Comparative Research   335

An Example of Causal-Comparative Research: "The Relation of Gender and Academic Achievement to Career Self-Efficacy and Interests"   336

■ Additional Examples of Published Causal-Comparative Studies   344

Chapter Summary   344

■ **APPLYING TECHNOLOGY**   More about Experimental and Quasi-Experimental Research Designs   345

List of Important Terms   346

Activities for Thought and Discussion   346

Answers to Chapter Exercises   347

References and Recommended Readings   347

Appendix A
Overview of Statistical Concepts and Procedures   348

The Nature and Uses of Statistics   348

Populations and Samples   349

Parametric Statistics and Nonparametric Statistics   350

The Calculation and Interpretation of Descriptive Statistics   351

Measures of Central Tendency   351

Measures of Variability   352

Relative Position   355

Relationships   355

Descriptive Statistics and the Normal Probability Curve   357

Relative Standings Associated with the Normal Curve   358

Percentile Rankings   359

Stanines   359

Z Scores   359

T Scores   360

Calculating and Interpreting Inferential Statistics   360

Chi-Square—Its Calculation and Interpretation   362

Calculating and Interpreting Standard Error and Confidence Limits   363

Testing for Significance   366

Type I and Type II Errors   368

Review of Statistical Terminology   369

List of Important Terms   369

Answers to Exercises   370

Appendix B
Using *TakeNote!* to Organize Your
Research Reports   371

Overview   371

A *TakeNote!* Sample Project   371

Glossary   382

Name Index   389

Subject Index   391

PREFACE

For Whom This Book Is Intended

Introduction to Educational Research, fifth edition, is designed specifically for educators who are new to research and seeking advanced degrees in graduate studies. Most users will be in-service teachers, administrators, special education personnel, coaches, and counselors, but the book is also appropriate for graduate students not yet actively teaching. No prior familiarity with the principles, procedures, or terminology of educational research is required in order to profit fully from this book.

Purposes of the Book

This book has two main purposes, which receive attention simultaneously. The first is to provide knowledge about educational research, sufficient for a clear understanding of the following:

- The ethical and philosophical principles adhered to in research
- The nature of research and the scientific process it employs
- Research questions, hypotheses, and hypothesis testing
- The various types of research and their purposes, traits, and designs
- The characteristics, sources, and collection of data
- Procedures for analyzing qualitative and quantitative data
- Published research, where it is found in the library, and how it is interpreted

The second purpose of this book, a purpose that has been made preeminent in this edition (as well as in its immediate predecessor), is to help graduate students conduct their own research. Toward that end, specific guidance is provided in

- Identifying satisfactory topics for research
- Framing research questions and subquestions
- Stating research hypotheses and null hypotheses
- Identifying the type of research called for in various topics
- Preparing a research proposal for a selected topic
- Conducting a thorough library search of literature
- Analyzing types of research appropriate for investigating selected topics
- Identifying needed data, their sources, and the procedures by which data are collected
- Analyzing data appropriately
- Answering research questions and testing hypotheses
- Stating findings and drawing conclusions
- Preparing research reports

Organization of the Book

In keeping with the purposes of helping students organize and undertake research while simultaneously acquiring fundamental knowledge about research, the book is organized into four parts, as follows:

Part One: Orientation to Educational Research. Clarifies the nature of research, explains its rules of operation, identifies standard types of educational research, and reviews the sources of data employed in those types of research.

Part Two: Preliminary Skills Needed for Conducting Research. Includes selecting, refining, and proposing a topic for research; locating published research in the library; and interpreting, summarizing, and annotating published research.

Part Three: Conducting Your Own Research Project. Shows users how to design their own research projects; clarifies the procedures and tools they need for gathering data in their investigations; explains how to analyze qualitative and quantitative research data, present findings, and draw conclusions; and takes students step by step through preparing an appropriate research report.

Part Four: Procedures and Exemplars in Eight Types of Research. Provides details about how the eight major types of research—ethnographic research, action research, evaluation research, descriptive research, historical research, correlational research, experimental and quasi-experimental research, and causal-comparative research—are planned and conducted. Published research reports that exemplify these types of research are reprinted in the chapters.

Chapters in the Book

The book is composed of 14 chapters, two appendixes, and a glossary. The first nine chapters are sequenced to provide direct guidance in planning, conducting, and reporting research. The last five chapters present types of research and exemplars for study and analysis. Chapter titles are:

Chapter 1.   Educational Research: Its Nature and Rules of Operation
Chapter 2.   Types of Educational Research and Corresponding Sources of Data
Chapter 3.   Selecting, Refining, and Proposing a Topic for Research
Chapter 4.   Locating Published Research
Chapter 5.   Interpreting and Summarizing Published Research
Chapter 6.   Designing a Research Project
Chapter 7.   Procedures and Tools for Gathering Data
Chapter 8.   Analyzing Research Data and Presenting Findings
Chapter 9.   Preparing a Research Report

Chapter 10. Ethnographic Research

Chapter 11. Action Research and Evaluation Research

Chapter 12. Descriptive Research and Historical Research

Chapter 13. Correlational Research

Chapter 14. Experimental, Quasi-Experimental, and Causal-Comparative Research

Certain courses may well require a sequence different from that presented here. Modifications can and should be made to meet the needs of instructors and students.

Chapter Formats

Chapters are formatted to include the following sections:

Preview. Presented at the beginning of each chapter, the preview provides a brief but thorough overview of what is to come in the chapter. These previews help readers anticipate and focus on the major topics presented in the chapter.

Targeted Learnings. After examining the preview, readers are directed to look especially for information related to specific chapter topics. These targeted learnings are repeated at the ends of chapters and are helpful for review and self-testing.

Chapter Information Organizer. Immediately following the targeted learnings, a graphic organizer is presented that shows chapter organization and content. These organizers are helpful as advance organizers for learning and as vehicles for review.

The Body of the Chapter. Here, the information, examples, and other explanations that convey chapter contents are presented. Interspersed within the body of the chapter are *application exercises* that call on readers to interpret or make realistic applications of what they have learned. These exercises are intended to enliven the reading, keep learners actively involved, and reinforce what has been learned.

Applying Technology. This section contains relatively brief presentations and/or discussions of topics related to the contents of the chapter and incorporates the use of technology. Specific topics for the Applying Technology section do not consist of a reiteration of the material in the chapter text; rather, this section contains material that could be considered secondary in nature but that can be used to exemplify or extend the content being discussed. Typically, these sections emphasize technology applications or related websites. Several chapters contain multiple Applying Technology sections.

Companion Website Highlight. This edition of the text is substantially enhanced by the inclusion of a Companion Website. Features of the Companion Website that are specifically highlighted in the chapters include supplemental materials that support the text material but that were not appropriate for inclusion in the text. These items appear in a format suitable for students to download and print out for their individual use. Examples of these highlighted items include:

- A sample guide for evaluating research
- A sample research proposal rating scale
- A research planning guide checklist
- Sample surveys
- Sample research proposals
- Statistical decision-making trees for both descriptive and inferential statistics
- A sample data file (which students can download and gain experience with data analysis)
- Several sample research studies

The Companion Website may be found at www.ablongman.com/mertler5e.

Chapter Summary. A brief résumé is presented at the end of each chapter that reiterates the major points covered in the body of the chapter. These summaries help readers tie the information together succinctly.

List of Important Terms. Following the chapter summary, a list of important terms discussed in the chapter is presented. Definitions of the terms are not provided; hence, the list is useful for review, discussion, and student self-testing. Although the definitions are not provided, a glossary has been provided near the end of the book.

Your Current Status. This section follows the list of important terms near the end of each chapter. It provides a cumulative look at the progress the reader has made through the specific chapter. This knowledge reinforces learning and fosters a sense of accomplishment.

Activities for Thought and Discussion. Presented at the end of each chapter are four to six additional activities that call on students to interpret or apply information presented in the chapter. Students are encouraged to explore the activities individually or in groups. The topics and their interpretations can be used for lively and informative class discussions.

Answers to Chapter Exercises. Suitable answers are presented for the in-text exercises included in the chapter. Alternative answers not presented are often correct; disagreement concerning answers provides students with a valuable opportunity for discussion and exploring concepts in greater depth.

References and Recommended Readings. In-chapter references are cited in this section. Also included are lists of works that have not been cited but that relate to the chapter contents and are recommended for additional supplemental reading.

Statistical Procedures

Fundamental statistical concepts and procedures appropriate for beginning students of educational research are presented as needed in various chapters. They are explained in relation to the analysis of specific research data and are clarified through many examples; thus, they are not intimidating to the reader. In-depth coverage of statistical topics is presented in Appendix A.

Appendix A

Following the final chapter of the text, an appendix is presented that presents an overview of statistical concepts and treatments in more depth than is offered elsewhere in the text. That information is assembled in Appendix A for reference or more advanced study.

Appendix B

A new appendix, containing an overview, explanations, and examples of the software program titled *TakeNote!* has been added to this edition. *TakeNote!* is an efficient and easy-to-use program that assists users in organizing and writing research reports that can be ordered as a package option by contacting your local sales representative.

Glossary

Research terminology introduced in the text is listed and defined in the glossary.

Changes from the Fourth Edition

Users familiar with the previous edition of this book will see several changes, the most substantial of which are intended only to enhance the previous editions of the text. These changes include:

- The incorporation of *Research Navigator*™, which provides free access to the EBSCO Information Services searchable database of published research articles, many of which are available in full-text format
- The inclusion of *TakeNote!* research report writing software as a supplement to the text (ordered as a package option by contacting your local sales representative)
- Revisions to Chapter 11 (Action Research and Evaluation Research)
- The reorganization of Part Four (Procedures and Exemplars in Eight Types of Research) such that the sequence of methods chapters flows from *less* formal and structured to *most* formal and structured
- The inclusion of a continuous activity (called a developmental activity) in Chapters 1 through 9 with the overarching theme of research proposal development that takes students step-by-step through many of the decisions they must make when designing a research study
- The incorporation of marginal notations in the published research articles that appear in Chapters 10 through 14
- A listing of additional or alternative research articles, available through *Research Navigator*™, for Chapters 10 through 14 that exemplify the particular type of research
- Verification of all website URLs that appear in the textbook, specifically in the Applying Technology sections
- A new appendix that contains explanations and examples of *TakeNote!* research report writing software

In addition, the Companion Website (www.ablongman.com/mertler5e) has been updated to reflect changes made to the fifth edition of the text.

Special Features

This book has several special features to increase the appeal and value to readers while also facilitating the instructor's presentation of material.

Sequenced to Assist Doing Research

As with the previous edition, the book remains organized to help users plan and conduct their first educational research projects. By proceeding through chapter contents, and by completing the in-text exercises as well as the developmental activities, users will simultaneously prepare a research plan on a topic of importance and will learn how to obtain and analyze data, answer research questions and test hypotheses, and prepare a proper report of their projects.

Readability: Organization and Style

This fifth edition demonstrates continued refinement in clarity and readability, a trait that many users consider to be a major strength. Throughout, unfamiliar terms are highlighted, and clear definitions are provided. Many examples are provided to make concepts and applications more understandable. At the same time, the material is kept concise, resulting in a book that covers essential concepts without overwhelming the reader.

Pedagogical Features

In keeping with the main purpose of helping users clearly understand and apply research concepts, many pedagogical features have been included in the book. These features include:

- Chapter previews—provide accurate anticipation of what is to be covered
- Chapter targeted learnings—provide lists of key understandings that students are to acquire
- Chapter organizers—offer graphic depictions of contents and organization of the chapters
- In-text application exercises—give periodic breaks for students to respond to new information, appearing in shaded boxes for emphasis
- Chapter summaries—help students comprehend chapter contents succinctly
- Current status—helps students see the progress they have made and what comes next
- Lists of important terms—provide opportunity for review and self-testing
- End-of-chapter activities—enable practice, reflection, and discussion
- Appendix of statistical concepts—reviews and expands statistical concepts and procedures introduced in other chapters as appropriate
- Expanded glossary—offers easy reference to research terminology

Reprinted Research Reports

Eight reprinted journal articles are included that exemplify various types of research. These relatively nontechnical articles have been specially selected to serve as exemplars to orient and encourage students who wish to conduct similar types of research. Guided activities and questions for discussion are provided to help students analyze the articles. In addition, each chapter in Part Four includes a list of additional published articles, easily accessible via *Research Navigator*™.

Glossary

A glossary of more than 250 terms important in educational research has been provided for easy student reference. The terms are highlighted in boldface when first appearing in the text. This is one of the most comprehensive glossaries presented in any educational research textbook.

Instructor's Manual

An instructor's manual is available online to instructors who adopt the text. The instructor's manual contains:

- Organizational suggestions—such as planning a course syllabus; selecting course assignments and activities; and establishing evaluation procedures
- Instructional suggestions—such as introducing the text to students; selecting and presenting contents and activities in class sessions; guiding students in critiquing research reports; guiding students in using the computer as a research tool; and helping students develop tools for data collection
- Test items—including short-answer tests and essay tests

Acknowledgments

We would like to acknowledge the contributions of several individuals who made the work on this edition proceed quite smoothly. We would like to thank the staff at Allyn & Bacon Publishing—in particular, Arnis E. Burvikovs, our editor, and Christine Lyons—for their feedback and support. We would certainly be remiss if we did not acknowledge the valuable comments and suggestions provided by the reviewers of this fifth edition:

Laura Shea Doolan, St. Joseph's College
Ncdra Skaggs Wheeler, Western Kentucky University

In addition, we would like to thank the following reviewers who have kindly analyzed previous editions of the text and have offered many valuable comments and suggestions over the years:

Beate Baltes, National University
Julie Bao, Shippensburg University
Kevin D. Crehan, University of Nevada at Las Vegas
Alvirda Farmer, San Jose State University
Charlotte Webb Farr, University of Wyoming
Jane A. Goldman, University of Connecticut
Laura D. Goodwin, University of Colorado at Denver
Bryan W. Griffin, Georgia Southern University
Robert L. Hale, Penn State University
Joseph Khazzaka, University of Scranton
Vicki LaBoskey, Mills College
Alex G. Ober, Western Maryland College
Pietro J. Pascale, Youngstown State University
William T. Phelan, University of Massachusetts
Steven Pulos, University of Northern Colorado
Sylvia Roberts, City College of New York
Dale G. Shaw, University of Northern Colorado
Lowell Wade Smith, Tennessee State University
William B. Ware, University of North Carolina at Chapel Hill
Douglas C. Wiseman, Plymouth State College
Terrence D. Wong, Marquette University

USING RESEARCH NAVIGATOR™

This edition of *Introduction to Educational Research* is designed to integrate the content of the book with the following resources of Research Navigator™, a collection of research databases, instruction, and contemporary publications available to you online at www.researchnavigator.com.

- **EBSCO's ContentSelect Academic Journal Database** organized by subject, with each subject containing leading academic journals for each discipline.
- *The New York Times,* one of the most highly regarded publications of today's news. View the full text of articles from the previous year.
- **Link Library** connects users to thousands of websites for discipline-specific key terms.
- **Research Review and Preparation.** A special section called "Understanding the Research Process" helps you work your way through the research process.

Connecting the Book with RN

As you read this book, you'll see special Research Navigator™ (RN) icons cueing you to visit the ContentSelect database on the Research Navigator™ website to expand on the concepts of the text and to further explore the work being done in the field of Educational Research. RN learning aids in the book include:

Research
Navigator.com
class size

1. **Marginal keyword search terms.** Appearing in the margins of the text, these already tested terms will guide your search on topics relevant to the course content and will yield an abundance of sources from a variety of perspectives that will broaden your exposure to key topics. Begin by searching the ContentSelect database, and then check out the other databases as well.
2. **Applied research activities and projects.** At the end of each chapter, special RN exercises provide more practice using the ContentSelect database in Research Navigator™ and move you beyond the book to library and field research.

It's now time to enter Research Navigator™. Purchase of this book provides you free access to this exclusive pool of information and data. The following walk-through illustrates, step-by-step, the various ways this valuable resource can make your research process more interesting and successful.

Registration

In order to begin using Research Navigator™, you must first register using the personal access code found on the inside of the front cover of your book. Follow these easy steps:

1. Click "Register" under New Users on the left side of the home page screen.

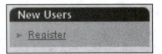

2. Enter the access code exactly as it appears on the inside front cover of your book or on your access card. (Note: Access codes can only be used once to complete one registration. If you purchased a used text, the access code may not work.)

1 **Your Access Code**

Please enter your six-word code without dashes. You can type the letters in lowercase or uppercase.

Example

SMPLE FRILL TONLE WEIRS CHOIR FLEES

2 **Do You Have an Account?**

If you've previously registered for any **Pearson Education** online product, please enter your existing Login Name (also called User ID) and Password so our system can identify your account and fill in most of the information requested on the next pages.

⦿ **No**, I am a new user.

(You will create a Login Name and Password at the end of this registration process.)

Next ▶

○ **Yes**, look me up.

Login Name   Password

Next ▶

Forgot your Login Name/ Password?

3. Follow the instructions on screen to complete your registration—you may click the Help button at any time if you are unsure how to respond.
4. Once you have successfully completed registration, write down the Login Name and Password you just created and keep it in a safe place. You will need to enter it each time you want to revisit Research Navigator™.
5. Once you register, you have access to all the resources in Research Navigator™ for six months. Each time you enter Research Navigator™, log in by simply going to the "Returning Users" section on the left side of the home page and type in your LoginID and Password.

Getting Started

You're now official! The options available to you on Research Navigator™ are plenty. From Research Navigator™'s home page, you have easy access to all of the site's main features, including a quick route to the three exclusive databases of source content. If you are new to the research process, you may want to start by browsing "Understanding the Research Process."

This section of the site can be helpful even for those with some research experience but who might be interested in some helpful tips. Here you will find extensive help on all aspects of the research process including:

- Introduction to the Research Paper
- Gathering Data
- Searching the Internet
- Evaluating Sources
- Organizing Ideas
- Writing Notes
- Drafting the Paper
- Academic Citation Styles (i.e., MLA, APA, CMS)
- Blending Reference Material into Your Writing
- Practicing Academic Integrity
- Revising
- Proofreading
- Editing the Final Draft

Completing Research

The first step in completing a research assignment or research paper is to select a topic. Your instructor may assign you a topic, or you may find suggested topics in the margins or at the end of chapters throughout this book. Once you have selected and narrowed your research topic, you are now ready to *gather data*. Research Navigator™ simplifies your research efforts by giving you three distinct types of source material commonly used in research assignments: academic journals (ContentSelect), newspaper articles (*The New York Times*), and World Wide Web sites (Link Library).

1. EBSCO's ContentSelect

The first database you'll find on Research Navigator™ is ContentSelect, which contains the EBSCO Academic Journal and Abstract Database containing scholarly, peer-reviewed journals (such as *Journal of Education Policy* and *Assessment & Evaluation in Higher Education*). The information obtained in these individual articles is more scientific than information you would find in a popular magazine, in a newspaper article, or on a Web page. Searching for articles in ContentSelect is easy!

Within the ContentSelect Research Database section, you will see a list of disciplines and a space to type keywords. You can search within a single discipline or multiple disciplines. Choose one or more subject databases, and then enter a keyword you wish to search. Click on "Go."

> **Search for Source Material**
>
> EBSCO's
> **Content**Select Academic Journal Database
>
> Exclusive to instructors and students using Pearson Education textbooks, the ContentSelect Research Database gives students instant access to thousands of academic journals and periodicals from any computer with an Internet connection!
>
> Search by Keyword
> You must select a database to search. To select multiple, hold down the alt or command key.
>
> Communication
> Communication Sciences & Disorders
> Computer & Information Science
> Criminal Justice
> Education
> Engineering
>
> Mixed Methods   Go ⚠ Log in to search.

Now you'll see a list of articles that match your search. From this page you can examine either the full text or the abstract of each of the articles and determine which will best help with your research. Print out the articles or save them in your "Folder" for later reference.

2. *The New York Times*

Searching *The New York Times* gives you access to articles from one of the world's leading newspapers. The first step in using the search-by-subject archive is to indicate the subject area you wish to search. You have the option of searching one specific subject at a time by highlighting the subject area or searching all subjects by highlighting "All." Click on "Go" now for a complete listing of articles in your chosen subject area that have appeared in *The New York Times* over the last year, sorted by most recent article first. For a more focused search, type a word, or multiple words separated by commas, into the search box and click "Go" for a list of articles. Articles can be printed or saved for later use in your research assignment.

> **The New York Times** Search by
> ON THE WEB   Subject Archive
> Archive of New York Times articles from January 1, 2002.
> Search by Subject
> Education Research ▼ Go ⚠ Log in to search.
> Search by Keyword
> Mixed Methods   Go ⚠ Log in to search.

3. "Best of the Web" Link Library

The third database of content included on Research Navigator™ is a collection of Web links, organized by academic subject and key terms. To use this database, simply select a subject from the dropdown list and find the key term for the topic you are searching. Click on the key term and see a list of editorially reviewed websites that offer educationally relevant and credible content. The Web links in Link Library are monitored and updated each week, reducing your incidence of finding "dead" links.

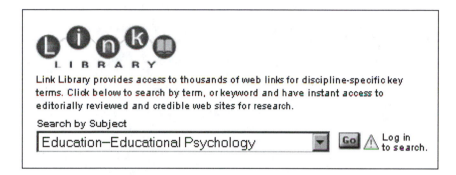

Using Your Library

While Research Navigator™ does contain a vast amount of information to assist you with your research, it does not try to replace the library. After you have selected your topic and gathered source material from the three databases of content, you may need to go to your school library to complete your research. Finding information at the library, however, can seem overwhelming. Research Navigator™ provides some assistance in this area as well. Research Navigator™ includes discipline-specific "library guides" for you to use as a road map. Each guide includes an overview of the discipline's major subject databases, online journals, and key associations and newsgroups. Print them out and take them with you to the library!

CAUTION! Please note that the Research Navigator™ site undergoes frequent changes as new and exciting options are added to assist with research endeavors. For the latest information on the options available to you on Research Navigator™, visit www.ablongman.com/aboutrn.com.

Introduction to Educational Research

1

Educational Research

Its Nature and Rules of Operation

PREVIEW

This chapter presents four clusters of information fundamental to educational research:

- The nature of educational research
- The value of the scientific method in answering perplexing questions
- The process by which educational research is done
- The operating rules for conducting educational research

You will see that

- Research is a careful, systematic, patient investigation that employs the
- Scientific method, which seeks facts and relationships, following a
- Research process that obtains, analyzes, and interprets data, while adhering to
- Operating rules of legality, ethics, and established research procedures

Targeted Learnings

This chapter describes the nature of educational research, explains why the scientific method is valuable in answering perplexing questions about education, outlines the process by which educational research is conducted, and identifies the operating rules for conducting research. As you read the chapter, look especially for information related to the following questions:

1. What *sources of information* do people usually consult first for answers to difficult questions? Why are those first sources of information often of so little value?
2. What is meant by *scientific method?*
3. What is *research?* How is educational research similar to and different from research in the natural sciences?
4. What is the *general procedure* by which research is done?

5. What are the legal, ethical, philosophical, and procedural *operating rules* for conducting educational research? What is an example of each?

6. Why should the operating rules of educational research be thought of as unwritten law?

Chapter Information Organizers

This chapter and those that follow present *information organizers,* graphic frameworks that show the organization and contents of the chapter. They are provided to help you see the chapter organization and coverage as a whole and to anticipate information you will encounter. You will find the organizers helpful for reviewing chapter contents.

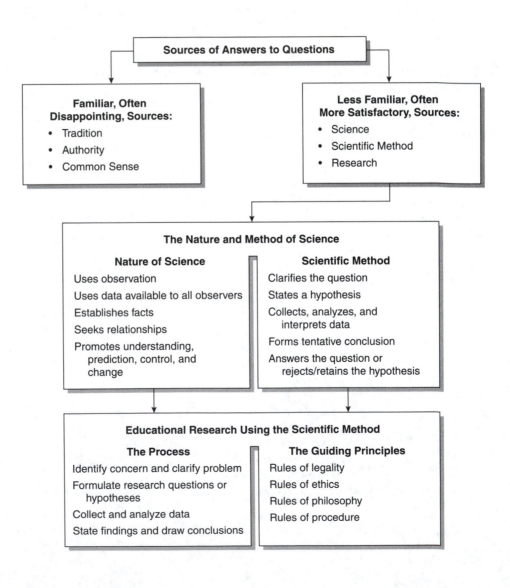

New Questions about Elmwood's Schools

To facilitate an introduction to educational research and the agreements by which it operates, let us consider the fictitious example of the Elmwood Urban School District, serving a city that in recent years has been undergoing dramatic change. Once a predominantly Anglo community, Elmwood has grown to reflect wide racial, ethnic, and cultural diversity. More than 70 different languages are spoken by students in Elmwood schools. Many of those students do not speak English well, and some of their parents do not speak English at all. In many ways Elmwood is richer because of this growing mix of cultures and viewpoints, but the changes have also brought difficulties. Gangs have formed. Some ethnic groups do not get along well with others. Overall academic achievement has declined, with certain groups performing well below national norms. Dropout rates have increased. Parents and students complain more frequently about racism, insensitivity, lack of fairness, and inappropriate curricula.

In an attempt to improve conditions, Elmwood district's community coordinating council has asked the superintendent to prepare a formal report on achievement, curriculum, and race relations in Elmwood schools. This effort will first require that a number of answerable questions be posed, of which the following might be examples:

- How does student achievement in Elmwood compare with that of other urban areas?
- Which segments of the student population are achieving less than expected?
- What is causing the lower-than-expected rates of achievement?
- What is the transiency rate of students? How does it compare with transiency rates 10 and 20 years ago?
- What relationship, if any, exists between students' English language proficiency and their success in school?
- Which areas of the present school curriculum are of most benefit to Elmwood's students? Which are of least benefit?
- Would Elmwood students profit from instructional procedures different from those presently used?
- What are Elmwood students' thoughts about school and its value?
- What are the students' major concerns about school? What are their parents' major concerns about school?
- How well do students of various ethnic groups interact and get along with each other?
- What might be done to improve ethnic and racial relations?
- What are Elmwood students' lives like outside of school?

Positing such questions is an important first step in addressing Elmwood's concerns. But having done that, how does one go about finding answers to the dozens or hundreds of such questions that might be asked about Elmwood schools, students, and community?

Seeking Answers to Questions

Whenever pressing questions arise, human nature prompts us to try to find answers as quickly as possible, and the sources we usually consult first are those most convenient to us—tradition, authority, and common sense. *Tradition* refers to how we collectively have judged, reasoned, and behaved in the past. Elmwood school personnel remember that the district's curriculum was considered to be exemplary many years ago, well delivered and well received. Tradition, therefore, tells them that the Elmwood curriculum needs no change, that something else must be at fault. This answer may possibly be correct, but present concerns suggest strongly that while the curriculum was effective in the past, it is no longer meeting the needs of Elmwood students.

When tradition fails to provide a suitable answer, we look next to *authority,* seeking the opinions of insightful experts who, we hope, know what is best. This source of answers remains popular: Witness the variety of bandwagons schools have jumped onto—and almost as quickly off of—as new problems arise in the schools. Elmwood district officials would almost certainly look to school districts in Los Angeles, Atlanta, New York, Miami, or elsewhere in hopes of finding answers to its problems. But Elmwood may find that Atlanta recommends one solution, while Chicago recommends another that is entirely different. Chances are that since no other urban area is closely similar to Elmwood, recommendations from elsewhere will not prove satisfactory.

With authoritative answers plentiful but not particularly helpful, Elmwood school personnel may decide to work things out for themselves, using a *commonsense* approach. Although human reason can be formidable, as evidenced by incredible accomplishments in technology and culture, it is clear that common sense also misses the mark regularly, as is equally evident in the social and economic difficulties in which we find ourselves. Good reasoning is dependent on reliable information: Without that, it is subject to serious error. Unfortunately, Elmwood personnel do not presently seem to have the reliable information needed for making sound educational decisions.

So after all is said and done, Elmwood district's council will probably find that no matter where it turns for help, sooner or later it will have to find its own solutions to its pressing problems. It will have to identify the specific concerns it wishes to address, formulate and clarify the questions it wants answered, obtain reliable information for answering those questions, and based on those answers, determine the changes that may, and may not, be needed.

But how can reliable information be obtained? Life swamps us with information, most of it irrelevant to our concerns. Of the information that interests us, a great portion comes from media whose stock in trade is the sensational. Much also comes from people and organizations with axes to grind and agendas to advance. No small amount comes from our own personal experience, which is sometimes objective and useful, but not always so. With information from these readily available sources, almost everyone in make-believe Elmwood has already formed conclusions about Elmwood schools—what is good and bad about them, what the students and teachers are like, what is wrong with the curriculum, what is holding students back, and why the entire enterprise is better or worse than it used to be. But in the absence of reliable, objective information, citizens' conclusions may or may not be correct.

The crucial task for Elmwood then—and coincidentally for any person or group intending to conduct research—is to obtain information that is reliable and valid. This is best accomplished by using what is called the *scientific method.*

The Scientific Method

Today we take for granted a level of comfort and convenience undreamed of only a few decades ago. We are among the best-fed, best-clothed, best-housed, and healthiest people the world has ever known. Exchange of information occurs with speed and accuracy beyond belief. Mobility is such that any part of the earth can be reached within hours. These advances in health and technology have been brought about through use of the scientific method of thinking.

The **scientific method** is a specific strategy used to answer questions and resolve problems. Essentially, it focuses on discovering valid facts and relationships. We should note that the term *fact* does not mean the same thing as truth. Facts are not immutable; they are merely agreements concerning observations made by impartial people who are judged to be competent to observe. For example, if competent people measure the heights of the players on Elmwood High School's basketball team and find that the average height of the players is six feet two inches, then that average height is considered to be a fact. However, if two new players enroll who are each seven feet tall, the previous average height will no longer be fact; a new fact will replace it. The key point is that fact depends on observation and, when possible, accurate measurement. Fact is not established through speculation, hunch, or inner vision.

Facts by themselves can often help us to understand conditions and events. If we desire to know what Elmwood's schools, curricula, teachers, and students were like 100 years ago, we can uncover a great number of facts that allow us to piece together a fairly accurate picture. But facts in and of themselves do not always provide answers to questions that intrigue us: It may be necessary to go further and search for relationships among various facts. We may wish to know, for example, why certain groups of students continually outdo other groups in achievement. To answer this question we seek out cause–effect relationships, such as traits or conditions (the cause) that produce higher or lower scholastic achievement (the effect). Or we may want to know how we can organize and implement an effective race-relations program in Elmwood schools. Here we seek out means–end relationships; we know the desired end (improved relationships among various groups) and, therefore, seek the means to bring it about.

Relationships among facts—the most powerful quality of science—give us the ability to predict, control, and even change human behavior and aspects of the world in which we live. If we can determine how traditional ethnic group values correlate with student behavior, we can *predict* with some accuracy how certain students are likely to behave in school. If we can determine that a new discipline system causes students to exhibit higher incidence of positive behavior, we can *control* the amount of disruptive classroom behavior, thus allowing students to gain more from their educational experience. And if we determine that students learn better when taught by a new instructional approach, we can teach in ways that permanently *change* (in this case increase) the amount of student learning.

The discovery of valuable relationships of these types is more likely to occur when the scientific method of thinking and problem solving is used. What is this method? In 1938, the American philosopher John Dewey described his concept of the scientific method, depicting it as a procedure for thinking more objectively. He presented the procedure as a series of steps. As you will see later, these steps parallel the procedures followed in conducting research. The steps Dewey listed are as follows:

1. Clarify the main question inherent in the problem.
2. State a hypothesis (a possible answer to the question).
3. Collect, analyze, and interpret information related to the question and hypothesis.
4. Form conclusions derived from the information analyzed.
5. Use the conclusions to verify or reject the hypothesis.

Although Dewey's popularization of the scientific method has helped us think more productively, it would be misleading to suggest that researchers always follow the steps he described exactly. Many research problems are simply interesting questions that nag at people's minds and can be answered without using a hypothesis (Dewey's step 2). Collecting, analyzing, and interpreting data (Dewey's step 3) is always done in research, but sometimes may be the first or second step taken rather than the third. Such could be the case if someone had an interest in the life of Elmwood's first superintendent of schools and, after finding out a good deal about him or her, decided to do further research into that person's life. Despite exceptions such as these—and they are numerous—Dewey's scientific method remains useful both in conducting research and in helping neophytes understand the research process.

Research and the Scientific Method

How closely does the research process mirror the scientific method, and why does it follow the scientific method at all? To understand the relationship between research process and scientific method, let us explore more closely the nature of research and how it is done.

The Meaning of Research

The word **research** comes from the French *rechercher* ("to search after or to investigate") and is defined as "a careful, systematic, patient investigation undertaken to discover or establish facts and relationships." We would do well to remember the words *careful, systematic,* and *patient investigation,* because they emphasize that research is more than a hurried process of looking up information in reference books. Research is called for when one is confronted with a question or problem that has no readily available answer. One must obtain information and make sense of it in order to answer the problematic question.

Research
Navigator.com
scientific research

Many topics of great human interest can be explored scientifically but others cannot. In **scientific research,** information is obtained by using the senses to observe objects and events. Not all topics can be investigated in this manner. For example, scientific research is of little value in exploring the major questions in philosophy, religion, and ethics. Such questions as, What is truth? What is the nature of God? and How should people treat each other? are certainly explored vigorously, but as they cannot be approached through impartial observation, they cannot be investigated scientifically.

Exercise 1.1

To what extent do you believe the following activities involve a careful, systematic process? Indicate (H) high, (M) medium, or (L) low for each activity.

_____ 1. Finding the year in which Elmwood Urban School District was established

_____ 2. Preparing student achievement profiles for the nation's 10 largest urban school districts

_____ 3. Identifying the ethnic group affiliations of 100 students randomly selected from Elmwood schools

_____ 4. Describing the daily lives of 10 randomly selected students from Elmwood schools

_____ 5. Developing instructional activities that best promote achievement in Elmwood's high school students

---

The Process of Educational Research

Educational research is typically carried out in a manner using the following steps. (Note the parallel with Dewey's scientific method.)

A Concern Exists.   A concern is identified for which there is no ready answer. The concern may have arisen because of a need, an interest, a requirement, or a commissioned work, and may have been present for a long time or may have arisen unexpectedly. For example, Elmwood educators have identified a disturbing pattern of academic achievement in Elmwood schools—students from certain ethnic groups seem to progress more rapidly than others, despite the educators' efforts to provide equal educational opportunity for all.

The Concern Is Addressed.   After being identified, the concern is addressed by following these steps:

Step 1.   The concern is clarified and stated succinctly, after which it becomes known as the **research problem.** In large-scale research, as would be called for in Elmwood schools, a number of smaller, more manageable concerns are also clarified. All told, a number of problems may be identified for research.

**Research
Navigator.c⊕m**
research question

Step 2.   One or more main **research questions** are posed to guide an investigation into each of the problems. If the use of research questions is not appropriate, one or more **hypotheses** may be stated for each problem. Often an investigation makes use of both research questions and hypotheses. Research questions indicate what the researcher actually hopes to determine. An example of a research question is: What are the achievement levels in tenth-grade English and algebra among students whose primary affiliations are in the following ethnic groups:…(group names are stated)?

Hypotheses differ from research questions in that hypotheses are statements that can be tested statistically. Often they do not indicate what the researcher truly expects to find.

An example of an hypothesis is: No differences exist in the average achievement levels in tenth-grade English and algebra among students whose primary ethnic affiliations are as follows (groups are named).

Both research questions and hypotheses are useful in orienting research, and both receive additional attention in subsequent chapters.

Step 3.   When research questions and/or hypotheses have been stated, information (referred to as **data**) pertinent to them is sought from various sources such as people, records, physical objects, environments, social settings, journal articles, books, and other printed materials.

Step 4.   As data are accumulated, they are summarized, organized, and analyzed. Statistical treatments are normally used to analyze numerical data, whereas verbal logic is used to analyze narrative data. (These analytical procedures are introduced in Chapters 8 and 10 through 14 and are more fully developed in Appendix A.) The steps taken to obtain, summarize, organize, and analyze information are called the **procedures** of the study. Once data are analyzed, they are presented as the **findings** of the study.

Step 5.   When the findings have been stated, researchers endeavor to interpret the meanings of those findings in terms of the original research questions or hypotheses. The interpretations they finally make are called the **conclusions** of the study.

In summary, the research process usually includes these activities:

- Identifying the matter about which concern exists
- Clarifying the specific problem on which the research will center
- Formulating research questions and/or hypotheses concerning the central problem
- Carrying out procedures by which data are collected, summarized, and analyzed
- Stating the findings determined through data analysis
- Drawing conclusions related to the original research questions and/or hypotheses

But let us remember that in practice these phases do not always occur so neatly as this summary might suggest, nor are they always accomplished in the sequence shown.

Exercise 1.2

José Gomes investigated the reading achievement of seventh-grade Vietnamese, Cambodian, Korean, and Filipino students who had been in the United States for four years or less. Identify each of the following from his research as (P) problem, (Q) research questions, (H) hypothesis, (PR) procedure, (F) finding, or (C) conclusion.

_____   1. The mean raw score for Korean students was 78.7.

_____   2. Average achievement for Korean students was two months above grade level.

_____   3. Twenty-five students were randomly selected from each ethnic group.

--------- 4. The purpose of this study was to investigate comparative reading achievement of seventh-grade students from selected ethnic groups.

--------- 5. A two-year average difference was found between the highest-achieving and the lowest-achieving group.

--------- 6. Average performance in reading was above the level anticipated.

--------- 7. No difference exists in reading achievement among seventh-grade students of selected ethnic groups.

--------- 8. The hypothesis was rejected.

--------- 9. The median test scores are shown in Table 23.

--------- 10. What differences, if any, exist in reading achievement among seventh-grade students of Vietnamese, Cambodian, Filipino, and Korean descent who have been in the United States for four years or less?

Research and Educational Research

To this point, the terms *research* and *educational research* have been used interchangeably. Scientific research follows the same general process regardless of the discipline in which it is employed, whether biology, astronomy, forestry, sociology, psychology, education, or elsewhere. Educational research is, therefore, simply scientific research applied to educational matters. As previously noted, for research to be considered scientific, its data must come from the observation of objects and events, and those same observational opportunities must be accessible to all interested individuals.

How can the scientific method be used to address the concerns about Elmwood schools? Suppose Elmwood wants to identify the student population groups whose scholastic achievement is lagging and then pinpoint the causes of low achievement, so that groups in need can be better served. Using a scientific approach, one must obtain reliable information for establishing pertinent facts. This can be done by administering achievement tests to students, in conjunction with interviewing those students and observing their behavior. Once data are collected and facts established, relationships can be explored—in particular, causative relationships that might indicate factors responsible for the low achievement of certain groups. This search for relationships might lead one to consider language proficiency, work expectations outside the home, and the value students and parents place on education. All could be explored objectively.

Rules of Operation in Educational Research

The research process, though it can occur in a rambling manner, is best done systematically by following certain operating rules. As we proceed, we will see that by following these rules, researchers can credibly obtain reliable information from which to draw valid conclusions. We will see, further, that the rules are neither obscure nor difficult to follow. Before we examine the operating rules of research, let us be mindful of what R. S. Peters wrote regarding educational research in *The Philosophy of Education* (1973):

> There must be respect for evidence and a ban on "cooking" or distorting it; there must be a willingness to admit that one is mistaken.... To learn science is not just to learn facts and to understand theories; it is also to participate in a public form of life governed by such principles of procedure. (p. 25)

Peters's words help explain why the **operating rules of research** are emphasized so strongly. You would do well to think of these rules as laws to be followed scrupulously: Indeed, two of the 13 actually are law. Before you progress beyond this chapter, you should fix these rules so firmly in your mind that any violation of them will immediately raise a flag of caution. The 13 rules have to do with protection of people involved, confidentiality of those involved, beneficence, honesty, accurate disclosure, significance of the research, generalizability, replicability, probability, researchability, parsimony, credibility, and rival explanations. We can think of these rules as the guiding principles of research. For consideration here, the principles are grouped into four categories—legal, ethical, philosophical, and procedural.

Legal Principles

Legal requirements of protection and confidentiality are placed on research in which humans are used as **participants** (people being studied). Researchers may not violate these restrictions.

Rule 1: Protection.   The National Research Act of 1974 ensured **protection** of individuals invited to participate in research studies. The law does not allow research to place individuals in physical danger, nor does it permit inquiry, without advised consent of the participants involved, into personal matters considered sensitive in nature. The intent of the law is to protect individuals against physical, mental, or emotional harm.

Rule 2: Confidentiality.   The Family Educational Rights and Privacy Act (known as the Buckley Amendment), also passed in 1974, put into law the **principle of confidentiality.** Without express permission to the contrary, the anonymity of human participants who participate in research is to be maintained.

To ensure compliance with laws of protection and confidentiality, colleges and universities where research is conducted have established institutional review boards (sometimes referred to as "human subjects review boards") whose function is to examine proposed research and make sure participants' rights are not violated. The review board does not have to evaluate all research proposals because many, especially in education, pose no physical, mental, emotional, or degradational danger to participants. Specifically exempt by law from having to undergo institutional review (meaning it is all right to proceed without a review board's approval or at least approval of the *full* review board) are the following kinds of research:

Research
Navigator.c⊕m
confidentiality

1. Research conducted in established or commonly accepted educational settings, involving normal educational practices. This would include research on administration, classroom practices, methods of teaching, instructional strategies, classroom management, use of new materials, testing procedures, and the like.
2. Research involving the use of educational tests, provided information from those tests is recorded in such a way that individuals are not named or readily identifiable (thus maintaining confidentiality).
3. Research involving survey or interview procedures, but such research is not allowed if
   a. responses are recorded in such a manner that individual students can be identified;
   b. a participant's responses could place him or her at risk of civil or criminal liability or could damage financial standing or employability;
   c. the research deals with sensitive aspects of the participant's behavior, such as illegal conduct, drug use, sexual behavior, or use of alcohol.
4. Research involving the observation of public behavior, but such research is not allowed if
   a. observations are recorded in such a manner that individuals are readily identifiable;
   b. recorded information could put the participant at risk of civil or criminal liability or could damage his or her financial standing or employability;
   c. the research deals with sensitive aspects of the participant's behavior, such as illegal conduct, drug use, sexual behavior, or use of alcohol.
5. Research involving the collection or study of existing data, documents, records, pathological specimens, or diagnostic specimens, if these sources are publicly available or if the information is obtained in such a way that no potential risk is foreseen for individual participants.

Most educational research topics fall within permissible areas, and the only legal prohibition to be observed is that of confidentiality. Graduate research topics therefore seldom have to be reviewed by the entire institutional review board. Oftentimes, even when sensitive topics such as drug use are proposed for investigation, the research will be allowed by the institutional review board if participants give their written consent.

If there is any question about the legality or ethics of proposed research, it is best to check with the institutional review committee or the institution's grants officer before proceeding.

Ethical Principles

Ethics have to do with moral aspects of research. Although not stipulated in law, researchers must be scrupulously ethical if their work is to have credibility. Operating rules in this category relate to beneficence, honesty, and accurate disclosure.

Rule 3: Beneficence. The **principle of beneficence** indicates that educational research is done to garner knowledge and shed light on the human condition. It is never conducted as a means of doing harm to individuals or groups or to denigrate, cast blame, find fault, deny opportunity, or stifle progress. The researcher's aim is always to increase understanding and, where possible, to promote opportunity and advancement for the population at large.

Applying Technology: **Human Subjects Research Approval**

Many institutions of higher education have begun placing the forms required for human subjects approval on the institution's website so that they are easily accessible by students, faculty, and other researchers. The URLs for sample forms from two institutions have been included here.

Bowling Green State University, Office of Sponsored Programs and Research (SPAR)

(www.bgsu.edu/offices/spar/orc/hsrb): Bowling Green State University uses a more streamlined form; many of the questions require the applicant only to check applicable boxes. Based on the information provided, the initial reviewers determine if the project is eligible for an "expedited review," meaning that it is not necessary to go before the entire Review Board. The Human Subjects Review Form is a downloadable file, in Microsoft Word format.

University of Minnesota, Office of the Institutional Review Board

(www.irb.umn.edu): The University of Minnesota utilizes specific forms for the social and behavioral sciences (www.irb.umn.edu/download/social.cfm). This application form, as well as related appendixes, are available in Rich Text Format (rtf) and are designed to work with Microsoft Word for both Mac and PC.

Rule 4: Honesty.   The **principle of honesty** is absolutely essential in the research process. This is such an obvious requirement that it might seem unnecessary to mention it. However, with dismaying frequency we hear of important research data being "fixed" to yield findings the researcher had hoped for or else suppressed because they are contrary to what was desired. Such dishonest manipulation of data is inexcusable and renders the research meaningless or dangerously misleading.

Occasionally bona fide researchers risk loss of reputation and career by tampering with data. This shows how high the stakes can be in certain research, especially when it involves large grants of money or affects career advancement. The temptation to alter data may even arise in research at the graduate level. That temptation, if experienced, must be put aside without hesitation.

Once the process of data collection is under way, data should be reported exactly as obtained; no data are to be suppressed, no alterations made in them, and no exceptions made in the procedures by which they are collected. If for any reason these stipulations cannot be adhered to, the entire research process should be terminated and replanned.

Rule 5: Accurate Disclosure.   The **principle of accurate disclosure** indicates that individuals selected to serve as participants in research must be informed accurately about the general topic of research and any unusual procedures or tasks in which they will be involved. They should receive assurance that their names will be kept confidential and that they will not be subjected to unusual discomfort or risk. In school research that involves entire classes, it is sufficient to inform (and obtain permission from) the head administrator rather than the students. If the research involves an unusual procedure, teaching method, set of materials, or the like, it may sometimes be necessary to obtain written consent from the students' parents and from the governing board of the school district.

Note that accurate disclosure does not mean full disclosure. Full disclosure would provide participants with all the details of the research, but in so doing would introduce the possibility of error that might render the research invalid. For example, one group of participants might, because of information they receive, try harder than another, believe they are superior or inferior and behave accordingly, or think they are receiving special treatment, good or bad, that is not being given to other groups. As a result, the research findings might differ from what would otherwise have been the case. For that reason, researchers try to provide equally to all participants knowledge of the topic, its importance, and its general requirements.

Following these guidelines, if one wanted to investigate the relative effects of two different sets of materials in teaching composition to high school students whose English capability is below national norms, accurate disclosure might be akin to the following: "We are going to investigate two different sets of instructional materials to see which works better for the students in our schools. Both sets of materials are considered to be good and are published by reputable companies. You will not undergo any unusual activities or testing procedures, and you will be under no risk of harm whatsoever. Your names will be kept strictly confidential."

Figure 1.1 shows an example of a cover letter that accompanied a survey as part of a research study. Notice that, at a minimum, the letter addresses the principles of protection, confidentiality, beneficence, and accurate disclosure.

Exercise 1.3

For each of the following, indicate the research operating rule(s) complied with or violated: (P) protection, (C) confidentiality, (B) beneficence, (H) honesty, or (AD) accurate disclosure.

_____ 1. Jones's research assistant inadvertently mentioned the names of three high school students identified by Jones as alcohol abusers.

_____ 2. Jones noted poor test performance by a bright student. Realizing the performance did not reflect the student's ability, Jones changed the score to what he believed the student should have made.

_____ 3. Jones informed the students, though not in detail, of the nature of the research in which they would be involved.

_____ 4. In the outdoor performance trials one of the participants succumbed to heat prostration and had to be hospitalized overnight.

Bowling Green State University

College of Education & Human Development

EDFI Program
School of Leadership and Policy Studies
Bowling Green, Ohio 43403
(419) 372-7322
FAX: (419) 372-8265

November 1, 2002

Dear <*name of school district*> Teacher,

Purpose of study; beneficence; importance

I am currently conducting a survey research study titled "Classroom Teachers' Assessment Literacy," the purpose of which is to examine teachers' general knowledge and understanding of testing and assessment.

Accurate disclosure

The purpose of this letter is to ask for your participation in the study. I am asking you to participate in the study by simply completing the survey as honestly and openly as you can. The survey should only take about 10-15 minutes to complete. When you have completed the survey, simply return it to me using the enclosed postage-paid envelope. Additionally, please complete the survey by **Friday, November 22, 2002.**

Anonymity and confidentiality, honesty

Please be assured that your responses will be anonymous. The code number that appears on the cover of your survey will be used only for record-keeping purposes. Please do not place your name or other identifying characteristics anywhere on the survey. No one other than you will know if you have or have not participated in this study. Additionally, your responses will remain confidential. No individual information will be shared; only aggregate results will be reported.

Protection

Your participation in this study is voluntary. By completing the survey, you are giving your consent to participate. If you do not wish to participate, simply do not complete the survey. If you have any questions regarding this survey study, I may be contacted at mertler@bgnet.bgsu.edu. You may also contact the Chair, Human Subjects Review Board, Bowling Green State University, (419) 372-7716 (hsrb@bgnet.bgsu.edu) if any problems or concerns arise during the course of the study.

Best Regards,

Craig A. Mertler

Craig A. Mertler, Ph.D.
Associate Professor of Assessment and Research Methodologies

A Caring, Competent, & Qualified Teacher in Every Classroom: A BGSU Tradition

FIGURE 1.1   Sample cover letter demonstrating adherence to crucial principles of research

Philosophical Principles

Philosophical principles have to do with the anticipated value of a particular investigation, as regards significance (worthwhileness), generalizability (findings applicable elsewhere), replicability (repeatable by others), and probability (the understanding that research findings are considered probabilities, not certainties).

Rule 6: Importance.   The topic of any research other than that done purely for personal interest should be justified in terms of the **principle of importance**—that is, whether the research findings are likely to contribute to human knowledge or be useful elsewhere. Research to be taken seriously must show promise of being worth the time, effort, and expenditures entailed. This applies to research done in graduate-degree programs as well. Graduate research topics are not acceptable if trivial or superficial or if their potential findings are likely to be inconsequential. It is the researcher's responsibility to justify the research under consideration. Ordinarily this can be done by pointing to the educational importance of a topic, establishing a need for information about it, and showing that the research has the potential to supply needed information.

Research
Navigator.c⊕m
generalizability

Rule 7: Generalizability.   The **principle of generalizability** means that the findings of research can be applied, or generalized, to other individuals and settings. For example, suppose an investigation is being done into the learning styles of Elmwood students who have immigrated to this country during the past two years from Central America. If the research is to have maximum value, the findings should do more than illuminate learning style patterns of the students in the sample: They should also promote understanding of similar students attending schools elsewhere.

But how does one predict whether, or to what extent, research findings might be generalizable? Indications of potential generalizability can be forecast by analyzing the proposed research locale, participants involved, time required, and treatments and measurements used. But a far more valuable predictor of generalizability is the degree to which the sample of individuals being studied (e.g., 70 sixth-grade students in Elmwood) represents the larger population to which the sample belongs (e.g., 20,000 sixth-grade students nationwide). Close correspondence between sample and population is assumed when participants are randomly selected from the larger population. This does not guarantee but does vastly improve the likelihood that the sample is representative of the population. When that is not possible (as it would not be for students attending Elmwood schools, who are already there and are, thus, preselected), then participants are scrutinized to see if their socioeconomic status, language ability, gender, age, and background seem consistent with those of the larger population.

The principle of generalizability, although normally of great importance, does not apply in all research. Historical research, for example (described in Chapters 2 and 11), is done to learn about a particular event or group of people at a particular place at a particular time. Its purpose is to provide understanding, not to predict what might happen elsewhere. One might be able to discover what Elmwood's first school was like, but that information could not, without considerable support, be generalized to the historical development of school systems in other cities, whose populations might have been dissimilar in culture, religion, language, wealth, customs, and other traits.

Similarly, action research (described in Chapters 2 and 13) is by definition pertinent only to the solution of a particular problem in a particular place. It is not done to help resolve concerns in other locations, though in some instances it might do so. If Mr. Branca decides to develop and test a community awareness project for his students in high school civics, he does not do so with the thought that his efforts will be noted across the country. His concern is to find something that works for him and his students in Elmwood Lincoln High School.

Rule 8: Replicability.   We often hear of new findings in medicine or physics or biology that have important implications for human well-being. Occasionally we later hear that those same findings have become suspect because other scientists, when repeating the original research, made different findings.

It is very important that any research be **replicable,** or repeatable, for that is a prime means of establishing credibility. Research is made replicable by keeping records of exactly what was done, and why, in each phase of the investigation. If another researcher follows the same recipe, he or she ought to come up with the same results. If not, the original research should be strongly questioned. Educational research is not often replicated, but the anticipation that it might be should remind researchers to be circumspect in procedure and report.

Rule 9: Probability.   Both beginning researchers and those who wish to make use of published research findings should understand that educational research rarely turns up hard-and-fast answers to the questions it explores. Research deals in **probabilities,** likelihoods, or the best answers among a variety of possibilities. *It almost never provides certainty.* This point will become clearer later when we consider statistical procedures for analyzing and interpreting data. Many of those procedures make reference to probability levels. A researcher might find, for example, that the average reading level of Latino students entering Elmwood's sixth-grade classes is "fifth year–eighth month, plus or minus three months." This finding would mean that while the average measured reading level was "fifth year–eighth month," potential errors inherent in sample selection and testing make it very unlikely that measurements will be absolutely accurate, and further, that the likely margin of error extends three months on each side of the "fifth year–eighth month" average.

Probability as related to data analysis is explained in detail in Appendix A. For the time being, remember that research conclusions hinge not on absolute certainty but on probability. For research findings to be taken seriously, there must be a very strong probability that if the research were repeated numerous times, the findings would almost always be approximately the same.

Procedural Principles

Procedural rules of research pertain to the selection of researchable topics, parsimony (keeping everything as succinct as possible), credibility (ensuring believability), and acknowledgment that rival (alternative) explanations might be made of the study's findings.

Rule 10: Researchability. It is difficult for most graduate students to determine whether a topic that interests them is consistent with the **principle of researchability,** that is, whether it can be approached and resolved through established research procedures. A preliminary test of researchability includes four questions: (1) Can the scientific method be used to investigate the topic under consideration? (2) If the answer to the first question is "no," can the topic be limited or reworded to make it researchable? (3) If the topic statement is, or can be made, approachable through the scientific method, is it possible to obtain required data? (4) Can the topic be investigated within existing constraints of time, facilities, distance, money, and other such practical matters? Let us consider each of these questions briefly.

Question Concerning Scientific Method. We have noted that science depends on reliable information. To what degree do you believe reliable information could be obtained for the following questions?

1. What are the grade point averages among students that comprise five different ethnic groups attending Elmwood's secondary schools?
2. Does spirituality affect student academic performance at the secondary school level?
3. What are the comparative effects of teaching spelling through two different methods at the third-grade level?
4. To what extent is student attitude toward school affected by the values that those students' parents and grandparents have placed on education?

As you can see, reliable information could easily be obtained for questions 1 and 3 but could not for question 2. (That is because agreement could not be reached concerning the existence, definition, or measurement of spirituality, which is not to say that spirituality does not exist.) Question 4 presents near-insurmountable difficulties, in that it would be next to impossible to obtain reliable information about the extent to which a given group of parents and grandparents might have valued education. Questions 1 and 3 would, therefore, be considered researchable, whereas questions 2 and 4 would not.

Question Concerning Rewording the Topic. Topics that are not researchable can often be reworded to make them researchable. Consider question 2. If the researcher restated the question as follows, it would easily be researchable: "What is the relationship between school achievement and frequency of church attendance among students at the secondary level?" Both achievement and church attendance could be determined objectively, making the topic approachable through the scientific method. However, frequency of church attendance can hardly be considered synonymous with spirituality, if that is what the researcher wants to explore.

Question Concerning Availability of Data. Even when research topics can be stated in a manner approachable through science, they may still be unresearchable because needed data are unavailable. Consider this question:

> To what extent is student compliance with teacher expectations related to the compliance levels displayed by parents of those students during the parents' own childhoods?

Levels of compliance shown by parents when they were children would be extremely difficult to ascertain.

Question Concerning Practicality.   Even when data are available for a topic, many practical matters can render the topic unresearchable. Consider this question:

> What is the relationship between patterns of behavioral compliance among first-
> grade students and the grade point averages of those same students when they grad-
> uate from high school?

This study could certainly be done, but only if one were willing to spend 12 years on it,
hardly practical for most people.

Rule 11: Parsimony.   In science the **principle of parsimony** holds that the simpler a
theory is, the better it is, provided it adequately explains the phenomena involved. This
simpler-is-better principle applies equally to research: Given a topic's guiding questions or
hypotheses, the best research procedures are those that most *simply* and *efficiently* obtain
necessary data and provide proper analysis. In research, more is not better. The principle of
parsimony reminds us that research should be guided by questions or hypotheses stated as
clearly and simply as possible. Only necessary data should be collected, and the process
should be kept efficient. Data analysis should be to the point. Findings resulting from that
analysis should be reported clearly and the conclusions stated succinctly. This is not to imply
that research is a simple endeavor, or that all statements can be made in three-word sentences.
Complexity is almost always present in research and its interpretation. Nevertheless, research
should be kept as clear, simple, efficient, and to the point as conditions allow.

Rule 12: Credibility.   It is an absolute waste of time to conduct research that, when
completed, lacks credibility. Nothing is gained by doing so; in fact, much is lost. Fortunately, almost all research remains credible if one adheres to the established procedures of
research, which help ensure significance, reliability, and validity.
     The **principle of credibility** is established as follows: First, the topic selected must
be significant and researchable. Second, the operating principles of research explored in
this chapter must be adhered to. Third, reliable and valid data must be obtained (*reliable*
means consistent, and *valid* means on target). Fourth, appropriate methods must be used to
analyze the data. Fifth, findings must be supported by the data. And, sixth, conclusions related to research questions or hypotheses must be logically persuasive and reported clearly
and accurately.

Rule 13: Rival Explanations.   In some ways, reporting one's research is like throwing
down a dare. Although not saying so in words, the researcher implies, "Here are my findings and my explanation of them; I dare you to find fault with what I say or come up with
a better explanation." According to the **principle of rival explanations,** researchers should
always anticipate that others will scrutinize their methods and make interpretations different from their own. For that reason, researchers should take measures to forestall criticism
and other possible interpretations. This can be accomplished by following procedures
properly, accounting for undesired influences (called *confounding variables*), analyzing
data appropriately, pinpointing possible *bias,* and foreseeing and ruling out alternative in-

terpretations. If alternate possibilities cannot be explained, they can be acknowledged in discussions of the findings. Ideally, investigators should feel complimented if their research attracts attention, but not if rival interpretations are clearly superior to their own. That would suggest they had not been meticulous in conducting, analyzing, and reporting their efforts.

Exercise 1.4

Indicate which research principles have been observed or violated in the following: (S) significance, (G) generalizability, (RE) replicability, (PR) probability, (RS) researchability, (PS) parsimony, (C) credibility, or (RV) rival explanations.

_____ 1. For his master's thesis in education, Altamura wanted to study genealogical family roots in Italy.

_____ 2. Professor Allen complimented Altamura's revised research plan as one of the most concise and direct she had ever seen.

_____ 3. Norton wanted to repeat an earlier experiment on learning but found that the documentation available was insufficient.

_____ 4. Professor Allen told Norton, "The differences you found could as easily have been due to motivation as to intelligence."

_____ 5. Norton wrote, "The data firmly prove the existence of a full year's difference in achievement."

_____ 6. Professor Allen determined that Norton's conclusions were not valid.

Educators as Researchers

You may be wondering, in view of the requirements and rules considered so far, whether genuine research can be carried out by educators, and if so, whether such research can shed light on topics of educational concern. Rest assured that educators can, even while busy on the job, do research of quality and importance. Indeed, it is now considered that practical inquiry undertaken by educators is more likely to lead to classroom change than is formal research conducted by research specialists (Richardson, 1994). In truth, educators have rarely found traditional educational research to be of much practical use (Foshay, 1994); they prefer action research into matters directly related to their work. Radebaugh (1994) contends that educational research should not be left to experts but should involve educators much more extensively; educator-conducted research is especially powerful in shedding light on topics such as educators' personal and professional lives and the problems educators regularly encounter in their work (Fleischer, 1994; Goodson, 1994). Considerable recent thought proposes that teaching should, itself, be viewed as ongoing action research, where teachers routinely raise questions about their work with learners, collect data, interpret it, and share their conclusions with fellow teachers (Cochran-Smith, 1995).

Educators have shown an aversion to doing educational research because they have considered it unrealistically esoteric, especially its statistical analysis and hypothesis testing.

Applying Technology: Ethics and Standards of Research

The community of educational researchers most prides itself on ethical and moral behavior with respect to the practice of their profession. A lack of ethical behavior on the part of educational researchers will lead only to a lack of credible research studies; this ultimately benefits no one, including teachers and students. The guiding principles of educational research and the subsequent protection of participants originated from the Federal Policy for the Protection of Human Subjects (Title 45 Code of Federal Regulations Part 46). The guidelines were developed by the Office of Human Research Protections (OHRP), now part of the U.S. Department of Health and Human Services. For those who might be interested, these revised federal guidelines are available online (http://ohrp.osophs.dhhs.gov/humansubjects/guidance/45cfr46.htm).

Furthermore, many professional organizations in education have developed their own standards to guide practice and professional behavior. As a prime example, the premier professional association in education, the American Educational Research Association (AERA), has developed its own set of ethical standards. As stated in the Foreword of the Ethical Standards of AERA,

> A main objective of this code is to remind us, as educational researchers, that we should strive to protect these populations, and to maintain the integrity of our research, of our research community, and of all those with whom we have professional relations. We should pledge ourselves to do this by maintaining our own competence and that of people we induct into the field, by continually evaluating our research for its ethical and scientific adequacy, and by conducting our internal and external relations according to the highest ethical standards.

Individuals who conduct or plan to conduct research studies in the field of education or its related disciplines should, *at a minimum*, take time to familiarize themselves with these ethical standards. The complete standards are available online (www.aera.net/about/policy/ethics.htm) and are organized as follows:

I. Responsibilities to the Field
II. Research Populations, Educational Institutions, and the Public
III. Intellectual Ownership
IV. Editing, Reviewing, and Appraising Research
V. Sponsors, Policymakers, and Other Users of Research
VI. Students and Student Researchers

We urge all current and future educational researchers to read these brief, but substantially meaningful, standards.

As a final example of organizational-level standards, the American Association for Public Opinion Research (AAPOR) has developed its own set of standards, titled "Code of Professional Ethics and Practices" (www.aapor.org/pdfs/ethics.pdf). Although different from AERA's Ethical Standards, one should quickly notice the parallel between the two. The AAPOR Code of Professional Ethics and Practices is organized as follows:

I. Principles of Professional Practice in the Conduct of Our Work
II. Principles of Professional Responsibility in Our Dealings with People
III. Standard for Minimal Disclosure

Regardless of the specific organizations responsible for developing these, as well as other, standards of ethical research practice, it should be obvious to researchers—both current and future—that the 13 guiding principles of educational research presented in the text are addressed in these standards. It is the responsibility of educational researchers everywhere to adhere to these critical guidelines.

With today's desktop computers, statistical computation is no longer a concern. Moreover, Ornstein (1995) points out that newer concepts of research into teaching rely on storytelling, narrative, autobiography, language, and dialogue, all of which affirm the wisdom of teachers while allowing them to share their knowledge using ordinary language. Flake, Kuhs, Donnelly, and Ebert (1995) explain that, when compared to research conducted in universities, research based on educational practice is usually the more meaningful—the questions addressed are more appropriate to education, the investigations more straightforward, and the findings more valid for school practice.

Thus, be assured that not only *can* you involve yourself successfully in meaningful educational research, it is likely that any investigation you conduct will be *more beneficial* than formal research to your work in education and probably more beneficial to other educators as well. You may even wish to involve your students as coresearchers in your investigations, which seems to help them take more ownership for their learning (Pearson & Santa, 1995).

DEVELOPMENTAL ACTIVITY

Guiding Principles of Research

A common project for students enrolled in a research methods course is to develop their own research proposals and/or final research reports. Integrated throughout Chapters 1 through 9 are "developmental activities" designed to help you navigate the stages in formulating a research proposal. These activities follow the overarching theme of research proposal development, focusing on various aspects of research you must consider and strategic decisions you must make when putting together your plan for a research study of your own design. Furthermore, these activities are intended to lead you step-by-step through the process. Following are the topics addressed in each individual chapter:

- Chapter 1—Guiding Principles of Research
- Chapter 2—Type of Research
- Chapter 3—Research Topic Refinement
- Chapter 4—Locating Published Research
- Chapter 5—Reviewing Published Research
- Chapter 6—Planning for Your Research
- Chapter 7—Data Collection Decisions
- Chapter 8—Statistical Analysis Decisions
- Chapter 9—Preparing to Write Your Report

In this chapter you read about the 13 guiding principles for research. It is important to not only consider them while you conduct your study but also probably even more during the planning stages and actual development of your proposal. In the early stages of the development of a research proposal, the budding researcher begins by considering a general topic and then gives thought to the various principles. Use the following questions to help you with these considerations.

1. A possible topic or problem I am thinking of researching is: _____

    _____.

2. Potential harm to participants in my study might include: _____

    _____.

3. I would address these potential sources of harm by doing the following: _____

    _____.

4. Potential violations of confidentiality might include: _____

    _____.

5. I would address these potential violations by doing the following: _____

    _____.

6. I could adhere to the *ethical* principles by doing the following: _____

    _____.

7. I could adhere to the *philosophical* principles by doing the following: _____

    _____.

8. I could adhere to the *procedural* principles by doing the following: _____

    _____.

9. My proposed topic for research is/is not eligible for "exempt" status because of the following: _____

    _____.

(A downloadable, interactive version of this developmental activity is available from the Companion Website, www.ablongman.com/mertler5e)

Chapter Summary

Educational research, a careful, systematic, patient investigation, leads to new knowledge through use of the scientific method, which involves clarifying a problem, formulating research questions or hypotheses, obtaining pertinent information, analyzing data, describing the findings, and drawing conclusions that answer the questions or test the hypotheses. Rather strict operating procedures are followed in scientific investigations to ensure that participants are protected, information is reliable, data are analyzed properly and reported accurately, and findings and conclusions are persuasively drawn from the data.

Several operating principles orient the research process. They include (1) the legal principles of participant protection and confidentiality; (2) the ethical principles of beneficence, honesty, and accurate disclosure to participants; (3) the philosophical principles of significance, generalizability, replicability, and probability; and (4) the procedural principles of researchability, parsimony, credibility, and rival explanations.

Traditionally, educators have been reticent about involving themselves in educational research, believing that it requires sophisticated skills that only highly trained professional researchers possess. That view has changed dramatically in recent years. Educators can and do conduct research into meaningful educational topics. Research design and data analysis and interpretation no longer present obstacles. Not only can educators successfully conduct research, but also the findings they make are often of great value, both to themselves and to fellow educators.

LIST OF IMPORTANT TERMS

The following terms, important in educational research, were presented in the chapter.

conclusions	principle of confidentiality	principle of researchability
data	principle of credibility	principle of rival explanations
educational research	principle of generalizability	procedures
findings	principle of honesty	research
hypothesis	principle of importance	research problem
operating rules of research	principle of parsimony	research question
participants	principle of probability	scientific method
principle of accurate disclosure	principle of protection	scientific research
principle of beneficence	principle of replicability	

YOUR CURRENT STATUS

You now have a preliminary understanding of the nature of educational research. You recognize the general tasks involved in conducting research, the major characteristics of the scientific method, and the operating principles researchers are expected to follow. You are now ready to examine the sources of data used in educational research. Before proceeding to that topic in Chapter 2, try your hand at the following activities presented for thought and discussion.

ACTIVITIES FOR THOUGHT AND DISCUSSION

1. Here once more are the questions presented at the beginning of the chapter. Check yourself to see how well you can answer them.
   a. What *sources of information* do people usually consult first when they need to find answers to difficult questions? Why are those first sources of information often of so little value?
   b. What is meant by *scientific method*?
   c. What is *research*? How is educational research similar to and different from research in the natural sciences?
   d. What is the *general procedure* by which research is done?
   e. What are the legal, ethical, philosophical, and procedural *operating rules* that are to be followed when one conducts educational research? What is an example of each?
   f. Why should the operating rules of educational research be thought of as unwritten law?

2. Recall the chapter information organizer that was presented at the beginning of the chapter.

Without looking back in the chapter, explain briefly what you now understand about each item in the organizer.

3. Suppose you wanted to investigate the effects of two different methods of teaching reading to third-grade students. How would you comply with the principles of (a) accurate disclosure, (b) significance, (c) replicability, and (d) rival explanations?

4. Suppose you wanted to investigate the after-school activities of adolescent students from various ethnic groups. How would you comply with the principles of (a) protection, (b) confidentiality, (c) beneficence, (d) significance, and (e) credibility?

5. In terms of intent, procedure, and results, compare science with a nonscientific endeavor such as philosophy or religion.

ANSWERS TO CHAPTER EXERCISES

1.1. 1. L 2. M 3. L 4. H 5. H

1.2. 1. F 2. F/C 3. PR 4. P 5. F 6. F/C 7. H/C 8. C 9. F 10. Q

1.3. 1. C 2. H 3. AD 4. P

1.4. 1. S/G 2. PS 3. RE 4. RV 5. PR 6. C

REFERENCES AND RECOMMENDED READINGS

Akers, W., & Schubert, W. (1992). Do the right thing: Ethical issues and problems in the conduct of qualitative research in the classroom. *Teaching and Learning, 6*(2):19–24.

Best, J., & Kahn, J. (2003). *Research in Education* (9th ed.). Boston: Allyn and Bacon.

Cochran-Smith, M. (1995). Color blindness and basket making are not the answers: Confronting the dilemmas of race, culture, and language diversity in teacher education. *American Educational Research Journal, 32,* 493–522.

Dewey, J. (1933). *How We Think.* Boston: Raytheon Education Co.

Dewey, J. (1938). *Logic: The Theory of Inquiry.* New York: Holt, Rinehart, & Winston.

Family Educational Rights and Privacy Act of 1974. Washington, DC: Family Educational Rights and Privacy Office.

Feigl, H., & Broadneck, M. (1953). *Readings in the Philosophy of Science.* New York: Appleton-Century-Crofts.

Flake, C., Kuhs, T., Donnelly, A., & Ebert, C. (1995). Teacher as researcher: Reinventing the role of teacher. *Phi Delta Kappan, 76,* 405–407.

Fleischer, C. (1994). Researching teacher-research: A practitioner's retrospective. *English Education, 26,* 86–126.

Foshay, A. (1994). Action research: An early history in the United States. *Journal of Curriculum and Supervision, 9,* 317–325.

Gall, M., Borg, W., & Gall, J. (2003). *Educational Research: An Introduction* (7th ed.). Boston: Allyn and Bacon.

Goodson, I. (1994). Studying the teacher's life and work. *Teaching and Teacher Education, 10,* 29–37.

Krathwohl, D. (1994). A slice of advice. *Educational Researcher, 23,* 29–32, 42.

Lederman, N. (1992). Students' and teachers' conceptions of the nature of science: A review of the research. *Journal of Research in Science Teaching, 29,* 331–359.

McMillan, J. (2004). *Educational Research: Fundamentals for the Consumer* (4th ed.). Boston: Allyn and Bacon.

McMillan, J., & Schumacher, S. (2001). *Research in Education: A Conceptual Introduction* (5th ed.). Boston: Allyn and Bacon.

National Research Act of 1974. Bethesda, MD: National Commission for the Protection of Human Subjects.

Ornstein, A. (1995). The new paradigm in research on teaching. *Educational Forum, 59,* 124–129.

Padak, N., & Padak, G. (1995). *Guidelines for Planning Action Research Projects: Research to Practice.* Kent State University, OH: Ohio Literacy Resource Center.

Pearson, J., & Santa, C. (1995). Students as researchers of their own learning. *Journal of Reading, 38,* 462–469.

Peters, R. (1973). Aims of education—a conceptual inquiry. In R. S. Peters (ed.), *The Philosophy of Education,* (pp. 11–29). London: Oxford University Press.

Radebaugh, B. (1994). Democratizing educational research or why is our nation still at risk after ten years of educational reform? *Thresholds in Education, 20*(2–3):18–21.

Reichardt, C. (1992). The fallibility of our judgments. *Evaluation Practice, 13,* 157–163.

Richardson, V. (1994). Conducting research on practice. *Educational Researcher, 23*(5):5–10.

Strometz, D., & Skleder, A. (1992). The use of role-play in teaching research ethics: A validation study. *Teaching of Psychology, 19,* 106–108.

2 Types of Educational Research and Corresponding Sources of Data

PREVIEW

This chapter introduces the principal types of educational research, differentiated on the basis of:

- Practicality
- Research methodology
- Questions addressed

Differentiated in terms of its immediate practicality, research is either:

- Basic research or
- Applied research

Differentiated in terms of methodology used, research is either:

- Qualitative research or
- Quantitative research

and

- Experimental research or
- Nonexperimental research

Differentiated in terms of questions addressed, research is either:

- Ethnographic
- Historical
- Descriptive
- Correlational
- Action
- Evaluation
- Causal-comparative or
- Experimental

The chapter also introduces concepts and terminology related to data, regarding:

- Sources of data
- Procedures in obtaining data
- Types of data

Targeted Learnings

This chapter introduces the principal types of educational research—two types differentiated on the basis of *practicality,* four types differentiated on the basis of the *research methodology employed,* and eight types differentiated on the basis of the *research questions addressed.* The eight types based on questions addressed are reviewed, and their data sources, data characteristics, and procedures are examined. (These eight types are explored in detail in Chapters 10 through 14.) Finally, terminology important in understanding research procedures and data is presented and defined. As you read the chapter, look especially for information that answers the following questions:

1. How do the concepts of *practicality, methodology,* and *questions addressed* serve to differentiate among types of educational research?
2. What are the eight types of educational research differentiated by questions addressed?
3. What are the differences between *primary* and *secondary data sources*? Which, if either, is more valued in research?
4. What are the seven procedures commonly used in obtaining data?
5. What is meant by the terms *external criticism, internal criticism, reliability, validity, variable, continuous variable, discrete variable, independent variable, dependent variable,* and *confounding variable*?

In Chapter 1 we saw that the purpose of educational research is to help find answers to perplexing questions that have no immediate solutions and that those answers often lead to improvement in education. We saw that research employs scientific procedures for obtaining valid information, clarifying facts, and exploring relationships among those facts. We saw further that educators can, and often do, conduct research within their institutional settings.

Variables and Educational Research

Before noting the various types of research, it is important to recognize that research helps us understand *variables* and the relationships that exist among them. **Variables** are sets of data that differ from one individual, object, or procedure to another, such as physical height, achievement scores, family incomes, styles of teaching, and varieties of books. A trait that does not differ from individual to individual is called a **constant.** The number of variables extant is enormous. Variables are of different types, including continuous variables, discrete variables, dichotomous variables, independent variables, dependent variables, and confounding variables.

Continuous, Discrete, and Dichotomous Variables

Variables can be continuous, discrete, or dichotomous. **Continuous variables** show gradational differences; individuals possess more or less of the same trait, which varies in small

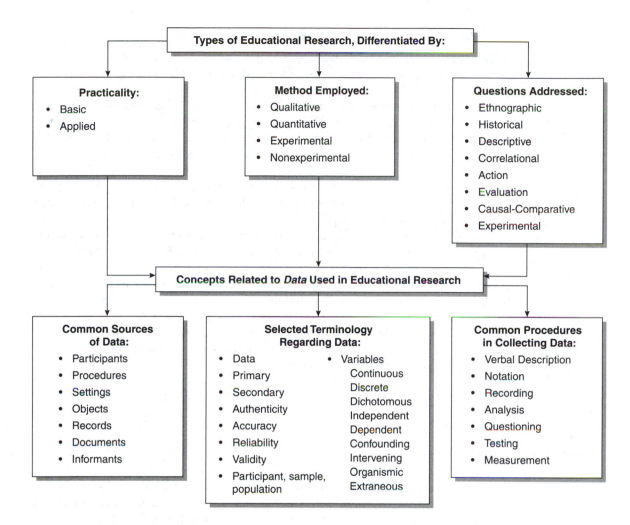

increments along a continuum. Examples of continuous variables are height and weight. Using the fictitious Elmwood Schools illustration we began in Chapter 1, we could identify several examples of continuous variables, such as "achievement" and "language proficiency" (as measured by standardized tests). **Discrete variables** are categorical in nature. Individuals may be classified into one of several categories. Examples of discrete variables are socioeconomic status, ethnicity, and ratings such as high-medium-low. Again returning to the Elmwood Schools example, specific discrete variables would include "ethnic group membership" and "type of instruction received." **Dichotomous variables** are simply special cases of discrete variables where there are only two possible categories. Examples of dichotomous variables include handedness (right, left) and sex (male, female). Examples of specific dichotomous variables from the Elmwood example might include "school district" (Elmwood, other urban districts) and "language spoken" (English, non-English).

Independent and Dependent Variables

Independent and dependent variables play important roles in experimental and causal-comparative research. The terms *independent* and *dependent* are always linked together: You cannot have an independent variable without a dependent variable, and vice versa. The **independent variable** precedes in time and exerts influence on the **dependent variable,** which may change when influenced by the independent variable. For example, level of intelligence (independent variable) may influence how quickly students learn (dependent variable), or different methods of teaching (independent variable) may influence students' enjoyment of school (dependent variable). In the Elmwood Schools example, the two levels of the independent variable "school district" (Elmwood versus other urban districts) might be compared in order to determine if differences exist with respect to "student achievement" (the dependent variable).

Confounding variables are traits or conditions, whose presence may or may not be recognized by the researcher, that may taint research outcomes. Types of confounding variables include (1) **intervening variables** (innate traits such as motivation and intelligence of participants); (2) **organismic variables** (relatively permanent physical traits that cannot be changed easily, such as poor eyesight, hearing, and coordination); and (3) **extraneous variables** (temporary conditions in nature, such as fatigue, distraction, excitement, discomfort, and test anxiety). Confounding variables must be controlled if research results are to be valid. Otherwise, conclusions drawn from research studies in which their effects were not controlled would very likely be misleading.

We now move ahead to consider various types of educational research and the general procedures used in each to obtain desired information, or data.

Types of Educational Research

Research is categorized in a number of ways. Best and Kahn (2003) note that various writers present their own systems of categorization, which indicates the absence of a standardized classification scheme. In this book, types of research will be differentiated according to (1) whether the research is done with a practical end in mind, (2) the overall methodology employed, and (3) the kinds of questions that prompt the research. Emphasis is placed on this third system of categorization, as it is the most helpful for beginning researchers.

Types of Research Categorized by Practicality

Research is often carried out to satisfy a strong interest about people, practices, and the natural world. Such research, done with no practical application in mind, is called **basic research.** This type of research is done to satisfy a need to know, just as researchers use the Hubble telescope to learn more about the farthest reaches of the universe, with no intention of resolving an immediate social or personal problem. Basic research is often conducted in the natural sciences but seldom in education, where most research is aimed directly at resolving immediate problems.

Research done to find practical solutions to pressing problems is called **applied research.** With few exceptions, this is the type of research done in education. The distinction between basic and applied research is informative but provides little guidance in selecting research topics or designing research.

Types of Research Differentiated by Methodology

Research is also categorized in terms of the *general methodology* it employs. Four different **research methods** are used in educational research. They are called *qualitative, quantitative, experimental,* and *nonexperimental.* Any given investigation is characterized by *two* of these labels. An investigation may be qualitative and nonexperimental, or quantitative and either experimental or nonexperimental. For reasons you will come to find out about later, a research study cannot be qualitative and experimental.

Research
Navigator.c⊕m

qualitative
research

quantitative
research

Qualitative versus Quantitative Research.   All research can be differentiated on the basis of whether its methodology produces mostly numerical data (e.g., scores and measurements) or mostly narrative data (e.g., verbal descriptions and opinions). Research that relies on narrative data is called **qualitative research,** while research that relies on numerical data is called **quantitative research.** We would use qualitative research if we wished to investigate and describe the after-school activities of a group of high school students that recently arrived from El Salvador. We would try to document carefully who did what, and the data thus obtained would be mostly verbal, acquired through observation, notation, and recording. On the other hand, if we wished to assess the language and mathematics abilities of those same students, we would use quantitative research. We would administer tests that yield numerical scores we could analyze statistically. At times, qualitative and quantitative methods are used in the same study.

Research
Navigator.c⊕m

experimental
research

Experimental versus Nonexperimental Research.   Though not often used in school settings because it disrupts normal groupings and teaching methods, **experimental research** can, more persuasively than any other type of research, show cause–effect relationships. It is this knowledge of cause and effect that enables us to predict and control events. The classical methodology of experimental research is as follows: Two or more groups are selected at random from a large population. Those groups, say, group A and group B, are given different treatments: Group A might receive normal instruction while group B receives instruction that involves extensive use of computers. After a time, the two groups are tested to see whether differences in learning have occurred. If differences are found, they are said to be the *effect* of the new treatment, while the new treatment (use of computers) is considered to be the *cause.* This is commonly called a **cause–effect relationship.**

Research
Navigator.c⊕m

cause and effect

Experimental research is carefully designed to control the influence of all variables except those whose specific relationship is being explored. Types of variables were discussed earlier in the chapter. Experimental research can be illustrated as in Table 2.1.

Nonexperimental research is used to (1) depict people, events, situations, conditions, and relationships as they currently exist or once existed; (2) evaluate products or processes; and (3) develop innovations. In these cases, experimentation is not appropriate or

TABLE 2.1 **Experimental Research**

Two Equal Groups	Taught Differently	Results Compared
Group A	Normal instruction	Achievement?
Group B	Computers used	Achievement?

else is not used because the independent (causative) variables, such as gender or ethnicity, cannot be manipulated—that is, varied—by the researcher in order to see whether a resultant change is produced in the dependent variable. The average person equates scientific research with experimentation, a view that is often correct in the natural sciences. But in education and the social sciences, experimentation is difficult to accomplish. Therefore, in education, nonexperimental research is the rule rather than the exception.

Exercise 2.1

Identify each of the following possible research projects as (B) basic or (A) applied; (E) experimental or (NE) nonexperimental; and (QA) qualitative or (QN) quantitative. Three or more labels should be applied to each research.

_____ _____ _____ 1. LaToyne Marshall, a retired teacher, becomes interested in describing the present-day lives of community residents who were his students in Cutter Elementary School at least 30 years ago.

_____ _____ _____ 2. Nativadad Rojas, bilingual coordinator for Elmwood schools, wants to determine how achievement is affected by instructing students part of the day in their native language.

_____ _____ _____ 3. Teachers at Fairfield High School want to produce and field-test an instructional packet on cultural diversity they believe will benefit all students at their school.

_____ _____ _____ 4. Alana Hopkins, a teacher at Magnolia Middle School, wants to determine, as a requirement for her master's degree, whether a relationship exists between school achievement and the number of schools previously attended by Magnolia students.

Types of Research Defined by Questions Addressed

A third means of categorizing research focuses on the nature of the research questions addressed. Eight types of research are commonly identified based on the nature of their central questions. Those types are ethnographic, historical, descriptive, correlational, action, evaluation, causal-comparative, and experimental research. Consider the following questions.

1. What is a typical week like in the lives of five selected students attending Elmwood's Lincoln High School?

2. What cultural, ethnic, and linguistic groups made up Elmwood schools' student population in 1955, and how successful were those groups academically?
3. What cultural, ethnic, and linguistic groups comprise Elmwood schools' student population today, and how successful are those groups academically?
4. What is the relationship between English vocabulary proficiency and school achievement among Elmwood students?
5. Can a schoolwide disciplinary system be designed to improve the overall behavior of students in Elmwood's Cutter Elementary School?
6. How effective is Elmwood's bilingual education program in promoting scholastic achievement?
7. What is the effect of bilingualism on school achievement among Elmwood students?
8. Can cultural sensitivity training improve interpersonal relationships among Elmwood's students of diverse ethnic backgrounds?

Each of these questions calls for a different type of research, as shown in the following explanations.

Question 1: What is a typical week like in the lives of five selected students attending Elmwood's Lincoln High School?

This question calls for **ethnographic research,** which documents and explains social behavior within groups. Unlike other types of research, ethnography explores behavior holistically within a social setting of customs, values, and styles of communication. Data sources are people, objects, environments, and communication patterns inherent in the context under study. Findings are usually presented in narrative form, sometimes enhanced by graphic illustrations. This type of research is nonexperimental, largely qualitative, and is heavily dependent on investigator perception and skill in making observations and interpretations.

Question 2: What cultural, ethnic, and linguistic groups made up Elmwood schools' student population in 1955, and how successful were those groups academically?

This question calls for **historical research,** which explores conditions, situations, events, or people of the past. Historical research is nonexperimental and may be qualitative, quantitative, or a combination of the two. It is typically guided by research questions and uses as sources of data original documents, newspaper accounts, photographs and drawings, historical records, locales, objects, and people who have some knowledge of the time and place under investigation. Findings from historical research are normally presented in narrative form illuminated by numerical, categorical, and graphic illustrations.

Question 3: What cultural, ethnic, and linguistic groups comprise Elmwood schools' student population today, and how successful are those groups academically?

This question calls for **descriptive research,** which is done to depict people, situations, events, and conditions as they currently exist. Descriptive research is nonexperimental and can be either qualitative, quantitative, or a combination of the two. Hypotheses are

TABLE 2.2   Correlational Research

A Single Group	Two Traits Measured	Relationship between Traits
Several individuals	English vocabulary School achievement	Might range from none to high

frequently used in descriptive research, as are research questions. The major sources from which information is obtained are physical settings, records, documents, objects, materials, and people directly involved. Additional information may be obtained from newspaper accounts, photographs, and people who possess knowledge of the situation but were not directly involved. Findings are presented in narrative form enhanced by numerical, categorical, and graphic illustrations.

Question 4: What is the relationship between English vocabulary proficiency and school achievement among Elmwood students?

This question calls for **correlational research,** which can explore the degree of correlation between two or more variables. In correlational research, data are obtained from the individuals serving as participants in the study. At least one pair of measures must be obtained for each of the people involved. To answer the foregoing question, we need to obtain a measure of each person's vocabulary proficiency (one of the variables) and a measure of each person's achievement level (the other variable). Those measures—probably numerical—give us a pair of scores for each student. From that information we can calculate the degree of relationship—the *correlation*—that exists between vocabulary proficiency and academic achievement for the sample. Correlational research, which is quantitative and nonexperimental, may strongly suggest cause–effect relationships but cannot demonstrate them nearly so convincingly as can experimental research. We must be cautious when inferring cause–effect from correlations. In themselves, correlations merely show that two traits covary with each other. For example, student intelligence and grade point average (GPA) are known to be correlated, which means that people high in one tend to be high in the other, and vice versa, though not always. But this does not say that either of the traits necessarily "causes" the other. It is foolish to suggest that a high GPA causes one to be more intelligent. Our minds tell us that intelligence is very likely an important contributing factor to high GPA, but so are motivation, perseverance, and good study habits.

In addition to suggesting possible causation, correlations give us the valuable ability to predict one of the variables from the other. If we know that 16-year-old Kareem is very intelligent, we can predict that he will probably graduate with a high GPA. If a university admissions official looks at Kareem's high GPA on his transcript, that official can predict with some certainty that Kareem is quite intelligent and has the capability to do well in college. Correlational research can be illustrated as in Table 2.2.

Question 5: Can a schoolwide disciplinary system be designed to improve the overall behavior of students in Elmwood's Cutter Elementary School?

TABLE 2.3 Action Research

Undesirable Condition	New Development Implemented	Result Evaluated
Unruliness	New discipline system	Better behavior?

This question calls for **action research,** which is done to improve conditions within a particular setting, without concern for applying the findings elsewhere. If the Cutter Elementary School faculty is worried about classroom discipline and wishes to make improvements at their school, then action research might be undertaken to identify the specific problems, formulate possible solutions, apply those solutions, and evaluate the results, all the while keeping records that document problems, procedures, and results. Action research can be illustrated as in Table 2.3.

> *Question 6:* How effective is Elmwood's bilingual education program in promoting scholastic achievement?

This question calls for **evaluation research,** done to make judgments about the quality of particular programs, procedures, materials, and the like. In Elmwood schools, evaluation research can determine the value of the bilingual program in terms of student learning and teacher satisfaction. Data in evaluation research are obtained by assessing student performance, analyzing materials, and interviewing teachers, students, administrators, parents, and community members. The data collected are then compared against a set of criteria used to indicate quality—the bilingual program, for example, might be judged against criteria such as student learning, ease of implementation, cost-effectiveness, availability and quality of materials, student and teacher morale, and high level of commitment from parents, teachers, and students.

> *Question 7:* What is the effect of bilingualism on school achievement among Elmwood students?

This question calls for **causal-comparative research,** which explores the influence of a preexisting condition—in this case bilingualism—on a variable such as learning. This type of research can suggest causality more persuasively than correlational research, but less persuasively than experimental research. For the question posed here, the researcher first randomly selects a group of monolingual students and a group of bilingual students, making sure that the two groups are otherwise as similar as possible, especially in ability and curriculum experienced. Then academic achievement of the two groups is measured. Finally, assuming that other factors are equal between the groups—an assumption that is tenuous in this case—any difference in scholastic achievement (the effect) can be attributed to bilingualism (the cause). This is not considered to be experimental research because the independent variable (bilingualism) cannot, except over long periods of time, be altered (manipulated) by the researcher as is essential in experimental research. Causal-comparative research is nonexperimental and quantitative and uses data obtained from the people involved. It can be illustrated as in Table 2.4.

TABLE 2.4   Causal-Comparative Research

Otherwise Equal Groups	Hypothesized Causal Factor	Observed Effect
Bilingual group A	Bilingualism	Achievement?
Monolingual group B	Monolingualism	Achievement?

Question 8: Can cultural sensitivity training improve interpersonal relationships among Elmwood's students of diverse ethnic backgrounds?

This question calls for **experimental research,** which might be designed as follows: A number of students are randomly selected from the population and then randomly assigned to two groups. None of the students has previously undergone cultural sensitivity training. One group (the experimental group) is given sensitivity exercises—an example of what is meant by "manipulating the independent variable." The second group (the control group) is given "placebo" exercises, activities believed to have no effect on participants except to make them think they are receiving special attention, as is the experimental group. After the sensitivity training is completed, the two groups are assessed to see if differences become apparent in individuals' relationships with others. Experimental research, which is usually quantitative, focuses on independent and dependent variables, called *cause* and *effect,* respectively. The *independent* (causal) variable in this question is cultural sensitivity training. The *dependent* (effect) variable is interpersonal relationships. If the two sample groups are originally very similar, and if other cautions to be described later are satisfied, then subsequent changes in interpersonal relationships tentatively may be attributed to the effects of sensitivity training.

Experimental research is difficult to conduct in education because in true experiments students are randomly assigned to groups receiving the different treatments. However, random assignment is impractical where students already belong to classes that cannot be reconstituted easily. Even when possible, many parents object to their children being "experimented on." Yet, as we have noted, experimental research is highly valued because it indicates cause–effect relationships more convincingly than any other type of research. Experimental research can be illustrated as in Table 2.5.

TABLE 2.5   Experimental Research

Two Equivalent Groups	Treatment (Independent Variable)	Result (Dependent Variable)
Group A	Sensitivity training	Interpersonal relationships?
Group B	Placebo training	Interpersonal relationships?

Exercise 2.2

Label each of the following research topics as (ET) ethnographic, (H) historical, (D) descriptive, (C) correlation, (A) action, (EV) evaluation, (CC) causal-comparative, or (EX) experimental. In some cases more than one label can be correctly applied.

_____ 1. The Cutter school PTA wants to describe the facilities, staff, and students of Cutter school when it first opened in 1952.

_____ 2. Mr. Sánchez wants to determine whether teaching Anglo students Spanish vocabulary also improves their vocabularies in English.

_____ 3. Miss Wharton wants to compare the daily lives of five randomly selected African American students.

_____ 4. Principal Medeiros wants to find out whether there is a relationship between student achievement and parents' responses to a questionnaire.

_____ 5. Mrs. Alonzo is developing what she calls a "cultural equity program" to see if it will improve relations among her sixth-grade students.

_____ 6. Mrs. Andrade wants to determine how well the new language books are serving their intended purposes.

_____ 7. Mr. Rekkas wishes to determine why teachers' professional lives 30 years ago seem to have been more satisfying than they are now.

Given the foregoing overview of standard types of educational research, let us consider the sources and requirements of the data they employ.

Primary and Secondary Sources of Research Data

Research
Navigator.c⊕m
primary data
secondary data

The information researchers obtain about people, settings, objects, and procedures is called **data,** which can be recorded in verbal or numerical form. Data are obtained from two broad sources of information, called **primary sources** and **secondary sources.** Information from those sources is correspondingly called **primary data** and **secondary data.** Usually a third type of information is sought as well—reports of previous investigations related to the matter under consideration.

Primary data sources are highly valued because the firsthand information they supply tends to be more accurate than information obtained from secondary sources. Examples of primary data sources are physical objects, original reports, records, and eyewitness accounts. In studying Elmwood schools, primary data sources would include such things as test scores, demographic records, attendance records, minutes of meetings, transcripts of testimony, photographs, instructional materials, student informants, parent informants, teacher informants, and transcripts of hearings. Although the primary data obtained from such sources are prized for accuracy, they nevertheless can be erroneous. It is well established that personal reports about the same incident usually differ, sometimes substantially.

Secondary data sources provide reports or interpretations of primary data, made by people who did not directly experience the events under consideration. Examples of secondary data sources are hearsay testimony, histories (not autobiographical), selected compilations, encyclopedia entries, newspaper reports, and analyses and interpretations of events not experienced firsthand. Secondary data sources are quite valuable and, at times, highly accurate—sometimes even more accurate than primary sources—but they are subject to errors of interpretation, emphasis, memory, and personal bias and are, therefore, generally considered less reliable than primary sources. In research involving Elmwood schools, secondary data sources might include newspaper accounts of meetings and incidents, editorials, radio and television reports, abstracts of hearings and court cases, what students say their parents believe, and what parents say their children experience and believe.

**Research
Navigator.c⊛m**
meta-analysis

Additional information sought by researchers includes the findings made in other investigations similar to their own. Researchers always review the literature to see if they can find such related studies. The information thus obtained is used for the following purposes: (1) to orient, guide, and define the limits of a study; (2) as secondary data possibly useful in the topic under investigation; and (3) as primary data in what are called **meta-analytical** studies, which analyze numerous existing studies to draw new conclusions. Usually, however, the questions, procedures, and findings in studies similar to one's own provide only context and guidance for research.

Specific Sources of Research Data

Data in educational research are obtained from several different sources, including participants, procedures, settings, objects, records, documents, and informants.

Participants, as we have noted, are individuals from whom data are obtained. They often, but not always, comprise a **sample,** which is a group of individuals one hopes represents the population at large.

Procedures are formalized ways of operating in the educational setting—the way things are done. How lessons are presented and how homework is assigned are two examples of procedures, from among hundreds in education.

Settings are the specific environments within which educational behavior occurs. Examples include classrooms, athletic fields, libraries, laboratories, playgrounds, and homes.

Objects are inanimate things such as books, supplies, materials, and artifacts.

Records are highly summarized reports of performance, expenditures, and the like, kept for later reference.

Documents are written papers and reports in their entirety, such as journal articles, technical papers, and curriculum guides. Photographs, drawings, and other illustrations are also considered documents.

Informants are people, other than participants in the study, from whom opinion, informed views, and expert testimony are obtained.

Exercise 2.3

For the following indicate the most likely source of data: (P) participant, (PR) procedure, (ST) setting, (O) object, (R) record, (D) document, or (I) informant.

_____   1.   Study of old textbooks

_____   2.   Average achievement scores in 1957

_____   3.   Observations of how primary teachers begin the day

_____   4.   Children's playgrounds

_____   5.   A comparative analysis of secondary school curriculum guides

_____   6.   What students say about self-directed work

_____   7.   What one "insider" says about the value of faculty meetings

_____   8.   School districts' mission statements

_____   9.   Live testimony before a committee

_____   10.   The group's reading level today, as yet undetermined

Procedures Used in Collecting Data

Data are collected from the sources just listed by means of seven general procedures: verbal description, notation, recording, analysis, questioning, testing, and measurement.

Verbal description is a data collection procedure used in the study of settings, procedures, and behaviors. It depends on observation and is a written or spoken depiction of what is observed. It attempts to capture fairly complete pictures. Verbal description is indispensable in researching topics where measurement and numerical representation are not feasible. It is the primary method used to obtain data in ethnographic research and is frequently used in historical and descriptive research as well. It enables researchers to capture full pictures of situations and dynamics within and among schools, classrooms, teachers, administrators, parents, community members, and students both inside and outside of school (Zaharlick, 1992).

Notation refers to making tally marks or brief written notes about people, objects, or other data sources. One sees a particular behavior and makes a note of its occurrence. One examines a textbook and lists its characteristics. One finds important information in a document and summarizes contents and bibliographical information. Notation is tied to observation. One observes and makes notes about what is seen or heard.

Recording refers to capturing scenes and interactions by means of camera or audio- or videotape recorders. Recordings are replete with detail that might go unnoticed until scrutinized. Data obtained in recordings must be converted to words, scores, or tally marks before they can be analyzed properly.

Analysis, which should not be confused with statistical analysis of data, involves breaking entities down into constituent parts in order to determine their composition, how they are organized, and how they function. Many sources can be accessed through analysis, but this procedure is especially useful in obtaining data about objects, relics, documents, and procedures, as follows:

Objects routinely analyzed include products made by students—art, handicrafts, handwriting, timed tests, constructions, portfolios, and the like—as well as those made by teachers and others concerned with education, examples of which include textbooks, curricula, guides, instructors' manuals, supplementary materials, and discipline systems.

Relics, which are objects recovered from prior times, are invaluable sources of data in historical research. For example, over a half century ago, all the inhabitants of the mining town of Bodie, California, abruptly departed when the mining operation closed. The weather at Bodie was so inhospitable that no one wanted to stay. Rather than try to move the town, the populace simply left their homes, stores, shops, buildings, and school more or less intact, with furniture, merchandise, supplies, and equipment in place. Now restored and protected, the ghost town of Bodie is replete with relics from which researchers have pieced together a detailed picture of life and education there in earlier times.

Documents analyzed in research include published papers, curriculum guides, newspaper accounts, photographs and other illustrations, transcripts of proceedings, and the like. Documents provide much of the data used in descriptive and historical research.

Procedures related to education are also analyzed, to determine who does what, when, and with what effect. Analysis of procedures was used by both Kounin (1971) and Jones (1987) in their pivotal studies on the relationship between instructional procedures and classroom discipline. By analyzing classroom procedures, Kounin and Jones identified those that facilitated or inhibited student attention and work, and from that knowledge new procedures were developed that reduced the incidence of classroom misbehavior.

Questioning involves researchers asking questions directly of participants or informants. Questioning is not done haphazardly but in a carefully planned manner. It uses both surveys and personal interviews, which can be carried out through correspondence, telephone contact, or personal contact, as follows:

Surveys are used in educational research to determine such things as opinions about education, attitudes toward the school system, home reading habits, and teachers' perceptions of their workloads. Surveys typically make use of questionnaires whose formats and contents are carefully prepared and refined before final use. Surveys stick scrupulously to the written format and do not provide for probing or clarifying.

The personal **interview** is organized around a predetermined set of questions but allows the questioner to provide encouragement, ask probing questions, and request additional information. The interview can obtain more useful information than can the questionnaire, but the reliability of that information can be suspect. Respondents are easily influenced by the interviewer's manner, encouragement, and requests for clarification, so that a person's responses to the same questions may vary substantially from one interviewer to another (Smith, 1992).

Testing, which calls on participants to perform cognitive and/or psychomotor tasks, is probably more frequently used to collect educational research data than any other method. Most tests are administered in written form, but many are administered orally. They usually yield a numerical score, but not always. Sometimes they provide ranked or categorical data and sometimes only verbal data. Validity (accuracy) and reliability (consistency) are matters of great concern in testing; therefore, research that makes use of tests must give close attention to the validity and reliability of test instruments used.

Measurement is used to obtain data by checking performance or status against an established scale. Testing, one means by which measurement is done, is often used synonymously with measurement, but measurement is the broader and more inclusive term and is used herein to refer to obtaining data by means of scales other than tests. Examples of measurement include determining height and weight, blood pressure, number of books read, distance run, time spent on lesson segments, and hours spent watching television.

Exercise 2.4

Which of the following data collection procedures is best associated with each of the following numbered items: (N) notation, (D) description, (A) analysis, (Q) questioning, (T) testing, or (M) measurement?

_____   1. Granger administered the Stanford Achievement Test.

_____   2. Morris carefully studied samples of student art work.

_____   3. Torres found the names in court records.

_____   4. Nguyen mailed out 1,000 questionnaires.

_____   5. Truk spoke with each of the top administrators.

_____   6. Michaels kept detailed accounts of classroom interactions.

_____   7. Oliphant wanted to determine students' pulse rates during final examinations.

Qualities Required in Research Data

Research conclusions cannot be taken seriously if there is question about the quality of the data from which the conclusions are drawn. Researchers, therefore, scrutinize data to make sure they are authentic, believable, valid, and reliable.

Authenticity and Believability

Researchers use two informal, unstructured means of assessing data for authenticity and believability. These two means are called the tests of *external criticism* and *internal criticism.*

External criticism has to do with determining whether the data come from legitimate sources. This test is one of analysis and judgment. It is unwritten and uses no statistical calculations. Let us suppose researcher Ms. Jordan, investigating past funding and expenditures of Elmwood schools, has discovered an unusual letter in Elmwood's archives. The letter bears the signature of Dr. Lehman, a former superintendent of schools who recently died in a mental institution. The letter is one of confession, in which Dr. Lehman admits falsifying over a period of five years both attendance and achievement records, in order to obtain increased federal funding for Elmwood schools. According to the letter, the admission of wrongdoing was made to assuage feelings of guilt and to set the record straight.

Ms. Jordan has the obligation of determining whether the information is legitimate. In applying the test of external criticism, she must satisfy such questions as: Is this letter genuine, or is it a fake? Can the signature be verified as that of Dr. Lehman? Was it really written on the date indicated, when Dr. Lehman was already a resident in the mental institution? If so, how did the letter get in the archives? Is there evidence that Dr. Lehman had enemies who wished to discredit him and might have attempted to do so in this manner?

While authenticity of data is fundamentally important, educational researchers do not often encounter situations that raise questions about authenticity of data. That is, there is relatively little likelihood of encountering fabricated scores or informants who misrepresent facts intentionally. Still, there remains the question of believability of the data, which calls for application of internal criticism.

In keeping with **internal criticism,** even if Ms. Jordan concludes that Dr. Lehman wrote the letter, she must still decide whether the information is believable. Researchers do regularly encounter information of questionable veracity. Ms. Jordan must, therefore, apply a second test to the letter she has found. That test is called *internal criticism* and has to do with data accuracy and lack of bias. Let us assume she determined that the signature on the letter was similar to that of Dr. Lehman in his declining years. Ms. Jordan knows that even legitimate sources can provide erroneous data. People do not perceive things exactly the same, nor do they remember them the same. Their recollections may be slanted by existing bias, and sometimes they believe to be true things they have only imagined. Ms. Jordan applies the test of internal criticism by asking questions such as: Did Dr. Lehman have his facts correct? Might he have believed he falsified records when in fact he did not? Was Dr. Lehman known to have made other unusual assertions? Do other experts believe that Dr. Lehman could have obtained funding through the misrepresentations he admits?

All researchers should ask themselves similar questions about the data they acquire. Is the source legitimate? Do the data come from real people, objects, or events? Are the data accurate? Is there possibility of bias? Such questions are usually answered through corroborating evidence from another source—in this case perhaps from a colleague who worked closely with Dr. Lehman at the time in question.

Research
Navigator.c⊕m
validity and
reliability

Validity and Reliability

Data must not only be authentic and believable but are worthless unless they are also valid and reliable. Data are **valid** to the extent they depict or deal directly with the topic under consideration. For example, information in Dr. Lehman's letter is valid if it pertains to a real occurrence but invalid if it does not. Data in the form of scores made on geometry tests are valid if they have to do with knowledge of geometry rather than some other ability (such as reading, which could unduly affect understanding of written directions and responses to word problems). Historical information about Scotch-Irish migration patterns in the United States is valid if it depicts movements of the Scotch-Irish, rather than of English or other immigrants contemporaneous with the Scotch-Irish.

Data are **reliable** to the extent they are consistent. Geometry test scores are reliable if individuals make approximately the same scores when again taking the test. Research data are considered reliable if there is consistency among the reports provided by different observers. Information presented in Dr. Lehman's letter would be considered reliable if verified by others who had knowledge of what Dr. Lehman did. On the other hand, if information about a topic is inconsistent—if it varies noticeably from test to test, observation to observation, or competent person to competent person—it is considered unreliable and is, therefore, of no value to the researcher. The concepts of validity and reliability will be discussed in greater detail in Chapter 7.

Exercise 2.5

Which of the following labels can best be associated with each of the following eight items: (P) primary data source, (S) secondary data source, (E) external criticism, (I) internal criticism, (R) reliable data, or (V) valid data?

_____ 1. It was determined that data obtained from the use of Mr. Collins's new algebra test did in fact have to do mainly with knowledge of algebra.

_____ 2. Students from whom information was obtained when Mr. Collins's test underwent validation procedures

_____ 3. Parents who offered information concerning what their children said they liked about Mr. Collins's test

_____ 4. Test data obtained from a selected group of students were, the second time they took Mr. Collins's test, almost the same as when those students first took his test a week earlier.

_____ 5. Mr. Collins, when explaining how he constructed his test

_____ 6. A lead story that appeared in the local newspaper concerning what students and administrators said about Mr. Collins's new algebra test

_____ 7. It was determined that Mr. Collins did author the new test, as he claimed.

_____ 8. Mr. Collins's conclusions were verified by two independent authorities.

Treatment and Presentation of Data

Once data are obtained, they are treated and presented in various ways. They may simply be identified, listed, described, or given as written narrative. Data presented in these ways can show the condition or status of people, objects, or processes, and are common in

---

Applying Technology: **More about Variables and Questions**

Dr. William Trochim, a professor at Cornell University, has developed an extensive online research methods textbook (http://trochim.human.cornell.edu/kb). His electronic text, titled *Research Methods Knowledge Base,* is an excellent resource and may prove very beneficial as a supplement to readers throughout this text. Dr. Trochim's *e-text* is organized into six major sections:

- *Foundations of Research*
- *Sampling*
- *Measurement*
- *Research Design*
- *Data Analysis*
- *Writing Up Research*

For the purposes of topics addressed in this chapter, Dr. Trochim provides a discussion of the various types of variables encountered in educational research (http://trochim.human. cornell.edu/kb/variable.htm). His discussion is quite good, as he presents specific examples of the classifications of variables. He is also quite frank in confessing that he had much difficulty in learning the distinction between independent and dependent variables—a problem often encountered by graduate students.

A discussion of types of data, specifically qualitative and quantitative, is also presented (http://trochim.human.cornell.edu/kb/datatype.htm). The discussion focuses on the distinction between qualitative and quantitative data but also enlightens future researchers as to the "intimate relationship" shared by these two types of data. This is a "must read" for all researchers, as it will surely improve understanding the basic nature of data.

Although it may not be specifically mentioned in subsequent chapters, the *Knowledge Base* can be an excellent supplement for topics covered later in this text.

---

ethnographic, historical, and descriptive research. But data may often be analyzed further for confidence testing, hypothesis testing, and to show comparisons, trends, relative placement of scores, differences among groups, relationships among variables, or effects produced by different treatments or conditions. Data analysis is described, as appropriate, in Chapters 8, 10 through 14, and Appendix A.

Additional Terminology Related to Data

So far, we have considered the labels used to differentiate among types of research, noted the sources of data used in research, and become acquainted with some of the necessary qualities of data. At this point, additional important concepts related to data are introduced.

Participants, Samples, and Populations

Researchers obtain data from participants who are often members of samples in order to learn about populations. People and other living things, when being studied in research, are referred to as *participants.* Participants are usually, but not always, members of *samples,* which are groups of individuals selected from a larger population. (Sometimes a single participant is studied in depth.) A **population** contains all the individuals within certain descriptive parameters, such as those of location, age, or sex. For example, a population might be all the 10-year-olds in the world, all the third-grade students in the United States, all the teachers in Elmwood, or all the parents and guardians of students attending Cutter Elementary School.

Researchers usually want to learn about entire populations, but it is impractical to study a population unless it is quite small—there are simply too many individuals to deal with. Therefore, researchers use samples drawn from the larger population. In order for their findings to apply to the entire population, the sample must fairly accurately represent the population. Random selection of participants from the population is a preferred method for establishing samples, but random selection is not often practical in educational research because it disrupts preestablished classes. When random selection is not possible, or for some reason is not appropriate, other procedures are used to select samples. Those procedures are discussed in Chapter 7.

DEVELOPMENTAL ACTIVITY

Type of Research

In the developmental activity at the end of Chapter 1, you began your process of planning a research study by thinking of a possible research topic, considering potential pitfalls you might encounter along the way, and brainstorming various ways to overcome them. Another important decision that you must make as a researcher in the early stages of planning a research study is to determine what type (or types) of research might be most appropriate in order to adequately address your topic. Consider the topic with which you began working in Chapter 1 and answer the following questions:

1. A possible topic or problem I am thinking of researching is: _____

   _____ .

2. The type of research that seems most appropriate to my chosen topic is (*check one*):

   ☐ ethnographic research

   ☐ historical research

   ☐ descriptive research

   ☐ correlational research

(continued)

☐ action research

☐ evaluation research

☐ causal-comparative research

☐ experimental research

3. The reason that I chose that particular type of research, and why I think it is most appropriate for my topic, is: _____

_____.

4. Other types of research (if any) in the preceding list that *might* also seem appropriate for my topic include: _____

_____.

5. Based on my responses to questions 3 and 4, criticisms by experienced researchers of my topic using these approaches might include: _____

_____.

6. Based on my responses to the preceding questions, I believe that _____ research would be most appropriate.

(A downloadable, interactive version of this developmental activity is available from the Companion Website, http://www.ablongman.com/mertler5e)

Chapter Summary

Research usually focuses on variables, which are sets of data that show ranges of difference in people, objects, and procedures. Terms used for variables include *continuous* (a wide range), *discrete* (several categories), *dichotomous* (two categories), *independent* (a manipulated variable), *dependent* (changes in accord with changes in the independent variable), and *confounding* (variables not subjected to research but which may taint research findings).

Types of educational research, sources of data, and means of obtaining data are intertwined. For individuals new to research, the most useful way of differentiating types of research is by the nature of the research questions addressed. Types of research thus differentiated include ethnographic, historical, descriptive, correlational, action, evaluative, causal-comparative, and experimental. Other labels that serve to differentiate among types of research are basic, applied, quantitative, qualitative, experimental, and nonexperimental.

Research information obtained about people, places, things, interactions, and the like is called *data*. Important concepts related to data include authenticity (genuineness), accuracy, reliability (consistency), validity (on target), primary (firsthand), secondary (secondhand), participants (people being studied), sample (a group of participants selected from, and representative of, a larger population), population (all the individuals within selected parameters), and variable (a characteristic that tends to differ from person to person or item to item).

Various procedures are used to obtain research data. Seven common procedures are notation, recording, description, analysis, questioning, measurement, and testing.

LIST OF IMPORTANT TERMS

action research

analysis

applied research

basic research

causal-comparative research

cause–effect relationship

constant

confounding variable

continuous variable

correlational research

data

dependent variable

descriptive research

dichotomous variable

discrete variable

ethnographic research

evaluation research

experimental research

external criticism

extraneous variable

historical research

independent variable

internal criticism

intervening variable

interview

measurement

meta-analysis

nonexperimental research

notation

organismic variable

population

primary data

primary source

qualitative research

quantitative research

questioning

reliability

research method

sample

secondary data

secondary source

survey

validity

variable

YOUR CURRENT STATUS

To your previous knowledge of the nature, principles, and procedures of educational research, you have added knowledge of various types of educational research, as defined by practicality (basic versus applied), method (quantitative versus qualitative; experimental versus nonexperimental), and questions addressed (ethnographic, historical, descriptive, correlational, action, evaluation, causal-comparative, and experimental). You know what is meant by data, recognize the differences between primary and secondary data, and can identify many of the major data sources. You understand the concepts of authenticity, accuracy, reliability, and validity and recognize their importance in research. Finally, you understand the meanings of the terms *population, sample, participant,* and *variable.* You are now ready to move on to a consideration of how one selects, refines, and proposes a topic for research. Before proceeding to Chapter 3, please take time to complete the following activities for thought and discussion.

ACTIVITIES FOR THOUGHT AND DISCUSSION

1. Suppose you wanted to investigate the effects of two different methods of teaching reading to third-grade students.
   a. Which of the eight types of research would be indicated?
   b. What would be the independent and dependent variables in your research?
   c. Identify your likely sources of primary data.

2. Suppose you wanted to compare the history and development of an urban school (Cutter) with that of a rural school (Greenleaf).

   a. What type of research would be called for?
   b. Name important primary and secondary sources of data.
   c. Would you orient your research by means of research questions, hypotheses, or both? Give examples.
   d. To what approximate degree do you believe this research would be qualitative, as contrasted with quantitative research?

3. Here are the questions presented at the beginning of the chapter. How well can you answer them?

a. How do the concepts of *practicality, methodology,* and *questions addressed* serve to differentiate among types of educational research?

b. What are the eight types of educational research differentiated by questions addressed?

c. What are the differences between *primary* and *secondary data sources*? Which, if either, is more valued in research?

d. What are the seven procedures commonly used in obtaining data?

e. What is meant by the terms *external criticism, internal criticism, reliability, validity, variable, continuous variable, discrete variable, independent variable, dependent variable,* and *confounding variable*?

4. Recall the information organizer presented at the beginning of the chapter. Without looking back, explain briefly what you now understand about each item in the organizer.

A N S W E R S   T O   C H A P T E R   E X E R C I S E S

2.1. 1. B/NE/QA 2. A/E (NE)/QN 3. A/NE (E)/QA (QN) 4. A/NE/QN

2.2. 1. H 2. EX 3. ET 4. C 5. A 6. EV 7. H/EV

2.3. 1. O 2. R 3. P 4. ST 5. D 6. P 7. I 8. D 9. I 10. P

2.4. 1. T 2. A 3. N 4. Q 5. Q 6. D 7. M

2.5. 1. V 2. P 3. S 4. R 5. P 6. S 7. E 8. I

R E F E R E N C E S   A N D   R E C O M M E N D E D   R E A D I N G S

Best, J., & Kahn, J. (2003). *Research in Education* (9th ed.). Boston: Allyn and Bacon.

Brandt, R. (1992). On research on teaching: A conversation with Lee Schulman. *Educational Leadership, 49*(7):14–19.

Crowl, T. (1993). *Fundamentals of Educational Research* (pp. 3–9). Madison, WI: WCB Brown & Benchmark.

Edyburn, D.L. (1999). *The Electronic Scholar: Enhancing Research Productivity with Technology.* Upper Saddle River, NJ: Merrill.

Gay, L., & Airasian, P. (2000). *Educational Research: Competencies for Analysis and Application* (6th ed.) (pp. 3–16). Upper Saddle River, NJ: Merrill.

Howe, K. (1992). Getting over the quantitative-qualitative debate. *American Journal of Education, 100*(2):236–256.

Jones, F. (1987). *Positive Classroom Discipline.* New York: McGraw-Hill.

Kounin, J. (1971). *Discipline and Group Management in Classrooms.* New York: Holt, Rinehart, and Winston.

Lederman, N. (1992). You can't do it by arithmetic, you have to do it by algebra! *Journal of Research in Science Teaching, 29*:1011–1013.

Lytle, S., & Cochran-Smith, M. (1992). Teacher research as a way of knowing. *Harvard Educational Review, 62*:447–474.

Sawin, E. (1992). Reaction: Experimental research in the context of other methods. *School of Education Review, 4* (Spring):18–21.

Schmidt, T. (1992). Assessment and evaluation of technology in education—the teacher as a researcher. *Computing Teacher, 20*(1):9–10.

Smith, J. (1992). Interpretive inquiry: A practical and moral activity. *Theory into Practice, 31*(1):100–106.

Smith, M. (1987). Publishing qualitative research. *American Educational Research Journal, 24*(2):173–183.

Trochim, W.M. (2000). *The Research Methods Knowledge Base* (2nd ed.). Available at http://trochim.human.cornell.edu/Kb/index.htm.

Winkler, K. (1992). Researchers leave labs, flock to schools for a new look at how students learn. *Chronicle of Higher Education, 39*(8):6–7.

Zaharlick, A. (1992). Ethnography in anthropology and its value for education. *Theory into Practice, 31*(1):116–125.

3 Selecting, Refining, and Proposing a Topic for Research

P R E V I E W

This chapter introduces four clusters of research skills important to graduate students:

1. Choosing a topic for research
- Identification of promising topics
- Selection of a specific topic to investigate
- Refinement of the selected topic

2. Stating the problem to be investigated
- Purpose of the study—what it is supposed to accomplish and how
- Importance of the study—why it is worth pursuing, what it can contribute
- Limitations of the study—restrictions that limit its scope
- Special terms that are used in the study

3. Orienting the research
- Formulating research questions—what one hopes to discover or resolve
- Formulating hypotheses—forecasts of results of the study

4. Preparing the research proposal
- Organization and presentation—how to put a proposal together

Targeted Learnings

This chapter introduces four important clusters of research skills. The first cluster includes identifying, selecting, and refining a promising *topic* for research. After the topic is refined, it becomes known as the *problem*. The second cluster includes *stating the problem* in a way that describes the purpose of the study, explaining why the problem is important, identifying the limitations that affect the study, and defining special terms that will be

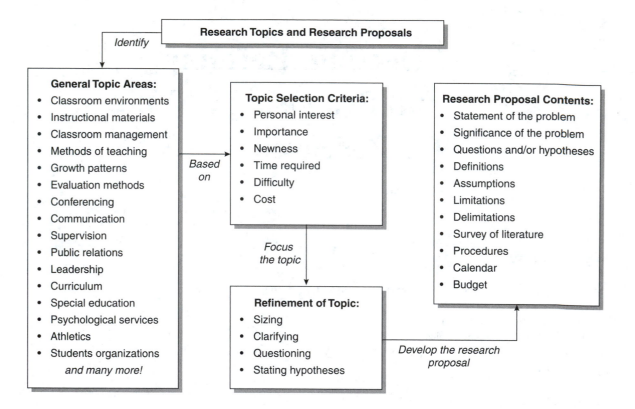

used. The third cluster includes phrasing *research questions and hypotheses* so that they can be used to guide the investigation, and the fourth cluster deals with how one organizes and presents *research proposals*. As you read the chapter, look especially for information related to the following:

1. Where can good educational research topics be found?
2. What should one keep in mind when selecting a topic for research?
3. Why do modifications and refinements usually have to be made in research topics after they have been selected?
4. What are the purposes of research questions and hypotheses?
5. How are research questions and hypotheses best stated?
6. What are the similarities and differences between research questions and hypotheses?
7. What is the distinction between a research topic and research problem?
8. What is a research proposal and how is it prepared and presented?

We now move ahead to learning skills involved in doing research of one's own. We begin by exploring how potentially fruitful research topics are identified, selected, refined, and ultimately presented as research proposals.

Where to Find Good Research Topics

All educators have concerns about educational matters and many questions for which they would like to find answers. They might like to know whether biculturalism facilitates, impedes, or has no discernible effect on school learning. They might like to determine whether the use of computers can, as is often claimed, actually improve teaching and learning. They might like to learn about the degree to which certain achievement tests correspond to or differ from the curricula and materials used in their school. They might want to determine how to help beginning teachers be more successful during their first years, and how to help experienced teachers avoid burnout, which seems to be the fate of so many.

Concerns such as these can suggest innumerable topics for research, and personal concerns are one of the best places to look for good research topics. But there are other excellent sources as well (see Ginsburg, McLaughlin, & Plisko, 1992). Pick up any education journal and you are likely to find several potential topics. Ask teachers what bothers them about teaching or what they would most like help with; their answers will identify a number of topic ideas. Or go to the university library and leaf through a recent volume of the *Education Index* or the *Current Index to Journals in Education*. There you will find hundreds of topics that call for further investigation. Many of these topics will be especially interesting to teachers, while others will appeal to administrators, counselors, psychologists, librarians, and any of the number of professionals working in schools.

Topics for Teachers

Teaching offers a broad range of good topics to be researched. Reflect on the imaginary Elmwood school district. The following are but a few of the topics that call for investigation there.

Classroom Environment.   Consider the numerous aspects of the physical and psychosocial environments in Elmwood classrooms. What impact might they have on student learning, behavior, attitude, interests, assumption of responsibility, relations with one another, and relations with the teacher? How could those classrooms make better use of time, movement, grouping, and management of materials?

Instructional Materials.   Consider to what degree textbooks and other printed materials are appropriate for Elmwood's multicultural makeup. Are they consistent with the racial and ethnic balance that Elmwood values? How familiar and useful do teachers find the materials? Do the materials hold student attention, provide enjoyment, allow for creativity, and spur achievement?

Classroom Management.   How efficiently are Elmwood classrooms operated? How satisfactory are the methods of managing student behavior? Do the routines currently in use make efficient use of time? Are teachers able to teach as they would like? Are students able to learn without undue distraction?

Instructional Methods.   There remains a great need for research into how different teaching methods and teacher personality styles affect learning among students of various ethnic groups. However, a note of caution: Research comparing different racial and ethnic groups moves onto sensitive ground. Proposed research must follow the legal requirements discussed in Chapter 1 and avoid suggesting, even inadvertently, that one ethnic group is somehow inherently better than another. Given that caution, let us note that teachers are always interested in new and workable information on

- Factors that motivate and hold attention
- Effective means of giving directions, cues, and signals
- The best ways to teach to reach stated goals and objectives
- Effective teaching methods and strategies—their nature, timing, and delivery
- Ways of providing effective oral and written feedback for student work efforts

The Relation of Human Growth Patterns to Education.   Although much information is available on human intellectual, social, physical, and emotional growth and development, relatively little research has been done into teaching strategies that best match or promote

- Individual interests and learning preferences
- Individual rates of learning
- Concerned, responsible, and self-disciplined behavior
- Natural student attentive behavior and teachable moments
- Classroom esprit de corps, joy and pride in learning

Evaluation.   More information is needed about the effects that grades, grading systems, and evaluative feedback have on student motivation, stress, attitude, and achievement. More information is needed on authentic assessment and on other nontraditional means of assessing student growth.

Conferencing.   Research is needed on how to maximize the value and improve the efficiency of personal conferences among teachers, students, and parents.

Topics for Administrators

Administrators experience many of the same concerns as teachers, and, in addition, they always need more reliable information and better procedures related to topics such as the following.

Effective Communication.   There is an increasing need for better styles of communication and links among teachers, students, parents, other administrators, and the general community.

Effective Supervision.   Administrators are always on the lookout for better ways of motivating, guiding, assisting, and supporting quality teaching in faculties where personalities and competencies are diverse.

Effective Public Relations. Administrators need to know effective strategies for obtaining the support of, and high regard from, parents and the community.

Effective Leadership. Administrators are continually searching for more effective ways of organizing, directing, encouraging, supporting, and otherwise getting the best from teachers, students, and support staffs in their schools.

Topics for Other Educators

We have noted but a few of the educational concerns that persist in schools, and, as you can see, they offer a multitude of possible research topics. Your interest may lie in yet another aspect of education—perhaps curriculum, special education, counseling, psychological services, athletics, the arts, or student organizations. Whatever the case, you will have no difficulty identifying a concern related to education that you will find enjoyable to research. Your own interests and needs are your best guides to good topics.

Exercise 3.1

Identify three topics you might be interested in investigating. You can name them from your current interests or from the topic areas just presented.

1. _____

2. _____

3. _____

Preliminary Considerations in Selecting Topics

When you first identify a research topic that interests you, you should evaluate it against the following considerations:

1. You should have a *personal interest* in the topic you select. Perhaps the topic is new and intriguing or is one that you associate with pleasant experiences. Perhaps it is one that has caused you unpleasant concern. Any topic that repeatedly suggests itself to you should be strongly considered.
2. The topic should be *important* and should make a difference in some aspect of education. If it does not, it should not be pursued, even if it is highly interesting to you personally.
3. The *newness* of a research topic may affect your enthusiasm and satisfaction. Although there is value in repeating previous research—to validate methods and see if findings hold true over time—it is ordinarily more exciting to explore topics that may lead to new information.

Applying Technology: Sources for Research Topics

The idea for a research topic is the first real decision with which a student is faced when engaging in the research process. The student's areas of interest often provide the best starting point. Initial interest in a topic may serve as the driving force behind the development of the research study. However, there are several sources of information of which students may take advantage in order to identify and evaluate initial topics (Edyburn, 1999). An excellent source of information is individuals who are knowledgeable in a particular field and *e-mail* serves as an efficient means of contacting them with initial questions. One might request further information on a topic, or the names of important researchers or research articles which address the topic. One note of caution, however: be sure to ask your contact person *specific* questions; a student should not submit an e-mail request such as, "Please send me everything you have done related to…" (Edyburn, 1999). If you are lucky, this may be the beginning of an important professional relationship.

Browsing the Web can also provide valuable information regarding possible research topics. There is a wide variety of search engines on the Web. *Search engines* organize websites by keywords. The results of a search for a specific topic will yield a list of related websites and an attempt is made to rank those sites in terms of relevance to the topic keyword(s). Some of these available search engines, listed with their respective URLs, include:

- Excite (www.excite.com)
- InfoSeek (www.infoseek.com)
- Google (www.google.com)
- Yahoo! (www.yahoo.com)
- WebCrawler (www.webcrawler.com)
- Ask Jeeves (www.ask.com)

Many *professional associations* operate websites and include links to other Web pages. These sites may be useful in identifying an initial topic or in narrowing the focus of a research topic. The premier professional association in education is the American Educational Research Association (AERA). AERA is divided into 12 divisions, based on broad disciplines. In addition, there are numerous special interest groups (SIGs). The AERA Web page can be found at www.aera.net. A sampling of other prominent professional associations is listed here:

- American Psychological Association (www.apa.org)
- Association for Supervision and Curriculum Development (www.ascd.org)
- Association for Educational Communications and Technology (www.aect.org)
- Council for Exceptional Children (www.cec.sped.org)
- International Society for Technology in Education (www.iste.org)
- National Education Association (www.nea.org)
- Phi Delta Kappa (www.pdkintl.org)

Additionally, the U.S. Department of Education (ED) maintains a list of professional organizations and links to their websites. The list currently includes over 30 professional organizations and can be found at www.ed.gov/about/contacts/gen/othersites/associations.html

Internet discussion groups can also be invaluable sources of information regarding ideas for and additional questions about research studies. A series of these discussion forums, or *LISTSERVs,* is maintained by AERA. The topical discussions take place via e-mail messages sent to everyone who has subscribed to a particular LISTSERV. AERA maintains one general LIST, 12 division LISTs, and one LIST for graduate students. Specifically, these lists are:

ERL-L	General discussion LIST for AERA
AERA-A	Division A: Administration
AERA-B	Division B: Curriculum Studies
AERA-C	Division C: Learning & Instruction
AERA-D	Division D: Measurement & Research Methodology
AERA-E	Division E: Counseling & Human Development
AERA-F	Division F: History & Historiography
AERA-G	Division G: Social Context of Education
AERA-H	Division H: School Evaluation & Program Development
AERA-I	Division I: Education in the Professions
AERA-J	Division J: Postsecondary Education
AERA-K	Division K: Teaching & Teacher Education
AERA-L	Division L: Politics and Policy in Education
AERA-GSL	Graduate Students List

In order to subscribe to any of the LISTSERVs, one simply sends an e-mail message to *listserv@asu.edu,* where the content of the message reads as follows:

```
SUB list-name your-first-name your-last-name
```

For example, if Mary Smith would like to subscribe to the research methodology LIST-SERV, she would send the following e-mail message:

```
SUB AERA-D Mary Smith
```

AERA also maintains a *hypermail archive* of all LISTSERV activity, organized by division. Some divisions have topic discussions archived as far back as 1993. To access the AERA LISTSERV archive, simply point your browser to www.aera.net/resource/listarch.htm. Then click on the appropriate division in order to access the archived discussions.

4. In selecting research topics, always give attention to the amount of *time* the investigation will require. Compare that against what you have available. Other things being equal, you should select a topic that can be completed in a relatively short time.

5. Reflect on the *difficulty* of researching the topic. Many extremely interesting topics are difficult or impossible to research for a number of reasons. You would find it difficult to do a descriptive study of education among the Eskimos of Siberia and impossible to determine what happens to students' brain cells as they learn mathematics.

6. Consider the *monetary costs* that investigating your topic would entail. If you would have to pay for costly supplies, materials, travel, and consultant services, find a different topic. There are many good topics you can investigate with very little expense.

7. A final consideration has to do with *ethics*. As pointed out in Chapter 1, it is unethical and sometimes illegal to conduct research that slanders, does physical or psychological harm to, implants undesirable ideas in the minds of, or otherwise mistreats human or animal participants.

Exercise 3.2

A. Which of the preceding considerations is most probably being overlooked in contemplating the following five topics: (PI) personal interest, (I) importance, (N) newness, (T) time, (D) difficulty, (C) cost, or (E) ethics?

_____ 1. The effects of early childhood trauma on later school learning

_____ 2. Graduate student Mary involves herself in a research project about which she cares nothing

_____ 3. The average income of male students versus the average income of female students enrolled in teacher education classes

_____ 4. An experiment to explore the effects of active involvement on learning, a topic already reported on in more than 1,000 studies

_____ 5. The effect on learning in classrooms where the temperature is kept excessively hot or excessively cold

B. Evaluate each of the three topics you selected in Exercise 3.1 against the seven considerations just presented. Reword your topics as you see fit.

1. _____

2. _____

3. _____

We now move ahead to consider how topics are refined to make them more easily researchable.

Refining the Research Topic

Once a topic has been selected, it usually must be refined before it can be researched effectively and efficiently. That is because most topics are at first too broad, too narrow, too vague, or too complex. Such defects are corrected by refining the topic, as follows.

First, the topic must be properly *sized,* that is, reduced—or occasionally expanded—in scope. Graduate students typically select topic ideas that are too broad to be dealt with efficiently, especially under constraints to time and resources. Such topics must be pared down so that the research can be accomplished expeditiously. Occasionally, a research topic is too narrow. In that case, the topic must be fleshed out. Examples of topics that are overly broad and overly narrow are presented later in this chapter.

Second, the topic may need to be *clarified,* reworded so that it states clearly and unambiguously the matter to be investigated, the variables to be investigated, and the participants, if any, that will be involved. Examples of how topics can be reworded are also presented later in the chapter.

Third, a series of *research questions* or one or more *hypotheses,* or both, should be stated. Such questions and hypotheses orient the study, add cohesiveness, and are essential in helping resolve the primary concern that prompted the investigation.

Research questions and hypotheses are both valuable in orienting research, and each offers an advantage the other does not. The advantage of research questions is that their several subquestions serve as guideposts and markers that, as they are reached, keep the research on track and ultimately lead to a successful conclusion. The advantage of hypotheses is that they can be tested statistically, thereby adding credibility to the research findings. Remember that researchers do not say that a hypothesis is true, correct, or proved, only that it is retained or supported, or else rejected or not supported. Guidance for composing research questions and hypotheses is given later in the chapter. Once these refinements have been made, what has heretofore been called the *research topic* becomes known as the *research problem.*

Some Necessary Terminology

Before proceeding to a discussion of how to regulate the size of a topic, it will be helpful to examine the meanings of these terms and phrases, which you will encounter often: *topic, broad topic, narrowing the topic, amorphous topic, clarifying the topic, problem, problem statement, research question, subquestions, hypothesis, research hypothesis, null hypothesis,* and *theory.*

The **topic** refers to the matter to be investigated. The topic is usually stated as a sentence fragment, such as:

- Successful teaching practices for multiethnic students
- School success and age of entry into kindergarten
- Using computers in the classroom to increase student achievement

A **broad topic** has no specific definition but generally means that a topic is too large in scope for the time or resources available. Examples of topics too broad to be pursued by a graduate student in education are:

- The formulation and field-testing of a new English curriculum for bilingual students in the elementary schools
- What teachers' lives are like outside school
- The factors that affect learning among culturally diverse students

Even if adequate expertise were available for investigating these topics, which is unlikely, the investigations would require far more time and resources than are available to graduate students.

Narrowing the topic refers to paring the topic down to manageable size. The previous broad topics might be narrowed down to:

- A program for developing English language vocabulary among bilingual students at the third-grade level
- Leisure activities of elementary teachers and the amount of time spent on them
- Hispanic students' perceptions of factors that interfere with success in school

An **amorphous topic** is stated so vaguely that it cannot be understood without further clarification. Examples of amorphous topics are:

- Using the library to confront students' main life views of themselves
- Daily family routines and students' involvement in the school setting
- Administrators' compulsions and teachers' stress factors

In these examples, one gets no sense of what the research is actually aimed at or how it might be carried out.

Clarifying the topic involves changing the wording to make the topic statement understandable. The preceding topics could be clarified thus:

- Using bibliotherapy to improve attitude toward school among middle school students with low self-concept
- The relationship between home chore assignments and the degree of responsibility shown in school by fifth-grade students
- Teachers' opinions concerning the nature and frequency of required staff meetings

The **problem,** as previously noted, is the term used for a topic that has been refined appropriately for research. The preceding topics, as clarified, would be called problems if accompanied by research questions or hypotheses.

A **problem statement** is a sentence or paragraph that explains the purpose of a given investigation. Problem statements are presented in future tense in research proposals and in past tense in research reports. An example of a problem statement for a research proposal is:

> The purpose of this study will be to develop and subject to preliminary testing a program for English-language vocabulary development among third-grade bilingual students.

An example of a problem statement for a research report is:

> The purpose of this study was to develop and subject to preliminary testing a program for English-language vocabulary development among third-grade bilingual students.

Problem statements are usually presented in one sentence, which often makes the statement a bit cumbersome to read, as in the examples just presented. Though not frequently done, it is perfectly acceptable to state the problem in two or more shorter sentences, as follows:

> The purpose of this study will be to construct and test an English vocabulary program. The program will be designed for use in third-grade classrooms and will be field-tested in five selected classes in Elmwood schools.

A **research question** is the fundamental question inherent in the research topic. Such questions, normally supplemented by a number of subquestions, are often used to guide the research process. For a topic such as using bibliotherapy to improve student attitude, a main research question could be:

> Can bibliotherapy be used to improve attitude toward school among students with low self-concept?

Subquestions are questions subordinate to the research question. Their effect is complementary and cumulative; as the subquestions are answered, the main question is also ultimately answered. Three examples of subquestions that might be used in the investigation involving bibliotherapy are:

1. In what ways has bibliotherapy been used to help students deal with problems in their lives?
2. What have been the positive and negative results of bibliotherapy?
3. What specific books might have bibliotherapeutic value for adolescent students with a low self-concept?

Hypotheses are succinct statements that forecast the findings of the study. They usually make predictions about future events, existing differences among groups, or existing relationships among variables. Hypotheses are of three types: *directional research hypotheses, nondirectional research hypotheses,* and *null hypotheses* (Charters, 1992).

A **research hypothesis** is a statement of what the investigator truly expects to find in the study. An example of a research hypothesis might be

> Students with low self-concept who participate in a program of bibliotherapy will show improvement in their attitude toward school.

This hypothesis is called **directional** because it indicates the direction of the results—in this case, a positive direction (improvement). It would also be a directional hypothesis if it stated that participating students would show a deterioration in attitude (a negative direction). A research hypothesis can also be **nondirectional.** Here is such an example:

> Students with low self-concept who participate in a program of bibliotherapy will show changes in their attitude toward school.

This research hypothesis is called nondirectional because it does not specify the direction of change, but only that change will occur. The change could be positive or negative.

The third type of hypothesis, the **null hypothesis,** states that no effect will occur, or that no differences or relationships will be found, even if that is not what the investigator expects to find. Here is an example of a null hypothesis:

> Students with low self-concept who participate in a program of bibliotherapy will show no change in their attitude toward school.

This statement would also be a research hypothesis if "no change" was what the investigator did expect to find, but in this example there would be little point in conducting research to try to show that bibliotherapy is of no value. Sometimes, however, investigators do set up research to demonstrate that no change, difference, or relationship is occurring. For example, suppose you hoped to show that the achievement of physics students taught with inexpensive equipment was just as high as that of students taught with expensive equipment. You would state a null hypothesis, believing or hoping it would be supported by the data.

There is a reason, however, for using null hypotheses even when they do not state what the investigator expects to find. The reason is that, generally speaking, it is easier to disprove a statement than to prove it. And remember, in most cases researchers hope to "disprove"—or, more accurately, find *in*adequate support for—the null hypothesis. Consider the following: Suppose you implement your bibliotherapy program. You hypothesize that at the end of the year, Elmwood students who complete your program will demonstrate an overall better attitude toward school than will matched groups of students attending other schools in your area. Note that this is a directional research hypothesis, not a null hypothesis. In order to *retain* your hypothesis as it is stated, your students must almost always outperform students in other schools. You might repeat this investigation five times and find each time that your students are better. Even then you cannot be certain that the results will not be different next time. For reasons discussed in the Appendix, for you to retain the research hypothesis, you must project that similar differences will occur at least 95 percent of the time, given hundreds of repetitions of the study.

But suppose you stated the hypothesis in the null form, saying that after your students completed your program, no difference would exist in attitude toward school between your students and those attending the other schools in your area. Now if you do find a difference, you have greater confidence in rejecting the null hypothesis. Again, for reasons explained in Appendix A, you need project, on average, only six "differences between groups" out of every 100 repetitions of the study in order to reject the null hypothesis. Tests of significance are designed so that you can find many compliances with a statement you have made without providing compelling evidence that it is correct. But only very few contradictions of your statement are required to suggest it is incorrect. For that reason, researchers state hypotheses in the null form and then see if they can find contradictions to those hypotheses.

In many cases, researchers do not limit themselves to just a null hypothesis or a research hypothesis. Instead, they use both (Gay & Airasian, 2000). In the example we have just considered, the investigator might state a null hypothesis and then pair a directional research hypothesis with it, the latter indicating the expected finding. The reason for doing this would be, first, to reject the hypothesis of no difference in attitude toward school and,

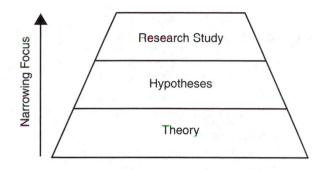

FIGURE 3.1   The relationship between theories, hypotheses, and research studies

second, to begin building the case that since a difference does seem to exist, it is very likely that the difference is being caused by the bibliotherapy program. It must be understood, however, that rejecting the null hypothesis does not, in itself, provide verification of the research hypothesis (McMillan & Schumacher, 2001). How hypotheses are tested for significance is explained in Appendix A.

A **theory** is an overall explanation of *how* things are or of *why* things are as they are. The term is defined here because many people confuse the terms *theory* and *hypothesis*. *Theory* is the much broader term: It explains but does not predict. It would be improper to say, "My theory is that these two boys will turn out to be behavior problems when they reach sixth grade." Hypotheses, on the other hand, do predict, and they can be drawn from theory. Take as an example psychologist Jean Piaget's theory of human intellectual development—his explanation of how the intellect is formed (Piaget, 1947). From the basis of Piaget's theory, one can hypothesize, or make predictions, about how children will behave as their intellects develop, then ultimately test that hypothesis in a research study (see Figure 3.1).

Exercise 3.3

A. Indicate whether each of the following is most in keeping with the definition of (RQ) research question, (SQ) subquestion, (DRH) directional research hypothesis, (NRH) nondirectional research hypothesis, (NH) null hypothesis, or (T) theory.

_____ 1. What do Elmwood's high school students believe to be true about the nature and frequency of sexual harassment by and among their peers?

_____ 2. No overall difference exists in job satisfaction among teachers at different grade levels.

_____ 3. One's sense of morality grows out of socialization and feedback from others.

_____ 4. To what degree do eighth-grade teachers look forward to going to work each day?

(continued)

Exercise 3.3 *Continued*

_____   5. Students given a year's course in Latin will develop better English vocabularies than will students who do not study Latin.

_____   6. Students given a year's course in Latin will develop English vocabularies that are inferior to those of students who do not study Latin.

_____   7. Students taught algebra through method Z will reach different achievement levels than those reached by students taught algebra through
method X.

B.   Answer the following (T) true or (F) false.

_____   1. Hypotheses are statements that predict occurrences or relationships between or among variables.

_____   2. Null hypotheses cannot be tested statistically.

_____   3. Null hypotheses assume that no differences originally existed among
samples drawn from the same population.

_____   4. If the null hypothesis is rejected, one can conclude either that the
sample was not accurately drawn or that differences now observed between groups have resulted from variables intentionally or unintention-
ally introduced during the investigation.

_____   5. Null hypotheses are usually statements of what the investigator really
expects to find.

_____   6. A directional research hypothesis should be tested for significance
before it is tested in the null form.

_____   7. *Nondirectional research hypothesis* and *null hypothesis* are different
names for statements that say the same thing.

_____   8. Hypotheses are more valuable in orienting almost all kinds of research
than are research questions.

With this background of terminology, to which you may need to refer occasionally, we proceed to consider how one regulates the size of research topics.

Regulating the Size of Research Topics

As mentioned, most graduate students at first select problems that are much too broad to be
investigated within existing constraints of time, skill, and resources. Occasionally, they
select topics that are too narrow; those topics need to be broadened to make them worth-

while. How does one get a sense of the proper size of a topic, in order to pare it down or flesh it out to acceptable dimensions? This "sizing" is best approached by anticipating what must be done to investigate a problem.

In Chapter 1 we noted that research begins with the identification of a concern for which there is no readily available solution, but for which a solution might be found. To obtain and process information so that the concern might be resolved, one follows a sequence of research steps. Assuming a topic has been selected and posed as a problem, the investigation will involve the following tasks:

1. *Reviewing the literature.* Some topics have had almost nothing written about them; others may have been covered extensively in journal articles, reference works, and other publications, all of which should be examined. Researchers, therefore, use the library to check indexes and other references, a process described in detail in Chapters 4 and 5. To help decide whether a given topic is of a size feasible for investigation, it is a good idea to consult in the library a reference book entitled *Resources in Education,* plus either the *Education Index* or the *Current Index to Journals in Education,* which will give you an idea of how much has been published on the topic. You would hope to find 20 to 50 recent publications related, but not identical, to your topic. But if you find hundreds, the review of literature might become overwhelming. In that case you might narrow the topic further or do only a selected review of the literature.

2. *Organizing the study.* This step gives you the clearest picture of what researching a proposed topic is likely to entail. Some studies are easy to organize, whereas others are difficult because they involve many arrangements, selection procedures, permissions, approvals, and the like. Think through what will be necessary to enable you to complete the investigation.

3. *Collecting and analyzing data.* Collecting good data is usually the most difficult—at least the most worrisome and time-consuming—part of conducting research. Statistical analysis, which once frightened beginners, is now easily done with computers. Data must be obtained in the appropriate kind and quantity, paralleling the investigation's research questions and hypotheses. You may have to prepare questionnaires, tests, or other assessment devices. It may be necessary to obtain published tests. You may need access to records from schools and elsewhere. Graduate students operate within stringent limitations of time and money, and their research skills are not yet sophisticated. Anticipating as precisely as possible the procedures involved in data collection will give you a good idea of whether a particular research topic can be investigated, given your constraints.

Foreseeing the Research Report Format

When reporting research, one follows conventions that make reading easier and allow the reader to analyze the topic, procedures, findings, and conclusions critically. The components of a research report generally parallel the steps by which the research is conducted

and, thus, provide further insight into the time and labor requirements of the topic you select. Research reports contain the following components:

1. *Introduction.* This section specifies the topic and tells why it is worth investigating.
   In reports such as graduate theses the introduction may also contain a statement of
   the problem, hypotheses, research questions, definitions of terms, and limits placed
   on the study.
2. *Review of related literature.* This component is not difficult to accomplish but may
   be very time-consuming, especially when there is a vast amount of literature related
   to your topic.
3. *Method.* The **method** spells out how the study was designed and how data were obtained and analyzed. Listing the procedures followed is easy enough but actually carrying them out may involve an enormous amount of work. It is best to select a topic
   in which data can be obtained and analyzed easily. With the availability of computers
   and statistics programs, statistical treatments of the data no longer present a significant obstacle.
4. *Findings.* Often called *results,* this section summarizes the new information that has
   been discovered. Findings are reported verbally, graphically, and/or numerically.
5. *Conclusions and discussion.* Here the researcher clarifies the meaning of the new information discovered and uses that information to answer the research questions and
   to retain or reject the hypotheses. Also included are the investigator's speculations
   and other discussions about the study and conclusions reached.

The Value of Conventional Procedures and Reports

Attempting to foresee the research and report requirements helps greatly in selecting a
topic, limiting it, and investigating it to a conclusion. From beginning to end, a prime goal
should be to conduct and report research in a manner that quietly implies, "Here is my research; find fault with it if you can." This attitude explains why it is so necessary to select
a topic of importance, refine it, follow established research conventions, and report the
work clearly.

Exercise 3.4

Evaluate each of the following potential topics for research at the graduate level. Mark them
as V (too vague), B (too broad), N (too narrow), C (too affected by constraints), or R (about
right).

_____ 1. An investigation of the social problems evident among students attending
Elmwood's public schools.

_____ 2. An investigation of the relative effectiveness of two different systems of
discipline in selected sixth-grade classrooms.

3. An investigation of six Filipino students' global behavior as a function of the interplay of their values, social contexts, and familial patterns.

4. A comparison of the after-school responsibilities of selected sixth-grade students from three different ethnic groups.

5. Views that students of diverse ethnic groups hold of teachers and other adults.

6. The effect that monetary payment for improved grades has on high school Anglo student achievement.

7. Around-the-clock shadowing of 10 selected Elmwood high school teachers.

8. Improvement in written composition among selected high school sophomores as a function of same-day analysis and feedback concerning their written work.

9. An experiment to add 10 words to the vocabulary of an inner-city student.

Refining the Topic: An Illustrative Case

We have noted that the research topics selected by graduate students are at first usually too broad, too vague, or too narrow and must be refined before they can be researched. The case of Jan is presented to illustrate the process of sharpening research topics into research problems.

Jan's Concern about Students' Entry Age to Kindergarten

Jan, a kindergarten teacher, has long believed that students who have already reached age 5 when they enter kindergarten do better throughout their subsequent school years than do students who enter kindergarten while only 4 years old. She believes, therefore, that it is a bad idea to enroll children in kindergarten before they reach age 5. She thinks doing so harms the children. That is what she wants to demonstrate in her study. The topic she has submitted for approval is "The bad effects of early entry into kindergarten." Jan's thesis adviser tells her that the topic cannot be researched in its stated form. To help her, the adviser presses Jan to state exactly what she means by "bad effects." Jan replies that the children have trouble in later grades.

What kind of trouble, the adviser wants to know.

Emotional problems, Jan maintains. She says the children cry a great deal, get upset easily, don't show much responsibility, and generally act like babies.

The adviser asks Jan how she knows that early-entry students behave like that, and Jan says all the teachers in her school are aware of it and that she has heard many of them comment on the problem. The adviser wants to know if early-entry students all behave that way (not all, Jan says) and if they do so only in primary grades.

No, they do so throughout school, Jan maintains, claiming that most of the problem students in sixth grade entered kindergarten at age 4.

The adviser asks Jan if she believes she could, for three randomly selected schools, divide sixth-grade students into two groups: those who had begun school at age 4 and those who had begun at age 5. Jan says she could, that records were available in the schools, and that she is sure the respective building administrators would be interested.

On what basis would Jan compare the two groups, the adviser wanted to know.

On how well they are doing in sixth grade, Jan answers. When pressed to be more specific, Jan mentions learning, behavior, personal relations, and emotionality.

The adviser points out that Jan's topic is too large and unwieldy and that it needs to be narrowed. The adviser asks what would be at the heart of Jan's concern if she had to select only two variables to measure in the students? Jan identifies reading ability and overall maturity.

How would she assess reading ability? From achievement test records, Jan decides. And how would she assess maturity? After considerable thought and discussion, Jan decides she could prepare a rating scale with categories such as responsibility, personal relations with others, emotionality, and self-assurance. She could ask teachers to rate the students in her sample, using the scale.

The adviser asks Jan to restate her topic. After two more discussions, Jan states her topic: "The effects of entry age into kindergarten on later student learning and emotional maturity."

The adviser approves that topic, contingent on Jan's obtaining permission from school district officials to pursue the investigation and her obtaining access to pertinent school records.

Pending permission and access, Jan is directed to prepare a research question and subquestions for the topic. Jan submits the following, which are approved. She is directed at this point to define certain terms.

Research Question.   How do sixth-grade students who entered kindergarten at age 4 compare with those who entered kindergarten at age 5 in reading achievement and social maturity?

Subquestions (questions subordinate to the main research question)

1. By what rationales of intellectual and social growth might one predict reading and maturity differences between the groups?
2. What existing research, if any, tends to confirm or deny the existence of such differences?
3. What is the average reading level of "older students" (those who entered kindergarten at age 5)?
4. What is the average reading level of "younger students" (those who entered kindergarten at age 4)?
5. What is the average maturity level of older students, as judged by their present teachers?

6. What is the average maturity level of younger students, as judged by their present teachers?
7. What is the average incidence of "problem behavior episodes" among older students?
8. What is the average incidence of "problem behavior episodes" among younger students?
9. Does gender seem to influence achievement and behavior in the two groups?

Preparing a Research Proposal

The example of Jan illustrates something of the process of selecting an appropriate research topic and then refining and reworking it to make it researchable. Jan still has an important task to accomplish before proceeding with her investigation. That task is to compose and submit a research proposal that includes (1) a statement of the problem; (2) the significance of the problem; (3) the research questions or hypotheses; (4) definitions, assumptions, limitations, and delimitations; (5) a survey of existing literature; (6) general procedure to be followed; (7) a time calendar; and, possibly, (8) a budget. Let us note briefly what each of these elements entails.

1. *Statement of the problem,* mentioned earlier, explains the purpose of the study. This is usually a simple declarative statement that is kept short but identifies the key elements of the proposed study. For example:

   The purpose of this study is to determine whether age of entry into kindergarten has an effect on students' subsequent school learning and behavior.

2. *Significance of the problem* is a statement that explains why the problem merits investigation, including why it is worth the time, effort, and expense involved in carrying it out. For example:

   Many teachers have long believed that children who enter kindergarten at age 4 are not sufficiently mature intellectually or emotionally to work on equal terms with students who enter kindergarten at age 5. They believe they see in those students differences in learning and social behavior that persist through the elementary grades. This study is designed to yield evidence that will substantiate or negate such concerns about age of entry to kindergarten.

3. *Research questions and/or hypotheses* are posed to guide the study and lead to resolution of the central concern. The following research question, research hypothesis, or null hypothesis would be suitable for Jan's study:

   Research question—How do sixth-grade students who entered kindergarten at age 4 compare with those who entered kindergarten at age 5, regarding reading achievement and social maturity? (This main research question is accompanied by subquestions, such as those presented in Case 1 for Jan's research.)

Research hypothesis—Students who entered kindergarten at age 4 will in sixth grade show lower reading achievement and lower levels of social maturity than will students who entered kindergarten at age 5.

Null hypothesis—No differences exist in reading achievement and social maturity between sixth-grade students who entered kindergarten at age 4 and sixth-grade students who entered kindergarten at age 5.

4. *Definitions, assumptions, limitations, and delimitations.* Here the investigator defines terms that are unclear or that have special meanings (insofar as such terms can be anticipated early in the study; modifications may be made later). In Jan's study, the term *social maturity* would be defined, as would *reading achievement* and such special terms as *younger students* and *older students*.

The investigator also states any known **assumptions** that are being made but cannot be proved. Examples in Jan's study would include the assumption that social maturity can be judged through instances of student behavior and that teachers are competent to make valid judgments about student behavior.

Limitations refer to conditions outside the investigator's control that affect data collection. For Jan, limitations would include the availability of records needed to show age of entry to kindergarten, sixth-grade achievement scores in reading, and objections that might arise from parents and administrators.

Delimitations are the boundaries purposely put on the study, usually to narrow it for researchability. In Jan's case, the study would be delimited to certain identifiable students in certain schools and would have to do only with age of kindergarten entry, social maturity, and achievement in reading.

5. *Survey of the literature.* For the research proposal, one need not conduct a full review of the literature. It is advisable, however, to *survey* the literature—that is, to examine appropriate references and indexes in order to determine the amount and kind of literature that must later be reviewed. It is also important to scan titles of articles to see if any of them deal directly with the topic under consideration.

6. *General procedures.* Here one presents a preliminary listing of the steps to be undertaken in obtaining permission, selecting participants, composing questionnaires or selecting tests or similar materials, obtaining data, summarizing and analyzing data, and presenting findings and drawing conclusions. Of course, not all details of these steps, nor even all of the steps themselves, can be totally foreseen.

7. *Time calendar.* The time line, with dates and deadlines, is superimposed, figuratively if not literally, on the list of procedures. Time is of the essence in most research, especially so for research in graduate degree programs, where an investigation often must be completed in as little as five or six months. A time calendar is therefore of great help in keeping one on track and on time.

8. *Budget.* Depending on the type of investigation to be undertaken, it is often a good idea to prepare a budget that indicates direct and indirect costs. *Direct costs* are those that you will have to pay out of pocket for such things as tests, other materials, transportation, and clerical help. *Indirect costs* are those that someone (preferably not you) will have to pay for items such as utilities, space, computer access, custodial services, and the like. Indirect costs are normally provided to graduate students by the institutions in which they are enrolled.

Research
Navigator.c⊕m
limitations
delimitations

D E V E L O P M E N T A L A C T I V I T Y

Research Topic Refinement

Up to this point, you have been working with a general topic area or possible topic for your proposed research study. Based on the considerations you made in Chapter 1 and the determination of the most appropriate type of research for your topic or problem you made in Chapter 2, it is now time to refine—and further specify—your topic. In addition to refining your topic, you will begin to specify your research questions or hypotheses. Carefully consider your topic as you respond to the following questions:

1. A possible topic or problem I am thinking of researching is: _____
   _____.

2. A more *broad* research topic within my general topic area might be _____
   _____.

3. A more *narrow* research topic within my general topic area might be _____
   _____.

4. After *careful* consideration of my responses to questions 1, 2, and 3, I believe that my topic is researchable as stated (*check one*):

   ☐ yes

   ☐ no (if "no," you'll need to focus your topic before you go any further)

5. The problem statement for my proposed study is as follows:

   The purpose of this study will be to _____
   _____.

6. I intend to use hypotheses to guide this research study (check one):

   ☐ yes…why? _____ (proceed to question 7)

   ☐ no…why not? _____ (proceed to question 8)

7. My hypotheses (both null and research) are as follows: _____
   _____.

8. My research question(s) is(are) as follows: _____
   _____.

(continued)

Research Topic Refinement *(Continued)*

 9. Possible *assumptions* for my study include: _____

   _____.

10. Possible *limitations* for my study include:_____

   _____.

11. Possible *delimitations* for my study include: _____

   _____.

(A downloadable, interactive version of this developmental activity is available from the Companion Website, www.ablongman.com/mertler5e)

Chapter Summary

Research begins with the selection and refinement of a suitable topic for investigation. When refined and clarified, the topic becomes known as the problem. The problem, in turn, may be supplemented with additional information and presented as a proposal for research.

There is no dearth of topics for research in education. Various indexes and other references attest to the enormous range of possibilities, but the most fruitful topics for graduate research usually lie in personal concerns about aspects of education. Certain cautions and considerations should be kept in mind when selecting a topic. Key considerations include one's personal interest and the topic's importance, relative newness, amenability to time constraints, and ease of management. The topic should be inexpensive to investigate, and it must incorporate impeccable standards of ethics at all times.

Once a research topic is selected, it ordinarily must be refined by limiting its scope, wording it clearly, and supplementing it with research questions or hypotheses that guide the investigation and help resolve its central questions. The difficult matter of regulating topics so they will be of a suitable size for graduate-level investigation can be managed by foreseeing the tasks that research requires. It is also helpful at this state to anticipate the format required for the final research report.

When a topic has been refined into a problem, graduate students are usually asked to prepare and submit for approval a research proposal that includes a statement of the problem; commentary on the significance of the problem; research questions or hypothesis; certain definitions, assumptions, limitations, and delimitations of the problem; a brief survey of the literature; a description of probable procedures for organizing the study and obtaining and analyzing data; a calendar, or time line, for accomplishing various aspects of the research process; and sometimes a budget that lists direct and indirect costs.

LIST OF IMPORTANT TERMS

amorphous topic

assumptions

broad topic

clarifying the topic

delimitations

directional research

hypothesis

limitations

method

narrowing the topic

nondirectional research

null hypothesis

problem

problem statement

research hypothesis

research question

subquestions

theory

topic

YOUR CURRENT STATUS

Building on what you already know about the nature of educational research, its purposes, types, and data sources, you have now become acquainted with how and from where one selects a worthwhile research topic, refines the topic to make it researchable and manageable, supplements the topic with useful research questions and/or hypotheses, and prepares a research proposal. Your next task is to learn how to locate published reports in the research library, the topic of Chapter 4. Before proceeding, please respond to the activities for thought and discussion.

ACTIVITIES FOR THOUGHT AND DISCUSSION

1. Name, in order of importance to you, five considerations you would keep in mind when selecting a topic for possible research.

2. For an investigation into the use of bibliotherapy to improve the attitude toward school of students with low self-concept, complete the following questions:

   Research question—Can bibliotherapy be used to help?

   Subquestions

   a. In what ways has bibliotherapy been used _____ ?

   b. What have been the positive and negative _____ ?

   c. What books, suitable for early adolescent readers _____ ?

   d. To what extent do students freely select _____ ?

   e. How do students react to _____ ?

   f. What changes in _____ ?

3. Look back at the three topics that you selected in Exercise 3.1 as interesting possibilities for research. For one of those topics (a) compose a directional research hypothesis and (b) compose a null hypothesis. Discuss your efforts with others in the class.

4. For that same topic, outline on a single page a brief research proposal that contains the elements normally included in research proposals. Discuss with others in the class.

5. The questions presented at the beginning of the chapter are shown here. See how well you can answer them.

   a. Where can good educational research topics be found?

   b. What should one keep in mind when selecting a topic for research?

   c. Why do modifications and refinements usually have to be made in research topics after they have been selected?

   d. What are the purposes of research questions and hypotheses?

   e. How are research questions and hypotheses best stated?

   f. What are the similarities and differences between research questions and hypotheses?

    g. What is the distinction between a research topic and research problem?

    h. What is a research proposal and how is it prepared and presented?

6. Recall the organizer that was presented at the beginning of the chapter. In your own words explain the chapter contents as suggested by the organizer.

ANSWERS TO CHAPTER EXERCISES

3.2. 1. D 2. PI 3. I 4. N 5. E

3.3. A. 1. RQ 2. NH 3. T 4. SQ 5. DRH 6. DRH
    7. NRH

B. 1. T 2. F 3. T 4. T 5. F 6. F 7. F 8. F

3.4. 1. B 2. R 3. V/B 4. R 5. R/B 6. C 7. C
    8. R 9. N

REFERENCES AND RECOMMENDED READINGS

Best, J., & Kahn, J. (2003). *Research in Education* (9th ed.). Boston: Allyn and Bacon.

Charters, W. (1992). *Understanding Variables and Hypotheses in Scientific Research.* (Report No. ISBN 0-86552-115-8). Eugene, OR: ERIC Clearinghouse on Educational Management. (ERIC No. ED 342 056).

Current Index to Journals in Education. (1969 to present). Phoenix: Oryx Press.

Edyburn, D. L. (1999). *The Electronic Scholar: Enhancing Research Productivity with Technology.* Upper Saddle River, NJ: Merrill.

Encyclopedia of Educational Research (6th ed.). (1992). New York: Free Press.

Gall, M., Borg, W., & Gall, J. (2003). *Educational Research: An Introduction* (7th ed.). Boston: Allyn and Bacon.

Gay, L., & Airasian, P. (2000). *Educational Research: Competencies for Analysis and Application* (6th ed.). Upper Saddle River, NJ: Merrill.

Ginsburg, A., McLaughlin, M., & Plisko, V. (1992). Reinvigorating program evaluation at the U.S. Department of Education. *Educational Researcher, 21*(3): 24–27.

Lesourd, S. (1992). A review of methodologies for cross-cultural education. *Social Studies, 83*(1): 30–35.

Mann, T. (1987). *A Guide to Library Research Methods.* New York: Oxford.

McMillan, J., & Schumacher, S. (2001). *Research in Education: A Conceptual Introduction* (5th ed.). Boston: Allyn and Bacon.

Piaget, J. (1947). *The Psychology of Intelligence.* Trans. M. Percy and D. Berlyne. London: Routledge and Kegan Paul, 1950.

Review of Research in Education. (1973 to present). Washington, DC: American Educational Research Association.

Wittrock, M. (ed.). (1986). *Handbook of Research on Teaching* (3rd ed.). New York: Macmillan.

CHAPTER

4 Locating Published Research

PREVIEW

This chapter deals with using the university research library to locate
- Secondary (not firsthand) sources of information, such as

  - Encyclopedias
  - Reviews of research
  - Scholarly books
  - Yearbooks
  - Handbooks of research
  - Magazine and newspaper articles
- Primary (firsthand) sources of information, such as

  - Journal articles
  - Dissertations
  - Scholarly books
  - *Digest of Educational Statistics*
  - Conference papers
  - Monographs
  - Technical reports

Locating sources of information is accomplished through
- The use of indexes, such as

  - *ERIC Descriptors*
  - *Resources in Education*
  - *Education Index*
  - *CIJE*
  - *Dissertation Abstracts*
  - *Psychological Abstracts*
- Computer-assisted searches of library resources

Targeted Learnings

In Chapter 3 you learned how to identify a research problem, refine it for investigation, formulate appropriate questions and hypotheses, and compose a research proposal. In this chapter you will learn how to use the research library to access major sources of information related to a given topic. As you read this chapter, look especially for information having to do with the following questions:

1. Why are secondary sources a good place to begin looking for information on a topic?
2. What are four specific examples of secondary sources?
3. How are primary sources located in a library?

71

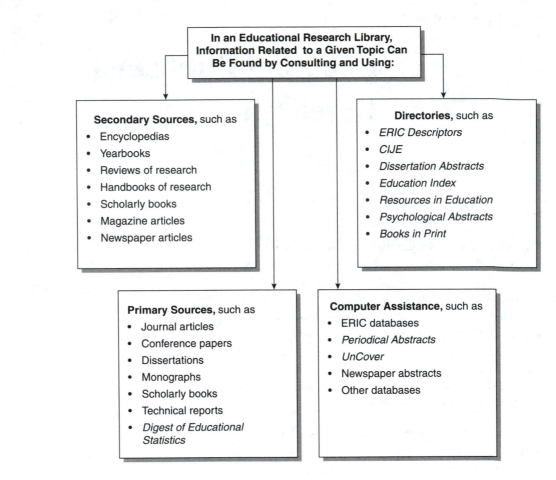

4. Which library holdings are usually considered to be primary sources of information?

5. What are three specific examples of directories to primary sources?

6. What advantages do computer searches of the literature offer over manual searches?

Using the Research Library

All researchers explore the literature for material about their topic to see, first, what has already been done and, second, to profit from findings, cautions, and suggestions made by other researchers. The guidance they gain from this review helps keep their research on course toward a satisfactory conclusion.

The skills of locating information in a library are best learned not from reading about the library but from actually using its resources. For that reason this chapter does not go into great detail about important library references and indexes. Instead you will find them listed and briefly described, accompanied by a guide for their use. That makes this chapter relatively short. But remember, in order to grasp the potential of the research library—and to ready yourself for conducting your own research—you must personally explore the library's resources. Those specific details are described in this chapter.

Secondary Sources in the Library

All research libraries contain a number of **secondary sources** of information. "Secondary" means that these sources do not provide firsthand or eyewitness accounts. Rather, they provide expert compilations, analyses, and interpretations of primary information by other individuals. As a rule, it is best to leave primary sources aside at first and begin a literature search by examining secondary sources, which indicate trends and general conclusions. They usually contain extensive bibliographies of primary source materials. The secondary sources you will find profitable include encyclopedias of research, yearbooks and handbooks of research, reviews of research, scholarly books, and sometimes magazine and newspaper articles. Generally speaking, you will find that among secondary sources

> *Reference books* such as handbooks, yearbooks, and encyclopedias give the best overall coverage of various topics but tend to become dated three or four years after publication.
>
> *Reviews of research* provide the best compilations and critiques of research on selected topics, but the topic selection is limited, and the material begins to become dated three or four years after publication.
>
> *Scholarly books* offer the best overviews and in-depth analyses of certain topics, but the topics are typically few in number and are treated in great detail, as is the case with single-theme works, or else are many in number and are treated more superficially, as with textbooks. (Note that scholarly books are considered primary sources if they report an investigator's own work and conclusions.)
>
> *Magazine and newspaper articles* offer the most current information about particular topics but are more subject to bias and error than are other secondary sources.

Let us briefly note specific examples of some of the more useful secondary sources of information.

1. *The Encyclopedia of Educational Research* (1992). This is a prime source of research information about a large number of topics. Consisting of four volumes, this reference comprises articles written by experts who review, analyze, and interpret research pertinent to broad topics. Each article contains an extensive bibliography. This reference is a key starting place when reviewing research literature.
2. The ***NSSE Yearbooks*** (1902 to present). The National Society for the Study of Education (NSSE) has, every year since 1902, produced two volumes, Part 1 and Part 2,

each of which deals in depth with research done on one or more education topics. The titles of the volumes usually reveal the topics covered; for example:

Education and the Brain (Vol. 77, pt. 2)

The Gifted and Talented (Vol. 78, pt. 1)

Classroom Management (Vol. 78, pt. 2)

The central themes selected for new volumes reflect matters of particular concern at the time the volume is published. The works are written by experts in the topic areas, and extensive bibliographies of significant research are included. The works provide some of the very best in-depth treatments available. But each volume covers only a few topics, and several years may pass before a given topic receives attention a second time, if ever. Thus, the material becomes dated rather quickly.

3. *Handbooks of research* on a number of educational topics are available in the library. For example, the *Handbook of Research on Teaching* (third edition, 1986) provides 35 articles that analyze and interpret research related to five areas: (1) theory and methods of research on teaching; (2) the social and institutional context of teaching; (3) research on teaching and teachers; (4) adapting teaching to differences among learners; and (5) research on the teaching of subjects and grade levels. Extensive bibliographies accompany the articles.

This reference was, for a few years after its publication, one of the best for research topics having to do with teachers and teaching. But because so much research has been done since the 1986 edition, this resource is dated for most current topics. When the new edition appears, the handbook will again be one of the most valuable references available to educational researchers.

The following are among the many excellent handbooks of research on specific topics in education:

Handbook of Research on Early Childhood Education

Handbook of Research on Educational Administration

Handbook of Research on Language Development

Handbook of Research on Curriculum

Handbook of Research on Math Teaching and Learning

Handbook of Research on Multicultural Education

Handbook of Research on Music Teaching and Learning

Handbook of Research on Science Teaching

4. *Review of Research in Education,* published yearly, provides expert critical review and analysis of important research on selected topics. The articles typically include more research citations than do the articles in a reference such as *The Encyclopedia of Educational Research.* The articles are written by expert researchers and vary in number in each issue. Volumes tend to emphasize one to three current issues. The

1984 volume, for example, emphasized various aspects of human development and education of the handicapped, whereas the 1990 volume emphasized mathematics and science instruction and parental choice of schools, and the 1994 volume emphasized teaching knowledge and practice and equity issues in educational access and assessment.

5. *Review of Educational Research* is published quarterly and, as the title indicates, contains reviews of research on selected topics in education. The reviews are quite complete, and the authors provide extensive bibliographies.

6. *Educational Leadership* is a journal published by the Association for Supervision and Curriculum Development. It is widely read by professors, school administrators, and school district personnel who work in curriculum and supervision. Periodically, the journal presents reviews of recent research literature on given topics. These reviews are accurate but nontechnical and reveal the current status of the topic reviewed.

7. *Scholarly books* written by academicians can, on occasion, be of great value to researchers. They are generally of two types: single-theme books and textbooks. **Single-theme books** go into great depth in addressing a particular matter and can provide much insight into the topic's nature and history. Usually these books present the author's interpretations of what others have done. They are, therefore, considered secondary sources, although sometimes they report a scholar's own research, in which case they are considered primary sources. Single-theme books tend to be technical and detailed. Often they report a scholar's views, interpretations, and speculations; in those cases, the author's biases are usually evident. Bearing this caveat in mind, investigators should not overlook this source of potentially valuable information.

    Textbooks contrast with single-theme books in that textbooks usually treat a great many topics, although rarely in much depth. They can be of considerable value in depicting the history, stages, and trends within various topics. Textbook authors are selective in the references they include. This makes most textbook bibliographies short but of high quality.

    Books in Print (annual editions) is the best source for identifying books that are of recent publication or that have stood the test of time. This reference lists books by author, title, and topic and indicates where the book can be obtained. Summaries of a few selected books are given. University libraries, unfortunately, do not quickly acquire recent books. Acquisition time is slow and financial considerations preclude the purchase of many books. If you need to obtain a book your library does not have, it can often be acquired on interlibrary loan from one university to another. It may be more convenient to purchase a needed book through booksellers or by writing or calling the publisher directly.

8. *Magazine and newspaper articles* can, for some topics, be especially important, as they often report the latest occurrences, findings, and controversies. If cited as literature related to a research topic, articles from these sources must be carefully evaluated for accuracy, completeness, and lack of bias. Remember that they are written by reporters who rarely have scholarly backgrounds in the topics presented. The writers' presentation may not have been subjected to scrutiny by authorities before publication. Too, the popular media thrive on controversy, and their articles are rarely

presented in a calm, evenhanded manner. Nevertheless, magazines and newspapers sometimes provide the most up-to-date information available.

Locating Secondary Sources

The library's main catalog is used to locate encyclopedias, yearbooks, handbooks, and scholarly books. The main catalog formerly consisted of drawers of index cards, one card for each book or series of books, containing complete bibliographic information and a Library of Congress number or other code that indicated the material's location in the library. A few libraries still use card catalogs, but most have converted to computer cataloging. Now, instead of leafing through drawers of cards, you use a computer terminal and follow on-screen directions to locate reference materials. The computer brings to the screen the source you are seeking and provides full bibliographic citation and the source's location in the library.

Reference books such as the *Encyclopedia of Educational Research, Review of Research in Education,* and various handbooks are shelved in the library's main reference section. Other secondary sources, such as certain abstracts, journals, and yearbooks, may be bound and shelved in the stacks or put onto microfiche and kept in the microfiche reading room. If you have trouble locating guides or resources, ask a librarian for assistance— librarians are most helpful.

Newspaper stories related to given topics can now be located and reviewed through library computers via *Newspaper Abstracts.* This is an index that abstracts articles published since 1989 in 25 major regional, national, financial, and ethnic newspapers. "Education" is one of approximately 20 topic categories for which abstracts are provided. Your library also keeps contents of various newspapers on microfiche, available in the microfiche reading room.

Magazine articles related to given topics can be located and reviewed in *Periodical Abstracts,* via library computers. Topic coverage, including education, is the same as for *Newspaper Abstracts.* Ask a librarian for directions. Your library keeps a selection of periodicals on microfiche or bound in original form and shelved.

Primary Sources in the Library

After you have explored secondary sources, you should examine primary sources in order to judge original research for yourself and to obtain more current information than is normally available in reference works. Common **primary sources** are journal articles, monographs, and papers presented at conferences. You can locate primary sources through specialized indexes, bibliographies, abstracts, and reviews of research. The Educational Resources Information Center **(ERIC)** provides marvelous assistance in locating primary sources through its listings and abstracts of published research.

Abstracts (summaries) of original works can be found in publications such as *Psychological Abstracts* and ERIC's *Current Index to Journals in Education (CIJE).* Published without evaluation or comment, abstracts help you decide whether the original publication merits further examination.

Reviews, listed previously as a secondary source, provide extensive bibliographies of journal articles and other publications that can be consulted as primary sources.

Indexes are especially valuable because they list primary sources of information such as monographs and journal articles that would otherwise be difficult to locate. Several excellent indexes, many of which can be accessed through computers, are available in research libraries.

Exercise 4.1

Indicate whether each of the following is most likely a (S) secondary source or (P) a primary source of information.

_____ 1. Professor Oldshanks's report of his own research on the aging process

_____ 2. Professor Oldshanks's in-depth analyses of other investigators' research on the aging process

_____ 3. Dr. Apodaca's book that criticizes the treatment of Hispanic students in Texas schools

_____ 4. The published article "How We Improved Multicultural Understanding in Elmwood Schools," written by the director of the project

_____ 5. The book entitled *A Review of Progress in Bilingual Teaching*

_____ 6. A conference address, "Stress and the Workplace: One Teacher's Personal Perspective"

Specific Directories of Primary References

Here we will note several of the most commonly used directories of primary sources.

The ERIC Materials.   The Educational Resources Information Center, or ERIC, publishes the most widely used indexes for locating education materials published since 1981. (For articles published before 1981, consult a reference called *The Education Index.*) ERIC consists of 16 regional clearinghouses and four adjunct houses that locate, catalog, abstract, and index research articles and other documents. Each clearinghouse is responsible for a subject area. The subject areas are (1) adult, career, and vocational education, (2) counseling and personnel services, (3) reading and communication skills, (4) educational management, (5) handicapped and gifted children, (6) languages and linguistics, (7) higher education, (8) information resources, (9) junior colleges, (10) elementary and early childhood education, (11) rural education and small schools, (12) science, mathematics, and environmental education, (13) social studies/social science education, (14) teacher education, (15) tests, measurements, and evaluation, (16) urban education, (17) art education, (18) United States—Japan studies, (19) literacy education for limited-English-proficient adults, and (20) matters related to Chapter 1 (federal law regarding instructional assistance for disadvantaged students). ERIC publishes a thesaurus of descriptive terms and two indexes that provide abstracts and complete citations of materials reviewed.

1. The ***Thesaurus of ERIC Descriptors*** is a book that lists the specific topics and labels under which various articles and documents are indexed. The *Thesaurus* is mainly used for accessing ERIC abstracts via computer, a topic to which we shall return.

2. The ***Current Index to Journals in Education (CIJE)*** is the ERIC index that cites and presents abstracts of articles published in education and closely related fields. Two bound volumes of new citations are published each year, and supplements are issued each month. The bound volumes of *CIJE* are typically shelved with the general reference books and/or in the education section of the library. Most larger libraries provide computer access to *CIJE* on CD-ROM (compact disk with read-only memory), which, as will be described later, provides wonderful benefits to the researcher.

3. ***Resources in Education (RIE)*** is the ERIC index that cites and abstracts documents such as papers read at conferences, descriptions of new programs, technical reports, reports from federally funded programs, selected books, and much original research that has not been published elsewhere, specifically in academic journals. The *RIE* is shelved in bound form and is also accessible via the library computer. Until recently, the materials it indexes were not usually available in libraries and had to be ordered from the addresses provided in the citations. Increasingly, libraries are making *RIE* materials directly available to researchers, predominantly in the form of microfiche.

Both *CIJE* and *RIE* are available on CD-ROM, and are also accessible via the Internet (see *Applying Technology:* Searching ERIC Online).

Abstracts Publications.   Some journals specialize in publishing short abstracts of unpublished papers and of previously published articles. The following are among the most useful for educational researchers:

1. *Psychological Abstracts* is the monthly publication of the American Psychological Association. It provides summaries of works selected from almost 1,000 publications, including journals, technical reports, and monographs. Some of the articles have to do with psychological aspects of teaching, learning, counseling, child development, and the learning process.

2. *Child Development Abstracts and Bibliography* is published three times per year and provides summaries of articles on child development selected from approximately 200 publications. Book reviews are included, as are extensive bibliographies. The publication is organized into six categories, of which two—"Cognition, Learning, and Perception" and "Educational Processes"—are related to education in the school setting. This source is especially valuable to researchers interested in child development and early childhood education.

3. *Dissertation Abstracts International (DAI)* provides abstracts of doctoral dissertations completed each year in more than 300 universities in the United States and Europe. The abstracts are grouped into nine different subject areas, or volumes. Volume VII, *Education,* is of most interest to educational researchers. The abstracts are complete, indicating what the researcher was attempting to explore, the procedures used, and the results obtained. Doctoral dissertations have been relatively little used in ed-

ucational research, despite the fact that they often contain some of the most recent and reliable scholarly information available.

Social Science Citation Index.   The *Social Science Citation Index (SSCI)* lists research reports having to do with education, social science, and behavioral science. This index provides the valuable service of indicating where a given author has been cited by other authors in later research, which provides one indication of how important the research was considered to be by later investigators. In addition, the index provides bibliographic citations for the articles that made reference to that particular author. For example, if Jones in 1975 published research on multicultural education, the *SSCI* would provide a list of reports published later that made reference to Jones's work.

Digest of Educational Statistics.   This reference book is unlike other sources in that it does not list, review, or analyze research. It nevertheless may be of much value in a particular investigation. Researchers often need reliable statistics concerning such things as the number of students in bilingual education, the percentages of the national school population that belong to various ethnic groups, and the amount of money each state spends on students, teachers, and buildings.

Exercise 4.2

Indicate the index or source that would most likely contain recent information for the needs presented below: (N) *NSSE Yearbooks,* (C) *Current Index to Journals in Education,* (D) *Dissertation Abstracts International,* (H) *Handbook of Research on Teaching,* (RI) *Resources in Education,* (S) *Digest of Educational Statistics,* (E) *Encyclopedia of Educational Research,* or (SS) *Social Science Citation Index.*

_____   1. You have lost the title of an important article.

_____   2. You want a copy of a paper presented at a major convention.

_____   3. You want to know your state's ranking on expenditures per student.

_____   4. You want to know what sorts of topics doctoral students in England are researching.

_____   5. You want to look at a research review book published this year.

_____   6. You need a reference book devoted specifically to research on teaching.

_____   7. You want to read analyses of educational research into many different topics.

_____   8. You want to know how much influence a given report might have had on later research.

Locating Primary Sources

Journal articles and unpublished documents are normally found in bound volumes on library shelves or on microfiche adjacent to the microfiche readers. Very recent articles are shelved in the current reading room for use prior to being bound. Specific articles and documents are identified and located through the indexes described earlier. This procedure can be done manually or, in most libraries, by means of computer.

The Computer Search.   Computers greatly facilitate the search procedure by covering great quantities of information rapidly, by surveying many different **databases,** and by limiting the searches in accord with selected **descriptors,** such as key words and dates of publication. Already mentioned were *Newspaper Abstracts* and *Periodical Abstracts,* which provide abstracts of stories and articles via computer. Also very useful is a computer capability called ***UnCover*** (available at www.ingenta.com). *Ingenta,* a UK-based Web service, provides a free online search service of published content from reliable research sources. With the acquisition of *UnCover* in March 2000, the most widely used search service in the U.S. academic sector, *ingenta* became the world's largest online resource for the search and delivery of research articles. *UnCover* produces and makes available on the Internet tables of contents from over 27,000 journal titles from over 6,000 publishers which have appeared since fall 1988. The merging of *ingenta* and *UnCover* content offers Internet users an unequaled *14 million* article citations—many of which are linked to full text articles. *UnCover@ingenta* offers researchers the opportunity to link to the full text of many articles and order fax copies of many of the other articles. However, there are some articles that are not available for delivery via any method. *UnCover@ ingenta* is relatively easy to use, with keyword access to article titles and summaries. Figure 4.1 shows (a) the search page for *ingenta* and (b) the search page for *ingenta select,* which contains only full-text, online publications.

Among the major education-related indexes accessible through library computer terminals are the following:

> *Current Index to Journals in Education*
> *Resources in Education*
> *Education Index*
> *Psychological Abstracts*
> *Sociological Abstracts*
> *Social Science Citation Index*
> *Dissertation Abstracts*
> *Exceptional Child Education Resources*
> *Resources in Vocational Education*
> *Bilingual Education Database*
> *Books in Print*

Some libraries have these indexes available online; most make them available on CD-ROM. In some cases, depending on your library, you may need to check out the compact disk from the librarian and use it in a computer equipped with a CD-ROM player. These disks contain the same information as do the bound volumes of the indexes, and they are updated every few months to keep them current.

As previously mentioned, ERIC is the most widely used index for locating published educational materials. Specific information regarding an online search of ERIC is provided in the section titled *Applying Technology:* Searching ERIC Online.

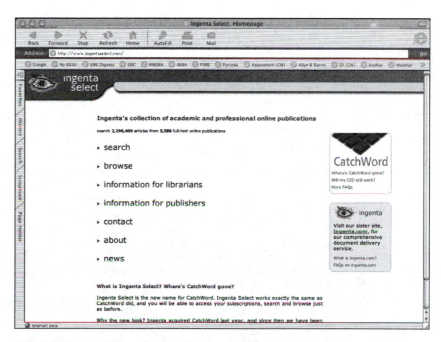

FIGURE 4.1 (a)   The main page for *ingenta*

FIGURE 4.1 (b)   The main page for *ingenta Select* (Courtesy of ingenta, Inc., a subsidiary of ingenta PLC.)

Applying Technology: Electronic Journals

In addition to the major divisions of AERA (American Educational Research Association) that you read about in *Applying Technology:* Sources for Research Topics in Chapter 3, AERA also supports the existence of many *Special Interest Groups* or (*SIGs*). The more than 150 AERA SIGs "provide a forum within AERA for the involvement of individuals drawn together by a common interest in a field of study, teaching, or research when the existing divisional structure may not directly facilitate such activity" (www.aera.net/sigs). One of these SIGs, "Communications among Researchers," maintains a website (aera-cr.ed.asu.edu), which includes a second page containing links to over 50 electronic journals (or *e-journals*). This site, titled "Electronic Journals in the Field of Education," may be found by pointing your Web browser to http://aera-cr.ed.asu.edu/links.html.

The SIG has included only links to e-journals that are:

- Scholarly
- Peer-reviewed
- Full-text
- Accessible without cost

These last two factors are key for the beginning researcher. First, the fact that only full-text articles are available means that you can view, read, and/or download them directly on your Web browser—there is no need to go to the library to retrieve these articles. Second, because a goal of the SIG is to promote free worldwide access to scholarship in education, all articles in these e-journals are available free of charge—there are no subscription fees, as there usually are with all print journals, or fees of any other kind.

A sampling of the e-journals to which links are provided by the "Communications among Researchers" SIG includes:

- *Action Research International*
- *Advancing Women in Leadership Journal*
- *Bilingual Research Journal*
- *Compute~Ed: An Electronic Journal of Learning and Teaching with and about Technology*
- *Contemporary Issues in Early Childhood*
- *Early Childhood Research & Practice*
- *Current Issues in Education*
- *Educational Insights: Electronic Journal of Graduate Student Research*
- *Educational Technology and Society*
- *The Electronic Journal of Science Education*
- *International Education Journal*
- *Journal of Technology Education*
- *The Ontario Action Researcher*
- *Practical Assessment, Research and Evaluation*
- *Reading Online: An Electronic Journal of the International Reading Association*
- *Research & Reflection: Leadership and Organizations*
- *Teaching English as a Second Language*

Applying Technology: Searching ERIC Online

As we have seen up to this point, the arrival of the Internet has resulted in wonderful resources of which researchers can take advantage in order to facilitate their research endeavors. The development of CD-ROM technology made the process of locating published research much easier. Prior to that, one had to scan nearly every volume of *CIJE* and *RIE* in order to locate published work relevant to a given topic. However, today's researchers are able to locate relevant articles and other documents without even *going* to the library. The entire ERIC database (both *CIJE* and *RIE*) is available online. Furthermore, the ERIC database is available at several different websites. One of the most popular locations from which to search ERIC is:

- **The Educator's Reference Desk** (www.eduref.org).

This site accesses the ERIC database via servers at Syracuse University. The main page for this site is shown in Figure 4.2. One simply clicks on "Search ERIC Database" and then on "Advanced Search" to arrive at the common search page, shown in Figure 4.3.

Notice that, initially, one can search for up to five terms in ERIC. Furthermore, notice that the search can be conducted based on one of several criteria (located in the drop-down

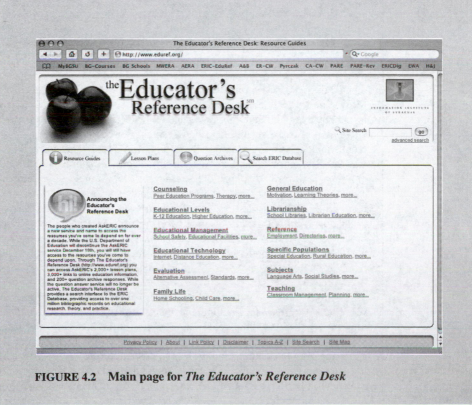

FIGURE 4.2   Main page for *The Educator's Reference Desk*

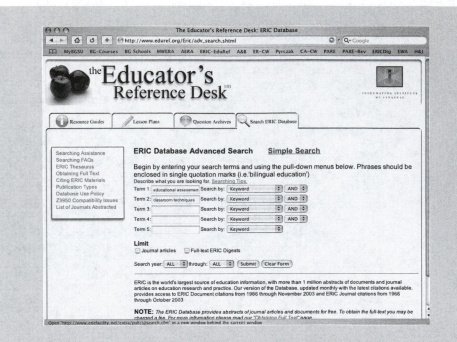

FIGURE 4.3   Search page for *The Educator's Reference Desk*

menus, or *selection buttons*), including searching by `Keyword`, `Author`, and `Title`. Most searches are conducted by `Keyword`, at least during the initial stages. Let us consider a concrete example: Suppose we wanted to locate published research on the topic of teachers' classroom assessment practices. We might search under the terms "educational assessment" and "classroom techniques" (see Fig. 4.3). Notice that located next to the criterion `Search by` button is another selection button containing boolean operators. *Boolean operators* are key words that enable the retrieval of terms in specific combinations. The most common operators are "and" and "or"—if "and" is used, only those documents which contain *both* keywords as descriptors will be retrieved (i.e., a narrower search); if "or" is used, *every* document with *either* of these two keywords as descriptors will be retrieved (i.e., a broader search). We will use "and" for our example—therefore, we are searching for documents that contain both "educational assessment" *and* "classroom techniques." We then click on `Submit` to begin our search of the database. The results of our search are shown in Figure 4.4.

First, you will notice that ERIC retrieved 164 documents containing these two descriptive keywords. The resulting documents are returned in sets of 25—to continue scanning the results, one simply clicks on `[Next]` at the bottom of the page. The documents are initially screened for relevance by examining the titles. If the researcher is interested in exploring a given document more closely, this can be accomplished by simply clicking on the ERIC accession number (i.e., the ED or EJ number). This will provide the entire citation information for that document. For example, if you scan down the list, you will notice that

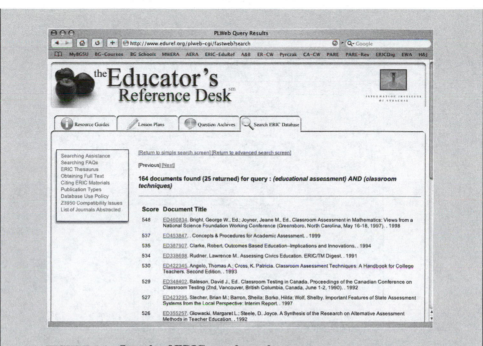

FIGURE 4.4   Sample of ERIC search results

a document written by one of the coauthors of this text appears on the list. By clicking on the accession number (in this case, ED 428 085), you are provided with the document's citation (see Figure 4.5).

Recall that the ERIC accession number (ERIC_NO, as shown in Figure 4.5) not only serves as the document's identification within ERIC but also informs the researcher as to whether the document was published in an academic journal (EJ) or exists in one of several unpublished forms (ED). Documents listed as EJ will include the citation information for the journal in which the document appears. This is important information because you will need it in order to locate the article in the appropriate library shelves.

Documents listed as ED may have originally been written as papers to be presented at academic conferences, position papers, technical reports, research reports, and so on. The accession number is again of vital importance here, because all ED documents appear on microfiche and *are cataloged by the six-digit ED number.* This number is the *only* means of locating the correct microfiche in your library's microfiche stacks.

Also of great importance to the researcher is the ABSTRACT. This is a brief summary of the contents of the document, including the results and conclusions of the study, if appropriate. Only by reading the document abstract can the researcher really be sure if he or she wants to obtain the full document for complete review. It is always best to study the abstract prior to investing the time required to locate the complete article.

Finally, the section titled NOTE includes any miscellaneous comments related to the document. With ED documents, for example, these comments provide information related to the purpose or development of the article. Based on the information provided in Figure 4.5,

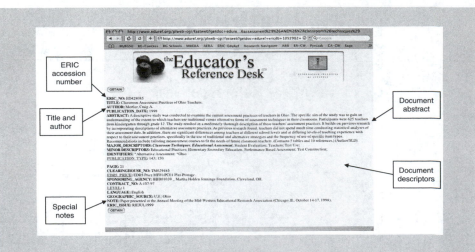

FIGURE 4.5   **Document citation from ERIC**

we know that this particular document was a paper presented at an academic conference—the name, location, and dates of the conference meeting are provided in this comment section.

Because of the flexibility of the searchable ERIC database, it does take some practice and experience to be able to work with it effectively. The idea of combining keywords in a single search—or even combining keywords with authors' names and so on—can be a little intimidating to the beginning researcher. However, novice researchers should not hesitate to "experiment" with searches of ERIC. Online access to the ERIC database is certainly a valuable research tool of which all researchers—at any level of experience—should take advantage.

As you can see, computer searches can save much time over manual searches. However, they only give you citations and, at best, brief abstracts of the original work. You must still go to the library stacks or microfiche room because the abstracts do not contain important details that you require; the summaries are presented only to help you decide whether the original is worth finding and reading.

A word to first-time computer searchers: Think of your first attempts as *learning experiences*. Most people, especially those not accustomed to using computers, at first make mistakes, need assistance, and have to start over again more than once. To ease initiation into a computer search, start small and learn how the process is done. If possible, get an experienced user to walk you through the process. Take notes to help you feel secure when you begin to work on your own. Although the procedure may at first seem intimidating, it is easily learned and will save you many, many hours of hard work.

A Purposeful Visit to the Library

In order to learn how to use the library profitably, you must go there in person and explore the resources and procedures described in this chapter. A guide for such an exploration is presented in the following exercise.

Exercise 4.3

Make a visit to the university library to familiarize yourself with the location and nature of the main sources and guides. Use the following guide.

Guide for Exploring the Research Library

Source or Element	Located		Found my topic		Value of source		
	Yes	*No*	*Yes*	*No*	*High*	*Fair*	*Little*
Library main catalog							
Current Index to Journals in Education							
Resources in Education							
Encyclopedia of Educational Research							
Review of Educational Research							
Review of Research in Education							
Psychological Abstracts							
Dissertation Abstracts International							
Social Science Citation Index							
Digest of Educational Statistics							
NSSE Yearbooks							
Research on Teaching							
Child Development Abstracts							
Books in Print							
Computers for search							

INTRODUCTION TO EDUCATIONAL RESEARCH

Companion Website Highlight

The Companion Website that accompanies this text (www.ablongman.com/mertler5e), and specifically this chapter, includes a downloadable, printable version of the guide to assist you in your efforts in exploring the research library, as shown in Exercise 4.3. Save or print the form and use it to summarize the benefit of each source when researching your topic in your university library.

Not Just for Conducting Research—Valuable Sources for Professional Development

Although your primary and immediate focus may be on learning about and actually conducting graduate level research, it is important to realize that you will have a long career in education or an education-related field. The sources of information, both primary and secondary, that have been presented and discussed in this chapter will continue to be excellent and invaluable sources of up-to-date research. True professionals continue to develop themselves in their respective fields throughout their careers. These individuals maintain membership in professional organizations and continue to read journals and other sources of current information specific to their disciplines. As current and/or future members of your respective professions, you too should avail yourselves of such opportunities.

D E V E L O P M E N T A L   A C T I V I T Y

Locating Published Research

Now that you have specified your research topic, it is time to begin reading and learning more about it. The best source for further information on your chosen topic is previously conducted—and preferably *published*—research. It is important to approach your search for published research in an organized manner, maintaining records as you proceed. Keep this in mind as you respond to the following questions:

1. A possible topic or problem I am planning to research is: _____

_____.

2. The main question or hypothesis for my study is: _____

_____.

3. *Secondary* sources that I consulted for information included: _____

_____ .

4. I searched for *primary* sources through the use of the following database(s): _____

_____ .

5. The search descriptors that I used were (*list single descriptors, and any combinations of descriptors, in the order in which they were searched*):

_____

_____

_____

_____

_____

_____

6. A summary of the results of my search using these descriptors is as follows:

Search Number	Descriptor(s) Used	Number Retrieved

(A downloadable, interactive version of this developmental activity is available from the Companion Website, www.ablongman.com/mertler5e)

Chapter Summary

It is important that you review existing literature related to the topic you wish to research, in order to learn more about the topic, determine the contexts in which the topic might have been researched previously, and obtain guidance that will help you in your research efforts.

When you use the university library to review research literature, begin with secondary sources, such as the *Encyclopedia of Educational Research, Review of Research in Education,* and *NSSE Yearbooks,* which contain excellent reviews and summaries of research done on various topics, plus extensive bibliographies that can direct you to good primary sources.

To find primary sources, next consult directories such as *Current Index to Journals in Education, Psychological Abstracts,* and *Dissertation Abstracts International,* all of which provide summaries of the materials indexed. The summaries will suggest whether the original source is worth reading carefully, and the index will provide the bibliographic citation for locating the article, conference paper, monograph, dissertation, or technical report that interests you.

L I S T   O F   I M P O R T A N T   T E R M S

abstracts	manual search	secondary sources
CIJE	*Newspaper Abstracts*	single-theme books
DAI	*NSSE Yearbooks*	*SSCI*
database	*Periodical Abstracts*	*Thesaurus of ERIC Descriptors*
descriptors	primary sources	*UnCover*
ERIC	*RIE*	

Y O U R   C U R R E N T   S T A T U S

Chapter 3 showed you how to select a research topic, refine the topic into a problem, and compose a proposal for research. In Chapter 4 you have learned to locate secondary sources of research information related to a given topic or problem and to use various indexes to locate primary sources, a process facilitated by library and home computers that can search the ERIC database and other indexes with amazing speed. You are now ready to learn how to interpret and annotate materials you have located that are important to your research, the topic of Chapter 5. First, however, please respond to the following activities for thought and discussion.

A C T I V I T I E S   F O R   T H O U G H T   A N D   D I S C U S S I O N

1. From your perusal of the research literature, what do you consider to be the most valuable traits of secondary sources? What do you consider to be the major limitations of secondary sources?

2. Describe what you consider to be the advantages and disadvantages of a computer search of ERIC and other databases, as compared to a manual search.

3. Based on what you discovered in the *CIJE* article abstracts, why is it often necessary to locate and read the original articles or papers rather than rely on the information in the abstracts?

4. Here are the questions presented at the beginning of the chapter. See how well you can answer them.

   a. Why are secondary sources a good place to begin looking for information on a topic?

   b. What are four specific examples of secondary sources?

   c. How are primary sources located in a library?

   d. Which library holdings are usually considered to be primary sources of information?

   e. What are three specific examples of directories to primary sources?

   f. What advantages do computer searches of the literature offer over manual searches?

5. Recall the chapter information organizer you saw at the beginning of the chapter. Without looking back, explain your understanding of each element of the organizer.

ANSWERS TO CHAPTER EXERCISES

4.1. 1. P 2. S 3. P/S 4. P 5. S 6. P   **4.2.** 1. C 2. RI 3. S 4. D 5. N 6. H 7. E 8. SS

REFERENCES AND RECOMMENDED READINGS

Alkin, M. (ed.). (1992). *Encyclopedia of Educational Research* (6th ed.). New York: Macmillan.

Batt, F. (1988). *Online Searching for End Users: An Information Sourcebook.* Phoenix: Oryx Press.

Books in Print (1995). New Providence, NJ: R. R. Bowker.

Burek, D. (ed.). (1992). *Encyclopedia of Associations* (26th ed.). Detroit: Gale.

Buttlar, L. (1989). *Education: A Guide to Reference and Information Sources.* Englewood, CO: Libraries Unlimited.

Child Development Abstracts and Bibliography. (1927 to date). Chicago: University of Chicago Press.

Completed Research in Health, Physical Education and Recreation Including International Sources. (1958 to date). Washington, DC: American Alliance for Health, Physical Education and Recreation.

Current Index to Journals in Education. (1969 to date). Phoenix, AZ: Oryx Press.

Dissertation Abstracts International. (1955 to date). Ann Arbor, MI: Xerox University Microfilms.

Education Index. (1929 to date). New York: H. W. Wilson.

Edyburn, D. L. (1999). *The Electronic Scholar: Enhancing Research Productivity with Technology.* Upper Saddle River, NJ: Merrill.

Exceptional Child Education Resources. (1969 to date). Arlington, VA: Council for Exceptional Children.

Houston, J. (ed.) (1990). *Thesaurus of ERIC Descriptors* (12th ed.). Phoenix, AZ: Oryx Press.

Huck, S., & Cormier, W. (1996). *Reading Statistics and Research* (2nd ed.). New York: HarperCollins.

Husén, T., & Postlethwaite, T. (eds.) (1994). *The International Encyclopedia of Education: Research and Studies.* New York: Pergamon.

National School Law Reporter. (1955 to date). New London, CT: Croft Educational Services.

Physical Education/Sports Index. (1978 to date). Albany, NY: Marathon Press.

Psychological Abstracts. (1927 to date). Washington, DC: American Psychological Association.

Readers' Guide to Periodic Literature. (1900 to date). New York: H. W. Wilson.

Rehabilitation Literature. (1940 to date). Chicago: National Society for Crippled Children and Adults.

Resources in Education. (1966 to date). Washington, DC: Superintendent of Documents, Government Printing Office.

Review of Educational Research. (1931 to date). Washington, DC: American Educational Research Association.

Review of Research in Education. (1973 to date). Washington, DC: American Educational Research Association.

Social Science Citation Index. (1973 to date). Philadelphia: Institute for Scientific Information.

Social Sciences Index. (1974 to date). New York: H. W. Wilson.

Sociological Abstracts. (1952 to date). San Diego, CA: Sociological Abstracts, Inc.

Subject Index to the Christian Science Monitor. (1960 to date). Boston: Christian Science Monitor.

The New York Times Index. (1913 to date). New York.

Thomas, R. (ed.) (1990). *The Encyclopedia of Human Development and Education: Theory, Research, and Studies.* New York: Pergamon.

Wegner, L. (1992). The research library and emerging information technology (pp. 83–90). *New Directions for Teaching and Learning, 51 (Teaching in the information age: The role of educational technology).*

Wittrock, M. (ed.). (1986). *Handbook of Research on Teaching* (3rd ed.). New York: Macmillan.

5 Interpreting and Summarizing Published Research

PREVIEW

This chapter provides practical suggestions to help you

- Review
- Interpret
- Annotate

published literature related to your topic. Included are suggestions to help you rapidly peruse reports to determine

- Topic and purpose
- Type of report
- Findings and conclusions

and to

- Skim information
- Summarize information
- Make annotated citations

Most reports, by type, are status reports, group comparison reports, and relationship reports. Interpretation of these reports often requires some knowledge of statistical analysis techniques. You may see:

For status reports:	For group comparison reports:	For relationship reports:
Mean, median, mode	Chi-square	Coefficient of correlation
Standard deviation	Difference between means	Statistical significance
Norms	Analysis of variance	
Percentiles	Statistical significance	

Targeted Learnings

In Chapter 4, you learned how to locate and use some of the most valuable secondary and primary sources of information in the research library. In this chapter, you will find suggestions on how to peruse published reports, interpret their contents, summarize them quickly, and make effective notes for bibliographic use. As you read the chapter, be sure to look for information related to these questions:

1. Why should research reports be skimmed rapidly before they are read carefully?
2. What specifically does one look for when skimming reports?
3. What entries should one make on note cards when annotating published reports?
4. What are the three general types of research reports encountered in published literature?
5. What characterizes the three different types of research reports?
6. What common analysis terminology—verbal and/or statistical—is usually associated with each of the three types of reports?
7. Why do the different types of research reports utilize different verbal and statistical procedures to analyze their data?
8. What two different meanings does the term *significance* have in the context of research?
9. Why is the term *significant* often misleading to uninformed readers of research?

You have already familiarized yourself with the major sources and locations of published research. That was the first phase in learning to use the library profitably. You are now ready to undertake the second phase, which involves accurately interpreting the published information in the sources you locate. This phase is completed in three parts, dealing with (1) how to read and summarize the material, (2) how to identify the type of report and interpret statistical analyses you might encounter, and (3) how to enter annotations on summary cards to maximize their value and ease of use.

Reading Research Reports

Research literature comes in various forms now familiar to you, such as references, handbooks, reviews, journal articles, technical reports, and scholarly books. After becoming able to locate relevant information, how does one make effective use of it? The first step is to learn how to *skim* the material quickly to ascertain its nature and the researcher's conclusions.

Skimming the Information

You know how to find a number of published reports related to almost any educational topic you choose. Because so much material is available, you need to be able to move through it quickly. The summaries presented in indexes such as *CIJE* and in journals such as *Psychological Abstracts* provide immeasurable help in pinpointing materials of value to your topic. However, summaries and abstracts omit many important details and can by no means replace reading the original material.

To move rather quickly through quantities of reports, you should practice skimming the materials so that you can quickly determine what the study is about and what the author concludes. By using this strategy, you can expeditiously obtain information and further identify reports that have direct bearing on your topic.

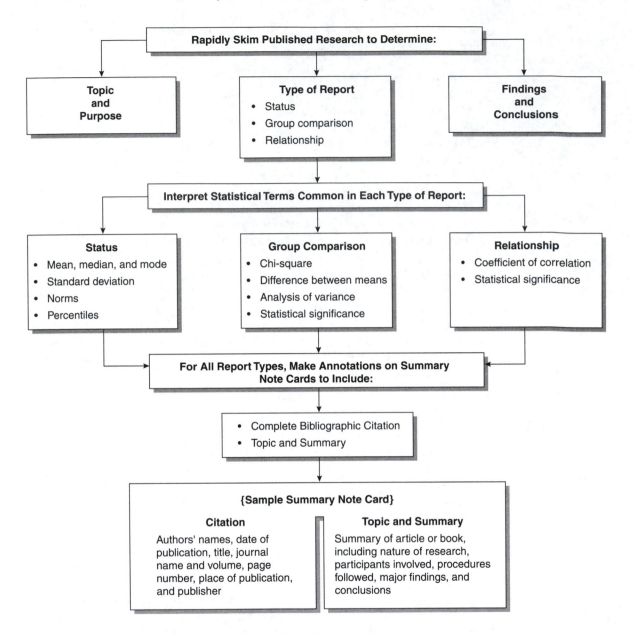

Determining What the Material Is About.   To pinpoint the focus of the article, look quickly for a *title* and an *introduction*. The title should clearly indicate the topic. Most researchers use descriptive titles for their reports, but such is not always the case. An example of a citation whose title makes clear the nature of the research being reported is

Cipielewski, J., & Stanovich, K. (1992). Predicting growth in reading ability from children's exposure to print. *Journal of Experimental Child Psychology, 54*(1):74–89.

In contrast, fictitious examples of titles that would leave one guessing are

> Onward and upward in educational research
>
> The golden egg of bilingual education

These two titles suggest that the reports have something to do with educational research and bilingual education but little else.

Once you have examined the title, you are ready to scan the introduction of the report, which may be labeled as such. If not labeled, the first paragraph or two usually introduces the report and tells why the topic is considered important.

Identifying the Writer's Conclusions.   To find the conclusions presented by the writer of the report, look for an abstract, summary, or a section near the end of the report entitled *Findings, Conclusions,* or *Discussion.* If there is no such heading, the conclusions are usually presented in the final paragraphs of the report or article.

Some journals—the exceptions rather than the rule—present an abstract at the beginning of the article. This is helpful to readers since it provides a brief synopsis of the article. If there is no abstract at the beginning, flip to the end of the article to see if there is a summary, which will indicate concisely what the article is about and what are its conclusions.

Cautions to Keep in Mind.   As you skim documents that describe (1) ethnographic research (such as patterns of interaction among teachers), (2) historical research (such as the backgrounds of the first teachers in Elmwood schools), or (3) action research (such as development of a special spelling program for Cutter Elementary School students), remember that the conclusions presented in those reports may be correct for the specific groups and locales investigated, but that does not necessarily make them applicable elsewhere.

On the other hand, if you are reading technical reports of research funded by grants or reports published in research journals, most of the information you encounter will be intended for wide dispersion and will have been subjected to close scrutiny by experts in their respective fields, who judge the research methodology, analysis of data, and appropriateness of conclusions. When reports meet these criteria, the results can nearly always be generalized to similar locales and populations. This is not to say that the conclusions are invariably correct, nor that you should *never* analyze critically the methods and conclusions of reports published in prestigious journals. But the likelihood is great that researchers reporting those investigations have followed established procedures, analyzed the data appropriately, and formulated conclusions that follow from the analyses and seem logically correct.

Summarizing the Reports

Suppose you have read a journal article reporting a large study on high school students' attitudes toward the use of alcohol. You have gleaned the following information:

> Lazerus surveyed 2,000 high school students in four eastern states concerning their attitude toward the use of alcohol…found that 42 percent approved of the use of alcohol in general, but that only 17 percent approved of their parents' using alcohol.

In what form should you make your notations, so they will be most accurate and useful? Good notations should not only summarize information, as the preceding entry does, but also indicate the *topic* and include a *complete bibliographical citation*. If you do a preliminary search via computer, you can print out the citations, thus ensuring completeness and accuracy. If you do a manual search, it is very important that you make your notes clear and complete. It is irritating and a frustrating waste of time—not to mention a sometimes *unrealistic* task—to have to go back later to find an item of information that was omitted or written illegibly.

If you have note-taking software and a laptop computer, the computer can enter, organize, and rearrange your notes in a number of ways. If you do not have that capability, it is suggested that you enter your summary notes on 5-inch by 8-inch index cards. Place each reference on a separate card. These cards are large enough to hold a good deal of information, and they are easy to store, organize, regroup, and retrieve. Index cards are valuable even if you have used a computer to print out citations and summaries. Simply cut and tape the citations onto the cards. But keep in mind that the article abstracts seldom contain all the details you need for your research. Those important notations must be made by hand.

One helpful suggestion is to write the topic of the report in the upper-right-hand corner of the card and write the author's name and date of publication in the left-hand corner. By doing this, you can easily group cards by topic, publication date, or alphabetized authors' names. This will save time when you begin organizing your references and preparing your bibliography.

An article citation *must* include all of the following:

- Author's name
- Date of publication
- Title of article
- Name of journal
- Volume of journal and issue (issue optional)
- Page numbers of the article

A book citation *must* include:

- Author's name
- Year of publication
- Title of book
- City where published
- Name of publishing company

As previously mentioned, make sure to record the citation correctly in its entirety. Make sure, also, that you enter notational information accurately, and if you quote material directly, indicate so clearly. Your card for a journal article might look like that shown in Figure 5.1. Note the author, date, topic, complete citation, and notes about principal findings. (All aspects of this particular entry are fictitious.) Your card for a book citation might look like that shown in Figure 5.2. (Again, the information is fictitious.)

Lazerus, F. 1997   High School Students' Attitude toward Use of Alcohol

Lazerus, F. (1997). What high school students say about their parents' use of alcohol. *Journal of Alcohol and Drug Education 35*(4), 37–42.

Lazerus surveyed 2,000 high school students in four eastern states concerning their attitude toward the use of alcohol. He found that 42 percent approved of the use of alcohol in general but that only 17 percent approved of their parents' using alcohol.

FIGURE 5.1   Summary note card for a journal article citation

---

Czeminski, P. 1998   High School Students' Attitude toward Alcohol

Czeminski, P. (1998). *Student Use of Alcohol: A Historical Perspective* (pp. 21–25). New York: Clearview Press.

Use of alcohol by high school students, on a per capita basis, has increased little, if any, in the six decades that accurate records have been kept. However, efforts to reduce alcohol consumption by high school students have been effective.

FIGURE 5.2   Summary note card for a book citation

Exercise 5.1

From the following fictitious information, write note cards in the manner suggested:

1. James F. Roberts did research on teacher partnering that showed that men are two points lazier than women when it comes to doing menial tasks. That finding was reported in his 1995 book, *Unequal Teacher Partners,* which was published in New York by the Domestic Press.
2. Cecilia A. González studied role acceptance in teacher partnering. In her article "Parameters of Teacher Role Acclimatization," published in the July 1993 (volume 4, pp. 12–18) *Journal of Teacher Partnering,* González reported that she found no gender differences in teachers' ability to adjust to new roles in the partnering process.

INTRODUCTION TO EDUCATIONAL RESEARCH
Companion Website Highlight

The Companion Website that accompanies this text (www.ablongman.com/mertler5e) includes a downloadable, printable form that will help you evaluate published research. It is organized as a checklist/rating scale and allows you to evaluate or critique all important aspects of a written research report. Save or print the form and use it to assist you in interpreting published research.

Interpreting the Statistical Information You Encounter

Researchers use words and phrases in special ways to express concepts clearly with an economy of language, but the special terms they use are usually confusing to people not schooled in research. If you are to understand the research reports you read, you must have a grasp of the fundamentals of this research language, especially having to do with statistics, significance, and conclusions.

Suppose you have read a report that said, "The difference between the groups was not significant." Or, "The coefficient of correlation was .85." Or, "The standard error of the mean was 1.72." What would these statements mean to you? If you are a beginner in research, they would mean little or might even be misleading.

Chapter 8 and Appendix A present considerable information about statistical terms and procedures. However, certain terms must be introduced here if you are to read research reports—even their conclusions—with adequate understanding. You can learn the meanings of these terms more easily when they are presented in relation to types of research findings. These types of findings generally consist of one or more of the following:

1. The *status* of one or more groups—say, a school, a community, a peer group, the eleventh grade in Elmwood High School. This status describes people, places, events, objects, and the like, as they now exist or once did.

2. *Comparisons* between two or more groups. Again, this might involve schools, communities, grade levels, gender, ethnic groups, and so forth. These comparisons are done to determine the existence and nature of differences that might exist between or among groups—differences such as preferences, lifestyles, achievement, rates of learning, or access to resources. These differences may exist inherently in the groups or may have been produced by introducing a variable that caused one group to become different from the other.

3. *Covarying relationships* between two or more sets of measurements (such as between scores of language ability on the one hand and reading ability on the other) obtained from the same group of individuals. Such relationships, when confirmed, enable you to predict one of the variables from the other, and the relationships may *imply*—although they do not convincingly demonstrate—the existence of cause and effect between the variables.

Applying Technology: **Writing a Review of Literature**

Writing a review of literature is an integral part of any formal proposal or design of a research study. A literature review involves the "systematic identification, location, and analysis of documents containing information related to the research problem" (Gay & Airasian, 2000). Once you have obtained documents related to your topic, you must analyze them for several reasons:

- To determine what has already been done
- To learn about specific research strategies, procedures, and instruments that have been shown to be effective in researching your topic
- To form the basis for interpreting your results (Gay & Airasian, 2000)

However, you must avoid the temptation to include everything you have found in your search for published literature. Additionally, a literature review is *not* simply a compilation of summaries of articles, one after another. On the contrary, a literature review is an opportunity for you to demonstrate your ability to "recognize relevant information…and to synthesize and evaluate it" according to the overall purpose and goals of your study (Taylor, 1998).

Writing the literature review is quite honestly not an easy task. There is no "recipe" for developing the actual written review. It will likely take several iterations of written drafts, perhaps organizing and reorganizing the analysis of your related literature. Although there exists no formula for this important research activity, several websites offer many suggestions that can be especially helpful. We review a sampling of those sites here:

- Writing a Literature Review in the Health Sciences and Social Work (www.utoronto.ca/hswriting/lit-review.htm)—this site poses several sets of questions to help you look critically at your literature review; the questions focus on your review as a whole and on your assessment of each book or article you have included.

In addition to this site, Purdue University has developed an Online Writing Lab (http://owl.english.purdue.edu), which includes links to several helpful pages, many of which incorporate activities for understanding and reinforcement:

- Paraphrase: Write It in Your Own Words (http://owl.english.purdue.edu/handouts/research/r_paraphr.html)—This site explains what paraphrasing is, why it is an important skill in technical writing, and includes an example containing an original passage, a legitimate paraphrase, and a plagiarized version; also provides six steps to effective paraphrasing.
- Quoting, Paraphrasing, and Summarizing (http://owl.english.purdue.edu/handouts/research/r_quotprsum.html)—Building on the previous site, this one offers explanations of the differences between quoting, paraphrasing, and summarizing published work. A brief sample essay is included, along with guiding instructions, for writing a summary of the piece—a good activity.
- Avoiding Plagiarism (http://owl.english.purdue.edu/handouts/research/r_plagiar.html)—This site defines *plagiarism* (the unacknowledged use of someone else's work or ideas) and provides examples of actions that might be considered plagiarism, as well as some not

considered to be such. The site is further composed of specific examples document-ing when credit should be given to an author. Included is an activity that provides sample situations in which the reader must decide the degree to which there exists a risk of plagiarism.

Also affiliated with the development of a written review of literature is the associated list of references, which must follow a prescribed format. In education, the preferred guide-lines are provided by the *Publication Manual of the American Psychological Association* (5th ed.), commonly referred to as the "APA Manual." Since the citation of electronic sources of information continues to be an evolving entity, and since citation format may change as technologies change, the American Psychological Association has provided this information on its website titled *Electronic References* (www.apastyle.org/elecref.html). In-cluded on this site are the recommended citation formats for:

- E-mail communications
- Web sites
- Specific documents on a web site
- Articles and abstracts from electronic databases
- Web citations within the text of your document

The APA has also included specific examples of reference citations on this Web page.

Finally, as mentioned in the text, it is important to maintain accurate records of all of the sources that you have referenced in your literature review. This can be a time-consuming and tedious task, but for obvious reasons it is a crucial part of the research process. How-ever, several types of bibliographic software now exist that can simplify the portion of the research task by allowing you to create bibliographies within your research paper or create stand-alone bibliographies (Gay & Airasian, 2000). One such program is *EndNote*. End-Note comes complete with over 300 predefined reference citation styles and works with your word processing program to enter citations from your EndNote database directly into your document. Additionally, EndNote can store Web pages containing full-text articles, and so on, and can automatically start your Web browser, taking you directly to that page. It essentially becomes the "card catalog of the electronic library" (Gay & Airasian, 2000). It will take some time and effort to learn how to use bibliographic software effectively, but it can certainly simplify the research process by making this aspect a less careless procedure.

Let us examine some of the terms you can expect to encounter in reports that present these three different types of findings.

Status Reports

Status reports describe things as they are or once were. Often status studies are qualitative in nature and do not make use of statistical procedures; the findings in qualitative research are ascertained through verbal logic and are presented as verbal statements. Such is often the case for ethnographic and historical research. But other status studies are quantitative in nature and involve numbers and testing. In those reports, you are likely to encounter the use of the following types of descriptive statistics and terms.

Raw Numbers or Raw Scores. Raw numbers or **raw scores** are numerals that indicate individuals counted (e.g., 35 adolescents) or scores made on tests before they are converted in any way (e.g., 78). You can expect to see entries such as these:

- Elmwood High School was opened in 1874, with *32* students attending grades 8 through 12. Today it serves *2,750* students, grades 9 through 12.
- Samuel's raw score on the math section of the Stanford Achievement Test was *43*. Raw scores of other students in Samuel's class ranged from a high of *45* to a low of *6*.

Terms That Indicate Typicality or Central Tendency. Three terms are commonly used to depict what is average or typical for a group of raw numbers or scores:

mean

1. **Mean,** symbolized M or $\overline{X}$. The mean is the arithmetic average of a group of raw scores or other measurements that are expressed numerically. Commonly thought of as synonymous with the term *average,* the mean is calculated by adding the raw scores together and then dividing the sum by the number of scores.

median

2. **Median,** symbolized *Mdn* or *Md*. The median is the point halfway between the highest and lowest scores of a particular array (group of scores). In other words, it is the value that separates the bottom 50 percent of scores from the upper 50 percent of scores. The median is determined by arranging the scores in order from lowest to highest, then counting halfway through the number of scores. For example, the median for the following array of scores would be 4:

   1, 2, 2, 3, 4, 6, 12, 13, 13

   If there is an even number of scores in the array, the median is the arithmetic average of the two middle scores. The median in the following array would be 7.5 (the average of 7 and 8):

   4, 5, 5, 7, 8, 9, 10, 10

   The median is less affected than is the mean by unusually high or low scores (also known as *extreme* scores) and for that reason is frequently used to report information such as average personal income or price of housing. Its usefulness in educational research is limited.

3. **Mode,** symbolized *Mo,* is simply the most frequently occurring score. The mode has no other use in statistics.

Terms That Indicate Spread or Diversity. Researchers are interested not only in what is average for a group but also in the dispersion of values within that group—that is, how spread out the scores or measurements are. Dispersion is often expressed in the following terms:

1. **Range,** which is the group spread from the highest through the lowest score or measurement. It is calculated by subtracting the lowest score from the highest score. For example, the range of an array of scores, in which the highest score is 45 and the lowest 15, would be 30: $45 - 15 = 30$. The concept of range has no further application in research statistics.

2. **Standard deviation,** symbolized *SD* or *s*. Standard deviation indicates the divergence of scores away from the mean of the group. Standard deviation is a concept not encountered in ordinary experience and is, therefore, difficult to describe empirically. It is analogous to the concept of an *average* deviation, which indicates how much each score, on average, differs from the mean. But average deviation is not a stable measure, statistically speaking; therefore, standard deviation, a stable and widely applicable measure, is used instead. Mathematically, standard deviation is closely associated with the normal curve. If a group of scores or measurements is normally distributed, 68.26 percent of them fall between plus one standard deviation and minus one standard deviation from the mean. The area beneath the normal curve between 11.96 and 21.96 standard deviations includes 95 percent of all scores, and the area between 12.58 and 22.58 standard deviations includes 99 percent of all scores (see Figure A.3 in Appendix A). These relationships are illustrated and further explained in Chapter 8 and Appendix A.

Converted, or Transformed, Numbers and Scores.   Raw scores are frequently converted or transformed into comparable scores to make them more understandable and more easily compared. For example, educators frequently work with **norms,** charts that show what is typical for certain ages, groups, or grade levels. It is important to remember, however, that once raw scores have been converted, they cannot be treated as if they were still raw scores. For example, converted scores cannot be averaged in an effort to obtain a composite (i.e., overall) converted score. Converted scores you are likely to encounter in research reports include the following:

1. **Grade equivalents** are shown in **grade norms** that accompany standardized achievement tests. They indicate the average scores made on a particular standardized test by students at different grade levels in various localities. The grade levels are further divided into months; they might, for example, show the mean score for students at seventh grade, sixth month; fourth grade, third month; and so on. Let us assume that Manuel, a second grader, has a raw score on a standardized reading test equal to 22, which, when compared to the norms accompanying the test, is seen to have a grade level equivalency of 3.3 (third grade, third month). A research report that contains this information might say that Manuel's reading level was 3.3. This does not imply that Manuel should be moved to the third grade, however. It simply indicates that Manuel's current level of reading ability is above the norm, or average, for second-grade students.

2. **Age equivalents** tell us the average performance of students at particular age levels. **Age norms** that show age equivalents accompany standardized intelligence tests. If Ricardo makes a raw score of 74 on his IQ test, one could look in the norms and find, perhaps, that 74 is the score made by the average person when 12 years, 6 months of age. It could then be said that Ricardo has a mental age of 12 years, 6 months, which may or may not be the same as his chronological (calendar) age.

3. **Percentile ranks** (symbolized *%ile* or *PR*) are converted scores that indicate one's **relative standing** in comparison to others who have taken the same test or have been included in the same measurement. Percentiles have nothing to do with percent correct but instead indicate relative position. Suppose you were informed that your raw score on a graduate aptitude test was 89. That would tell you virtually nothing. But if you were also informed that your score placed you at the 73rd percentile, you would understand that you did as well as or better than 73 percent of all people who had taken the test.

4. **Stanines** are conversions not into individual scores but into wider bands of scores. The word *stanine* comes from *standard nine,* in which the range of possible scores is divided into nine bands. The first stanine is the lowest, the ninth stanine is the highest, and the fifth stanine normally includes the mean of all scores made. Many raw scores fall into the fourth, fifth, and sixth stanines but few into the first or ninth.

Review of Terminology Used in Status Reports

Raw scores—scores made or numbers involved

Mean (M or $\overline{X}$)—the arithmetic average

Median (Mdn or Md)—the midpoint between highest and lowest in an array of scores

Mode (Mo)—the most frequently occurring score or measure in an array

Standard deviation (SD or s)—indicator of the dispersion from the mean for a set of scores

Grade equivalents—the average scores made by students at particular grade levels

Age equivalents—the average scores made by students of particular age levels

Percentile rank (%ile or PR)—indicator of a given score's standing, relative to others made on the same test or measurement

Stanines—nine bands, showing relative position within which all scores are distributed

The reader is reminded that specific information concerning the calculations of measures of central tendency and diversity—accompanied by sample exercises—has been included in Appendix A.

Comparison Reports

We have considered some of the statistical and other special terms often employed in research that describe the status of individuals or groups. Now let us consider **comparison**

reports, which typically involve the application of inferential statistics and which you are likely to encounter in evaluation, causal-comparative, and experimental research. Suppose a researcher compared the levels of self-esteem among various groups of students attending Elmwood Lincoln High School or the levels of reading progress of groups in Elmwood elementary schools. Reports of those studies would be likely to include one or more of the following:

Research
Navigator.c⊕m
chi-square

Chi-square (χ^2). You will usually see this term spelled out as a word in the report, then symbolized afterward. **Chi-square** is a statistical procedure that allows one to determine, when measurements are expressed as categories in the form of frequency counts, whether a difference exists (1) between two groups, (2) between before-and-after measurements of the same group, or (3) what is expected for a group compared to what is actually observed for the group. Suppose Mr. Michael wants to improve his students' regard for algebra II. To determine their present attitude he asks them to respond anonymously by checking one of the following:

_____ I like algebra II.

_____ I don't like algebra II very much, but I don't dislike it either. I'm neutral.

_____ I don't like algebra II.

Mr. Michael tallies responses from his four sections of students and finds that:

- 5 like the class (that number is placed in the "like" category)
- 27 are neutral (that number is placed in the "neutral" category)
- 71 dislike the class (that number is placed in the "dislike" category)

He then organizes and presents his classes in a different way which he believes will cause his students to like the class better. Two months later he asks them to respond as before. This time he finds that:

- 27 like the class
- 42 are neutral
- 34 dislike the class

It seems to Mr. Michael that student regard for the class has improved considerably, but he is uncertain whether the change indicates a real improvement or simply a chance difference in the way students responded. Chi-square is a procedure that enables Mr. Michael to *statistically* answer his question. Chi-square compares what one expects to see against what one actually observes. In Mr. Michael's case, a null hypothesis would assume that after the new approach to teaching had been used, one would still expect to find that 5 students like algebra II, 27 were neutral, and 71 disliked it. But the actual observation is now that 27 like the class, 42 are neutral, and 34 dislike it. The frequencies (or counts) of responses for students' opinions before the instructional change (*expected*) and after (*observed*) follow:

	Observed	Expected
Like	27	5
Neutral	42	27
Dislike	34	71

It is from a table like this that chi-square is computed in order to determine whether the difference between the observed frequencies and expected frequencies is, or is not, attributable to chance errors made in selecting the participants. The procedure by which this is done, along with a complete example, is provided in Appendix A.

Research Navigator.c⊛m
t-test

Difference between Means (using the t test). You saw that if responses are made by categories, as in Mr. Michael's case, chi-square can be used to determine differences between groups. If, however, responses are obtained as scores or other numerical measurements, the difference between groups can be assessed in terms of group mean scores, through an analysis technique called **difference between means.**

Suppose that Miss Jones, a colleague of Mr. Michael, also teaches algebra II in Elmwood High School. She has followed with interest Mr. Michael's efforts to improve student liking for his class, but while she admits he might have caused students to like his course better, she doubts his students are learning any more than hers. If fact, she bets Mr. Michael that her traditional way of teaching the class will produce higher student achievement than does Mr. Michael's new approach.

At the end of the grading period, the two teachers give the same final test to their students. They exchange classes, each administering the test to the other's students, and they arrange for impartial scoring. They find that Mr. Michael's students make a mean score of 88 on the exam, while Miss Jones's students make a mean score of 90. She gloats, but Mr. Michael contends that the difference between the groups' scores is not significant, that it is due only to chance or sampling error. Which teacher is right?

The *t* **test** enables us to answer that question. This procedure (called an *independent-samples t test*) analyzes the difference between the means of the two groups, to determine whether the difference is significant—that is, whether the difference of two points can, or cannot, be attributed to chance errors made in selecting the participants. The procedure for computing *t* tests is presented in Appendix A. A variation of this design (called a *repeated-measures,* or *dependent-measures, t test*) allows us to analyze the difference between the means of pre- and postmeasures taken on the same group of individuals, again looking for a significant difference.

Research Navigator.c⊛m
analysis of variance

Analysis of Variance (ANOVA). **Analysis of variance** is used to test for differences between two groups when the sample sizes are relatively large and unequal, provided the discrepancy between sample sizes is not extreme (Gravetter & Wallnau, 2002), and to compare three or more groups of any size.

Suppose Mr. Michael's efforts to increase students' regard for algebra II stirred up interest in other Elmwood high schools. While many teachers preferred continuing with their customary teaching approaches, several began changing, some using individualized self-paced teaching, others large-group instruction followed by small-group tutorials, and still others using algebra to solve real-life problems. They decided to ask that the results of their efforts be analyzed statistically. All used the same final examination. They found that the mean score for traditionally taught students was 91; for those taught individually the mean was 89; those using small-group tutorials made a mean score of 92; and students using real-life situations made a mean score of 85.

Differences in test performance seem evident, but even assuming that no intervening variables unduly affected the results, the question remains: Do the mean scores reflect *real* achievement differences—possibly the result of methods of instruction—or are the observed differences simply attributable to chance? ANOVA, considered further in Appendix A, is used to answer that question. Variations of ANOVA include designs with more than one independent variable (*factorial ANOVA*) and designs with more than one dependent variable (*multivariate ANOVA,* or *MANOVA*). If, while reviewing published research, you encounter any of these variations and believe that they are beyond your understanding, do not panic. You should simply remember that they all have the same underlying purpose—to compare groups.

Review of Terminology Used in Comparison Reports

Chi-square (χ^2)—a procedure for determining the significance of differences when data are categorical in nature

Difference between means—assessment that uses the *t* test, a procedure for determining the significance of a difference between means obtained from two different groups of participants or from the same group measured twice

Analysis of variance (ANOVA)—a procedure for determining the significance of differences among means obtained from two or more groups of participants; also used to explore interactions among several variables

Research
Navigator.c⊕m
correlations

Correlational Reports

Researchers are always interested in discovering **correlations,** which are relationships between individuals' performances on two or more measures, such as between intelligence test scores and reading test scores. Such correlation between variables, where individuals' performances on one of the variables tends to accompany similar (or inverse) performances on the other, permit greater understanding of observed phenomena. They also permit us to predict either variable from knowledge of the other. Such predictions cannot be made with absolute accuracy because correlations are almost never perfect, but the predictions can be useful nonetheless. Examples of useful but far-less-than-perfect predictions are forecasting weather from humidity, temperature, and air pressure, and predicting overall cardiovascular health from the amount of cigarette smoke inhaled over time.

In education, it is known that intelligence and reading ability are correlated, which enables us to predict one from the other. If we know that Juan, in fourth grade, is an outstanding reader, we can predict with fairly good accuracy that he has above-average intelligence. Or, if we give Juan an IQ test and find that he scores above the average, we can predict with fairly good accuracy that he is, or can become, a good reader.

Correlations do not, by themselves, *demonstrate* cause and effect. High intelligence cannot be said to cause one to be a good reader, nor does learning to read well cause one's intelligence to increase. True *cause–effect relationships* are shown when one (independent) variable is manipulated such that a second (dependent) variable then changes as a result of that manipulation. In correlational studies, variables are not manipulated. However, correlations often *suggest* cause–effect relationships, which are then sometimes verified through experimental research.

Correlational reports that you encounter in the literature will prominently feature a term called **coefficient of correlation.** The coefficient is shown as a decimal number that indicates the degree of relationship between the two or more variables being investigated. The coefficient of correlation, symbolized by the italicized letter *r,* ranges from a possible value of –1.00 to +1.00. Both –1.00 and +1.00 indicate extremely high (actually, perfect) correlations. A coefficient of 0 indicates no correlation—the absence of a relationship.

The coefficient of correlation may be positive or negative. If it is a **negative correlation,** a minus sign is used (e.g., –.48); if it is a **positive correlation,** no sign is used (e.g., .48). Positive and negative correlations are of equal magnitude; that is, positive .48 (.48) is not larger or stronger than negative .48 (–.48). Positive and negative simply show the *direction* of the relationship. In a positive relationship, high scores on one variable tend to accompany high scores on the second variable, while low scores accompany low scores. In a negative relationship, high scores on one variable tend to accompany low scores on the other variable. For example, quality of diet is *positively* correlated with overall health—the better the diet, the better the health. Quality of diet is *negatively* correlated with incidence of disease—the better the diet, the less frequent or serious the incidence of disease. Generally speaking, correlations, whether positive or negative, are considered high if the absolute values are equal to .70 or above, medium if between .40 and .60, and low if below .30.

Review of Terminology Used in Correlational Reports

Correlation—a relationship that exists between two or more variables, such that individuals' standings on one of the variables tend to be accompanied by similar, or inverse, standings on the other variable(s)

Positive correlation—high standing on one variable tends to accompany high standing on the other variable(s), average standing tends to accompany average, low tends to accompany low

Negative correlation—high standing on one variable tends to accompany low standing on the other variable(s), average tends to accompany average, and low tends to accompany high

Coefficient of correlation (r)—a decimal number that indicates the degree of relationship in a correlation; virtually always a decimal value, the coefficient can vary from 0, which indicates an absence of relationship, to 1.0 or –1.0, both of which in-dicate perfect relationships but are almost never encountered in research; the positive and negative values have nothing to do with strength or closeness of relationship—they only show the direction of the correlation; generally speaking, correlations, whether positive or negative, are considered high if they are ±.70 or more extreme, medium if between .40 and .60 (or between –.40 and –.60), and low if between .30 and 0 (or between –.30 and 0).

Exercise 5.2

Indicate, for each of the following findings, whether the research expresses (S) status, (C) com-parison, or (R) relationship.

_____ 1. The valedictorian at Elmwood Lincoln High School has been a female 37 times.

_____ 2. Girls score better in reading than do boys at Cutter Elementary School.

_____ 3. Student grades can be predicted, though not perfectly, from family income.

_____ 4. The inquiry approach produced higher achievement than did memorization.

The Concept of Significance

The terms *significant* and *significance* appear in a majority of research reports. Two sepa-rate meanings are associated with these terms. The first has to do with whether or not the topic being investigated is worth the time and effort involved. We read that the topic was significant, or that the research made a significant contribution.

The second meaning is associated with statistical treatment of data. Quite different from the first, this meaning has nothing to do with importance. To say a finding is "statis-tically significant" is to say it is very likely the finding exists in the population as well as in the sample—that it has not appeared just because of errors made in selecting a representa-tive sample.

Research
Navigator.c⊕m
statistical
significance

It is this second meaning—**statistical significance**—to which we give attention here. For a finding to be deemed significant, it must meet stringent levels of probability, usually either the .05 level or the .01 level. The .05 level of significance means there is only a 5 percent chance, on average, that a finding of a particular magnitude occurred because of errors made in selecting the sample. The .01 level means there is only a 1 percent chance that the finding is due to sampling error.

Thus, significance tests help us determine whether a finding made in a sample also exists in the population. Suppose a difference or a correlation is found in the sample. We are now left with the questions: Does the finding for the sample also exist in the popula-tion? Or has the finding appeared because a sample was erroneously selected that does *not* mirror the population? Or has something occurred to bring about differences between sam-ples that were once equal, something that would affect the population as well?

If the significance test strongly suggests that the finding cannot be attributed to error made in selecting the sample, the finding is called *significant.* However, if there is even a slight chance (usually just over 5 percent) that the finding is due to sampling error, the finding is deemed *not significant.*

Let us suppose that in a study we have found an apparent relationship between bibliotherapy and student attitude toward school. Our **null hypothesis** was that "No difference exists in attitude toward school between students who have participated in bibliotherapy and students who have not participated." We know that the sample might, or might not, accurately reflect the population. To determine whether it does, we test the null hypothesis statistically. Gall, Borg, and Gall (1996) point out that, before administering the test of significance, we should have decided on the level of probability we will accept. This is called the **alpha (α) level** when stated in advance. We might have selected the .05 level (odds of 19 to 1 against the results being due to sampling error, shown as $p < .05$) or the .01 level (odds of 99 to 1 against the result being due to sampling error, shown as $p < .01$). If we selected an alpha level of .05 and our test showed a probability level less than that, we **reject the null hypothesis** and call the finding significant. In so doing, we move ahead to assume that the finding in our sample is probably real—that it reflects the population and is not due to errors we made in selecting the sample (Bartz, 1976). Following that conclusion, logic allows us to conclude that improved student attitude was brought about by bibliotherapy.

The .05 and .01 **probability levels** of significance are traditional in research, but there is nothing magic about them. They are very low levels of probability of sample error, and until recently were the two levels commonly shown on probability charts used by researchers. Nowadays, statistics packages for computers can show all probability levels. In any case, researchers want to be very sure that they do not **retain a hypothesis** when in fact it is not true. Therefore, they set the probability level so it is very unlikely they will make such an error. But even the very strict odds of .05 and .01 (or .001 often seen reported) leave room for some doubt about any finding. That is why researchers never report any finding with absolute confidence.

Shaver (1992) presents a concise summary of what significance testing does and does not do. He says that significance testing *does* provide a statement of probability of occurrence in the long run. He cautions however, that significance testing

- *Does not* indicate the probability of a given finding's having occurred by chance. (The concept of chance applies to numerous future repetitions of a study, not to one particular instance of the study.)
- *Does not* indicate that the null hypothesis is true or false. (It only suggests levels of probability.)
- *Does not* indicate whether a treatment being studied had an effect. (It only helps rule out the possibility of procedural error.)
- *Does not* indicate the magnitude of a result. (The result can be very small and still significant, or very large and not significant, depending on the number of participants involved—*the more participants, the greater the likelihood of significance.)*
- *Does not* indicate the importance of a result. (As noted previously, statistical significance has nothing to do with importance.)

In light of these facts, Shaver recommends that researchers minimize their reliance on tests of significance and place emphasis instead on the size of differences or correlations they find.

Exercise 5.3

Explain what the italicized phrases mean.

1. Jones found that girls scored higher than boys on 18 of 30 tasks but that the difference between the groups was *not significant.*
2. Adolescent boys from the Midwest were an average of one-quarter inch taller than boys from other parts of the country. The difference was *highly significant.*
3. A *correlation of* −.83 was found between the two variables.
4. The correlation was significant at the .05 *level of significance.*
5. The null hypothesis was *rejected.*

D E V E L O P M E N T A L   A C T I V I T Y

Reviewing Published Research

In Chapter 4, you began searching for and reading published research related to your chosen research topic. As you read published research, it is imperative that you *analyze* what you are reading for several reasons—for example, you need to become a critical consumer of research, it is important to see what research has and has not been conducted on your topic, and because published research will help guide decisions that you will make for your particular study. This activity will help you get started in this process. For the article that you review, respond to questions 1 through 10. You should be able to respond to each item, although this may sometimes require you to make inferences. After reviewing several research studies, respond to question 11.

1. What was the purpose of the study?_____

_____.

2. What was (were) the research question(s)? _____

_____.

3. The following is a *brief* summarization of the literature review:_____

_____.

_____.

4. What was (were) the hypothesis(es)?_____

_____.

5. Based on the types of research previously discussed, this study would be classified as:

_____.

  6. What type of sampling was used? _____

      _____ .

  7. How were the data collected?_____

      _____ .

  8. How were the validity and reliability of the data assessed?_____

      _____ .

  9. What descriptive and/or inferential analyses were used?_____

      _____ .

10. The following is a *brief* summarization of the conclusions and recommendations: __

      _____ .

      _____ .

      _____ .

11. Now that you have reviewed several studies related to your topic, draft a *preliminary* outline for the review of related literature that you will eventually write for your study, highlighting the major sections, or subheadings, of your literature review.

        I. _____

       II. _____

      III. _____

      IV. _____

       V. _____

(A downloadable, interactive version of this developmental activity is available from the Companion Website, www.ablongman.com/mertler5e)

Chapter Summary

When reading research reports, scan them quickly to determine (1) the topic, purpose, and importance of the report, (2) the type of report you are reading—either status, difference between groups, or correlational—and (3) the report's findings and conclusions. When taking notes on material as you read, be sure to include subject, date, author, summary, and complete bibliographical citation.

Your ability to interpret research reports will increase as you familiarize yourself with some of the statistical terms and concepts you are likely to encounter. In status reports of a qualitative nature, you will find verbal descriptions of findings and conclusions, with little if any use of statistics. Few specialized terms will be encountered there. In status reports of a quantitative nature, you are likely to see mention of raw scores, mean, median, mode, standard deviation, grade equivalents, age equivalents, percentiles, and stanines. In reports that focus on differences between or among groups, you are likely to see mention of chi-square, difference between means, and analysis of variance. In correlational reports you are likely to see mention of correlation, coefficient of correlation, positive correlation, and negative correlation.

In reports of correlations and group differences, you are almost certain to see mention of the term *significance,* which in statistics refers not to importance but to whether the researcher's hypothesis can be retained or rejected at a given probability level, such as .05 or .01.

L I S T   O F   I M P O R T A N T   T E R M S

age equivalents	grade norms	range
age norms	mean	raw score
alpha (α) level	median	reject the null hypothesis
analysis of variance (ANOVA)	mode	relative standing
chi-square	negative correlation	retain the null hypothesis
coefficient of correlation	norms	standard deviation
comparison report	null hypothesis	stanines
correlation	$p < .01; p < .05$	statistical significance
correlational report	percentile rank	status report
difference between means	positive correlation	t test
grade equivalents	probability levels	

Y O U R   C U R R E N T   S T A T U S

Having earlier learned to locate published research, you are now familiar with procedures, concepts, and terms that help you read, interpret, and summarize quantities of research. That gives you the background necessary to begin planning a research project of your own. But before continuing to that phase of your development, please strengthen your ability by responding to the activities presented here for thought and discussion.

A C T I V I T I E S   F O R   T H O U G H T   A N D   D I S C U S S I O N

1. Outline the strategy suggested for rapidly assessing the large number of reports you are likely to encounter when reviewing literature on a given topic.

2. List the information you were advised to enter on note cards and where the information should be placed.

3. Why is the concept of significance so often employed in research that explores correlations and differences between groups? If you encountered the following statement: "The coefficient of correlation was significant at the .01 level," what would it mean to you?

4. Explain why knowledge of statistical terms and concepts enables you to interpret research reports more accurately.

5. Recall the information organizer presented at the beginning of the chapter. See if by referring to it you can summarize the chapter contents.

6. Here again are the questions presented at the beginning of the chapter. See how well you can answer them.
   a. Why should research reports be skimmed rapidly before they are read carefully?
   b. What specifically does one look for when skimming reports?

c. What entries should one make on note cards when annotating published reports?

d. What are the three general types of research reports encountered in published literature?

e. What characterizes the three different types of research reports?

f. What common analysis terminology—verbal and/or statistical—is usually associated with each of the three types of reports?

g. Why do the different types of research reports utilize different verbal and statistical procedures to analyze their data?

h. What two different meanings does the term *significance* have in the context of research?

i. Why is the term *significant* often misleading to uninformed readers of research?

ANSWERS TO CHAPTER EXERCISES

5.1. Discuss responses in class, in light of the style manual used at your institution.

5.2. 1. S 2. C 3. R 4. C

5.3.

1. The odds are unacceptably high that the finding does not exist in the population but has appeared because of errors made in selecting the sample.

2. The finding is probably true for the population.

3. A high inverse relationship exists between the two variables.

4. If the study were repeated thousands of times, similar findings would occur at least 95 percent of the time.

5. The finding is probably "real" and not the result of sampling error.

REFERENCES AND RECOMMENDED READINGS

Bartz, A. (1976). *Basic Statistical Concepts in Education and the Behavioral Sciences.* Minneapolis: Burgess.

Edyburn, D. L. (1999). *The Electronic Scholar: Enhancing Research Productivity with Technology.* Upper Saddle River, NJ: Merrill.

Gall, M., Borg, W., & Gall, J. (2003). *Educational Research: An Introduction* (7th ed.). Boston: Allyn and Bacon.

Gay, L. & Airasian, P. (2000). *Educational Research: Competencies for Analysis and Application* (6th ed.). Upper Saddle River, NJ: Merrill.

Gravetter, F. J., & Wallnau, L. B. (2002). *Essentials of Statistics for the Behavioral Sciences* (4th ed.). Pacific Grove, CA: Wadsworth.

Kutz, E. (1992). Teacher research: Myths and realities. *Language Arts, 69,* 193–197.

Lyne, L. S. (ed.). (1999). *A Cross-Section of Educational Research: Journal Articles for Discussion and Evaluation.* Los Angeles: Pyrczak.

Pajares, M. (1992). Teachers' beliefs and educational research: Cleaning up a messy construct. *Review of Educational Research, 62,* 307–332.

Patten, M. L. (ed.). (1991). *Educational and Psychological Research: A Cross-Section of Journal Articles for Analysis and Evaluation.* Los Angeles: Pyrczak.

Publication Manual of the American Psychological Association (5th ed.). (2001). Washington, DC: American Psychological Association.

Shaver, J. (1992, April). What statistical significance testing is, and what it is not. Paper presented at the annual meeting of the American Educational Research Association, San Francisco.

Taylor, D. (1998). *Writing a Literature Review in the Health Sciences and Social Work.* Available at www.utotonto.ca/hswriting/lit-review.htm

Vierra, A., & Pollock, J. (1988). *Reading Educational Research.* Scottsdale, AZ: Gorsuch Scarisbrick.

Zeuli, J. (1992, April). How do teachers understand research when they read it? Paper presented at the annual meeting of the American Educational Research Association, San Francisco.

6 Designing a Research Project

This chapter examines seven tasks to which you must give attention when planning your own research project:

- State topic, problem, and questions and/or hypotheses
- Outline the library search for related information
- Identify needed data and their probable sources
- List steps to be carried out in the study
- Specify procedures and tools for collecting data
- Foresee how data can best be analyzed and interpreted
- Anticipate the appropriate report format for your research

Targeted Learnings

This chapter is designed to help you plan a research project of your own. As you complete the chapter exercises, you will simultaneously be preparing a preliminary plan for researching a topic of your choice. Furthermore, you will see how investigations are planned in any of the standard types of educational research. As you proceed through the chapter, make sure to look for information related to the following concerns:

1. Stating a topic and problem, with appurtenant questions and/or hypotheses
2. Identifying the type of research called for in your topic
3. Learning more about the type of research you have selected
4. Organizing a library search for information related to your topic
5. Foreseeing needed data and their potential sources
6. Making a list of steps to be taken in conducting the study
7. Noting the procedures and tools you will require for collecting data
8. Anticipating the kinds of analyses your data will need
9. Drawing up conclusions from your data analysis
10. Selecting the appropriate format for reporting your research

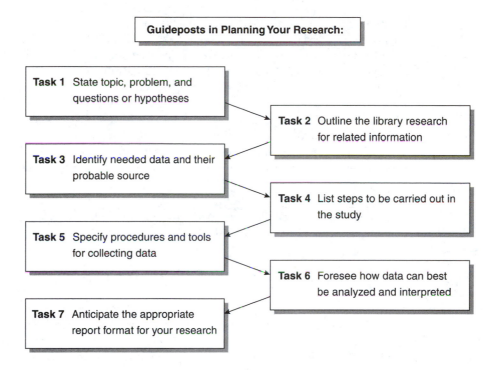

Guideposts in Planning Your Research:

Task 1 State topic, problem, and questions or hypotheses

Task 2 Outline the library research for related information

Task 3 Identify needed data and their probable source

Task 4 List steps to be carried out in the study

Task 5 Specify procedures and tools for collecting data

Task 6 Foresee how data can best be analyzed and interpreted

Task 7 Anticipate the appropriate report format for your research

How Planning Should Be Done

Authorities offer various suggestions as to how research should be planned. Gay and Airasian (2000), for example, say that a research plan should give attention to these elements:

1. Introduction, including statement of the problem, review of the literature, and statement of the hypothesis
2. Method, specifying participants, instruments, materials/apparatus, design of the study, and procedure
3. Data analysis
4. Time schedule
5. Budget

Wiersma (2000) emphasizes that planning should be done in accordance with whether the research is qualitative or quantitative. For *qualitative research*, he suggests the following:

1. A working design that specifies participants and possible variables
2. A working hypothesis
3. Procedures of data collection such as interview, observation, and document perusal
4. Procedures of data analysis and interpretation, including data reduction, data organization, and description

For *quantitative research*, Wiersma maintains that "explaining or controlling variance is an important part of quantitative research" (2000, p. 83). He suggests, therefore, that when planning quantitative research, one should describe not only the participants, hypotheses, and plans for collecting and interpreting data but also the procedures by which variance will be controlled, such as through the following:

1. Randomization, which tends to spread a variable evenly across groups being studied
2. Holding factors (e.g., ethnicity of participants) constant, thus reducing the effect that an irrelevant factor might have on the dependent variable
3. Making adjustments statistically, to remove the effects of an intervening variable such as intelligence

Wiersma (2000, p. 84) clarifies these points using an example of a study on the effects of different teaching methods on learning high school chemistry, from which Table 6.1 is adapted.

The Approach to Planning Advocated in This Book

The planning advice we have just seen is excellent, but experience shows that those new to research appreciate as much guidance as they can get. For that reason, an abundance of instructions and exercises is provided in this chapter to increase your ability to plan an investigation of your own. In addition to the material presented in this chapter, you will be asked to read at least one of the other chapters presented later—one that goes into detail about the type of research you wish to plan.

We will now proceed to the tasks you must accomplish when planning your own research. You will be guided through those tasks in order. Instructions are presented for planning each task, and exercises are provided to strengthen your understanding. Through completion of all the exercises, you will have simultaneously prepared a plan you can follow in researching the topic you have selected.

Tasks to Be Accomplished When Planning Research

Seven major tasks must be completed as you design a workable plan of research. These elements comprise your **research design.**

TABLE 6.1

Variable	Control of Variable
Student science background	Random assignments of students to groups
Teacher	An independent variable. Each teacher uses different methods.
School	A constant; students of only one school are included.
Ability level	Statistically controlled, by partialling out effects of intelligence

1. State the topic, problem, and questions and/or hypotheses.
2. Outline the library search for related information.
3. Identify data you will need and their probable sources.
4. List the steps you will need to carry out in order to complete the study.
5. Specify the procedures and tools you will employ in collecting data.
6. Foresee how data can best be analyzed and interpreted.
7. Anticipate the report format most appropriate for your research.

We will now proceed through these tasks and their related exercises.

Task 1. State the Topic, Problem, and Questions and/or Hypotheses

To begin your research plan, specify the topic, the problem, and the research questions and/or hypotheses. For the topic, you should

1. Select an educational matter that is of personal interest or concern to you.
2. Determine whether the topic is researchable, considering ethics, complexity, and time.
3. Compose a tentative working title for your research.

Exercise 6.1

Identify and jot down a topic (e.g., "student self-concept and reading achievement" or "home laboratories for biology students") that you have a genuine interest in exploring. Compose a tentative working title that describes the topic.

Example:

   Topic: student self-concept and reading achievement

   Working Title: The relationship between self-concept and reading achievement among fifth-grade students

   Your Topic:

   Working Title:

Now move to Exercise 6.2 and decide whether the topic can be researched from a practical standpoint, taking into account ethical considerations, amenability to scientific method, difficulty, time, and cost. If you believe it can be successfully researched, then proceed. If you find it questionable, go back and revise your initial research topic or select a different one.

For stating the problem you should

1. State the purpose of your intended research.
2. Explain why the topic is of sufficient importance to merit investigative attention.

Exercise 6.2

Appraise your topic to determine whether it can be researched by a graduate student in education, considering

- Ethics—Can the project be done ethically, or does it have questionable aspects?
- Scientific method—Can the topic be investigated scientifically?
- Difficulty—Does the project seem too easy, too difficult, or about right?
- Time—Does it seem that the project can be investigated in the time you have available?
- Cost—Is the investigation likely to entail undue expense?

Research Navigator.com

limitations

3. Specify the *limitations* (existing constraints) and *delimitations* (limits you will impose) under which your investigation will be conducted, together with the assumptions you are making, but cannot prove.
4. Define the terms central to your investigation, especially those that have unusual meanings.

Having selected your topic and given it a working title, you next describe the purpose of the study clearly and briefly. Simply state what you want to investigate, discover, or accomplish. This brief description is called the *statement of the problem*. In case you do not remember how to compose a statement of the problem, here are three examples to use as models:

- The purpose of this study is to determine whether age of entry into kindergarten has an effect on students' subsequent school learning and behavior.
- The purpose of this study is to construct and test an English vocabulary program. The program will be designed for use in third-grade classrooms and will be field-tested in five selected classes in Elmwood schools.
- The purpose of this study is to explore factors related to achievement levels in English and mathematics among high school students of Filipino, Hispanic, and Caucasian descent.

Exercise 6.3

State the purpose of the proposed investigation for the topic you identified in Exercise 6.1.

Purpose:

Along with the statement of the problem, you will be expected to indicate why the study is worth pursuing. This portion is referred to as the *importance* of the study.

Exercise 6.4

Write a one-paragraph justification of the importance of the study you have identified.

Limitations and delimitations of the study to be undertaken should be specified at this point. Because these concerns are not always immediately clear, you may not be able to state them precisely at this stage of planning—it may be necessary to revisit them later in the development of your study.

In the *limitations of the study* you identify existing restrictions that are outside your control, such as availability of records, problems in selecting a sample, or time allotments. The limitations can usually be presented as a list and then explained further in one or two additional paragraphs.

In the *delimitations of the study* you identify boundaries that you, the investigator, are placing on the study. Here you might state specifically what you will and will not investigate; the number of individuals, classes, or schools to be involved in the study; calendar time to which the study is restricted; or any other boundaries you might wish to impose on the investigation. Similarly, delimitations can be presented as a list and further explained in one or two paragraphs.

In this phase of planning you must also define any terms that are not commonly recognized or that you will be using in a special sense.

Exercise 6.5

For your topic, (1) write three limitations, (2) write three delimitations, and (3) define three terms you will use that a lay reader would not readily understand.

Regarding questions and/or hypotheses, you must (1) state the research questions you will attempt to answer, and/or (2) state the research hypotheses and/or null hypotheses you will use.

You know that some types of research are oriented by questions, others by hypotheses, and still others by both. If you intend to use questions to guide your research, you should pose a main research question and then supplement it with a number of related subquestions that help answer the main question, as shown in the following example:

Problem: The purpose of this study is to formulate and test a set of procedures for increasing the level of student attention during sixth-grade mathematics instruction.

Main Question: Can a set of procedures be devised and implemented that will increase the level of student attention during sixth-grade mathematics instruction?

Subquestions:

1. Does evidence indicate that student attention is important during mathematics instruction?
2. What is meant by *paying attention,* and what do students do when paying attention?

3. What materials, techniques, and activities naturally attract and hold student attention?
4. What other factors cause students to pay attention?
5. What have teachers traditionally done to attract and hold student attention during mathematics or other instruction?
6. Can teachers incorporate a planned set of "attention holders" into their lessons?
7. If so, will those efforts produce increases in student attention?

The subquestions are much more limited than the main question. They are also more easily answered and are sequenced so that their answers can help answer the main question. Subquestions provide valuable guidance in planning and conducting the investigation.

Exercise 6.6

A. Would you consider the following to be a good or poor main research question?

Are Latino students in Elmwood getting what they should out of school?

You probably see it is a poor question because it is too vague: "Getting what they should out of school" has no clear lmeaning. It is also too broad; even if clarified, it covers too much ground.

The question would be acceptable if put in this form:

How do Latino students compare to other students in Elmwood high schools regarding achievement and attitude toward school?

The question thus stated directs attention to what the research is to determine. It clarifies the topic and limits it to researchable size.
    With these considerations in mind, write a main research question for the problem you have stated.

B. We have noted that answering a main research question is easier when a number of subordinate questions are posed to help answer the main question. The subquestions should be clear and succinct. Evaluate the following subquestions for (C) clarity, (S) succinctness, and (A) answerability.

_____ 1. Do Latino students goof around a lot after school?

_____ 2. Why are Latino students so good in math?

_____ 3. Do Latino students' attitudes toward school differ from the attitudes of other groups of students?

_____ 4. Do Latino students learn math differently from the way students of Asian descent learn it?

_____ 5. Given the incredible disadvantages experienced by certain members of the Latino student community, why do Latino students so frequently, and to such a surprising degree, outstrip their peers in so many different academic areas?

(continued)

Exercise 6.6   *Continued*

Let us appraise the subquestions: Question 5 is not stated succinctly; all the others are sufficiently brief. Questions 2, 3, and 4 are stated clearly, while questions 1 and 5 are not. Only question 3 is readily answerable; the other questions range from difficult to virtually impossible to answer through research.

C. Subquestions should also be arranged in good sequence, either from simple to more complex or so that prior questions furnish beginning points for questions that follow. Given the main question,

> *Is Latino students' achievement in high school mathematics affected by their parents' support of education?*

evaluate the following subquestions. Indicate the five questions that contribute best to answering the main research question. If you find the sequence of questions to be unsatisfactory, rearrange them as you believe appropriate.

_____ 1. What are the mathematics achievement levels of Latino high school students?

_____ 2. What do Latino students' parents say about their children's enjoyment of school?

_____ 3. Does the literature suggest a relationship between parental support and school achievement?

_____ 4. How does mathematics achievement among Latino students compare with that of students in general?

_____ 5. Does Latino student achievement in mathematics remain constant through the school years, relative to that of other students?

_____ 6. Is there a correlation between Latino students' mathematics achievement and their parents' attitude toward education?

_____ 7. How does Latino high school students' attitude toward school compare with that of other students?

D. Write out five subquestions to help answer the main research question you composed in part A of this exercise.

If hypotheses are used to guide research, they may be *research hypotheses,* which state the outcomes the investigator expects, or *null hypotheses,* which usually are not what the investigator expects to find but are testable satisfactorily within the logic of inferential statistics (examined in Chapter 8 and in Appendix A). To assist you in completing Exercise 6.7, the following examples are provided:

Research hypothesis: Mathematics achievement among Latino high school students is positively related to parental support of education.

Null hypothesis: No relationship exists between mathematics achievement of Latino high school students and their parents' support of education.

Frequently, both types of hypotheses are used in the same study. The investigator states a research hypothesis to orient the study and then a null hypothesis for testing whether a finding can be attributed to errors made in selecting the sample.

Exercise 6.7

A. Which of the following hypotheses are stated suitably for guiding practical educational research?

1. No difference exists in grade point average between sixth-grade students of Asian descent and sixth-grade students of Hispanic descent.
2. Attitude toward school is better among African American students than among Caucasian students.
3. No difference exists between students of Japanese descent and students of Korean descent regarding genetic capabilities for learning mathematics.
4. All students should be given equal access to educational opportunity.

B. Compose a research hypothesis and a null hypothesis for the problem you stated earlier.

Task 2. Outline the Library Search for Related Information

In this task, you should accomplish four things:

1. Select the terms or descriptors for use in the library search.
2. Identify secondary sources to be searched.
3. Identify guides and directories for searching primary sources.
4. Assemble the materials needed for summarizing and citing references.

Descriptors are terms related to your research topic that can be found in reference indexes such as *Current Index to Journals in Education (CIJE)*. They are helpful when you use the indexes manually and are indispensable when you use the computer for your search. One of the best aids in identifying appropriate descriptors is the *Thesaurus of ERIC Descriptors*. It can be found in the reference section of the library next to the bound volumes of *CIJE*, near the computer terminals used to search ERIC. Additionally, it is included on the ERIC compact diskette (if your library uses the CD-ROM version of ERIC) and can be accessed online within the searchable ERIC databases. When you consult the *Thesaurus*, identify the descriptor that most closely matches the theme of your study and use it first. While it might lead to all the references you need, you should list related descriptors as well, as they sometimes lead to unexpectedly valuable resources.

Exercise 6.8

For your topic, write three descriptors that might be used in searching the indexes. To facilitate searching, each descriptor should consist of no more than two words.

Secondary sources, such as yearbooks, research reviews, and encyclopedias, should be checked manually, using the descriptors you have identified. You should consult secondary sources first because it is likely they will summarize existing research in your topic and provide a review of the topic's historical treatment. Secondary sources are also likely to contain critiques and extensive bibliographies but probably will *not* include the most current research.

Exercise 6.9

Refer to the list of secondary sources presented in Chapter 4. Write the names of five sources that seem promising for your topic.

Guides such as indexes and directories should be consulted next for indications of documents and journal articles that might contain primary information related to your topic. Plan on using first those that can be accessed by computer, such as *Current Index to Journals in Education, Resources in Education,* and *Dissertation Abstracts International.*

Exercise 6.10

Refer to the indexes and directories listed in Chapter 4. Write the names of four that seem most promising for researching your topic.

You should now plan procedures and materials for summarizing and citing information related to your study. Chapter 5 suggested procedures for surveying quantities of materials and accurately making summaries and bibliographical citations.

As you delve into the literature, you may have to make another decision about your topic, depending on what you find. If your topic has already been researched extensively, answers to your questions may exist in the literature, in which case the topic is probably not a good choice for your project. If references to your topic are few or nonexistent, you may need to think through your topic again; it may have inherent problems that have prevented its being researched.

Assuming you have identified a researchable topic you wish to pursue, you can complete the library search as described in Chapters 4 and 5. Remember to organize the citations so as to present first the information that is more *generally* related to your topic and *earlier in publication date,* and then proceed to materials that are more *recent* and more *specific* to your topic. That is, you should organize the references so they proceed:

from general → to specific

and from earlier research → to more recent research

The use of research subquestions to guide your research can also help organize your literature review.

Exercise 6.11

Indicate which of the following should probably be presented (E) earlier or (L) later in your review of the literature.

_____   1. In 1957 Wilkinson…

_____   2. Gange's 1995 research showed that…

_____   3. Historically, research on this topic has dealt with…

_____   4. Martínez (1994) described research done at the turn of the century…

_____   5. Present consensus seems to be that…

_____   6. Garibaldi's 1958 findings are still considered to be the most accurate available…

_____   7. Of several similar topics investigated, the following are representative…

_____   8. Of all research, the most pertinent seems…

Task 3. Identify Needed Data and Sources

A number of elements must be considered within this task and should be carefully organized. The elements are as follows:

1. Specify events or conditions about which you need data, usually *one* of the following:

    ■ Human social behavior, individually or in one or more groups
    ■ Events or conditions of the present
    ■ Events or conditions of the past
    ■ Correlations that permit making predictions and sometimes suggest cause–effect relationships
    ■ Innovative procedures or products
    ■ Existing group differences and trends
    ■ Quality of programs or operational units
    ■ Relationships that strongly indicate cause and effect

    When you identify, from the preceding list, the event or condition central to the research topic you selected in Exercise 6.1, you have pinpointed the type of research you will undertake. It is important at this point that you read more about the particular type of research you are to pursue, in order to gain a greater understanding of what is involved in obtaining and analyzing data.

Exercise 6.12

Use the following chart to select and read the chapter presented in this book that describes the type of research you have identified for your topic. Select the event or condition central to your topic, note the probable type of research, and then read the suggested chapter.

(continued)

Exercise 6.12 *Continued*

Within that chapter, you will find one or more reprinted research reports that exemplify the type of research described in the chapter. After you have read that chapter, return here to continue your planning.

It is assumed at this point that you have, as suggested in Exercise 6.12, selected and read a chapter, or portion thereof, pertinent to the type of research appropriate for your topic. We now continue with directions for planning your research project.

Central event or condition of your topic	Type of research	Read this chapter
Human social behavior	Ethnographic	Chapter 10: Ethnographic Research
Innovative procedures or products	Action	Chapter 11: Action Research and Evaluation Research
Quality of programs or operations	Evaluation	Chapter 11: Action Research and Evaluation Research
Events or conditions of the present	Descriptive	Chapter 12: Descriptive Research and Historical Research
Events or conditions of the past	Historical	Chapter 12: Descriptive Research and Historical Research
Co-relation (between variables)	Correlational	Chapter 13: Correlational Research
Existing group differences and trends	Causal-comparative	Chapter 14: Experimental, Quasi-Experimental, and Causal-Comparative Research
Relationships that show cause and effect	Experimental	Chapter 14: Experimental, Quasi-Experimental, and Causal-Comparative Research

2. List the kinds of data you need to collect for your research, usually one or more of the following:

   - *Descriptions*—verbal summaries of observations
   - *Scores or tallies*—test scores or frequency tallies
   - *Measurements*—assessments by measuring devices other than tests
   - *Opinions*—what people believe
   - *Statements*—authoritative pronouncements
   - *Analyses*—careful logical scrutiny

3. Pinpoint anticipated sources of data, usually including one or more of the following:

   - *Participants*—people participating in the study
   - *Procedures*—formal ways of doing things
   - *Settings*—physical environments
   - *Objects*—tangible things

- *Records*—highly summarized notations
- *Documents*—printed materials, such as articles
- *Informants*—people who provide desired information verbally

---

Exercise 6.13

For the topic you have identified for research, first list the kinds of data you will need to collect and then the probable sources of those data.

Task 4. List the Steps You Will Need to Carry Out to Complete the Study

Use the following suggestions:

1. If you need to select a sample of participants who will furnish data, indicate the kind of sample you believe obtainable and best for your study. Note that additional information and greater detail for methods of sample selection is provided in Chapter 7.

   - **Random sample:** Every person in the population has a chance of being selected.
   - **Stratified sample:** Sample is specially drawn to fairly represent elements of the population, such as various ethnic groups.
   - **Cluster sample:** Sample consists of existing groups, such as classes or schools.
   - **Convenience sample:** Sample consists of whoever happens to be available.

2. Indicate how you will select the sample.
3. Indicate what the participants, if any, will be expected or required to do. Expectations are normally categorized as one or more of the following:

   - Reorganize or regroup
   - Undergo assessment
   - Receive training, instruction, or other treatments
   - Demonstrate skills or knowledge
   - Interact and behave in their normal fashion

Exercise 6.14

1. Do you expect to select a sample for your study? If so, indicate the kind of sample and how you will select it.
2. If you use participants in your study, indicate what you will expect them to do.

---

4. Indicate how you will obtain data. In most studies, data are collected by one or more of the following:

   - *Notation*—observer makes notes of observations
   - *Description*—observer makes detailed recordings of observations
   - *Analysis*—investigator makes careful logical scrutiny of objects and procedures

- *Questioning*—investigator or assistant conducts interviews or surveys
- *Testing*—participants respond to formal tests
- *Measurement*—assessment is done through use of measuring devices other than tests

5. Indicate the tools that will be used in collecting data. This is usually one or more of the following:

   - *Recording devices*—pencil, paper, camera, audio and video recorders
   - *Guides*—structure for procedures and questions, as in interviews
   - *Criteria*—standards for judging existence or acceptability
   - *Tests*—commercial standardized tests; sometimes tests constructed by the investigator
   - *Measuring devices other than tests*—rulers, thermometers, weight scales, and the like
   - *Rating scales*—written prompts to which participants respond, such as Likert scales and semantic differential scales
   - *Questionnaires*—sets of questions to which participants respond in writing

6. Anticipate the form in which data will accumulate (typically one or more of the following):

   - Written descriptions
   - Numerical summaries
   - Categorizations—participants or responses placed in categories
   - Hierarchical listings—responses or participants placed in rank order
   - Tallies—marks indicating frequency of occurrences or responses

7. Give attention to how you will ensure the quality of your data, such as by

   - Determining legitimacy of source by verifying authenticity, credentials of provider, or measures of validity
   - Determining accuracy of data via credentials of the provider, preponderance of opinion, logical analysis, and statistical measures of reliability

Task 5. Specify the Procedures and Tools You Will Employ in Collecting Data

This topic was discussed in the preceding paragraphs. You will almost certainly use one or more of the following procedures to obtain data: notation, description, analysis, questioning, testing, and measurement. Depending on the procedures you envision, you will need to use tools such as recording devices, guides, criteria, tests, measuring devices other than tests, rating scales, and questionnaires.

Exercise 6.15

For the data you anticipate obtaining in your study

1. List the specific steps you will follow and tools you might use in collecting data.
2. Indicate how you expect to organize data prior to analysis.
3. Explain how you will attempt to ensure quality of your data.

Task 6. Foresee How Data Can Best Be Analyzed and Interpreted

Data Analysis.   Procedures for analyzing data vary according to type of data and research questions and/or hypotheses.

    Previously we saw that *qualitative* and *quantitative* are the two general types of data, and that they must be analyzed differently. Qualitative data are for the most part narrative or verbal, whereas quantitative data are for the most part numerical. A certain amount of overlap exists between the two types. The following is what you should give attention to:

Research
Navigator.c⊛m

qualitative data

quantitative data

1. State how you will analyze **qualitative data,** if such analysis is appropriate. This usually involves logically matching data with research questions. In ethnographic studies, analysis involves identifying topics, categories, and patterns that ultimately lead to interpretations, from which conclusions are reached concerning the research questions asked. (Techniques of qualitative data analysis are described in Chapter 8.)
2. State how you will analyze **quantitative data,** if such analysis is appropriate. This usually involves statistical procedures that result in

- Numerical descriptions of central tendency, variability, correlations, differences, and relative standings, and/or
- Statistical inferences about standard error, probability, and significance

Techniques for analyzing quantitative data are described in Chapter 8 and in Appendix A.

Exercise 6.16

For the data you anticipate

1. Will you need to use qualitative analysis or quantative analysis? Explain why.
2. If quantitative analysis is indicated, do you expect to explore status of groups, differences between or among groups, or relationships between or among variables?

Analysis Applied to Answering Questions and Testing Hypotheses.   *Research questions* are answered through logic and accumulation of evidence. *Qualitative analysis* requires a strong verbal argument, enough to be very persuasive. *Quantitative analysis* describes data numerically and often requires the application of statistical tests to help determine whether the findings exist in the population as well as in the sample.

    Hypotheses, as we have seen, are tested statistically. Statistical tests provide the rationale for either retaining or rejecting your hypotheses, thus suggesting whether or not your findings are probably "real." You also use logic to support the inferences you make about your hypotheses.

Findings.   *Findings* are statements that explain what your data analysis has revealed. Presented verbally, findings are commonly grouped in accordance with the research questions or hypotheses to which they pertain. For example, given the research question

How do Latino students compare to other students in Elmwood high schools regarding achievement and attitude toward school?

You might properly present your findings as follows:

Question 1:   How do Latino students compare to other students in Elmwood high schools as concerns achievement and attitude toward school?

Findings: With regard to this question, it was found that

1. Latino students' achievement test scores, compared to other students in Elmwood high schools, were….

2. Latino students' attitude toward school, compared to that of all other students in Elmwood high schools, was….

Although findings are expressed verbally, it is expected that they be referenced to the analytical procedures on which they are based, which might be shown as:

- Graphic summaries, shown in figures, tables, and graphs, and/or
- Tabular summaries shown in tables, with appropriate statistical tests applied

Conclusions.   *Conclusions,* which are the interpretations you make of your research findings, are also presented verbally. They are comprised of your reflections on the meaning, significance, and implications of what you have discovered. Using the previous example:

How do Latino students compare to other students in Elmwood high schools regarding achievement and attitude toward school?

You might write

Given the findings of this study, the following conclusions appear to be warranted:

1. Latino students in Elmwood high schools…(continue stating your interpretations).

Exercise 6.17

For the research questions and hypotheses you stated in Exercises 6.6 and 6.7:

1. Indicate the general procedures you would use to answer questions and test hypotheses.
2. Indicate how you would expect to present your findings and conclusions.

Task 7. Anticipate the Appropriate Report Format for Your Research

Relatively little has been said up to now about formats used for research reports, although you have had direct experience with many. (Chapter 9 provides detailed help with report formats.) For the present, simply recognize the existence of a *generic* format and three variations: the *thesis/dissertation* format, the *technical paper* format, and the *journal article* format.

The generic report format includes:

1. Specification of the problem
2. Review of related literature
3. Procedures and data collection
4. Data analysis
5. Findings
6. Conclusions

The report format that your institution expects you to follow will be a variation of this generic format. You most likely will be expected to use the thesis format adopted by your

---

Applying Technology: **More Guidelines for Reports**

Recall that earlier in this text we referred the reader to an electronic text authored by Dr. William Trochim of Cornell University (http://trochim.human.cornell.edu/kb). Included in his online text are two pages that provide excellent guidance in terms of planning for research and, specifically, the writing of a proposal or final research report. The first of these, titled "Key Elements" (http://trochim.human.cornell.edu/kb/guideelements.htm), presents an overview of important criteria that must be addressed in any research report. Even though the author focuses on writing up a completed study, his references to and descriptions of several aspects of a report would also apply to writing a research proposal or plan. In "Key Elements," Dr. Trochim addresses the following aspects:

- *Introduction*
- *Methods*
- *Results*
- *Conclusion, Abstract,* and *Reference* sections

Included in each of these sections are detailed descriptions of the specific components for each section (e.g., *Methods* includes descriptions of Sample Selection, Measurement Issues, and the Research Design and Procedures).

The second page, titled "Formatting" (http://trochim.human.cornell.edu/kb/formatting.htm), contains even more detailed descriptions of the specifics of how to format a research proposal or plan. These guidelines follow those provided in the *Publication Manual of the American Psychological Association* (5th edition). Included on this page are descriptions of the contents of individual sections of the research proposal or paper. In addition to the components listed above, Dr. Trochim has also included information on:

- Citing referencing within the text (i.e., within the literature review)
- Formats for citing references in a reference list
- Information on formatting tables, figures, and appendices

Finally, Dr. Trochim has also included the complete text of a sample research paper (http://trochim.human.cornell.edu/kb/sampaper.htm), exemplifying many of the guidelines presented on his previously mentioned Web pages.

graduate school. Two other variations frequently used by researchers are the technical paper format, specified by agencies that sponsor research, and the journal article format, specified by particular journals that publish research. By now you have seen many examples of the journal format, and you may also have seen some of the technical paper format.

This completes the instruction on how to prepare for your own research. The following case illustrates how one graduate student planned her research.

INTRODUCTION TO EDUCATIONAL RESEARCH
Companion Website Highlight

The Companion Website that accompanies this text (www.ablongman.com/mertler5e) includes three sample research proposals produced by groups of masters students, as well as a report from a completed research study. They have been provided as examples of various ways of planning a research study and of developing a research plan.

Illustrative Example of Planning a Research Project

Sheila Holly, an experienced teacher adept at working with student teachers, had for some time been interested in exploring whether success in student teaching could be predicted from the basis of student teachers' personal traits. She planned an investigation to pursue that question, following the research phases outlined in the planning guide you have just completed.

Topic and Problem

The process began when Holly decided she wanted to determine whether student teacher success could be predicted from personal traits. For her working title, she chose "Predicting Success in Student Teaching from Student Teachers' Personal Traits." She then formulated the following problem statement:

> The purpose of this study is to determine whether success in student teaching can be predicted from selected personal traits of student teachers.

Holly included a brief statement about the importance of the study, explaining that student teaching is very costly to taxpayers, that better prediction of success would save money and other resources, that reliable predictors of success in student teaching have not been available, and that there has been speculation but no proof that student teaching success depends more on personal factors than on intelligence or grade point average. She continued by describing the limitations of the study, which had to do with participants available, student teaching placements, and schools and master teachers involved. She also stated the delimitations of the study, which included time duration, personal traits to be investigated, and instruments and procedures that would be used to assess personal traits and success in student teaching. Finally, Holly defined the terms central to her study, including student teaching, success in student teaching, personality, and personal traits.

Holly used both research questions and a null hypothesis in her study. Her null hypothesis was:

> No relationship exists between success in student teaching and selected personal traits of student teachers.

Her main research question was:

> Can personal traits of student teachers be used to predict success in student teaching?

Subordinate to that main research question were the following subquestions:

1. What are some of the personal traits of student teachers that professors and master teachers consider important to success?
2. Can master teachers and professors of teacher education reach consensus concerning a cluster of personal traits that seem to be essential to success in student teaching?
3. If a group of such traits can be identified, can they be reliably observed and rated in student teachers?
4. If a group of reliably observable traits can be identified and agreed upon, can those traits be assessed by using an instrument such as a rating scale?
5. If student teachers can be assessed with such a scale, can the overall rating procedure be refined sufficiently that accurate predictions can be made from the scale?

Examination of the Literature

With those preliminary tasks completed, Holly went to the library to determine the extent to which her topic had been researched. She examined primary and secondary sources, systematically annotating references that had bearing on her research questions. She found some mention of her topic, but no research or practice that suggested that personal traits could, or could not, reliably serve as predictors. She, therefore, decided to proceed with her study.

Required Data and Data Sources

Holly saw that her study involved two main components. The first was the identification and validation of possible predictors of success that could be built into an assessment instrument. The second was to determine whether a correlation existed between personal traits thus identified and student teaching success. The focus of the first component was *innovation*. The needed data seemed to be expert opinion, and the best source of those data seemed to be experienced teachers and professors of education, accustomed to working with student teachers.

The focus of the second component was on correlations for *making predictions*. The needed data seemed to be (1) scores depicting traits of student teachers, and (2) measures of candidates' later success in student teaching. Those data would be obtained from participants (i.e., student teachers) involved in the study.

Holly used a cluster sample to obtain data. The cluster consisted of 38 student teachers under her direction during the fall term. She explained the proposed study to those students, and all of them agreed to undergo assessment regarding personal traits and performance in student teaching.

For developing the trait assessment instrument, Holly counted on the help of master teachers and university professors of education. She planned to conduct discussions and interviews with those colleagues, hoping they could identify a pool of personal traits that they believed important to success in student teaching. If they could do so, Holly would analyze the traits to determine which might be assessable through observation or measurement. She would then incorporate those traits, illustrated with example behaviors, into a rating scale that could be used by professional educators who were working with student teachers. She planned to have the professionals evaluate the rating scale, suggest modifications, and then use the scale to assess the selected personal traits of the students. Holly intended to assess all 38 student teachers personally as well, and in addition to ask student teachers to use the instrument to assess themselves.

Data having to do with success in student teaching would come from the end-of-term evaluations routinely completed for student teachers, plus the professionals' appraisals of where each student teacher seemed to rank among student teachers in general.

Holly planned to obtain both qualitative and quantitative data from the assessments and evaluations. Because she feared that the trait assessment instrument and the final evaluation form might produce unreliable or even misleading numerical data, she planned to have professionals participating in the study keep detailed records of each student teacher's performance.

Holly planned to make a dual analysis of the qualitative and quantitative data, in order to compare the ratings of each student teacher as made by the master teacher, the university professor, the student, and Holly herself. She planned to correlate the numerical data from the assessment instrument and the student teaching final evaluation forms. At the same time she planned to explore qualitatively the correspondence between personal traits and student teaching success.

INTRODUCTION TO EDUCATIONAL RESEARCH

Companion Website Highlight

The Companion Website for this text (www.ablongman.com/mertler5e) also includes a downloadable, printable proposal rating scale. It can be used to assist you in the development of a research plan or to evaluate an existing one. Save or print the form and use it to assist you in planning for a research study.

Appraisal of Holly's Plan

Holly may or may not be successful in what she proposes to accomplish. She must contend with serious questions about the validity and reliability of the trait assessment instrument she hopes to develop. Also, the reliability of student teacher evaluations is always in question.

These factors will leave some uncertainty about any conclusions Holly reaches. Despite these serious concerns, Holly's topic is important and worth exploring. She may well uncover valuable and generalizable findings. But she will have to obtain statistically significant results and build powerful logical arguments if she is to answer her questions convincingly.

D E V E L O P M E N T A L   A C T I V I T Y

Planning for Your Research

This chapter's developmental activity is essentially a compilation of many of the exercises that you have already examined earlier in this chapter but in a more streamlined format. Think about the work you have done in previous chapters' developmental activities and respond to the following:

1. My preliminary research problem or topic is: _____

   _____.

2. The type of research that seems most appropriate is: _____

   _____.

3. My research questions and/or hypotheses include: _____

   _____.

4. My justification for investigating this problem or topic (i.e., why would I argue that it is an important topic to investigate) is: _____

   _____.

5. The main variables for my study include: _____

   _____.

6. Descriptors that I am using for the identification of related literature include: _____

   _____.

7. The following constitutes a potential outline of the major sections of my literature review:

   I. _____

   II. _____

   III. _____

   IV. _____

   V. _____.

8. My intended sample consists of (who and how many): _____

   _____.

9. The type of sampling (if any) that seems most appropriate is: _____

   _____.

10. The type(s) of tool(s) that I plan to use to collect data is/are as follows:_____

   _____.

11. The following statistical techniques will be used to analyze my data—and ultimately
    answer my research questions/hypotheses: _____

   _____

   _____.

(A downloadable, interactive version of this developmental activity is available from the Companion
Website, www.ablongman.com/mertler5e)

Chapter Summary

Careful advance planning is *extremely* important if research is to give attention to necessary components, remain focused, and be finalized correctly and expeditiously. Attention must be given to each of the seven tasks as discussed in this chapter, as all are essential and critical components of the process of designing and conducting a research study.

INTRODUCTION TO EDUCATIONAL RESEARCH
Companion Website Highlight

Finally, the Companion Website for this text (www.ablongman.com/mertler5e) includes a downloadable, printable version of a comprehensive guide for planning educational research. It has been structured as a checklist and allows you to monitor your progress when planning for a research study. Save or print the checklist and use it to assist you in planning your research study.

LIST OF IMPORTANT TERMS

cluster sample	qualitative data	research hypothesis
convenience sample	quantitative data	stratified sample
null hypothesis	random sample	subquestions
problem	research design	

YOUR CURRENT STATUS

In this chapter, you have seen how research is planned. You are familiar with seven principal tasks to be completed when planning research. By completing the chapter exercises you have outlined a plan for actual research of your own that you should be able to use with confidence.

ACTIVITIES FOR THOUGHT AND DISCUSSION

Using the planning guide, develop an outline, consisting of no more than one page, of an investigation into one of the following topics:

1. Why students such as the members of your class pursue graduate studies in education

2. A comparison of the lecture-discussion method versus the self-guided study method for promoting achievement in classes in educational research

3. Factors that might serve to improve teacher morale and job satisfaction

4. The lines of work teachers believe they would prefer if they had career choices to make over again

REFERENCES AND RECOMMENDED READINGS

Bauman, J., Allen, J., & Shockley, B. (1994). *Research Questions Teachers Ask: A Report from the National Reading Research Center School Research Consortium* (Reading Research Report No. 30). Athens: Universities of Georgia and Maryland, National Reading Research Center.

Best, J., & Kahn, J. (2003). *Research in Education* (9th ed.). Boston: Allyn and Bacon.

Crowl, T. (1993). *Fundamentals of Educational Research*. Dubuque, IA: William C. Brown.

Eisner, E. (1992). A slice of advice. *Educational Researcher, 21*(5):29–30.

Fleischer, C. (1994). Researching teacher-research: A practitioner's retrospective. *English Education, 26*(2):86–126.

Gay, L., & Airasian, P. (2000). *Educational Research: Competencies for Analysis and Application* (6th ed.). Upper Saddle River, NJ: Merrill.

Glass, G. (1992). A slice of advice. *Educational Researcher, 21*(3):23.

Kagan, D. (1992). Professional growth among preservice and beginning teachers. *Review of Educational Research, 62,* 129–169.

Kutz, E. (1992). Teacher research: Myths and realities. *Language Arts, 69,* 193–197.

McMillan, J. (2004). *Educational Research: Fundamentals for the Consumer* (4th ed.). Boston: Allyn and Bacon.

Padak, N., & Padak, G. (1995). *Guidelines for Planning Action Research Projects. Research to Practice.* Kent State University, OH: Ohio Literacy Resource Center.

Ross, S. (1992). Getting started as a researcher: Designing and conducting research studies in instructional technology. *TechTrends, 37*(3):19–22.

Schloss, P., & Smith, M. (1999). *Conducting Research.* Upper Saddle River, NJ: Prentice-Hall.

Trochim, W. M. (2002). *The Research Methods Knowledge Base* (2nd ed.). Available at trochim.human.cornell.edu/kb/index.htm

Wiersma, W. (2000). *Research Methods in Education* (7th ed.). Boston: Allyn and Bacon.

Zeuli, J. (1992, April). How do teachers understand research when they read it? Paper presented at the annual meeting of the American Educational Research Association, San Francisco, CA.

7 Procedures and Tools for Gathering Data

PREVIEW

All researchers require new information to help answer their research questions, information referred to as

- Data

They plan carefully how to obtain data that is

- Appropriate for their type of research
- Directed at their research questions or hypotheses

They give meticulous attention to

- Identifying fruitful sources of data
- Planning out procedures for obtaining desired data
- Selecting tools to use in data collection
- Selecting samples as data sources, when needed
- Obtaining and organizing the new data

They also do their best to ensure

- The validity of their data
- The reliability of their data

And to do so, they use specific procedures called

- Internal criticism
- External criticism

Targeted Learnings

In this chapter we explore in greater detail the procedures and tools that researchers use to collect data in their investigations. This exploration begins by identifying once more the typical foci of the eight types of educational research. Those foci provide guidance for identifying potential sources of data. Once data sources are identified, one can decide if a sample is needed from which to obtain data, and if so, what kind of sample would be best under existing circumstances. The data sources also suggest procedures for obtaining data and the tools that would be most useful.

As you read the chapter, look especially for information related to the following questions:

1. What are the typical foci of the eight types of educational research?
2. Which three types of educational research call for the careful selection of samples?
3. What are the differences among the various types of samples?
4. What is meant by *data source?* How does data source differ from type of research?
5. How do internal criticism and external criticism relate to the quality of data?

Steps to Follow When Considering Procedures for Collecting Data:

Identify the focus of research

- Social behavior
- Present status or events
- Past status or events
- Correlation/prediction
- Innovation
- Evaluation
- Causation

Decide what data are needed

- Descriptions
- Scores
- Measurements
- Opinions
- Statements
- Analyses
- Rankings
- Categorizations

Select appropriate data sources

- Participants
- Procedures
- Settings
- Objects
- Records
- Documents
- Informants

Decide if, and what type of, sample is needed

- Random
- Stratified
- Cluster
- Systematic
- Convenience

Select appropriate procedures for data collection

- Making notations
- Describing
- Analyzing
- Questioning
- Testing
- Measuring

Select tools appropriate for collecting needed data

- Marking devices
- Cameras
- Recorders
- Guides
- Criteria
- Tests
- Surveys
- Scales
- Measuring devices

Foresee the format in which the data will accrue

- Detailed notes
- Summary notations
- Scores
- Tallies
- Categories
- Rankings
- Measurements
- Analyses

6. What are the characteristics of the following data collection procedures: notation, description, analysis, questioning, measurement, and testing?
7. Which tools for collecting data are most likely to be used in each of the collection procedures named in question 6?
8. What is meant by *data collection profile?* Of what value are such profiles?

Although much valuable information can be located in the university library, research usually requires that firsthand data be acquired directly from the settings, objects, behaviors, procedures, animals, and/or humans being studied. As you gain ability to plan your own research, it is important that you learn to specify the following:

1. The information (data) needed to answer your research questions and/or test your hypotheses
2. The sources from which needed data can be obtained
3. Appropriate procedures for collecting data
4. Tools useful in collecting data
5. The form into which collected data will accrue

Types of Research and Their Typical Foci

Each type of educational research—ethnographic, historical, descriptive, correlational, action, evaluation, causal-comparative, and experimental—has a predominant central focus. Figure 7.1 shows the types of research and the typical focus of each.

Types of Research	Focus
Ethnographic	Social behavior
Historical	Past events or conditions
Descriptive	Present events or conditions
Correlational	Predictive correlations
Action	Innovation
Evaluative	Judgment about quality
Causal-comparative	Possible causation
Experimental	Causation

FIGURE 7.1   Types of research and corresponding foci

Types of Data Needed

Each research focus suggests the need for certain kinds of data, such as verbal descriptions, scores, measurements, opinions, statements, and analyses. As these labels do not adequately describe the data to which they refer, brief explanations follow:

Descriptions are verbal representations of participants, objects, procedures, and settings. They may be given in summary form or in great detail. Ms. Cauthern's explanation of how she assigns homework is a description.

Scores are the numerical values assigned to test performance. The 78 that Jason made on the spelling test is a score.

Measurements are appraisals made with measuring instruments other than tests. They are usually stated numerically, but are sometimes stated verbally. Alicia's height, 5 feet, 4 inches, is a measurement.

Opinions are views expressed by participants and informants. Although opinions are often informed and accurate, they may be uninformed and inaccurate, but nevertheless indicate status of thought, attitude, or value. What Mr. Jakes said about school politics is an opinion.

Statements are informed verbal depictions or opinions, as might be given by authorities or eyewitnesses. What Superintendent Morton said about discipline in Elmwood schools, when interviewed on television, was a statement.

Analyses are clarifications and conclusions reached through careful scrutiny and logic. When Mrs. Toler and Mr. Thornton studied the mathematics textbook to determine its attention to problem solving and abstract thought, they performed an analysis.

Sources of Data for Various Types of Research

Data are usually obtained from one or more of the following sources: participants, procedures, settings, objects, records, documents, and informants. The value of a particular source of data depends on the type of research being conducted. Let us take a moment to review the nature of each of these sources of data.

Research
Navigator.c⊕m
participants

Participants are the individuals specially selected to undergo scrutiny in research. For example, a student involved in an experiment is a participant. Traditionally participants were, and sometimes still are, called **subjects.**

Procedures are formalized ways of operating in the educational setting. They are the way things are done, such as how lessons are presented and how homework is managed.

Settings are the specific environments in which behavior occurs or is intended to occur. Classrooms, athletic fields, streets, and homes are examples of settings.

Objects are inanimate things, including books, supplies, materials, and artifacts.

Records are highly summarized reports of performance, expenditures, and the like, kept for later reference.

Documents are written papers and reports in their entirety, such as journal articles, technical papers, and curriculum guides. Photographs, drawings, and other illustrations are also considered documents.

Informants are people other than participants in a study from whom opinion, informed views, and expert testimony are obtained. When Mrs. James explained to the researcher how she dealt with the parents of her students, she became an informant.

Exercise 7.1

Indicate the principal data source most likely involved in the eight sentence fragments that follow. Sources: (PA) participant, (P) procedure, (ST) setting, (O) object, (R) records, (D) document, or (I) informant

_____   1. Mrs. Simpkins said she believed that…

_____   2. The illustrations appear to suggest that…

_____   3. Ted's heart rate just prior to the examination reached…

_____   4. The books had deteriorated…

_____   5. An expert on year-round schools testified…

_____   6. Directions on how to do the activity were given once, then repeated…

_____   7. This information indicates that David has never done very well in school…

_____   8. It was a large urban high school…

Samples and Their Selection

In research, the kinds of foregoing data help determine whether a sample should be selected from which to obtain data, and if so, what sort of sample it should be. As you learned previously, a sample is a subgroup of people, animals, or objects selected to represent the much larger population (in its entirety) from which it is drawn.

Are Samples Necessary in Research?

Samples are essential in some kinds of research but are not needed in others. In historical research, one does not usually decide in advance to accept data only from selected persons or objects and not from others that might have equal value to the research topic being investigated. In action research, one is concerned only with a particular group in its entirety, such as a class, grade level, or school. In such cases, there is no point in trying to obtain a sample that represents the population.

But where research is concerned with representing a population that is so large it cannot be investigated in its totality, samples are necessary. Those samples should be carefully selected so they will accurately reflect the distribution of trait variables (e.g., gender, age, socioeconomic status, years of education, and so on) within the population.

Can Small Samples Represent Large Populations?

Small samples can indeed accurately reflect the population, so that findings obtained from the sample can be generalized to the population. To help ensure that samples represent the population, the individuals that comprise them are selected randomly, whenever possible, although other alternative sampling procedures are often required. The various methods of selecting samples are categorized as either probability sampling or nonprobability sampling techniques.

Probability Sampling

Research
Navigator.com
random sample

Probability sampling is a category of sample selection procedures in which one can state the probability (likelihood) of each member of the population being selected for the sample and in which there is a constant probability of selection for each member of the population. Types of probability sampling include random sampling, stratified sampling, cluster sampling, and systematic sampling.

Random sampling, sometimes called *simple random sampling,* is done in such a way that each individual in the total population has an equal chance of being selected. Random sampling is the best way to obtain a representative sample, although no method guarantees perfect representation. To obtain a sample that would represent all students in Elmwood Lincoln High School, one might put all names on individual slips of paper, thoroughly mix them, and blindly draw out the number desired for the sample. Of course, this would only be a feasible procedure if the population from which you were selecting a sample was small. Random samples were once hand-selected using tables of random numbers. Now, computer programs greatly facilitate the selection process.

Stratified sampling may be used when researchers want to ensure that subgroups within the population are represented proportionally in the sample. The population of Elmwood high school students, for example, contains many different ethnic groups. For the sake of illustration, let us say that the makeup of that population is 33 percent Anglo, 28 percent Latino, 14 percent African American, 9 percent Japanese, 7 percent Korean, and 3 percent Chinese, with several other groups making up the remaining 6 percent. Suppose we wished to conduct a study using a sample that contained those same exact ethnic percentages. A purely random selection process would give us a sample that might or might not match the ethnic percentages of the population. To make sure we obtained an accurate sample, we might decide to use stratified selection. For a sample of 100 students, we would decide in advance that 33 of those students should be randomly selected Anglos, 28 randomly selected Latinos, 14 randomly selected African Americans, and so on until the sample of 100 participants was filled—therefore, our sample would be representative of the population, specifically with respect to ethnicity. This example describes a process of sample selection in which the various ethnic groups are *proportionally* representative of the population. Stratified samples may be selected so that various subgroups are represented *equally* in the sample (Gay and Airasian, 2000). Altering our previous example in this manner would have resulted in our sample consisting of roughly 15 randomly selected students from each of the seven ethnic categories—this would result in a sample of 105 students with each ethnic group being represented equally.

Research Navigator.c⊛m

cluster sample

Cluster sampling involves the random selection of groups that already exist. If we wished to conduct an experiment dealing with a new way of teaching spelling to fourth-grade students, it would be impractical to randomly select a sample of 50 students from the entire fourth-grade population in Elmwood schools and then teach only those 50 students the new spelling method. It would be much more feasible to use entire, intact fourth-grade classrooms. In a case such as this, at least five classrooms should be selected at random from all Elmwood fourth grades to receive the experimental treatment. But with such cluster sampling, it is improbable that those classrooms would accurately reflect the fourth-grade population of the school district. The convenience or necessity of cluster sampling is thus offset by a greater likelihood of obtaining an unrepresentative sample.

Systematic sampling is often done when all members of the population are named on a master list and the sample is drawn directly from that list. From the list, a name is chosen at random. Following that first selected name, every kth person (that is, every tenth, every fiftieth, every one-hundredth, or whatever) is selected for inclusion in the sample. The value for k is determined by simply taking the total number of subjects in the population and dividing it by the number needed for the sample. Systematic sampling has most of the virtues of random sampling and is usually more conveniently done. However, if the original list of names exists in a predetermined order, it is possible that the resulting sample may be biased. This ultimately results in systematic sampling being classified as a nonprobability sampling technique (see the next section). In this case, it is best to randomize the original list in an attempt to remedy the potential bias in a systematic sample.

The various types of probability sampling techniques are depicted in Figure 7.2.

Nonprobability Sampling

Research Navigator.c⊛m

convenience sample

Nonprobability sampling is a sampling procedure in which the probability of inclusion for each member of the population cannot be specified. It is used when probability sampling is not feasible. Types of nonprobability sampling include convenience sampling, judgmental sampling, snowball sampling, and quota sampling.

Convenience sampling uses groups of participants that simply happen to be available. Teachers often use convenience samples when doing research, selecting as the sample their own class, or the classes of two or three fellow teachers. Samples selected in this manner cannot be assumed to represent the population. The results obtained in such studies should only be generalized to the population with great caution.

purposive sample

Judgmental sampling, also known as **purposive sampling,** is used to select certain segments of the population for study. The researcher uses his or her judgment as to which segments should be included. For example, one might wish to do research into the lifestyles of 10 "deviant" students, who have a history of chronic misbehavior in school. Or one might wish to investigate the nurturing practices of parents of students named valedictorians of their graduating classes for a particular year. Judgmental sampling, as you can

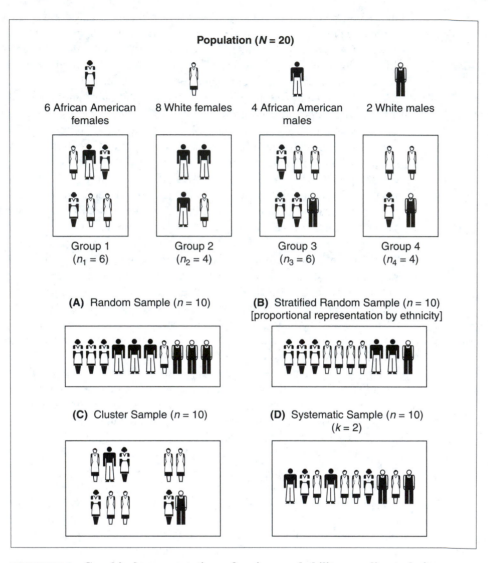

FIGURE 7.2 Graphical representations of various probability sampling techniques

see in these examples, is more appropriate for qualitative research—where making gener-
alizations to the entire population is *not* the focus—than for quantitative research.

Snowball sampling, also known as **network sampling** or **chain sampling,** is often
used in qualitative research endeavors. The basic technique begins with the identification
of a few initial participants to be interviewed. Following each interview, the researcher
simply asks each participant to recommend other individuals who meet certain criteria and
who might be interested in participating in the research study. The term *snowball* refers to
the accumulation of participants as one progresses through the data collection process.

Applying Technology: **Probability and Nonprobability Sampling**

We again refer you to Dr. Trochim's electronic research methods textbook (http://trochim.human.cornell.edu/kb) for a discussion of probability and nonprobability sampling techniques. In the first of these pages, titled "Sampling Terminology" (http://trochim.human.cornell.edu/kb/sampterm.htm), Dr. Trochim provides a brief but excellent general overview of sampling and its related terminology, including:

- Populations
- Samples
- *Target* populations
- *Accessible* populations

The second page (http://trochim.human.cornell.edu/kb/sampprob.htm) addresses the concept of probability sampling. Basic definitions and excellent examples, with very helpful graphic images, are provided for simple random sampling, stratified random sampling, systematic sampling, and cluster sampling. An example of *multistage sampling,* which involves combining two or more of the preceding probability sampling techniques, is also provided.

The final page to be referenced here addresses the various types of nonprobability sampling techniques (http://trochim.human.cornell.edu/kb/sampnon.htm). Explanations are provided for convenience, purposive, and quota sampling, as well as some lesser used nonprobability techniques.

Snowball sampling is seen as a useful technique for getting started when you are unable to identify another means of finding the participants you want; however, it should not be used in isolation as the sole means of sample selection (Glesne, 1999).

Quota sampling, not often used in educational research, is done when an investigator wants to do research applicable to the population but for whatever reason is not able to draw a sample from the population. The investigator may, therefore, intentionally construct a sample that seems to have the same characteristics as the population. If one wished, for example, to study the educational backgrounds of adult members of six different ethnic groups prominent in Elmwood, it might be very difficult to select a sample randomly. However, given existing information about those groups, it might be possible to contact individual members and thus put together a sample that is believed to represent the groups in the population regarding age, gender, socioeconomic status, and other pertinent criteria.

Finally, it should be noted that systematic sampling, previously described as a probability sampling procedure, may also be classified as a *non*probability technique in specific situations. If the list being used to select the sample is "ordered" in some manner (i.e., the names are not randomly arranged), the possibility exists for certain subgroups to be systematically excluded from the sample (Gay & Airasian, 2000). For example, certain ethnicities have distinctive last names that may group together when arranged alphabetically.

If a sample is being selected from a list arranged alphabetically, it is quite possible that one or more particular ethnic groups might be completely excluded from the sample.

Size of Samples

As indicated earlier, it has been found that samples smaller than 30 are not likely to reflect the trait distributions that exist in the population, a fault that could put one's research findings in doubt. Even when small samples do represent populations accurately, their size reduces the likelihood that research results based on their data will be found statistically significant. A given correlation or difference between means, for example, is more likely to be found statistically significant if obtained from a large sample; significance becomes less likely as the sample size becomes smaller.

How small is too small? A minimum sample size depends on the type of research study being conducted. Statisticians have seemed generally to agree that, as a rule of thumb, samples used in correlational research should be *no smaller than 30,* those used in experimental or causal-comparative research *no smaller than 15 per group involved,* and those that involve entire classrooms should include *at least five classrooms per different research treatment.* For descriptive research studies, a common recommendation is to sample approximately 10–20 percent of the population. With large populations, this can obviously become cumbersome. Gay and Airasian (2000) assert that once population sizes of a certain magnitude (about $N = 5,000$) are exceeded, population size becomes irrelevant and a sample size of $n = 400$ will provide adequate representation. Even large samples, if improperly selected, can lead to invalid conclusions. Bartz (1976) maintains that sample size is not nearly so important as sample accuracy. Best and Kahn (2003) agree that care in selecting the sample is more important than increasing the size of the sample.

Exercise 7.2

Mark these statements about samples (T) true or (F) false.

_____ 1. Samples are not necessary if data can easily be obtained from the entire population.

_____ 2. Convenience samples, because participants are included by happenstance, can be considered equivalent to random samples.

_____ 3. You might wish to use stratified sampling if you were studying the differences between males and females.

_____ 4. If a convenience sample is as large as 100, we can assume it reflects the population.

_____ 5. A carefully selected sample of 25 may well be more indicative of the population than a poorly selected sample of 1,000.

TABLE 7.1 Foci, Data, Sources, and Samples

Research Focus	Data Required	Data Source	Type of Sample
Social behavior	Descriptions	Participants Settings	Clustered Judgmental
Past status/conditions	Descriptions	Settings Records Documents Informants	Usually none
Present status/conditions	Descriptions Scores Measurements Opinions Statements Analyses	Participants Procedures Settings Objects Records Documents Informants	Random Stratified Clustered Systematic Judgmental
Correlation/prediction	Scores Measurements Categorizations Rankings	Participants	Random Stratified Clustered Systematic
Innovation	Descriptions Scores Measurements Opinions Analyses	Participants Procedures Settings Objects Documents Informants	Clustered Convenience
Evaluation	Descriptions Scores Measurements Opinions Analyses Statements	Participants Procedures Settings Objects Documents Informants	Random Stratified Clustered Systematic Judgmental
Causation	Scores Measurements	Participants	Random Stratified Clustered Systematic

Relationships among Research Focus, Data, Source, and Sample

We have noted that types of research have particular foci, that those foci suggest kinds of data required and the sources of those data, and that focus and data help indicate whether a sample will be needed when obtaining data. Table 7.1 depicts the relationships among research focus, data required, sources of data, and type of sample that might be indicated.

> **Exercise 7.3**
>
> Answer the following.
>
> 1. Which research focus is least likely to limit data to scores and measurements?
> 2. Which research focus is most likely to limit data to scores and measurements?
> 3. Why are cluster samples so often used in educational research?
> 4. What distinction was made between scores and measurements?
> 5. Why don't relationship/prediction studies make use of opinions and statements?

Validity and Reliability in Data Collection

Before we consider the general procedures involved in data collection, let us take a moment to review the concepts of data validity and reliability, which must be kept in mind when collecting data.

Validity of Data

Research Navigator.c⊛m
validity

Validity, an essential quality in research data, has to do with whether the data are, in fact, what they are believed or purported to be—in other words, did we *actually* measure what we intended to measure, based on the focus of our research? If you go to a writing clinic expecting to learn how to plot fictional stories but find that the information presented has to do only with how to sell your stories, the information you receive in the clinic is not appropriate for your purposes. Though the data might have been entirely accurate, the information was not what it was purported to be, or what you believed it would be. Hence, from your perspective, the information was invalid. In the same sense, scores obtained from a test of critical thinking are valid if they represent the ability to think critically, as distinct from knowledge of vocabulary or reading skill. The determination of the validity of data ultimately has a substantial effect on the interpretation of those data, once they have been analyzed, and the subsequent conclusions drawn from those results.

Determining Validity of Test Data

Presently, validity is seen as a unitary concept (AERA, APA, NCME, 1999), combining that which was previously described as four distinct types of validity: content, concurrent, predictive, and construct. It is defined as the "degree to which all the accumulated evidence supports the intended interpretation of test scores for the proposed purpose" (p. 11). Validity of data obtained from the administration of tests (usually quantitative data) can be determined through the examination of various sources of evidence of validity. Although similar to the four outdated types of validity, the five sources of validity evidence are unique in their own right.

***Evidence of Validity Based on* Test Content.**   This source of evidence is based on the relationship between the content addressed on a test, or other instrument used for data collection, and the underlying *construct* (or characteristic) it is trying to measure. This type of evidence often includes logical analysis of content coverage on the test, as well as the judgments of experts in the particular content field.

***Evidence of Validity Based on* Response Processes.**   This source of validity evidence often results from the analysis of individual sets of responses from a test. Examining patterns of response or questioning respondents about the performance or strategies they used on a particular test can provide insight into the specific characteristics actually being measured by a set of test items.

***Evidence of Validity Based on* Internal Structure.**   Analysis of the internal structure of a given test involves an examination of the extent to which the relationships among the test items conform to or parallel the construct actually being measured. Often subsets of test items that on the surface appear to be measuring the construct of interest actually are measuring something slightly or even drastically different.

***Evidence Based on* Relations to Other Variables .**   Analyses of the relationships between test scores and other measures of the same or similar constructs can provide evidence of the validity of the scores resulting from the instrument of interest. These other similar measures might include other tests or inventories or performance (e.g., "hands-on") criteria that purport to measure the same thing.

***Evidence Based on* Consequences of Testing.**   Testing, as well as any other type of data collection, is done with the expectation that some benefit will be realized from the intended and appropriate use of the scores. The process of validation should indicate whether these specific benefits are likely to be realized. Examples of these benefits include improved academic achievement, increased self-esteem, or improved motivation. At a minimum, testing (as well as other forms of data collection) should not have a detrimental effect.

Determining Validity of Non-Test Data

Validity of qualitative data, as well as quantitative data from non-test measurements, is usually established by experts applying what is called *external criticism*. **External criticism** has to do with establishing that a given information source is *authentic*. Suppose that in research on the history of Elmwood Urban School District, an informant claims to have been present at a closed school board meeting in 1958 at which scandalous information was purportedly discussed and suppressed. The data from the informant pass the test of external criticism only if the informant's presence at the meeting can be verified. Or suppose that it is reported that participants' temperatures were elevated by 0.5 degrees through a given exercise. The data would be considered valid if authentic thermometers were used in accordance with established procedures.

Reliability of Data

Research
Navigator.c✦m
reliability

Reliability, a second essential characteristic of data, refers not to authenticity but to consistency. If you hear three accounts of the aforementioned closed school board meeting, but each account differs as to what happened, who was involved, and what the results were, you can have little confidence in any of the versions you have heard. That is to say, the accounts (the data) are inconsistent and, therefore, unreliable. If, however, each account is essentially similar, the information you have received is consistent and may be considered reliable.

Similarly, if you administer a certain test repeatedly under identical circumstances but find that you get different results each time, you would conclude that the test is unreliable. If, however, you get similar results each time you administer the test, you would consider the results reliable and, therefore, potentially useful.

Determining Reliability of Test Data

Research
Navigator.c✦m
test-retest
reliability

Reliability of test data is usually established by correlating the test results with themselves. Three different methods are used—test-retest, equivalent forms, and split-half.

The *test-retest method* involves administering a given test to a group of participants and then, perhaps a week later, again administering the same test to the same people. The scores from the first and second administrations are correlated and the resultant coefficient of correlation provides an index of reliability—the higher the correlation coefficient (i.e., as it approaches 1.00), the more reliable the test.

The *equivalent forms method* of determining reliability is similar to the test-retest method, except that in this case two different forms of the test are available for measuring the same thing. Form A of the test is administered to a group of individuals, and soon thereafter form B is administered to those same individuals. The two sets of scores are correlated and the resultant coefficient serves as the index of reliability. Again, a high coefficient indicates the test has good reliability.

Research
Navigator.c✦m
internal
consistency

The *split-half method* determines a specific form of reliability known as *internal consistency.* The use of this approach is appropriate when testing a single group on two occasions is not feasible, or when an alternate form of a test is not available. The split-half method involves dividing a given test into two parts, such as the even-numbered items and the odd-numbered items. The test is administered to a group of individuals. Two scores are obtained for each person—in this situation, a score for even-numbered items and a score for odd-numbered items. Those two sets of scores are then correlated and the resultant coefficient is the test's index of reliability.

You may come across other measures of internal consistency reliability in the research literature. Two commonly reported measures are Kuder-Richardson (KR) reliability and Cronbach's alpha (α) reliability. Without going into great detail, these two measures are both basically averages of all possible split-half reliabilities. Their interpretations are similar to the split-half reliability coefficient—a high KR reliability or high α both indicate good reliability.

Determining Reliability of Non-Test Data

Reliability of quantitative data is established through consistency. If similar data are found by different but equally qualified researchers, the data are considered reliable. So are data that are similar when acquired before and after a time interval. Reliability of qualitative data, however, is relatively difficult to establish objectively (Vierra & Pollock, 1988). The prime requirement is consistency. Investigators, therefore, attempt to check multiple sources of qualitative data to reassure themselves that the information is consistent, and in addition they think carefully about the procedures used to obtain the data and about the trustworthiness of their sources of informants (Borg, Gall, & Gall, 1999).

In making this effort, investigators are applying **internal criticism,** which has to do with determining the *credibility* of data. In the example given of an informant reporting on a school board meeting held in 1958, even if the informant can substantiate being present at the 1958 board meeting (thereby satisfying authenticity of the source), internal criticism must be applied to determine whether the informant's contentions are reliable. One approach is to compare what the informant says against what is said by other informants, or against records or written accounts. Logical interpretation also plays a strong role in internal criticism, and researchers must answer for themselves questions such as: Do these contentions make sense? Could the events have happened? Can persuasive arguments be made for or against them? To reiterate, the use of internal criticism requires a high degree of subjectivity on the part of the researchers.

Relationship between Validity and Reliability

We often think of validity and reliability as two distinct concepts, but in fact they share an important relationship. It is possible for scores obtained from an instrument to be reliable (consistent) but not valid (measuring something other than what was intended). In contrast, scores cannot be both valid and unreliable—if scores measure what was intended to be measured, it is implied that they will do so consistently. Therefore, reliability is a necessary, but not sufficient, condition for validity. When establishing the validity and reliability of your research data, always remember the following adage: *A valid test is always reliable, but a reliable test is not necessarily valid.*

Procedures in Data Collection

Suppose an investigator has identified a research topic and has located appropriate sources of information. How does he or she now go about collecting the data needed to answer the research questions or test the hypotheses? The general procedures for collecting data were introduced in Chapter 2 and are discussed here more fully.

Data are collected by means of six general procedures: notation, description, analysis, questioning, testing, and measurement.

Notation

Characteristics.   Notation is the process of making very brief written notes, tally marks, or evaluation symbols about people, objects, settings, or events being observed. All types of research can make use of data collected through notation; descriptive research almost always does so. Notation is tied to observation: You observe and make notes about what is seen or heard. This procedure involves what its label implies.

Tools.   No tools other than paper and a pencil or other marking device are needed for notation.

Data Format.   Using notation, you may record data in the sequence they are observed or slot data into categories that correspond to elements receiving special attention in the research. In the first case, one might observe teachers interacting in meetings and attempt to make notes of what occurs at certain times. For example, you might observe ongoing interaction and make tally marks in categories such as who is talking, the nature of what is said, who responds to whom, who defers to whom, constructive comments, destructive comments, and so forth. This notational technique is frequently used in descriptive research.

Description

Characteristics.   Description is the process of putting observations into verbal form but goes further than notation by attempting to convey complete pictures, replete with detail. Description is used when information cannot be measured but only observed and described, as is typically the case for behaviors, routines, interactions, and linguistic patterns.

The descriptive process is usually used in ethnographic research, and often in descriptive and action research. Ethnographic research in particular relies heavily on the richness of observational data, especially detailed descriptions of settings, participants, and phenomena. The data are obtained by a careful observer who enters into a social setting and observes and records as much as possible. The investigator's mere presence will for a while influence participants' behavior; some time may pass before group members resume their natural behaviors. The observer ordinarily tries not to influence events or behaviors, but simply records fully what is seen and heard. However, because the observer sometimes becomes a functional member of the group being studied, the group's behavior is necessarily influenced by the investigator's presence.

The investigator usually makes a large quantity of notes, which must later be summarized and organized into an overall picture of occurrences, situations, and contexts. The objective of this data-gathering procedure is not simply to present an accurate picture, though accuracy is certainly important, but also to identify topics, categories, and patterns of behavior within the natural setting, to be used in answering the research questions.

Although naturalistic observation and description are difficult to do well, this type of research and data gathering is being used with increasing frequency, especially in educational settings. A kindergarten teacher, for example, might study patterns of personal interaction, dominance, and submission among children on the playground, observing and making careful notes about actions and verbal interchanges while an aide oversees the children. A middle-grades teacher might study changes, over time, in language patterns by students learning English as a second language. An administrative intern might study the dynamics of teacher adjustment to mandated curriculum changes, in an effort to describe and explain the natural patterns of cooperation, resistance, and scapegoating as the changes are implemented.

Tools.   No special tools are needed for collecting data by means of description. Many researchers use only pencils and notebooks, while others use audio and video recorders. Unfortunately, recording devices tend to affect human behavior being observed, thereby distorting the data.

Data Format.   The data obtained through written description may fill only a single page or, as is usually the case for ethnographic research, may result in voluminous quantities of notes. Structured formats may or may not be used to organize data as they are being collected, but the data must ultimately be organized so they relate to the research questions or hypotheses.

Analysis

Characteristics.   The term *analysis* has three separate meanings in research. One meaning is associated with obtaining data, as one might analyze a book, an article, or an individual's behavior as a part of data gathering. In this kind of analysis, objects, documents, procedures, and other behaviors are broken down into constituent parts, to determine the nature of those parts, how they relate to each other, and how they function together as a whole.

A second meaning of analysis refers to a product: It is the verbal or written result of the analytical process. For example, you might refer to a completed analysis of the school curriculum or the final analysis of Mr. Baker's teaching methods.

The third meaning of the term *analysis* has to do with making sense of data after they have been collected. This process involves applying statistical treatments to quantitative data or applying logical treatments to qualitative data. You already know something of the terms and meanings used in statistical data analysis, and in Chapter 8 and Appendix A you will find more about analysis of both quantitative and qualitative data.

Here we concern ourselves with the first of the three meanings of analysis, which has to do with obtaining data from objects, settings, and procedures. This involves careful scrutiny to discover traits, procedures, meanings, and relationships. Unlike observation, which is broad and all-encompassing, by using analysis you attempt to find specific information to answer specific questions. Journal articles may be analyzed to identify content, treatment, bias, or change over time. Apparatus may be analyzed to assess specific elements of form, function, and quality. Curriculum guides may be analyzed to determine concordance with a school system's stated goals.

Tool.   To help ensure the quality of data obtained by analysis, an analysis guide should be used in the process. This tool should stipulate what is being sought and might include criteria and examples for determining the presence and quality of the desired elements. For example, a guide for analyzing a series of elementary school science textbooks might include criteria such as:

- Corresponds to stated goals of the science program (Goals of the elementary science program are listed and can be checked off.)
- Provides clear, unambiguous statements of intended leanings
- Emphasizes a hands-on approach to learning science through classroom activities
- Is written at an appropriate level of difficulty
- In teacher's edition, specifies needed materials and provides suggestions for obtaining and using those materials

The analysis guide would continue in this way, including all the elements being considered in the textbook series.

Data Format.   Data resulting from analysis may be either verbal or numerical. Those data should be put into formats that parallel the structure of the analysis guide.

Questioning

Characteristics.   Questioning is a prompting process used to elicit and probe responses from participants and informants. In research, questioning is typically done through interview and survey.

The **interview** is conducted in person: The interviewer asks questions directly of respondents, either face-to-face or by telephone. The process involves a one-to-one exchange that permits the interviewer to pose questions and when necessary probe or otherwise follow up to obtain clearer responses in greater depth. Teachers doing graduate research often use interviews for purposes such as obtaining community opinion concerning quality of school programs.

Interviews, however, are time- and cost-intensive, which limits the number of respondents that can be included in most research projects, especially projects done by graduate students. If too few respondents are interviewed, the data are not likely to represent the population. Investigators, therefore, hope to interview at least 30 respondents, a number that is usually feasible in descriptive research, though historical research sometimes cannot identify more than a few respondents, if any.

**Research
Navigator.c⊛m**

cross-sectional
survey

longitudinal
survey

Surveys, a second structured procedure for questioning respondents, are usually done by means of printed questionnaires mailed to large samples, though surveys can also be done by telephone. Surveys are used to obtain data cross-sectionally as well as longitudinally. A **cross-sectional survey** collects data across different segments of the population at a particular time. It shows the status of those segments but cannot clearly depict changes that might be occurring. If one wished to determine the educational levels of parents of Elmwood students, for example, a cross-sectional survey would be appropriate.

In **longitudinal surveys** the researcher obtains data from the same or similar samples over time, and as a result can reveal changes in opinion or status. If one wished to document changes in Elmwood residents' evaluations of Elmwood schools, a longitudinal survey, in which the same questions would be asked of participants each time the survey was done, would be appropriate. Excellent examples of cross-sectional and longitudinal surveys can be seen in the annual Gallup Poll of the public's attitude toward the schools. This poll, sponsored by Phi Delta Kappa, has been conducted each year since 1969 and published in the journal *Phi Delta Kappan.*

Compared to the interview, the survey tends to be broader in scope and less personal in nature. Surveys do not typically probe responses as do interviews and normally do not provide for additional questioning that could clarify answers or allow respondents to raise concerns.

The questions used in surveys are sometimes open-ended but more frequently are accompanied by response choices preselected by the investigator. Asking respondents to select response *a, b,* or *c* makes it easier to tabulate and analyze survey results than if open-ended questions are used, but this approach may curtail important information being brought to light.

An advantage of surveys over interviews is that surveys usually require less time investment per respondent than do interviews. One might consider using written questionnaires mailed out to survey 1,000 people, but only under very unusual circumstances could 1,000 people be interviewed personally. At the same time, interviews provide 100 percent return, whereas a much smaller return results from written surveys; respondents are either disinterested or will not take the time to write and return their responses.

Tools. The collection of data through questioning is enhanced through the use of four tools: interview guide, questionnaire, Likert scale, and the semantic differential. Interviews are managed through the use of an interview guide, which contains questions sequenced in the order they are to be put to respondents. Follow-up questions should be included for probing or clarifying. Great care should be exercised here, as it is difficult for interviewers to pose questions and probe answers without improperly leading respondents' answers.

The questions included on the interview guide can be highly structured, semistructured, or open-ended, as shown in the following examples:

Highly **structured question:** Of the following three aspects of Elmwood schools, which one do you consider to be highest in quality?

1. Teachers
2. Buildings and grounds
3. Books and equipment

Semistructured question: Elmwood elementary teachers have made an effort to communicate with parents more frequently than in the past. What have you liked best about the communication you have received? What have you liked least about it?

Open-ended question: What suggestions can you make for improving the quality of Elmwood middle schools?

Research Navigator.com

questionnaire

A second tool useful in questioning is the **questionnaire,** employed in research in which data are collected by means of a written survey. The same types of items are included on questionnaires as on interview guides. Because it is essential that the respondents answer and return the questionnaires, the appearance of the instrument must be as appealing as possible. It should be uncluttered and pleasant to look at. Relatively few items should be included, directions should be simple, and responses should be easy to make; otherwise, respondents will put the material aside and neglect to return it. The response rate, always a concern when surveys are used, can be increased by indicating in the cover letter how little time will be required to respond thoughtfully and by stressing the potential value of the responses and the research. Other suggestions for increasing response rate include contacting respondents in advance and expressing appreciation, including a token monetary payment such as a dollar bill, and using follow-up mailings to respondents who do not reply (Clark & Boser, 1989; Hopkins & Gullickson, 1989).

Research
Navigator.c⊕m
Likert scale
Likert-type scale

A third tool useful in questioning is the **Likert scale,** an instrument composed of statements that permit responses along an "agree…disagree" continuum, such as: strongly agree, agree, neutral, disagree, strongly disagree. Likert scale items used in a questionnaire might appear as shown in Figure 7.3. *Likert-type* items also utilize response scales that exist on a continuum, but the continuum differs from the "agree…disagree" form of a true Likert item. For example, a Likert-type item might require participants to respond on a scale which examines quality ("excellent…poor"), frequency of occurrence ("always… never"), or level of comfort ("very comfortable…not at all comfortable").

Research
Navigator.c⊕m
semantic
differential

A fourth tool used in questioning, the **semantic differential scale,** presents pairs of adjectives related to a word or phrase. A continuum, usually consisting of seven blanks, is given between the pairs of adjectives. Respondents mark the blank along the continuum that represents their view. Figure 7.4 shows the typical appearance of the semantic differential scale.

In both Likert and semantic differential scales, a scoring system can be used that assigns values to the categories, such as 1 for the most negative to 7 for the most positive on the semantic differential, or 1 for "strongly disagree" to 5 for "strongly agree" on the Likert scale. The scoring must be done with care, for items on Likert and semantic differential scales are usually constructed so that their positive and negative sides are not always located in the same place, as shown in Figures 7.4 and 7.5. This is done to cause respondents to think about their responses rather than mark all items the same.

Data Format.   Two kinds of responses are obtained in interviews and surveys. They come from open-ended questions, where respondents provide unstructured comments, and

---

FIGURE 7.3   Format of the Likert scale

Instructions: For each statement, circle whether you strongly agree with the statement (SA), agree (A), are undecided (U), disagree (D), or strongly disagree (SD).

1. Teachers in Elmwood school district are, for the most part, overpaid.	SA	A	U	D	SD
2. Elmwood should pass a bond issue to raise money for new school buildings.	SA	A	U	D	SD
3. Racial integration efforts in Elmwood schools reflect community wishes.	SA	A	U	D	SD

FIGURE 7.4   Format of the semantic differential scale

Directions: Mark an X in the appropriate blank between each pair of words, so that your opinion is accurately expressed.

1. Elmwood's efforts concerning bicultural education

        effective — — — — — ineffective

             fair — — — — — unfair

        too little — — — — — too much

     well planned — — — — — haphazard

2. Elmwood's treatment of different ethnic groups

        considerate — — — — — inconsiderate

           ignorant — — — — — knowledgeable

        not helpful — — — — — helpful

structured questions, where respondents select from among responses provided. The open-ended responses are collated as they are written by respondents, and if categories of response can be foreseen, the responses can be channeled into those categories as they are received. Responses that do not fit any preselected categories must be analyzed and categorized at a later time. Structured responses, on the other hand, can be tabulated as they are received. If relatively few different responses are possible, the tabulations can be made directly on a copy of the interview guide or questionnaire.

Testing

Characteristics.   *Testing,* as the term is used here, is the process of obtaining data by having participants respond to written or oral examinations. More has been written about

INTRODUCTION TO EDUCATIONAL RESEARCH
Companion Website Highlight

The Companion Website that accompanies this text (www.ablongman.com/mertler5e) includes several examples of surveys which have been used in actual research studies. These surveys exemplify the use of Likert and Likert-type questions and include both open-ended and structured survey items. Examine these surveys, looking for differing characteristics as they have been described in the text.

test construction, administration, scoring, and interpretation than about all other aspects of educational measurement combined. Researchers like to use tests because the numerical data they offer seem more precise than verbal data. However, proponents of qualitative research generally disagree with that point, contending that a verbal description of Juan's mathematics achievement is more accurate and informative than the numerical scores that might be assigned to his test performance.

Research Navigator.com

criterion-referenced tests

norm-referenced tests

Tools.   Tests are the tools used in collecting data through testing. Two general types of tests are commonly used in educational research—criterion-referenced tests and standardized tests. **Criterion-referenced tests** are constructed so that each test item relates directly to an instructional objective, toward which classwork has been directed. Attainment of such objectives is the goal for both teacher and class, and the ideal result would be for all students to respond correctly to all items. No distribution of scores is desired. Criterion-referenced tests are used to judge the quality of educational programs and to assess minimum proficiency levels for students.

Norm-referenced tests are carefully constructed tests, usually commercial, that are designed not to show the attainment of specific objectives but to show how individuals

---

Applying Technology: **Survey Construction**

Often researchers have a specific research topic in mind and know what kind of data are needed in order to answer the related research questions. Unfortunately, as is many times the case, there may be no existing survey instrument available that could be used to collect these data. The researcher is left to develop the survey so that it specifically addresses his or her research needs. In his page titled "Constructing the Survey" (http://trochim.human.cornell.edu/kb/survwrit.htm), Dr. Trochim provides a superb discussion, complete with excellent examples, of:

- The various types of questions that can be used in survey research
  (http://trochim.human.cornell.edu/kb/questype.htm)

- Different methods of structuring response formats
  (http://trochim.human.cornell.edu/kb/quesresp.htm)

- Different ways to word questions in order to avoid misinterpretation
  (http://trochim.human.cornell.edu/kb/quesword.htm)

- Suggestions on where to place specific types of questions within the actual survey
  (http://trochim.human.cornell.edu/kb/quesplac.htm)

Developing surveys for research studies is not an easy task, as many people assume. It requires time, practice, and experience. Anyone who is considering collecting data via self-developed surveys is urged to examine the Web pages listed previously for critically important and essential suggestions and recommendations.

Research
Navigator.c⊕m
standardized tests

(and schools and school districts) compare with one another. The score that an individual makes on a norm-referenced test is translated into a converted score, such as a percentile, stanine, or grade-equivalent that enables relative standing to be shown.

Commercial **standardized tests,** typically norm-referenced, are constructed with great precision by professional test makers. These tests are intended to disperse scores across a wide range corresponding to the normal probability curve, thus differentiating among the individuals taking the test. Standardized tests are available in astonishing variety and number; more than 9,000 published and unpublished tests are listed in the Educational Testing Service database.

Standardized tests are accompanied by norms (hence, the label *norm-referenced*) that permit comparisons of individuals, schools, and school systems. The norms are compiled from the responses of thousands of individuals believed to reflect a cross section of the national population. Standardized tests usually have very high levels of validity and reliability.

As mentioned, a great deal has been written about tests, test construction, establishing validity and reliability, using tests properly, and interpreting results correctly. For information about commercial tests, one of the best sources is *The Fifteenth Mental Measurements Yearbook* (Plake, Impara, & Spies, 2003), which includes critical reviews of well over 250 tests, with more than 1,800 references related to the construction, use, and limitations of those tests. A similarly valuable reference is *A Consumer's Guide to Tests in Print* (Hammill, Brown, & Bryant, 1989). Good information on standardized and teacher-made tests can be found in textbooks such as those authored by McMillan (2001) and Mertler (2003).

Data Format.   Most of the data obtained through testing are, initially, raw numerical scores. In some cases they will be rankings or listings by category. Raw scores may be

---

Applying Technology: Searchable Online Test Locators

In many research instances, it is not necessary for researchers to develop their own survey or other data collection instrument. Researchers, as part of previous research studies, may have developed and/or utilized an instrument that ideally meets their needs in terms of desirable data to be collected. Fortunately, several organizations provide searchable databases of such tests and other survey materials. Two such databases are:

- The Educational Testing Service (ETS) Test Collection (http://testcollection.ets.org)
- The Mental Measurements Yearbook's Test Reviews Online (http://buros.unl.edu/buros/jsp/search.jsp)

These databases can be searched by keyword, author, publisher, or acronym. Search results typically provide a description of the instrument (including the authors, publisher, availability, descriptors, and abstract) and how it may be obtained. Both tests, inventories, and surveys that are free and those that are available for a nominal fee are included in the databases.

converted into percentiles, stanines, grade equivalents, or other derived scores. Rankings may be placed into ordered position as they are received and tallied. Categorical responses are tallied in the appropriate categories.

Measurement

Characteristics. Measurement assesses traits and abilities by means other than testing. The assessments are assigned numerical values or can be placed in categories or rankings. Measurement obtains information by comparing participants' performance or status against an established scale, a procedure that first helps determine the extent or quality of a variable trait and, second, permits assigning a value to it.

Research Navigator.com

measurement scale

Testing is sometimes used synonymously with *measurement,* especially in the context of educational research, but the two terms do not have the same meaning. *Measurement* is the broader generic term, widely applicable to human and other natural phenomena. It makes use of measurement scales, which include (1) **interval scales,** consisting of raw numbers (e.g., 34, 43, 48); (2) **ordinal scales,** which show position in rank (e.g., first, fifteenth, thirtieth); and (3) **nominal scales,** which assign individuals to named categories (e.g., fast, medium, slow). As indicated, the value obtained through measurement is most often a cardinal number but may also be an ordinal number or a named category.

Tools. Measurement tools used in data collection are numerous and varied, but all of these tools are scales designed to obtain indices of traits, such as physical characteristics (e.g., weight, height, temperature), physical performance (e.g., speed, accuracy, endurance), or mental acuity (e.g., sees the point, responds appropriately).

When ready-made measuring scales do not exist, researchers often prepare their own scales. This requires composing a list of traits or task elements, together with a set of scoring criteria. Task elements ensure that overall performance is observed. Scoring may be done in terms of accuracy, time required, or other criteria; the scoring procedures should be specified in advance. An example of such scales are instruments used to assess the performance of teachers and student teachers. In these instruments, assessment is done in several different categories, such as "relates positively with students" and "is well prepared to teach lessons." Within such categories, an evaluator judges teacher performance against a set of criteria such as:

Category:	relates positively with students
Criteria:	calls students by name
	makes positive, supportive comments
	takes time to talk with students individually
	gives regular attention to all students

Data Format. Data obtained through measurement are most often numerical, though they may also be verbal, nominal, or ordinal. All are categorized so as to parallel the study's research questions or hypotheses.

TABLE 7.2   Data Collection Procedures Typically Used in Eight Types of Research

	Data Collection Procedures						
	Research	*Notation*	*Description*	*Analysis*	*Questioning*	*Testing*	*Measurement*
Ethnographic	*	*					
Historical	*	*	*				
Descriptive	*	*	*	*	*	*	*
Correlational					*	*	*
Action		*	*	*	*	*	*
Evaluation		*	*	*	*	*	*
Causal-comparative					*	*	*
Experimental					*	*	*

Relationships between Types of Research and Data Collection

Table 7.2 shows the data collection procedures typically used in the eight types of research.

Exercise 7.4

From the following list, determine the best response to each of the 10 definitions: (L) Likert scale, (C) criteria, (R) raw score, (Q) qualitative data, (N) nominal scale, (V) validity, (RE) reliability, (T) test, (S) semantic differential, (NO) notation, (A) analysis, (M) measurement, (QS) questionnaire, or (P) percentile.

_____   1. A concern raised when a test is not measuring what it is supposed to measure

_____   2. Using symbols and tally marks in obtaining data

_____   3. A set of standards used in making judgments

_____   4. Breaking something down logically into its constituent parts

_____   5. Obtaining data through use of a thermometer

_____   6. A numerical score that has not been manipulated or converted

_____   7. A device for obtaining opinions in written form

_____   8. A device that prompts individuals to indicate whether they agree or disagree

_____   9. A broad type of data that is difficult to analyze through statistical procedures

_____ 10. A measurement scale that assigns individuals to categories

TABLE 7.3   A Composite of Research Types and Data Collection Procedures

Research	Focus	Pertinent Data	Sources	Collection	Tools
Ethnographic	Social behavior	Descriptions	Participants Settings	Description	Recorders Pencil-paper Camera
Historical	Past events and conditions	Descriptions Analyses Statements	Settings Objects Records Documents Informants	Analysis Questioning	Guides Criteria
Descriptive	Present events and conditions	Descriptions Opinions Analyses Statements Scores Measurements	Participants Procedures Settings Objects Records Documents Informants	Notation Descriptions Analysis Questioning Testing Measurement	Guides Criteria Questionnaires Measuring devices Tests Scales
Correlational	Relationships Prediction	Scores Measurements	Participants	Testing Measurement	Tests Measuring devices
Action	Innovation	Descriptions Opinions Analyses Scores Measurements	Participants Procedures Settings Objects Documents	Description Analysis Questioning Testing Measurement	Guides Criteria Questionnaires Tests Scales
Evaluation	Judgments	Opinions Analyses Scores Measurements	Participants Procedures Settings Records Objects	Analysis Testing Measurement	Questionnaires Tests Measuring devices
Causal-Comparative	Possible causation	Scores	Participants	Testing Measurement	Tests Measuring devices
Experimental	Causation	Scores	Participants Measurement	Testing Measuring devices	Tests

A Composite of Research Types and Data Collection Procedures

In this chapter we have explored types of research, their particular foci, the kinds of data they require, where those data can be found, how the data can be collected, and which tools are most useful in the various procedures of data collection. All of these elements are interrelated. Table 7.3 presents a juxtaposition of elements and procedures described in the chapter.

Data Collection Profiles

As you become able to organize and conduct your own research, you will find data collection profiles useful in both the planning and the operational phase of research. The information presented to this point enables you to construct data collection profiles for the eight types of educational research. The profiles include focus, data sources, data collection procedures, tools typically used in gathering data, and data formats. The following is a generic data collection profile for ethnographic research. This profile would be completed by supplying the specific information indicated by the question marks. Data profiles for other types of research would be constructed in the same manner.

Generic Data Collection Profile of Ethnographic Research

Focus: Social behavior (of what group?)

Data Sources: Participants (who?), settings (what, where?)

Data Collection Procedure: Description of observations (what is observed?)

Tools: Paper and pencil; camera; recording devices (specify)

Data Format: Detailed written verbal descriptions (of observations made)

▱ DEVELOPMENTAL ACTIVITY

Data Collection Decisions

In the developmental activity for Chapter 6, you began to consider issues of data collection. Here you will make more detailed decisions regarding your proposed data collection, specifically with respect to sampling, instrumentation, and quality assurance (i.e., validity and reliability).

1. My research problem or topic is: _____

   _____.

2. The sample for my study will consist of: _____

_____.

3. The following demographic characteristics are important in my study (*check all that apply*):

☐ age
☐ ethnicity
☐ gender
☐ other: _____

4. The type of sampling I will do is (*check one*):

☐ random
☐ stratified random
☐ cluster
☐ systematic
☐ convenience
☐ other: _____

5. The following is a brief description of the type of data collection instrument I plan to use: _____

_____

_____.

6. With respect to instrumentation, I plan to do the following (*check one*):

☐ use an existing instrument
☐ develop an instrument

7. My independent variable(s) is (are): _____

_____

_____

and can be classified as (*indicate for each variable listed*):

☐ continuous
☐ discrete

8. My dependent variable(s) is (are): _____

_____

_____

and can be classified as (*indicate for each variable listed*):

☐ continuous
☐ discrete

Based on your response to question 6, respond to either question 9 or question 10:

9. I am using an existing instrument. The following is a brief description of the instrument's validity and reliability: _____

_____

_____

_____

_____.

10. I am developing my own instrument. I plan to ensure the validity and reliability of my instrument in the following manner: _____

_____

_____

_____

_____

_____.

(A downloadable, interactive version of this developmental activity is available from the Companion Website, www.ablongman.com/mertler5e)

Chapter Summary

Each type of research has a particular focus—either social behavior, past events, present events, relationships or predictions, innovation, evaluative judgments, or causation. Recognition of focus helps provide guidance in identifying needed data, which can be obtained in the form of descriptions, opinions, analyses, statements, scores, and measurements. These data are obtainable from participants, procedures, settings, objects, records, documents, and informants, and are collected through procedures of notation, description, analysis, questioning, testing, and measurement. Tools helpful in collecting data include marking devices such as pencils, cameras, recorders, guides, lists of criteria, questionnaires, tests, scales (such as the Likert scale), and other measuring devices (such as thermometers or weight scales). The data obtained with these tools and procedures accrue as written verbal descriptions, summarized notations, raw scores, converted scores, categories, and rankings.

Samples are often, but not always, required for data collection. Certain types of research, such as correlational and experimental, depend on samples that accurately represent the population from which they are drawn. Other types of research, such as action and evaluation, use data from the participants and materials available at hand. If a sample is required, a decision must be made concerning whether it is to be random, stratified, cluster, systematic, convenience, snowball, or judgmental.

A further consideration has to do with ensuring validity and reliability of data. For test data, validity and reliability are usually computed through statistical procedures. For qualitative data and non-test quantitative data, validity and reliability are addressed through external criticism, to establish authenticity of source, and internal criticism, to establish accuracy of the information.

Although many aspects of data collection must be kept in mind, they can be summarized for various types of research by composing data collection profiles that specify focus, data sources, data collection procedures, tools, and formats into which data will accrue.

LIST OF IMPORTANT TERMS

chain sampling
cluster sampling
convenience sampling
criterion-referenced test
cross-sectional survey
external criticism
internal criticism
interval scale
interview
judgmental sampling
Likert scale
longitudinal survey

network sampling
nominal scale
nonprobability sampling
norm-referenced test
open-ended questions
ordinal scale
probability sampling
purposive sampling
questionnaire
quota sampling
random sampling
reliability

semantic differential scale
semistructured questions
snowball sampling
standardized test
stratified sampling
structured questions
subjects
survey
systematic sampling
validity

YOUR CURRENT STATUS

You now have a solid beginning knowledge of the procedures by which research data are collected. You know the fundamentals of sample selection. You are mindful of validity and reliability of data. You know the foci of the different types of research, the data they require, the sources of those data, the procedures by which those data are obtained, the tools most useful in obtaining them, and the formats into which data are likely to accrue. You are now ready to proceed to Chapter 8, which deals with analyzing research data and presenting findings. But, first, please respond to the following activities.

ACTIVITIES FOR THOUGHT AND DISCUSSION

1. Refer again to Table 7.4, which summarizes most of the information presented in this chapter. Select a research focus and see if you can talk your way through the elements corresponding to that focus.

2. Explain why samples are very carefully selected in some types of research and not in others.

3. Suppose you wish to investigate how non-Caucasian fictional characters were depicted in children's literature between the years 1900 and 1950. What type of research would this be? What would be its focus? What sources of data would you use? What would you do about selecting a sample? What data collection tools would you consider appropriate?

4. Explain how validity of test data and non-test data is established.

5. Select three types of research and compose a data collection profile for each, as shown in the data collection profile of ethnographic research.

ANSWERS TO CHAPTER EXERCISES

7.1. 1. I 2. D 3. PA 4. O 5. I 6. P 7. R 8. ST

7.2. 1. T 2. F 3. T 4. F 5. T

7.3. 1. Past status or events
2. Causation
3. For practical reasons—they are what is available, without disrupting the educational program unduly

4. Scores refer to test results; *measurement* is the broader term, referring to data obtained through use of measuring devices other than tests.
5. Verbal data, unless it can be categorized, cannot be correlated mathematically.

7.4. 1. V 2. NO 3. C 4. A 5. M 6. R 7. QS 8. L 9. Q 10. N

REFERENCES AND RECOMMENDED READINGS

American Educational Research Association, American Psychological Association, & National Council on Measurement in Education. (1999). *Standards for Educational and Psychological Testing.* Washington, DC: American Educational Research Association.

Babbie, E. (2001). *The Practice of Social Science Research* (9th ed.). Belmont, CA: Wadsworth/Thomson Learning.

Bartz, A. (1976). *Basic Statistical Concepts in Education and the Behavioral Sciences.* Minneapolis: Burgess.

Best, J., & Kahn, J. (2003). *Research in Education* (9th ed.). Boston: Allyn and Bacon.

Bogdan, R., & Biklen, S. (2003). *Qualitative Research in Education: An Introduction to Theory and Methods* (4th ed.). Boston: Allyn and Bacon.

Borg, W., Gall, J., & Gall, M. (1999). *Applying Educational Research: A Practical Guide* (4th ed.). White Plains, NY: Longman.

Clark, S., & Boser, J. (1989). *Seeking Consensus on Empirical Characteristics of Effective Mail Questionnaires: A First Step.* Paper presented at the annual meeting of the American Educational Research Association, San Francisco.

Gay, L., & Airasian, P. (2000). *Educational Research: Competencies for Analysis and Application* (6th ed.). Upper Saddle River, NJ: Merrill.

Glesne, C. (1999). *Becoming Qualitative Researchers: An Introduction* (2nd ed.). New York: Longman.

Hammill, D., Brown, L., & Bryant, B. (1989). *A Consumer's Guide to Tests in Print.* Austin, TX: PRO-ED.

Hopkins, K., & Gullickson, A. (1989). *Monetary Gratuities in Survey Research: A Meta-Analysis of Their Effects on Response Rates.* Paper presented at the annual meeting of the American Educational Research Association, San Francisco.

McMillan, J. (2004). *Educational Research: Fundamentals for the Consumer* (4th ed.). Boston: Allyn and Bacon.

McMillan, J. (2001). *Classroom Assessment: Principles and Practice for Effective Instruction* (2nd ed.). Boston: Allyn and Bacon.

Mertler, C. A. (2003). *Classroom Assessment: A Practical Guide for Educators.* Los Angeles: Pyrczak.

Plake, B., Impara, J., & Spies, A. (eds.). (2003). *The Fifteenth Mental Measurements Yearbook.* Lincoln, NE: University of Nebraska Press.

Trochim, W. M. (2002). *Research Methods Knowledge Base* (2nd ed.). Available at trochim.human.cornell.edu/kb/index.htm

Vierra, A., & Pollock, J. (1988). *Reading Educational Research.* Scottsdale, AZ: Gorsuch Scarisbrick.

PREVIEW

Research can yield two different kinds of data:

- Qualitative data
- Quantitative data

Both types of data must be analyzed as one attempts to:

- Answer research questions and/or
- Test hypotheses

Qualitative data are expressed verbally and are analyzed logically, using this process to

- Identify topics
- Cluster topics into categories
- Form categories into patterns
- Make explanations from the patterns
- Use the explanations to answer research questions

Quantitative data are expressed numerically and are analyzed statistically, which usually involves

- Making descriptions of the data, using measures of
  - Central tendency
  - Variability
  - Relative standing
  - Correlation
- Making inferences about the population, by means of
  - Confidence limits
  - Significance levels

Once data are analyzed, the results are reported as

- Research findings

Targeted Learnings

Chapter 7 explained how original data are obtained in various kinds of research. In this chapter, we explore how those data are typically analyzed in order to help answer research questions or test hypotheses, and further, how analyzed data are presented as research findings. The chapter examines the differences between analysis of qualitative data and analysis of quantitative data. General approaches used in analyzing both kinds of data are presented. With regard to statistical analyses, we concern ourselves more with the concepts of analysis than with actual calculations: Statistical calculations are treated in greater depth in Appendix A.

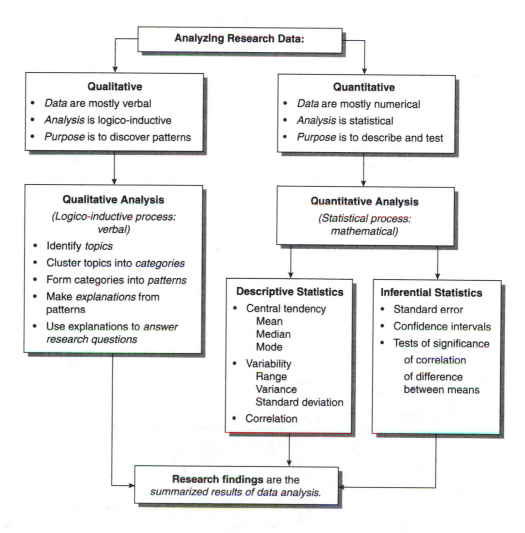

As you read the chapter, look especially for information related to the following questions:

1. What is the general purpose of data analysis in all types of research?
2. Why are qualitative data and quantitative data analyzed differently?
3. How are qualitative data analyzed?
4. How are quantitative data analyzed?
5. What are the relationships among populations, parameters, samples, and statistics?
6. What is the difference between descriptive statistics and inferential statistics?
7. What does *significance* mean in statistics?
8. What is the relationship between data analysis and research findings?

Qualitative Data and Quantitative Data

Research Navigator.com

qualitative data

quantitative data

Earlier you learned that research makes use of two kinds of data: *qualitative data,* which are mostly verbal, and *quantitative data,* which are mostly numerical. Sometimes, both kinds are collected and analyzed in the same study. The type of data one obtains is determined by the type of research being conducted. Table 8.1 shows the kinds of data that are most commonly sought in the various types of research.

Once collected, both qualitative and quantitative data usually must be analyzed before adequate interpretations can be made. Analysis helps to do four things: (1) describe the data clearly; (2) identify what is typical and atypical among the data; (3) bring to light differences, relationships, and other patterns existent in the data; and ultimately (4) answer research questions or test hypotheses.

TABLE 8.1   The Type of Data Analysis Most Commonly Used in Each Type of Research

	Typical Data Analysis Procedures	
Research	*Qualitative*	*Quantitative*
Ethnographic	•	
Historical	•	•
Descriptive	•	•
Correlational		•
Evaluation	•	•
Action	•	•
Causal-comparative		•
Experimental		•

While all data analysis aims at the same general goals, qualitative and quantitative data are analyzed quite differently. Qualitative data are analyzed **logico-inductively,** a thought process that uses logic to make sense of observations, in which

- Observations are made of behaviors, situations, interactions, objects, and environments
- Topics are identified from the observations and are scrutinized to discover patterns and categories
- Conclusions are induced from what is observed and are stated verbally
- Those conclusions are used to answer the research questions

Quantitative data, in contrast, are analyzed mathematically, and the results are expressed in statistical terminology. Essentially, statistical analysis is used to

- Depict what is typical and atypical among the data
- Show degrees of difference or relationship between two or more variables
- Determine the likelihood that the findings are real for the population as opposed to having occurred only by chance in the sample

Research Navigator.c⊕m

qualitative analysis

An Example of Qualitative Analysis

Suppose we are conducting historical research into education as it took place in 1935 in Bodie, now a ghost town. One portion of the research has to do with depicting a typical winter's day for sixth-grade students attending Bodie School. We pose the following main research question:

What was a typical January school day like for sixth-grade students attending Bodie School in 1935?

To help answer that question, we also state a number of subquestions, of which the following are examples:

1. What time did school start in the mornings?
2. What would students probably have to do before starting out for school?
3. What was the weather like in January?
4. How did the students get from home to school?
5. Of what did the morning curriculum consist?
6. What did students do for recess and lunch?
7. Of what did the afternoon curriculum consist?
8. What was the classroom environment like?
9. What books and instructional materials were used?
10. At what time was school dismissed?
11. What would students probably have to do after being dismissed from school?
12. What sort of homework was assigned, and how much time did it require?

By answering subquestions like these, we should ultimately be able to compile a satisfactory answer to the main research question. Some of the answers to subquestions might be found among the relics left in Bodie School. A class plan book or grade book might help answer questions about the curriculum, as would textbooks and other instructional materials. How students got from home to school and back might be revealed in the presence of skis or snowshoes, and student compositions might be found that would shed further light regarding how they traveled. The data obtained from these sources would be mostly verbal in nature and would be analyzed logically by matching evidence to research subquestions. It is unlikely that any mathematical or statistical treatments would be required.

Research
Navigator.c⊕m
quantitative
analysis

An Example of Quantitative Analysis

Suppose we have been asked by the Bureau of Indian Affairs to help explore various aspects of academic achievement among Native American students attending boarding schools on a large reservation. One of the specific requests is for information about science achievement among eighth-grade students. Many teachers on reservation schools say that their students retain cultural and religious beliefs about natural phenomena that contradict concepts presented in the school science program and that consequently affect science achievement. We are asked to determine whether students do in fact retain such beliefs and, if they do, to investigate whether adherence to those beliefs is related to achievement in science. To guide our research, we state two hypotheses, both in the null form:

Hypothesis 1. No difference exists between eighth-grade students attending schools on the reservation and a matched group of eighth-grade rural Anglo students, as concerns adherence to cultural beliefs that contradict science concepts taught in school.

Hypothesis 2. No relationship exists between science achievement and adherence to cultural beliefs that contradict science concepts taught in school.

For Hypothesis 1, we decide to administer to students a test designed to reveal the frequency with which they select culture-linked nonscientific responses rather than correct scientific responses to specially designed test items. From this test we can obtain mean scores and patterns of scores for a sample of Native American students and also for a sample of rural Anglo students, which we will use for comparison. If differences between the two groups are found, we will test the null hypothesis (tests for this purpose are described later in the chapter). If we are able to reject the null hypothesis—which would mean that any difference we found was probably *not* due to errors made in selecting the samples but actually represents *real* differences in the population—we could then conclude that the two populations are different in their adherence to nonscientific cultural beliefs.

To test Hypothesis 2, we will need to compute correlations between scores made by Native American students on two tests: the science achievement test and the test designed to indicate adherence to nonscientific beliefs. If we are able to reject the null hypothesis of "no correlation," we can conclude that a relationship probably *does* exist in the population between science achievement and adherence to nonscientific cultural beliefs.

Analyzing Ethnographic Data

The Bodie School and Native American illustrations indicate the general difference between approaches to obtaining and analyzing qualitative and quantitative research data. The analysis of ethnographic data, however, requires an approach that is distinct from the example provided for qualitative analysis in historical research. The reason for the difference lies in the nature of ethnographic research, which investigates people and their interactions within social settings. One of its peculiarities is that the questions answered by ethnographic research often emerge after data collection has begun, rather than before data collection, as in other types of research. This happens because pertinent questions in ethnographic research cannot always be foreseen; they may come to light only after considerable data have been collected. Thus, collection of ethnographic data is not necessarily guided by a clearly defined list of questions, where we only collect data that directly pertain to those questions. Instead, many of the most significant questions emerge during the investigation.

A second unusual trait of ethnographic research is that it attempts to draw conclusions from a broad, rather than a limited, picture of human behavior. Voluminous quantities of relatively unstructured data are typically collected in ethnographic research. It is only when preliminary data analysis has narrowed and structured some of the data that the final research questions can be clarified.

To make sense of such unstructured data, researchers employ a systematic procedure of analysis that involves (1) identification of topics, (2) clustering of those topics into categories, (3) forming the categories into patterns, and (4) making explanations from what the patterns suggest. This process does not occur in straight-line sequence but rather as *flux*, with ebb and flow, give and take. The process begins with notes and ends with interpretations, as shown in Figure 8.1. In this configuration, the notes that comprise the data should reflect very accurately what has actually been observed. Accuracy requires that the observer be astute in grasping the overall picture while noting significant details. Often video or audio recordings are used instead of pencil-and-paper notes in order to obtain a more detailed and accurate picture.

As the investigator begins to examine the notes or recordings, he or she identifies specific topics that emerged prominently during the observation periods. For example, if

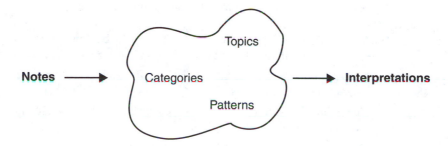

FIGURE 8.1   Procedure of analysis in ethnographic research

one were attempting to study "What Teachers Talk about in the Faculty Lounge," an enormous variety of topics would surface. During the first observation, examples such as the following might appear:

- Why someone was almost late to school
- Whose spouse has been sick
- Displeasure about the upcoming faculty meeting
- What that kid, Johnny Jackson, did (again!)
- The status of the hoped-for salary increase
- How disrespectful students have become
- A motion picture that you really ought to see
- What somebody said about seeing Jack with what's-her-name

The investigator might record notes about these topics as they are discussed and then, later, transfer the notes to separate cards. This transference can be made after the topics begin to reflect specific categories of concern, such as work, leisure, entertainment, and the like. At the same time, the investigator can use the categories as labels for the data cards. Each card can be given a category label that permits regrouping of cards, such as:

(Topic) **Hoped-for Salary Increase**   (Label) **Job Concerns**

—notes—

The labels permit the cards to be reorganized easily into categories such as Family, Employment, Incidentals, Sports, Entertainment, Gossip, Jokes, Problems, Complaints about Students, Complaints about Administrators, and Complaints about Parents.

The investigator does not wait until all data are in before beginning this analytical process. To the contrary, **interim analysis** takes place continually (Gall, Borg, & Gall, 2003). As topics are reorganized into categories, such as Complaints about Students, those categories in turn cause the observer to become even more attentive to behaviors specific to categories and simultaneously to flag behaviors that do not fit and, therefore, call for establishing new categories.

As observation and analysis proceed over time, it becomes evident that categories form themselves into patterns. It may take some time for this phase of analysis to evolve, but sooner or later the investigator will begin to note patterns such as:

Daily patterns: What teachers are likely to talk about on different days of the week, so that, for instance, different patterns might emerge for Mondays and Fridays.

Time-of-the-year patterns: What teachers are likely to talk about at various times of the year and near holidays.

Complaint patterns: The amount of time given over to complaining and the nature of those complaints.

Dominance and submission patterns: Who tends to dominate talk sessions, and who tends to defer to whom.

From such patterns, the investigator ultimately formulates overall interpretations that help depict interactions within the group and setting.

That leads to the interpretation phase, into which one should proceed cautiously. One might be tempted to say that patterns of complaint, for example, are attributable to frustration or insecurity, or that what certain teachers say about students suggests that they harbor an inner hostility toward kids. But such conclusions cannot be made with certainty, and the investigator must be very wary of making such statements. Vierra and Pollock (1988) point out that throughout the investigation, but particularly at the interpretation stage, researchers must remain mindful of questions such as:

- What do I know?
- How can I be sure this knowledge is accurate?
- What other explanations are possible?

Only when these questions can be answered satisfactorily should interpretations be put forward as research conclusions. This entire process is referred to as **logico-inductive analysis** or **hypothetico-inductive analysis,** terms that are used synonymously.

Exercise 8.1

Among the following research topics, which ones would probably be best analyzed though the notes-topic-categories-patterns-interpretation paradigm of qualitative research?

1. A comparison of achievement resulting from two different methods of teaching spelling
2. A listing of completion dates and contracting companies in the construction of Elmwood's 157 schools
3. Verbal interactions of children on the playground
4. The relationship between manual dexterity and learning to type
5. The progressive development of dramatic arts abilities among drama students
6. The effects of different levels of nitrogenic fertilizer on the growth of turf for football fields
7. The comparative achievement of adolescent boys and girls in Spanish I
8. What teachers say about administrators behind their backs, and vice versa
9. What Mondays are like for high school principals

Cautions and Reminders in Qualitative Data Analysis

Both the collection and analysis of qualitative data are prone to errors of subjectivity and imprecision. To counter these concerns, investigators, when collecting data, should strive to be *thoroughly* objective and impartial and to depict contexts and events as realistically as possible (Lancy, 1993). Data analysis is also easily affected by investigator bias. For that reason, great care should be taken to see that prejudices and preconceived notions do not improperly influence perceptions and interpretations.

Finally, when drawing conclusions, it is important to document the evidence on which the conclusions rest. The context should be carefully described as well—the place, the prevailing attitudes, the emotions, the motives, and the existent physical, social, and psychological realities. When making interpretations, investigators should force themselves to look for evidence other than what they first note and to make interpretations that are different from those anticipated or first identified. If alternative explanations can be found that are equally plausible, then questions, data, and interpretation should be reevaluated carefully.

Analyzing Quantitative Data

We have seen that in qualitative research investigators are keenly interested in contexts, values, attitudes, emotions, and social realities that affect human interaction, and that, in order to obtain better data, investigators often involve themselves closely with those they are observing. A different approach is usually taken in quantitative research. There, investigators try to keep themselves apart from participants. They fear that their involvement, or even their presence, might contaminate the study by causing participants to behave differently than they otherwise would. This is not to indicate, however, that quantitative research is value-free. To the contrary, all research is value-laden. Researchers investigate what they believe to be important, and they look for—and certainly hope for—results that can make a practical difference in education.

As shown earlier in Table 8.1, descriptive, correlational, evaluative, action, causal-comparative, and experimental research are all likely to include quantitative data that require statistical analysis. Until recently, students new to research looked on statistics with considerable trepidation, fearful of esoteric formulas and laborious calculations. It is still valuable to understand the processes involved in statistical calculations, but the calculations themselves need cause no fear. Now, computers can do the calculations in the blink of an eye, providing quick and accurate results that might formerly have taken hours or even days. University computer or media centers make such computational services available to graduate students, typically at no cost to the student. Also, with the appropriate software, students can perform statistical analyses on their home computers.

Populations and Parameters; Samples and Statistics

Before proceeding further, let us take a moment to note how populations, samples, parameters, and statistics are related.

A *population* consists of all the individuals who make up a designated group and whom we are ultimately interested in studying and, therefore, about whom we are interested in drawing conclusions. If we want to know about sixth-grade students in Alabama, the population to which we refer consists of all sixth-grade students in Alabama.

A *sample* is comprised of a small group drawn from a population, carefully selected in order to closely reflect the characteristics of the population. Samples are used in research because it is often impossible and almost always inconvenient—due to financial constraints, time factors, and so on—to study an entire population. If researchers are to suggest that what they have learned from the sample applies also to the population, samples need to be selected so they represent the population fairly closely.

Parameters are numerical indices that describe a population, such as the number of individuals included, measurements made of them, and descriptions that indicate average, dispersion, or relationships among those measurements. Parameter indices are usually symbolized with Greek letters, while their sample counterparts are usually symbolized with English or Roman letters. To illustrate, the population mean is symbolized μ, the twelfth letter of the Greek alphabet, pronounced *mew,* while the sample mean is symbolized M or $\overline{X}$.

Statistics are numerical indices and procedures that describe the sample and help one make inferences about the population. Statistics (which apply to the sample) are directly analogous to parameters (which apply to the population). Because samples almost never reflect populations exactly, statistics as a result almost never equal exactly the parameters to which they correspond. **Sampling error** is the term applied to this discrepancy between a sample statistic and a population parameter.

Research
Navigator.com

sampling error

Exercise 8.2

For the following, indicate which refers to (P) population, (PR) parameters, (S) sample, and (ST) statistics.

_____ 1. Thirty-two specially selected girls

_____ 2. The mean height of all sixth-grade girls in Elmwood schools

_____ 3. All the students in Elmwood schools

_____ 4. The mean IQ of 32 selected girls

What Statistics Are Used For

You might recall that the term *statistics* has multiple meanings. One meaning refers to summary *indices* resulting from data analysis, such as mean, median, standard deviation, and coefficient of correlation. Another meaning refers to the *procedures* by which data are analyzed mathematically. Statistics—the procedures—are used to describe and treat data in various ways, of which the following are most common:

■ *To summarize data and reveal what is typical and atypical within a group.* Research often yields hundreds or thousands of items of numerical data that, until summarized, cannot be interpreted meaningfully. Suppose you had the raw measurements of heights, weights, and intelligence quotient (IQ) scores for all the adult women in North Carolina. That would give you thousands of pages of numbers that would leave you baffled. Statistics can reduce such masses of data into terms more easily understood by showing what is average, how much difference exists between highest and lowest values, what the most commonly occurring value is, and how spread out the values are. Knowing those things, you would have a much clearer picture of what adult women in North Carolina are like.

- *To show relative standing of individuals in a group.* Statistics are frequently used to show where an individual stands for a given measurement in relation to all other individuals in the sample. Such standings are shown through percentile rankings, grade equivalents, age equivalents, and stanines—concepts discussed later in this chapter.

- *To show relationships among variables.* Investigators are often interested in determining whether correlations exist among variables—for instance, between people's ages and the amount of time they spend watching television or between students' self-concept and their scholastic achievement. Such relationships are often shown by means of statistical correlations.

- *To show similarities and differences among groups.* Researchers are often interested in ascertaining whether groups are similar to or different from each other. For example, they need to make sure, particularly for experimental research, that the two or more groups involved at the beginning of the experiment are approximately equal in the trait being investigated. Then later they check to see whether a special treatment given to one of the groups has changed it in some way, compared to the other.

- *To identify error that is inherent in sample selection.* Samples almost always differ to some degree from the population from which they are drawn. This introduces a degree of error—referred to earlier as *sampling error* or simply *error*—into research, so that we can never be sure that a statistical finding is also correct for the population. Error refers to the disparity between a given statistic and its corresponding parameter value—that is, between what is measured in a sample and what exists in the population. Statistical procedures enable one to determine the amount of error associated with measurements, means, correlations, and differences between means. When this error is known, one can specify the "confidence levels" for a particular value or finding. For example, if we find a sample mean of 6.2 and then determine its *standard error*—a quantitative measure of sampling error, defined as the average distance of samples means away from the population mean—we can conclude, with a specified degree of confidence (e.g., 95 percent), that the population mean lies somewhere within a given range, such as between 5.3 and 7.1.

- *To test for significance of findings.* When researchers discover apparent correlations between variables or differences between means, they apply statistical tests of significance. They do this to determine whether their findings might be due to the researchers' having, by chance, selected a sample that did not reflect the population or if, in fact, they represent *real* differences or relationships that exist in the population. If the likelihood turns out to be high that the sample does accurately reflect the population, the researcher will call the finding "significant," meaning that a particular finding resulting from sample data is probably also real for the population, rather than one that occurred only in the sample because of chance errors. However, if the test suggests that the finding might not be of sufficient magnitude to override errors in a sample selection, the investigator will deem the finding to be "not significant," meaning that the finding might not be real for the population.

- *To make other inferences about the population.* As noted, researchers are seldom able to investigate an entire population and must, therefore, work with samples. Yet, they hope to show that findings for the sample are true also for the population. Thus, when we determine a mean score for the sample, for instance, we wish to say that the same mean score exists in the population as a whole. Of course, since we have not investigated the entire population, we can only make inferences about the population mean. In doing this, we assign probability levels that allow us to say that the sample finding is "probably also correct" for the population, within specified limits.

The actual statistical techniques used to accomplish these ends are presented in Appendix A.

Descriptive Statistics and Inferential Statistics

Research Navigator.c⊛m
central tendency

Descriptive statistics are the procedures involved and their associated numerical indices that help clarify data from samples. We now present discussion of the most commonly used descriptive statistics. (The reader should note that when spelled out, the statistical terms are not italicized—e.g., mean, median. However, symbols and abbreviations used in place of those terms are usually italicized—e.g., *M, Mdn.*)

1. Measures of **central tendency,** including the mean, median, and mode.

   - Mean (symbolized $\overline{X}$ or *M*)—the arithmetic average.

     Example: What is the mean of the following set of scores?

     8, 7, 6, 5, 5, 5, 5, 4, 4, 1

     (Answer: 5)

   - Median (abbreviated *Mdn* or *Md*)—the midpoint in an array of scores, determined by counting halfway from highest to lowest.

     Example: What is the median of the following set of scores? (Remember, you must order the scores from highest to lowest first.)

     8, 7, 6, 5, 5, 4, 4, 4, 4, 3

     (Answer: 4.5)

   - Mode (abbreviated *Mo*)—the most frequently made score on a test or other measure.

     Example: What is the mode of the following set of scores?

     8, 7, 6, 5, 5, 4, 4, 4, 4, 3

     (Answer: 4)

Research Navigator.c⊛m
variability

2. Measures of **variability** (amount of spread or dispersion in the scores), including the range, variance, and standard deviation.

   - Range—the difference between highest and lowest score or measure.

Example: What is the range for the following set of scores?

8, 7, 6, 5, 5, 4, 4, 4, 4, 3

(Answer: 5)

- Variance (symbolized s^2)—a measure of dispersion; calculated as the average of the squared deviations from a particular value such as the mean. (The calculation of variance is shown in Appendix A.)

- Standard deviation (*SD* or *s*)—a stable and probably most useful measure of dispersion; calculated as the square root of the variance. (The calculation of a standard deviation is shown in Appendix A.)

3. Measures of **relative standing,** including percentile ranks, stanines, and converted or transformed scores.

- Percentile rank (*%ile* or *PR*)—a ranking assigned to a particular score that shows the percentage of all scores that fall below that particular score.

    Example: Juan's score fell at the 56th percentile. This percentile ranking means he equaled or excelled 56 percent of all other students who took the test.

- Stanine—a value from 1 to 9, with 5 being average, which shows where a score stands in relation to others.

    Example: Mary's score fell in the 6th stanine. This means she was slightly above average among all other students who took the test.

- Converted or transformed score—a value assigned to a raw score, such as the grade-level equivalency, that corresponds to the score a student made on a test.

    Example: Shawn made a score of 46 on the test, which places him at the seventh-grade, sixth-month level.

4. Measures of **relationship,** including coefficient of correlation.

- Coefficient of correlation (of which the most common is called a *Pearson correlation* and is symbolized *r*)—a measure of relationship between two or more sets of scores made by the same group of participants.

    Example: The correlation between reading ability and achievement test scores was +.32. This means there was a modest positive relationship between the two variables.

Inferential statistics are used to make inferences about the population, enabling investigators to make estimates about the population from what has been learned about the sample. They include the following:

1. *Error estimates* that indicate the range within which a given measure probably lies in the population.

    Example: If the study were repeated many times, the correlation would probably continue to fall between +.28 and +.36.

2. *Confidence intervals* that indicate the probability that a population value lies within certain specified boundaries.

   Example: There is a 95 percent probability that the correlation in the population lies between +.22 and +.42.

3. *Tests of significance,* which show the likelihood of a finding's having occurred because of sampling error, that is, chance errors made in selecting the sample. Tests include those for correlation, difference between two means, and difference between three or more means.

■ *Significance of correlation.*

   Example: If the study were repeated hundreds of times, a correlation of this absolute value or larger (e.g., less than −.83 or greater than +.83) would occur at least 95 percent of the time. This is symbolized by $p < .05$, which means that the probability (p) of the result being due to sampling error, or chance, is less than 5 out of 100.

■ *Significance of the difference between means of two samples* (*t* test).

   Example: If the study were repeated hundreds of times, a difference between means of this absolute value or larger would occur at least 95 percent of the time ($p < .05$).

■ *Significance of the difference between three or more means* (analysis of variance or *F* test).

   Example: If the study were repeated hundreds of times, a difference between three or more means of this absolute value or larger would occur at least 95 percent of the time ($p < .05$).

Procedures for calculating these inferential statistical indices are presented in Appendix A.

Exercise 8.3

Supply the appropriate name for each of the following:

1. The most frequently made score.
2. The relationship between two sets of scores made by the same individuals.
3. The arithmetic average of the scores.
4. The difference between the highest and lowest score in a group.
5. A finding is probably real—not due to sampling error.
6. The true measure for the sample probably lies within these boundaries.
7. There is a 95 percent probability that the population mean lies within these boundaries.
8. Statistics used to make judgments about the population.
9. John's score equaled or surpassed 68 percent of all scores.
10. Measures that show spread or diversion.

Applying Technology: **More about Statistics**

Statistical analysis of quantitative data often provides graduate students with some of their most difficult challenges. Statistics are frequently likened to a foreign language—new concepts, new terminology, and so on. We provide several Web pages to which the reader can refer in order to supplement understanding of statistical concepts and terminology. We, once again, refer you to Dr. Trochim's knowledge base. Dr. Trochim has included several Web pages that address various topics related to analysis of quantitative data. Brief descriptions of the contents of these pages, including their URLs, follow:

- Data Preparation (http://trochim.human.cornell.edu/kb/statprep.htm)—information includes discussions of methods of ensuring the accuracy of data, the entry of data into a data file or database, and various examples of simple data transformations;
- Descriptive Statistics (http://trochim.human.cornell.edu/kb/statdesc.htm)—discussions of the general nature of descriptive statistics and an example of univariate analysis, including the development of a frequency distribution, calculations of various measures of central tendency, and calculations of measures of dispersion;
- Correlation (http://trochim.human.cornell.edu/kb/statcorr.htm)—a discussion of the measure of a relationship between two variables, including graphical representation and sample calculation of correlation coefficient.

Another Web site that provides a multitude of information about statistics has been developed by Dr. David W. Stockburger of Southwest Missouri State University. It essentially consists of an online statistics textbook and can be found by pointing your browser to www.psychstat.smsu.edu/sbk00.htm.

This online text is the actual text used by Dr. Stockburger to teach an undergraduate course in statistics; however, the content and coverage of that content are also appropriate for graduate students taking an introductory course. Advantages of this online text include:

- The concepts are addressed in a brief, but very thorough, manner
- It is relatively easy to navigate your way around the text and, therefore, focus on a particular topic, by using the Table of Contents
- The text incorporates several interactive examples and exercises

Finally, the text also includes links to numerous additional online resources. By clicking on Bibliography and Web Resources (www.psychstat.smsu.edu/introbook/biblio.htm) in the Table of Contents, and then clicking on the button

> **Statistical Resources on the Web**

you will find a listing of several categories of resources. These categories include online statistics books, statistical resources, sources for data files, commercial textbooks, research articles, statistical software packages, and online statistics course home pages.

Applying Technology: **Interactive Statistical Calculations Using** *StatCrunch*

Although statistical software packages have become much more user friendly over the past 10 years, their high cost and lack of availability continue to limit access by graduate students. There are several good statistics packages including Statistical Package for the Social Sciences (SPSS), Statistical Analysis System (SAS), MYSTAT, and MINITAB. However, the cost of many of these packages is staggering, especially for the financially conscious graduate student. For example, SPSS retails for nearly $1,000, and SYSTAT has a retail price of nearly $1,300. Nonetheless, there are options available. One such option is *StatCrunch* (formerly known as *WebStat*) (www.statcrunch.com/).

StatCrunch is an online, Web-based data analysis software system developed by the Department of Statistics at the University of South Carolina. It works in similar fashion to any statistical software that you might purchase and install on your home or office computer. The main page for StatCrunch is shown in Figure 8.2. The analysis program is started by clicking on the `Fire it up!` link.

The resulting window—an interactive Java window—is shown in Figure 8.3. Analyses are run on StatCrunch by first simply entering data directly into this window. As with any analysis program, the columns represent variables and the rows represent cases, subjects, or participants. By clicking on the column headings, you can name the variables in your data set.

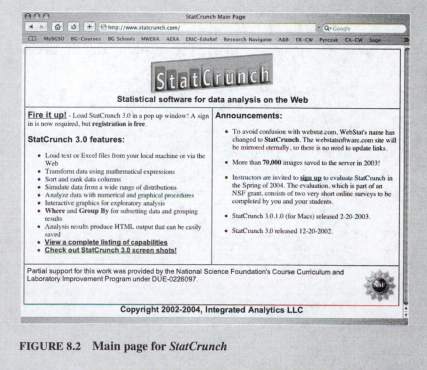

FIGURE 8.2   Main page for *StatCrunch*

(continued)

Applying Technology: **Interactive Statistical Calculations**
Using *StatCrunch*   *Continued*

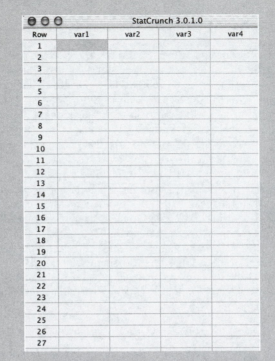

FIGURE 8.3   Initial Java window for *StatCrunch*

Let us examine a simple step-by-step example: Assume we have a random sample of students from three schools that we want to compare with respect to scores on some state-wide competency test. We would enter the data for our three variables—scores in school 1 (**school1**), scores in school 2 (**school2**), and scores in school 3 (**school3**)—into the Stat-Crunch window (see Step 1).

Step 1: Name variables and enter data.

Row	school1	school2	school3	var4	var5
1	25	24	22		
2	10	27	24		
3	15	24	27		
4	21	19	25		
5	23	28	30		
6					
7					
8					
9					
10					
11					
12					
13					
14					

Next, we would select the appropriate method of analyzing our data—because we have three groups we would like to compare on the dependent variable, the appropriate test is analysis of variance. We select this option by clicking on "Stat" and "ANOVA: One-way" (see Step 2).

Step 2: Select appropriate statistic from menu.

okmarks	Window	Help	StatCrunch	Data	Stat	Graphics	Results	Help	Thu

StatCrunc

Summary Stats
Tables
Z statistics
Proportions
T statistics
Variance
Regression
ANOVA ► One Way
Control Charts

Row	school1	school2	school3		var6	v:
1	25	24	22			
2	10	27	24			
3	15	24	27			
4	21	19	25			
5	23	28	30			
6						
7						
8						
9						
10						
11						
12						
13						
14						

Holding down on the SHIFT key, we then click on each variable in order to move it to the analysis box, located on the right (see Step 3). We then click on the Calculate button.

ANOVA

⦿ Compare selected columns

school1	school1
school2	school2
school3	school3

Step 3: Select variable for analysis and click **Calculate**.

○ Compare values in a single column

Responses in: Select Column

Factors in: Select Column

Where: --optional--

(?) (Cancel) (Calculate)

Applying Technology: **Interactive Statistical Calculations Using** *StatCrunch   Continued*

Finally, we see the results displayed in a new window (see Step 4). A standard ANOVA summary table is displayed—by the way, notice that since the *p*-value is not less than .05, our three schools are not significantly different from one another.

> **Step 4:** Examine the results shown in a new window.

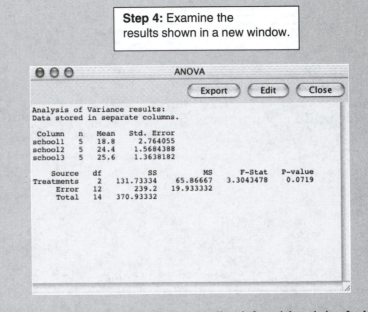

StatCrunch will calculate descriptive as well as inferential statistics. It also has the capability to plot various types of graphs. If you have a large amount of analyses to perform, we still recommend a software package; however, in a "pinch," StatCrunch provides an efficient and expedient alternative. Give it a try!

INTRODUCTION TO EDUCATIONAL RESEARCH
Companion Website Highlight

The Companion Website that accompanies this text (www.ablongman.com/mertler5e) includes a downloadable data file complete with descriptions of the variables and the methods by which they may have been coded. If you are interested in furthering your skills in quantitative analysis, we recommend that you save this file and practice various analysis techniques using the analysis software program of your choice.

Cautions in Using Statistics

Don't go overboard in using statistics. In your research, specify exactly what it is you want to know—what questions you wish to answer or which hypotheses you intend to test. Then select the statistics that are appropriate for describing your data and for performing the treatments you require. Make sure the statistical analyses contribute directly to the purposes you have in mind. Remember, too, that statistics do not prove anything, for in all findings there remains a degree of uncertainty. Confidence intervals and/or significance levels only help by showing what the chances are that one might be making an error in judgment.

As for significance, it is possible to determine that a particular finding is significant, statistically speaking, when in fact the magnitude of the finding is so small that it makes no practical difference whatsoever. Such results often occur when a researcher uses very large samples. This constitutes the very crucial distinction between *statistical significance* and *practical significance.* For example, it might be discovered that in the Elmwood high school population as a whole, students born in January have a mean IQ that is one point higher than that of students born in a different month and that the difference is significant. But what possible importance could that minuscule amount have? Conversely, it might be found, in a small sample of 10 students, that mathematics taught through a new method produced 30 percent more achievement gain than did the traditional teaching method. But because the sample is so small, the finding may be deemed not significant. Rather than reject that finding, which might have very important implications, one might wish to repeat the research using a larger sample.

Statistics are used to *assist* logical thought processes. They do not *replace* logic. They help investigators interpret data, answer research questions, and test hypotheses. But they do not make interpretations, nor can they be offered up as the final word in any research matter. So, regardless of how impressive statistics might appear, remember that it is the researcher's thought processes that count most in good research.

Research Navigator.com

statistical significance

practical significance

INTRODUCTION TO EDUCATIONAL RESEARCH
Companion Website Highlight

The Companion Website that accompanies this text (www.ablongman.com/mertler5e) also includes a statistical decision-making tree designed to assist you in selecting the appropriate analysis technique for your given research situation. This decision-making tree can be used by itself or in conjunction with Dr. Trochim's interactive "tree" (see *Applying Technology:* Selecting an Appropriate Statistical Test), which can be found at http://trochim.human.cornell.edu/selstat/ssstart.htm. The Companion Website also includes a downloadable monograph produced by the staff at SPSS titled *Basic applied techniques: Choosing the right stat to make better decisions.*

Applying Technology: **Selecting an Appropriate Statistical Test**

When analyzing quantitative data, students tend to realize rather quickly that one of the more difficult aspects of the process is determining the applicable statistical test to use. Again, Dr. Trochim has provided a wonderful, interactive, Web-based tool designed to aid researchers in deciding on the most appropriate statistical technique to use in a given situation. The page, titled "Selecting Statistics" (http://trochim.human.cornell.edu/selstat/ssstart.htm), is interactive in that you are asked a series of several questions about the design and variables you are trying to analyze.

The questions are asked in a specific order, leading you to the appropriate statistical technique:

- How many variables does the problem involve?
- Is a distinction made between a dependent and an independent variable?
- Do you want to treat the relationship as linear?

Depending on the nature of your research design and subsequent answers to the questions, there may be additional questions you will need to answer. It is, however, an efficient method of determining an appropriate test—the entire process will take only a minute or two. It certainly is better than the alternative—discovering after-the-fact that you have conducted the wrong procedure and now must return to your analyses.

Presenting Your Findings

Research findings comprise the information you bring to light through data analysis. The findings are statements of facts—at least as those facts are represented by the particular sample studied—the researcher has discovered. They may be accompanied by statements that help readers interpret the findings. Findings help provide answers to research questions and hypotheses and are most appropriately presented in conjunction with those questions or hypotheses.

In historical and descriptive research using qualitative data, the findings will be the summary statements about interactions, situations, environments, objects, and so forth, that have been scrutinized. For example, one might write statements such as:

The school register revealed that 73 students attended Bodie School in 1935.

The teacher record book contained marks for reading, mathematics, penmanship, history, geography, and spelling.

In the case of ethnographic research that is gathering qualitative data, findings will be your summary statements about the individuals, environments, and patterns of behavior you have observed. These findings are presented as verbal statements and might appear as follows:

Gossip was the category of talk most frequently heard in the faculty room.

Teachers' behavior before school was for the most part work oriented.

On the other hand, in quantitative research, you present your findings statistically, accompanied by verbal statements. For example, you might write

The mean score for Group A was 45, with a standard error of .38.

The correlation between measures of attentiveness and achievement was −.68, significant at the .01 level.

When you have a number of statistics to report, it is helpful (and customary) to present them in tabular form. Thus you might write

Means and standard deviations for the six groups are shown in Table 1.

Further information on presenting findings and conclusions is provided in Chapter 9.

D E V E L O P M E N T A L   A C T I V I T Y

Statistical Analysis Decisions

Closely associated with making important decisions about the collection of your data, as you did in the developmental activity for Chapter 7, are decisions about how you anticipate analyzing your resultant data. In this chapter's activity, you will strengthen choices about analytical techniques that you have likely already begun to consider. Bear in mind that decisions about analyses should focus on the information necessary to enable you to answer your questions or address your hypotheses.

1. My research question(s) or hypothesis(es) is(are): _____

_____

_____.

2. My main variables, and their associated classifications, include:

Variable 1: _____

☐ continuous
☐ discrete

Variable 2: _____

☐ continuous
☐ discrete

Others: _____

☐ continuous
☐ discrete

3. I plan to use the following *descriptive* statistics to summarize my variables (*check all that apply*):

Statistical Technique	Variable 1: _____	Variable 2: _____	Other: _____
Mean	☐	☐	☐
Median	☐	☐	☐
Mode	☐	☐	☐
Range	☐	☐	☐
Standard deviation	☐	☐	☐
Percentile rank	☐	☐	☐
Stanine	☐	☐	☐
Correlation coefficient	☐	☐	☐

4. The appropriate inferential statistical technique(s) for my study is(are): _____

_____

_____

_____.

5. As I consider again my questions or hypotheses, the reason(s) I chose the foregoing technique(s) is(are): _____

_____

_____

_____.

6. I ☐ will / ☐ will not (*check one*) perform a significance test because _____

_____

_____

_____

_____.

7. I ☐ will / ☐ will not (*check one*) calculate confidence intervals because _____

_____

_____.

8. The type of sampling I will do is _____.

9. The type of sampling to be used in my study places the following limitations and/or de-limitations on my use of inferential statistics: _____

_____

_____

_____.

(A downloadable, interactive version of this developmental activity is available from the Companion Website, www.ablongman.com/mertler5e)

Chapter Summary

Research data, whether qualitative or quantitative, must be analyzed in order to answer research questions or test hypotheses. Qualitative data, largely verbal in nature, are analyzed verbally, through the logico-inductive process. This analysis applies verbal data to research questions and examines the data's persuasiveness in answering related questions. Quantitative data, largely numerical in nature, are analyzed statistically, in order to describe samples and make inferences about populations. Descriptive statistics include measures of central tendency, variability, relative standing, and correlation. Inferential statistics include measures of standard error and tests of significance. Statistics do not prove anything in themselves, but do assist the logical thought processes of the investigator. Once data have been analyzed, the results are presented as findings, organized according to research questions and hypotheses and presented clearly so they can be understood easily by others.

LIST OF IMPORTANT TERMS

central tendency
descriptive statistics
hypothetico-inductive analysis
inferential statistics
interim analysis

logico-inductive analysis
parameters
probability levels
relationship
relative standing

sampling error
statistics
variability

YOUR CURRENT STATUS

In Chapter 7 you learned how to obtain appropriate research data, and in this chapter you have seen how those data, whether qualitative or quantitative, can be analyzed in order to help answer questions or test hypotheses. For specific statistical procedures, you were directed to explore the contents of Appendix A. You are now ready to learn how to put together a research report.

ACTIVITIES FOR THOUGHT AND DISCUSSION

1. Suppose you conduct research to test student preference among five colors for interior classroom walls. One thousand students are included in your sample. One of the colors is chartreuse. You use chi-square to analyze the data. Based on the null hypothesis, how many students do you expect to choose chartreuse?

2. For the eight types of research, indicate which are more likely to involve qualitative analysis and which are more likely to involve quantitative analysis.

3. Here are the questions presented at the beginning of the chapter. See how well you can answer them.

   a. What is the general purpose of data analysis in all types of research?
   b. Why are qualitative data and quantitative data analyzed differently?
   c. How are qualitative data analyzed?
   d. How are quantitative data analyzed?
   e. What are the relationships among populations, parameters, samples, and statistics?
   f. What is the difference between descriptive statistics and inferential statistics?
   g. What does *significance* mean in statistics?
   h. What is the relationship between data analysis and research findings?

ANSWERS TO CHAPTER EXERCISES

8.1. 3, 5, 8, 9

8.2. 1. S 2. PR 3. P 4. ST

8.3. 1. mode 2. correlation 3. mean 4. range 5. significance 6. error estimate 7. confidence interval 8. inferential statistics 9. percentile rank 10. measures of variability

REFERENCES AND RECOMMENDED READINGS

Bartz, A. (1976). *Basic Statistical Concepts in Education and the Behavioral Sciences.* Minneapolis: Burgess.

Best, J., & Kahn, J. (2003). *Research in Education* (9th ed.). Boston: Allyn and Bacon.

Borg, W., Gall, J., & Gall, M. (1999). *Applying Educational Research: A Practical Guide* (4th ed.). White Plains, NY: Longman.

Cronk, B. (1999). *How to Use SPSS: A Step-By-Step Guide to Analysis and Interpretation.* Los Angeles, CA: Pyrczak.

Gall, M., Borg, W., & Gall, J. (2003). *Educational Research: An Introduction* (7th ed.). Boston: Allyn and Bacon.

Green, S., Salkind, N., & Akey, T. (2000). *Using SPSS for Windows: Analyzing and Understanding Data* (2nd ed.). Upper Saddle River, NJ: Prentice Hall.

Lancy, D. (1993). *Qualitative Research in Education: An Introduction to the Major Traditions.* White Plains, NY: Longman.

Lortie, D. (1975). *Schoolteacher: A Sociological Study.* Chicago: University of Chicago Press.

McMillan, J. (1996). *Educational Research: Fundamentals for the Consumer* (2nd ed.). New York: HarperCollins.

Mertler, C. A., & Vannatta, R. A. (2001). *Advanced and Multivariate Statistical Methods: Practical Application and Interpretation* (2nd ed.). Los Angeles, CA: Pyrczak.

Norusis, M. (1991). *SPSS/PC+ Studentware Plus.* Chicago: SPSS Inc. Software manufacturers are SPSS Inc., 444 N. Michigan Ave., Chicago, IL 60611.

Stockburger, D. W. (1996). *Introductory Statistics: Concepts, Models, and Applications.* Available at www.psychstat.smsu.edu/sbk00.htm

Trochim, W. M. (2002). *The Research Methods Knowledge Base* (2nd ed.). Available at http://trochim.human.cornell.edu/kb/index.htm

Vierra, A., & Pollock, J. (1988). *Reading Educational Research.* Scottsdale, AZ: Gorsuch Scarisbrick.

9 Preparing a Research Report

PREVIEW

This chapter is designed to help you learn to prepare
- Research reports

Special attention is given to
- Conventions of reporting that have to do with

Format
- Introduction
- Relevant citations
- Procedures followed
- Results found
- Interpretations

Writing style
- Descriptive
- Clear, unemotional
- Third person, passive
- Tentative, not adamant
- Consistency in all

- And to sections usually contained in research reports, including:

Front material
- Title
- Acknowledgments
- Abstract

Body
- Introduction
- Review of literature
- Procedures
- Findings
- Conclusions

Back material
- Bibliography
- Appendixes

Targeted Learnings

The purpose of this chapter is to help you learn to write research reports appropriate to your needs. Formats for theses, project papers, and articles are examined, and important conventions of style are described and explained. As you read the chapter, look especially for information related to the following:

1. What is meant by *convention,* and why are conventions important in reporting research?
2. What are the conventions of style regarding person, voice, tense, and consistency?
3. What are the four to six sections usually included in research reports?

Reports of research conducted by graduate students are usually
submitted in one of three formats: thesis, project paper, or journal
article. The thesis format is the most common.

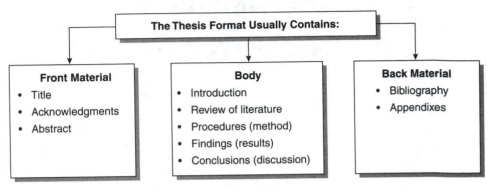

The research report is organized and presented according to
conventions consistent with the scientific method. Those conventions
are spelled out in the style book adopted by each graduate school.

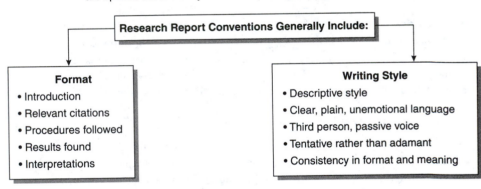

4. Which section explains the plan for obtaining data?
5. In which of the sections is the investigator permitted to speculate on meanings and implications?
6. What is meant by *front material* and *back material?*
7. Who ultimately specifies the style and format that graduate students must use when preparing reports required in their programs?

Conventions in Research and Reporting

You already know that the research process adheres to certain **conventions,** which are agreed-upon procedures that help ensure the accuracy of data and findings. These conventions contribute to the validity of research and increase the confidence one can place in it. When research conventions are not followed, the credibility of the research is brought into question.

The same is true for research reports. They, too, are prepared according to conventions that promote both readability and credibility. It is important that you recognize these conventions and follow them when preparing your research report. Failure to do so does not render research invalid, but just as one's credibility as an educator can be damaged by the use of incorrect grammar, so can a researcher's credibility be damaged by using unconventional report styles and formats.

Conventions of Style

Several conventions of research reporting have to do with writing style, chiefly those concerning (1) titles of reports; (2) person, voice, and tense; (3) tentative and definite statements; (4) simplicity of language; and (5) consistency of style and meanings. Let us briefly consider these conventions. Keep in mind that none is necessarily a hard-and-fast rule (unless, or course, your graduate adviser says it is), but you cannot go wrong by following conventional approaches.

Title

Earlier chapters stressed that the title of a research report should indicate clearly what the report is about. Catchy, clever titles should be avoided unless by chance they happen to describe the topic accurately. Readers of research rely on titles to indicate whether reports deal with topics they particularly wish to read about. For that reason, titles of research reports are sometimes rather long, though writers generally try to limit titles to no more than 15 words.

Exercise 9.1

Suppose you have completed a study of the history of racial integration of students in Elmwood schools. In view of the convention about titles, which of the following would be the best title for your report?

1. Elmwood Schools—When They Were Trying to Find the Way
2. Elmwood Schools Dismissed Color as a Criterion
3. A History of Racial Integration of Students in Elmwood Public Schools
4. In the Days When Elmwood Schools Learned to Say "No" to Segregation
5. Desegregation in Elmwood Schools
6. Elmwood Schools Find They Can Open Their Doors to All Students Without the System Collapsing

---

Person and Voice

Research reports are typically written in the third person, although this convention is beginning to change. Usually, the authors do not refer to themselves as "I," "we," or "the author," but as "the writer" or "the investigators."

The passive voice, rather than the active, is used extensively. Researchers write "It was found that…" or "The following conclusions were reached…" (both passive voice), rather than "The writer found…" or "The investigator reached the following conclusions…" (both active voice). This convention, too, is beginning to change.

Tense

Research reports are written mostly in the past tense. Such is almost exclusively true for sections that report the purpose of the study, the procedures, the findings, and the conclusions. (Note that *research proposals,* unlike reports, tend to use the future tense.) Typical statements in reports might be:

The purpose of this study was to…

The following steps were taken in obtaining data…

It was found that…

The data seemed to warrant the following conclusions…

Sometimes the present tense is used in the introduction of the report, together with the past tense. For example:

For *many years investigators have sought…and today they are still seeking…*

The present tense is used, too, in reports that describe ongoing research, from which additional reports will follow. The following is an example:

These are the principal implications as presently warranted by the data…

Tentative versus Definitive Statements

Researchers use tentative statements to report their conclusions. It is not considered correct to present any conclusions as absolutely certain, but rather to show that there always remains some room for doubt. That is why research reports contain statements such as:

The data seem to suggest…

The following conclusions appeared to be warranted…

The true mean probably lies between…

You can be a bit more definite when reporting data and statistics because an accepted margin of error is presumed to exist. It is proper to use statements such as:

The mean and standard deviation were…

Seventy-two percent of the respondents indicated…

The coefficient of correlation was…

And, of course, you should be quite definite and precise when describing procedures you followed in conducting the research.

Simplicity of Language

Research reports are written in plain, rather than flowery, language. You are supposed to get straight to the point, unemotionally, without attempting to use a "literary style." The following is an example of writing that contains unacceptably fancy wording:

> The purpose of this extremely involved study was to explore from every conceivable angle the impossible demands that have been placed on the dedicated faculty members of five highly touted middle schools.

More acceptable wording for that same introduction removes the flowery adjectives and adverbs, as follows:

> The purpose of this study was to investigate the working conditions of classroom teachers in five different middle schools.

Just remember that people read research reports not for entertainment but to make themselves better informed. You need not try to charm readers with your prose; they want you to get to the point quickly because their time is limited. Of course, you need to explain your research well enough so that readers can understand your procedures and findings, but while you do so, keep your message short and simple.

Consistency

When writing research reports you should strive for consistency in style, word usage, meanings, and special symbols. If you indent direct quotations on each side, do so the same way every time. When using statistical or other special symbols, be sure always to use the same marks in the same way, even though several interchangeable symbols (such as those used to indicate standard deviation) are in common use. You should also format chapters, sections, headings, charts, tables, and figures in a consistent manner.

Exercise 9.2

Find what needs to be improved in each of the following statements. Reword each statement according to recommended conventions.

1. I decided to undertake this study for two reasons.
   Reword:

(continued)

Exercise 9.2 *Continued*

2. The data conclusively prove the following:
Reword:

3. Until a scant two years ago, teachers who clung to the time-treasured ways of motivating their classroom charges were made the objects of derision.
Reword:

4. The following are the steps I was following in my study:
   a. January 13: I go to the district office to check school records.
   b. I spend January 15 through the 25 making notes of discrepancies in the entries.
   c. On January 26 the investigator meets with the personnel director to discuss the discrepancies.
Reword:

Conventions of Format

Research reports contain four to six major sections, depending on the report. Always included are an introduction, a description of the procedures followed, a presentation of findings, and a presentation of conclusions. Often, a short review of related literature is included, and many reports conclude with a discussion of the findings and new questions that have arisen.

These sections are sometimes, but not always, labeled in journal articles, as you have probably seen. Even when they are not labeled, you do not have much difficulty recognizing the sections; they are usually there, according to convention. (You may notice, however, that it is much easier to read reports that contain clear headings.) In theses and dissertations, the principal sections are clearly labeled either with headings or chapter titles. When you write your research report, you will very likely be expected to label the sections in that way.

Let us explore the typical sections of research reports and their contents.

Introduction

Introductions specify the topic and tell why it merits attention. In theses and dissertations, the introduction is presented as "Chapter 1." In journal articles and technical reports this section may be labeled "Introduction," but frequently you will simply encounter introductory paragraphs that indicate the topic (which should be made clear in the title), establish its importance, and tell the specific purpose of the research being reported.

In theses and dissertations, the introductory chapter contains additional items not normally found in short reports, such as the following.

Statement of the Problem. A concise description of the problem being investigated. In some formats this is simply called "The Problem," and it tells specifically what the investigation was intended to explore (e.g., "The purpose of this study was to explore the relationship between muscularity and running speed among high school basketball players").

Hypotheses. Hypotheses are conjectures the investigator intends to test. Recall that there are three types of hypotheses: directional research hypotheses, nondirectional research hypotheses, and null hypotheses. Examples could include:

1. More muscular players have a faster running speed than do less muscular players. (a directional research hypothesis)
2. A difference in running speed exists between more muscular players and less muscular players. (a nondirectional research hypothesis)
3. No difference in running speed exists between more muscular players and less muscular players. (a null hypothesis)

Research Questions. Questions may be used instead of hypotheses for orientation in many types of investigation. As you recall, research questions are often organized into one or more main questions and are followed by a number of related subquestions. As subquestions are answered, one hopes to become able to answer the main research question.

Definition of Terms. This is a section of the report in which definitions are given for words, acronyms, abbreviations, names, labels, and the like that are central to the study. In the investigation of the relationship between body weight and running speed among basketball players, for example, you would be expected to define what you mean by the terms *high school basketball players, muscularity, more muscular, less muscular,* and *running speed.*

Limitations and Delimitations. This section describes the limits that *naturally* affect your study (limitations) and limits that *you* have imposed on your study (delimitations). Limitations on the muscularity–speed study might be that only high school athletes are involved, that they can be measured only at a particular time of the year, and that they have agreed to be tested. Delimitations that you impose might be that the participants are males, that they are of selected ethnic groups, and that they are members of varsity and junior varsity basketball squads.

Review of Related Literature

You are expected to review literature related to the problem of your study in order to accomplish three things: (1) determine whether studies already exist similar to the one you propose to do, (2) possibly obtain guidance for the investigation of your topic, and (3) establish a point of departure or a platform on which to build your research.

With the literature review, you inform readers about what has been done that is related to, but different from, your topic. In theses and dissertations, the review you present is usually quite long; it typically constitutes a separate chapter. If the review is short, it may be included in Chapter 1. Journal articles and technical reports tend to mention in an early paragraph only a few of the most important related studies, as indicated in the following illustration (please note that the citations are fictitious):

> *In the later 1990s, discipline continued to rank highest among all teacher concerns (Smith, 1998). In fact, Allison and McCarthy (1998) found discipline problems to be the leading cause of teacher failure and the second leading cause of teacher stress. Concern about discipline has led several investigators to explore alternative discipline systems (Childers, 1997; Harrison, 1998), along with new training programs in behavior management (Paterno, 1997; Sánchez, 1997).*

There are no hard-and-fast rules for organizing longer literature reviews, but the following guidelines, presented previously in Chapter 5, facilitate reading and add to the persuasiveness of your report:

1. *Begin with the most general information and end with the most specific.* If you are studying school discipline, you would report studies that indicate it is a widespread problem before you report that it causes stress, and you would report that discipline skills can be taught before reporting on specific training programs.
2. *Begin with older studies and move toward more recent studies.* This progression shows lines of thought and refinement that have occurred over time.
3. *Group your references within the categories you have identified in your research problem.* If you are using research questions and subquestions, a natural organization is to report general findings related to the main question and then specific findings related to each of the subquestions. If you are conducting an historical study, you might group literature by years or decades; if a study is descriptive, you might group by various topics you wish to describe; if it is action research and/or development, you might group the reports according to their similarity to the innovation you have developed and implemented.
4. *When you report what you consider to be particularly important studies, use adjectives that indicate your evaluation;* for example, "In a landmark study, Jones (1995)…" or "Smith's (1996) controversial study…"

Exercise 9.3

Suppose you are reporting action research in which you have developed and implemented a new system of discipline in your school. For your review of the literature, you want to report research findings that cluster around certain themes, which are shown in the following list. Number the blanks to indicate the best order for presenting the themes and their related literature:

_____   1. Rules and practices that promote good classroom behavior

_____   2. The relationship of discipline to achievement

_____   3. Support from others that helps teachers enjoy better discipline

_____   4. The outcry over what is seen to be lack of discipline in the schools

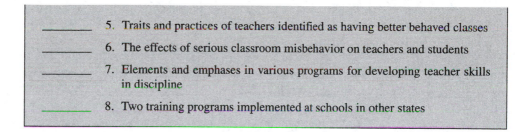

_____ 5. Traits and practices of teachers identified as having better behaved classes

_____ 6. The effects of serious classroom misbehavior on teachers and students

_____ 7. Elements and emphases in various programs for developing teacher skills in discipline

_____ 8. Two training programs implemented at schools in other states

Procedures or Method

The third major section of research reports is labeled either "Procedures" or "Method." Here, the investigator reports step-by-step what was done in the study. This section typically comprises Chapter 3 in theses and dissertations. Journal articles may or may not use a heading to indicate this section of the report, but, in any case, it can easily be found due to its contents.

There is no prescribed format for recounting procedures, but the following suggestions will make your presentation more easily understood by your readers.

1. In longer reports, especially in theses and dissertations, begin by repeating the purpose of the study (i.e., the problem statement). In short reports, this is not necessary.
2. Describe the design of your study. In this portion, indicate
   a. Hypotheses or questions
   b. Sources of information
   c. People involved and how they were selected
   d. Other important resources used in the study
   e. Tests, measuring devices, and other instruments
   f. Procedures used in data analysis

   In theses and dissertations, the research design should be described in detail. In shorter reports, a brief description is sufficient.

3. Group the procedures into categories—for example: sample, measurement, data analysis. Then describe, step-by-step, what you did in each.

All of this is done for two purposes: first, to show that in your research you proceeded scientifically and followed established conventions, and second, to enable readers to follow and understand what you did. This also encourages enlightened criticism of your work: You can expect others to ask questions about, or take exception to, the way you have conducted your investigation. It also permits your study to be replicated if someone wishes, which is important in building a reliable body of research evidence and conclusions.

Findings or Results

The next major section included in research reports is called either "Findings" or "Results" and is usually presented as Chapter 4 in theses and dissertations. Because this portion of the report is so important, it is usually given a heading of some sort, even in shorter papers.

In this section, you summarize the new information you have discovered. If your report is long, you may want to repeat the hypotheses or research questions, then show the results of the analysis of data related to each hypothesis or question.

Results are reported verbally and are usually supported with tables and figures. Tables frequently show numerical data and indicate statistical analyses. Figures are used to illustrate or clarify findings. Figures include graphs, charts, drawings, computer printouts, and the like.

You should use tables and figures whenever they can add clarity to what you are describing. Suppose you are a middle school English teacher, and a part of your action research explores students' preferences for the writings of Blume, O'Dell, and Bradbury. You could report verbally that out of a sample of 100 boys and 100 girls, a certain number preferred each of the writers; but doing so would require a long paragraph of information that could be confusing. You would do better to present the information in a table, as is shown in Table 9.1. (The data in the table are fictitious.) You can see how clearly the information stands out when presented in concise tabular form.

On the other hand, when you wish to make graphic presentations of data that cannot be presented as rows and columns of numerals, you can use figures to clarify the information. Any sort of graphic depiction, other than rows and columns, can be called a figure. Bar and line graphs are frequently used figures. You could use a bar graph to illustrate the comparative preferences of boys and girls for the writings of Blume, O'Dell, and Bradbury, as in Figure 9.1. (Note that in tables the title is placed at the top; in figures it may be placed either above or below the illustration. To be sure, you should consult the style guide used in your graduate program.)

Verbal descriptions accompany tables and figures to ensure that readers understand correctly what is being shown. To accompany the table in your report, you might write

Table 9.1 shows the preferences of boys and girls for the writings of the three authors. The difference between the two groups was significant at the .01 level, as shown in the chi-square analysis presented in Table 9.2.

To accompany the figure you might write

The graph shown in Figure 9.1 illustrates the comparative preferences of boys and girls for the writings of the three authors. Evident is the apparent preference among girls for the works of Blume and the apparent preference among boys for the works of Bradbury.

TABLE 9.1   Preferences among 200 Eighth-Grade Students for the Writings of Blume, O'Dell, and Bradbury

	Blume	O'Dell	Bradbury	Total
Girls	42	38	20	100
Boys	18	33	49	100

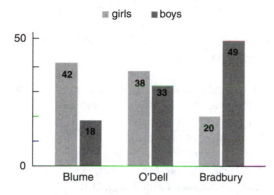

FIGURE 9.1   The preferences of 200 eighth-grade boys and girls for the writings of Blume, O'Dell, and Bradbury

TABLE 9.2   Chi-Square Analysis of Differences in Boys' and Girls' Preferences for the Writings of Blume, O'Dell, and Bradbury

	Observed			Expected		
	Blume	*O'Dell*	*Bradbury*	*Blume*	*O'Dell*	*Bradbury*
girls	42	38	20	33.3	33.3	33.3
boys	18	33	49	33.3	33.3	33.3

o	*e*	*(o–e)*	*(o–e)²*	*(o–e)²/e*
42	30	12.0	144.00	4.80
18	30	–12.0	144.00	4.80
38	35.5	2.5	6.25	0.18
33	35.5	–2.5	6.25	0.18
20	34.5	–14.5	210.25	6.09
49	34.5	14.5	210.25	6.09

$$\chi^2 = 22.14$$
$$df = 2 \quad sig < .01$$

The information shown in tables and figures should be related to specific hypotheses or research questions set forth in the study. If hypotheses are used, they may at this point be either retained or rejected, based on data analysis.

If you used research questions instead of, or in addition to, hypotheses, it is at this point that you state answers that you judge to be warranted by the data. In answering the questions, you proceed as follows:

- Take each subquestion separately and select data and the subsequent results related to it.
- Examine the data logically (there are no formulas for this process) and arrive at the answer you deem appropriate.

For example, if you had done an historical study of education in the ghost town of Bodie, one of your questions might have been, "How did students get to school in the winter?" You had obtained the following information: (1) Several pairs of long wooden skis still remain in the cloakroom of the classroom; (2) among the student compositions found in the classroom was one describing coming to school on skis when the snow was deep; and (3) a former Bodie student (now an elderly man) described to you how students used snowshoes or skis but preferred skis because they were faster. From that and the fact that some of the homes had horse corrals, you conclude that "students probably got to school on skis or snowshoes when the snow was deep but walked or rode horses when there was little snow." The answer to each of the individual subquestions contributes to answering the main research question.

In theses and dissertations, you would be obliged to present your data in sufficient detail so that other persons could apply their own logic to answering the questions. If you report your work in a shorter form such as a journal article, others might request sets of your data for further study.

Conclusions or Discussion

In the fifth section of most research reports you present and discuss the conclusions you have reached in your investigation. Sometimes, especially in theses and dissertations, this section is called "Conclusions and Recommendations." In shorter reports, it may be labeled "Findings" or "Findings and Implications."

In this final section, you at last have the opportunity to interpret, speculate on, and otherwise discuss the conclusions you have reached. This portion is often quite enlightening because it contains the thoughts of the person most intimately involved in seeking answers and exploring meanings and implications—the researcher herself or himself. Here you may discuss errors you inadvertently made, problems you encountered unexpectedly, your surprise at the findings, or other related matters that help readers understand your research efforts and the conclusions you reached.

More than anything else, it is this portion of the report that allows *you* to tell what you believe the findings mean, how you have interpreted them, what they imply for education, or what they suggest for further research. This is the one place in the report where you are allowed to speculate a bit, to move a little beyond hard evidence and stringent logic. Had you done the study of education in Bodie, you would be allowed to say:

> *A day at Bodie School, while unlike that in today's modern schools, was probably typical of most rural schools in the early 1930s. Everyone, students, teachers, and parents, seemed to have been a bit more resourceful than is now the case, because they had to make do with less. Yet the students still learned their subjects as well as do students today. Teachers had more authority then; their discipline and teaching methods were standardized and were supported by parents. But while they had fewer*

resources to use in teaching, their concerns about the growth and well-being of their students seem not to have been very different from those of teachers today.

Front and Back Material

Front and back material are portions of the report that come before and after the main body. Theses and dissertations contain both. Typical **front material** includes:

- Title page
- Signature page (for advisers to sign and date)
- Acknowledgment page
- Table of contents
- List of tables
- List of figures
- Abstract

Typical **back material** includes:

- Bibliography (complete list of references and other resources)
- Appendix or appendixes (materials used or produced in the study but that occupy too much space to be included in the body of the report)

Journal articles and other short reports typically have no front material, though some present a very helpful abstract at the beginning of the article. Their back material is usually limited to the list of references cited in the report.

Style Guides

Specific directions have not been provided here for preparing front and back material, for citing references, or for presenting tables and figures. That is because each graduate school or professional journal has adopted a style it prefers.

When preparing theses or dissertations, you are expected to follow the **style guide** used in the institution through which your work is done. Some colleges and universities have prepared their own guides. Others have adopted existing stylebooks, of which the following are well known and widely used:

Achtert, W., & Gibaldi, J. (1985). *MLA Handbook for Writers of Research Papers* (2nd ed.). New York: Modern Language Association of America. (Note: This is frequently called "MLA style.")

American Psychological Association. (2001). *Publication Manual of the American Psychological Association* (5th ed.). Washington, DC: American Psychological Association. (Note: This is frequently called "APA style.")

Campbell, W., Ballou, S., & Slade, C. (1990). *Form and Style: Theses, Reports, Term Papers* (8th ed.). Boston: Houghton Mifflin. (Note: This is often referred to as "Campbell.")

Turabian, K. (1980). *A Manual for Writers of Term Papers, Theses, and Dissertations* (5th ed.). Chicago: University of Chicago Press. (Note: This is often referred to as "Turabian.")

University of Chicago Press. (1993). *The Chicago Manual of Style: The Essential Guide for Authors, Editors, and Publishers* (14th ed.). Chicago: University of Chicago Press. (Note: This is frequently called "Chicago style.")

Scholarly journals also have styles they prefer, and when you submit an article for publication you are expected to use that journal's style. Journals will inform you of the required style or send you a style sheet on request; or you can examine published articles to determine the style expected.

A Composite Outline of Format Conventions

The following outline shows typical format conventions for theses, dissertations, journal articles, technical reports, and occasional papers.

Theses and Dissertations	*Articles and Papers*
■ Title page	■ Title
■ Signature page	
■ Acknowledgment page	
■ Table of contents	
■ List of tables	
■ List of figures	
■ Title	
■ Abstract (one page)	■ Abstract paragraph, optional
■ Introduction (Chapter 1) Identify problem Discuss importance Present background State hypotheses/questions Define terms State limitations and delimitations	■ Introductory paragraph(s) Identify problem Discuss importance Present background State hypotheses/questions
■ Review of literature (Chapter 2) General to specific Older to newer Relate to hypotheses/questions Organize into categories	■ Literature may be reviewed very briefly in introduction
■ Procedures or method (Chapter 3) Give step-by-step description of research design, participants, instruments, and what was done to collect and analyze data	■ Procedures section Summarize what was done, how, and when, in collecting and analyzing data

Theses and Dissertations

- Findings or results (Chapter 4)
  Organize by hypotheses or research questions
  Show data analyses and tests of significance
  Present in tables and figures
  Answer questions, test hypotheses

- Conclusions (Chapter 5)
  Present investigator's conclusions
  Discuss implications
- Bibliography
  List references cited and any used but not cited

- Appendix or appendixes
  Attach important material used or produced in the study but too lengthy to be included in the body of the report

Articles and Papers

- Findings section
  Organize by hypotheses or research questions
  Show data analyses and tests of significance
  Present in tables and figures
  Answer questions, test hypotheses

- Conclusions and discussion
  Present investigator's conclusions
  Discuss implications
- References
  List references cited

Applying Technology: **Organizing Research Papers with** *TakeNote!*

Academix Software Corporation has developed software to assist students in the process of writing research reports. The software program, in CD-ROM format, is titled *TakeNote!* and it not only assists students in formatting specific contents of the research paper but also in the overall organization of the paper. This software can be especially helpful to students with respect to the development of a review of related literature, among other aspects of the research report.

Please note that a comprehensive tutorial for *TakeNote!* has been provided in Appendix B. Many students will find *TakeNote!* an invaluable resource, for both their current and future work.

The *TakeNote!* software is available as an extra value package option; therefore, some students may have received the software package with their copies of this textbook.

Sample Pages

The following are samples that you can use as general guides or models when preparing research reports. Remember that each institution and journal has its own approved format that you will be expected to follow. We consider shorter reports first and then proceed to thesis formats.

For Research Papers and Journal Articles

[*fictitious*]

The Application of Selected School Effectiveness Factors
in Twelve Regional Secondary Schools
by
Ira Cartwright
Director of Instructional Improvement
Excellence, Michigan, Schools

Abstract

Four selected "school effectiveness factors" were systematically introduced into 12 regional high schools. At the end of the first year, student achievement showed significant improvement over what had been normal for the school. Student attitude toward school improved significantly, as did teacher professional satisfaction.

Introduction

For the past two decades, student achievement in secondary school has remained static or has declined. Yet at the same time, a number of schools have been identified as highly successful. Many investigators, notably Shumate and Hall (1994), Gromald (1995), Rimes and Cortez (1996), Colbertson (1997), and Khoury (1998), have explored factors that seem to characterize these successful schools and differentiate them from schools considered to be relatively ineffective. Their conclusions have been that highly effective schools show the following characteristics... [*continued*]

The Problem

The purpose of this study was to determine whether selected effectiveness characteristics, when incorporated into ongoing scholastic programs and maintained for one academic year, could raise student achievement and improve the attitudes of students and teachers. In particular, the study was intended to seek answers to the following questions... [*continued*]

Procedures

To obtain information for answering the research questions set forth in this study, the following steps were taken:

1. Twelve regional secondary schools were selected for inclusion in the study. The schools were [*names*]. Approval for involvement was obtained from school board, faculty, and administration.

2. The individuals from whom data were obtained included all the students and teachers in the 12 selected schools who were present on the date of final testing.

3. Four selected effectiveness factors were introduced into the scholastic programs of the participating schools. Those four factors were [*name and define*]. The factors were introduced as follows: [*describe how*]. Training and follow-up sessions were conducted [*describe when and how*].

4. At the end of the school year, student achievement was measured through use of [*name tests*]. The data were analyzed by [*describe*]. Student attitudes and teacher attitude were assessed by means of [*name instruments*]. The data were analyzed by [*describe*].

Findings

Data analysis revealed the following: [*explain in relation to each of the research questions*]. The findings are presented in Table 1, Table 2, and Table 3. [*Show tables and explain contents beneath each table.*]
[*continued*]

Conclusions

Concerning achievement, the findings show growth significantly beyond the levels reached by similar students over the past ten years and significantly higher than those of students in schools used as controls for this study. This result seems to be due to...

The attitude ratings of both students and teachers were also significantly higher than those of students and teachers in the control schools. This seems to have been due to... Based on the results of this study, it seems evident that...

It seems fair to suggest that school districts elsewhere consider...

References

[*list alphabetically by writers' last names*]

For Masters' Theses

The following are sample pages that can be used as *general* guides in preparing graduate theses. The first samples are from a thesis that reported an action research project. The second samples indicate what might be used in theses that report other types of research.

For a Thesis That Reports Action Research

[*title page—one page*]

CHILDREN'S LITERATURE BROUGHT ALIVE:

A LITERATURE PROGRAM TO ENCOURAGE STUDENTS TO READ

A Paper

Presented to the Faculty of

Excel University

in Partial Fulfillment

of the Requirements for the Degree

Master of Arts

in Education

by

Marcella Louise Cox

Spring 1998

[*next page—separate page*]

ACKNOWLEDGMENTS

The writer wishes to express her gratitude to the following people, who encouraged, supported, and assisted in the development of the project: [*list*]

[*new page*]

TABLE OF CONTENTS

	page
ACKNOWLEDGMENTS	ii
ABSTRACT	iii
CHAPTER	
I. Introduction and Statement of the Problem	1
II. Information and Resources	5
III. Procedures	14
IV. Findings	22
V. Conclusions	24
APPENDIXES	
A. Lesson Plans	26
B. Background Information	72
BIBLIOGRAPHY	107

[*new single page*]

ABSTRACT

The purpose of this project was to develop and implement a holistic procedure for encouraging intermediate-grade children to develop interest in reading, through exposure to and involvement with a variety of quality children's literature and activities related to it.

The project was designed to call on each student to read storybooks selected from various genres of children's literature. The students were involved in activities related to their reading, including readers' theater, choral reading, creative writing, drama, and art.

The program was put into effect as follows: First, students were assessed to determine their individual levels of reading ability. Second, they were given interest inventories to help in the selection of books. Third, appropriate books were selected for each student. Fourth, each student received a personalized plan that included assignments, schedules, and partners. Fifth, students read their books and participated in associated activities. Sixth, students prepared materials, worked on performances, and presented performances to family members and other classrooms.

Ongoing assessment of student involvement, enjoyment, and progress showed the program to be highly successful.

[*new page*]

CHAPTER I

INTRODUCTION AND STATEMENT OF THE PROBLEM

During the first year that the writer taught a fifth-sixth grade class, she noted how differently students behaved according to what they were asked to do during reading lessons. On the three days per week that they were to work from their grade-level reading books, they groaned and asked, "Do we have to read the whole story today?" and "Do we have to answer all the questions at the end of the story?"

In contrast, on the two days per week they were involved in children's literature, they showed interest and excitement. Typical questions for those days were, "Can we make scenery for readers' theater?" and "Can we make a skit out of the story?"

The writer began to believe that the reading program could contribute much more strongly to building student enjoyment of reading if it were based on selected literature, rather than on the grade-level readers.

Such a program would have to be well organized and balanced to include all areas of skill development. This would then permit...[*Continue in this vein so as to lead into a statement of the problem, but do not describe anything that was actually done in the project.*]

THE PROBLEM

The purpose of this study was to organize and implement
a holistic procedure for helping children develop
interest in reading through exposure to and
involvement with a variety of children's literature.
Such a procedure would include literature of the
following genres: picture books, traditional
literature, modern fantasy, poetry, contemporary
realistic fiction, historical fiction, biography,
and nonfiction. Further, it would engage the
children in creative and artistic activities, such
as painting, designing, acting, pantomiming, and
batiking. The program would be balanced to include
skill development in word attack, oral and
silent reading, and comprehension of theme, character,
and meaning.

DEFINITION OF TERMS

Terms central to this study are defined as follows:
Holistic [*define*]
Modern fantasy [*define*]
[*continued*]

DELIMITATIONS

The writer restricted the study as follows:

Program development: The writer selected the books and
     developed the materials, activities, and guides for the
     program.
Participants: Participants in the study were the students
     in the writer's fifth-sixth-grade combination class.
Time period: The time during which the project was planned
     and implemented was restricted as follows: The project

was prepared over a period of four months—September, October, November, and December. The project was implemented and appraised over a period of three months—January, February, and March.

[*continued*]

[*new page*]

CHAPTER II

INFORMATION AND RESOURCES

This project relied heavily on the collection of reading materials representing various genres, namely, picture books, traditional literature, modern fantasy, realistic fiction, historical fiction, biography, and nonfiction. It was anticipated by the writer that a minimum of 8 to 10 books within each genre would be required for the project.

The initial list of books developed by the writer contained a minimum of 15 books per each category. Several sources, including the local library, children's literature guides, and various school district reading specialists, were contacted in order to develop a preliminary list of books within each category and to determine the local availability of specific books within each category. Following the determination of the local availability of the necessary number of copies of each book, the final list of books to be used in the project was determined. These books, organized by genre, included:

[*continued*]

[*new page*]

CHAPTER III

PROCEDURES

The writer began by selecting children's literature in eight genres: picture books, traditional literature, modern fantasy, poetry, contemporary realistic fiction, historical fiction, biography, and nonfiction. Considerations in book selection included variety, overall story quality, depiction of various ethnic groups, balance between boys and girls as main characters, and quality of illustrations.

When the book selection process was completed, a number of different activities were planned for each book and genre. These activities were incorporated into a teacher's guide that consisted of three parts:

1. Assessment instruments to determine reading ability and areas of interest.

2. Contracts, schedules, and notebook formats for students to follow and use.

3. Books students were to read, activities they were to complete, and performances they were to make.

The writer then proceeded to collect and make quantities of materials, such as...

[*Proceed in this fashion to describe, step-by-step, what was done in the project.*]

[*new page*]

CHAPTER IV

FINDINGS

The writer was successful in producing a literature-based reading program that incorporated writing, art, music, and drama. Compared to the writer's previous reading program, the diversity and quality of these new activities attracted greater student interest and promoted greater degrees of student involvement.

Three problems were encountered when the project was first introduced into the writer's classroom. Those problems were...[*list and describe*]

To correct those problems, the following modifications were made in the program... [*list and describe*]

Preliminary assessment completed after the program had been in place for three months suggested that student achievement in basic reading skills was as high, or higher, than in the reading program the writer used previously.

[*new page*]

CHAPTER V

CONCLUSIONS

This project demonstrated how a reading program based on children's literature could be organized to include writing, art, music, and drama—a diversity of activity that greatly increases student interest in reading while maintaining necessary emphasis on the acquisition of reading skills.

The enthusiasm that students showed for the activities suggests that the program could be continued indefinitely and could perhaps be spread into other areas of the curriculum as well. [*Continue with observations about the project and thoughts about how it could be improved, expanded, and adopted by other teachers.*]

[*new page*]

APPENDIXES

[*Present here the guides, lists of materials, photographs, and so forth that depict what was developed and implemented in the project. If there is more than one appendix, present a heading for each—e.g., Appendix A: Description of the Project; Appendix B: Teacher's Guide for the Reading Program; Appendix C: Lesson Plans Used in the Program, etc.*]

Thesis Format for Other Types of Research

Theses that report types of research other than action research differ somewhat from the example just presented, in keeping with the characteristics of the research being reported. Let us take as an example a thesis that reports an experiment to determine the effectiveness of "quality school factors" applied in two secondary schools.

[*title page*]

THE EFFECTIVENESS OF QUALITY SCHOOL FACTORS

DETERMINED THROUGH IMPLEMENTATION

IN TWO SELECTED SECONDARY SCHOOLS

[*remainder of page the same as shown previously*]

ACKNOWLEDGMENTS

[*same as shown previously*]

ABSTRACT

[*a one-page summary of the study*]

TABLE OF CONTENTS

	page
ACKNOWLEDGMENTS	ii
ABSTRACT	iii
LIST OF TABLES	iv
LIST OF FIGURES	v
CHAPTER	
1. Introduction	
Concern about school effectiveness	1
Statement of the problem	5
Hypotheses and research questions	6
Rationale of the study	8
Definition of terms	9
Limitations of the study	12

Delimitations   14

Assumptions   16

Overview of the study   18

2. Review of the Literature

Organization of review   19

School effectiveness   20

Teacher effectiveness   26

Quality school factors   32

Implementation efforts elsewhere   35

Summary   41

3. Procedures

Review of hypotheses and research questions   42

Design of the study   44

Establishment of calendar   46

Selection of the samples   47

Description of quality factors   48

Orientation of school personnel   49

Training procedures for school personnel   50

Implementation, monitoring, and feedback   53

Assessment procedures   57

4. Findings

Student achievement   61

Student attitude   63

Teacher attitude   65

Parental acceptance   67

Program implementation feasibility   69

5. Conclusions

Commentary on implementation   71

Commentary on results   75

Implications   78

Recommendations for further research   82

BIBLIOGRAPHY

APPENDIX: Participating Schools and Personnel   93

CHAPTER I

INTRODUCTION

[Begins much the same as the sample provided for action research and development but contains more elements and background information, as indicated in the Table of Contents.]

CHAPTER II

REVIEW OF THE LITERATURE

[Describes literature related to the topic, grouped according to hypotheses and research questions. The presentation is organized to move from general to specific and from older to more recent literature.]

Remaining Chapters

[Similar to the samples provided for the action research report. See Table of Contents for specific differences.]

INTRODUCTION TO EDUCATIONAL RESEARCH
Companion Website Highlight

The Companion Website that accompanies this text (www.ablongman.com/mertler5e) includes additional examples of written research reports, including:

- A paper appropriate for presentation at a research conference
- A paper appropriate for publication in an academic journal

INTRODUCTION TO EDUCATIONAL RESEARCH
Companion Website Highlight

The Companion Website that accompanies this text (www.ablongman.com/mertler5e) includes a list of organizations that sponsor or publish journals as well as the names of those journals. This list is a great resource for individuals looking for specific types of journals or for an outlet to publish their research.

DEVELOPMENTAL ACTIVITY

Preparing to Write Your Report

Writing lengthy, comprehensive scientific reports requires some skill...and a great deal of practice. Novice researchers typically find it helpful to anticipate the "look" of their report and to do some degree of preparation *prior* to actually writing the final report. One helpful procedure is to develop a thorough outline of the report, specifying the major headings and subheadings you will use throughout. You then write your report around this outline. Such an outline has been started for you here, with the major section or chapter headings provided. For this activity, complete the outline by specifying the subheadings you anticipate using for your report. Be aware that, depending on your topic and research, you may require fewer or more entries than have been provided; you may also want to use another level of heading.

I. INTRODUCTION

    A. _____

    B. _____

    C. _____

    D. _____

    E. _____

II. REVIEW OF RELATED LITERATURE

    A. _____

    B. _____

    C. _____

    D. _____

    E. _____

III. METHODOLOGY _____

    A. _____

    B. _____

C. _____

D. _____

E. _____

IV. RESULTS

A. _____

B. _____

C. _____

D. _____

E. _____

V. CONCLUSIONS AND RECOMMENDATIONS

A. _____

B. _____

C. _____

D. _____

E. _____

(A downloadable, interactive version of this developmental activity is available from the Companion Website, www.ablongman.com/mertler5e)

Chapter Summary

Graduate students usually report their research in thesis format and sometimes in formats appropriate for technical papers or journal articles. The reports are done in keeping with conventions of style and format. Although there are differences among types of reports, certain conventions apply to all.

Conventions of acceptable style include descriptive titles, plain language, use of third person, passive voice, use of past tense, consistent organization, and consistent meanings of terminology.

Research formats are organized to include an introduction, statement of the problem, hypotheses or research questions, review of related literature, procedures, findings, and conclusions. Some variation exists in the terminology used to denote these sections of reports.

Reports often include front and back material. Examples of front material are tables of contents and abstracts; examples of back material are bibliographies and appendixes.

LIST OF IMPORTANT TERMS

back material

conventions

front material

style guide

YOUR CURRENT STATUS

You have completed the activities designed to enable you to conduct and report research of your own. The remaining chapters, Chapters 10 through 14, present detailed descriptions of the nature and procedures of the eight types of educational research as determined by the questions asked.

ACTIVITIES FOR THOUGHT AND DISCUSSION

1. Here are the questions listed at the beginning of the chapter. See how well you can answer them.
   a. What is meant by *convention,* and why are conventions important in reporting research?
   b. What are the conventions of style regarding person, voice, tense, and consistency?
   c. What are the four to six sections usually included in research reports?
   d. Which section explains the plan for obtaining data?
   e. In which of the sections is the investigator permitted to speculate on meanings and implications?
   f. What is meant by *front material* and *back material?*
   g. Who ultimately specifies the style and format that graduate students must use when preparing reports required in their programs?

2. Recall the information organizer that is presented at the beginning of the chapter. For a topic you are interested in researching, see how well you can use the organizer to plan a research report.

ANSWERS TO CHAPTER EXERCISES

9.1. Choice 3 is the best title.

9.2. 1. Reword something like this: "This study was undertaken for two reasons."

2. Reword as "The findings suggest the following conclusions."

3. Better wording: "Prior to [year], teachers who used traditional means of motivating students were considered old-fashioned."

4. Better wording:

   "The following steps were taken in obtaining data:
   a. Records were checked in the district office.
   b. Notations were made of discrepancies in the records.
   c. A meeting was held with the personnel director to discuss discrepancies."

9.3. The following arrangement would organize topics to proceed from more general to more specific.

5 Rules and practices that promote good classroom behavior

3 The relationship of discipline to achievement

7 Support from others that helps teachers enjoy better discipline

1 The outcry over what is seen to be lack of discipline in the schools

4 Traits and practices of teachers identified as having better behaved classes

2 The effects of serious classroom misbehavior on teachers and students

6 Elements and emphasis in various programs for developing teacher skills in discipline

8 Two training programs implemented at schools in other states

10 Ethnographic Research

P R E V I E W

This chapter focuses on the nature, intent, and procedures of
■ Ethnographic research

which is a type of research used for studying
■ Social groups

Characteristics specific to ethnographic research include:
■ Holistic in nature, replete with detail
■ Data gathered through naturalistic group observation
■ Observer-researcher may function as member of group
■ Verbal data are analyzed logically and contextually

Strengths of ethnographic research include:
■ Best for learning about group behavior
■ Rich in details
■ Provides complete pictures

Major concerns about ethnographic research include:
■ Reliability of data
■ Validity of conclusions
■ Generalizability of findings

Targeted Learnings

This chapter deals with *ethnographic research,* an investigative technique for studying social groups in natural settings. Ethnography has long been a principal research method in anthropology. Until fairly recently, it was not used much in education, but its popularity is now growing rapidly. In this chapter you will learn more about the nature of ethnographic research, why it is used, and how it is conducted. To further your understanding, two ethnographic article reprints are included for your examination and analysis. As you read this chapter, look especially for information related to the following:

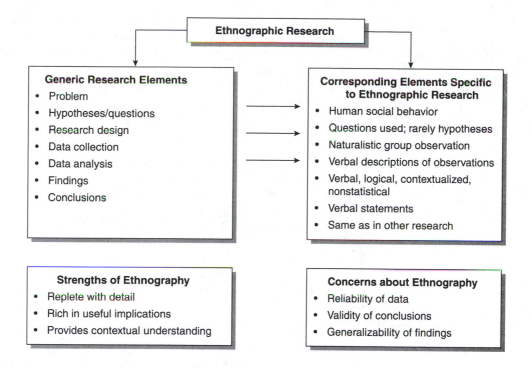

1. What is the main purpose of ethnographic research?
2. What distinctive characteristics set ethnographic research apart from other types of research?
3. What roles do hypotheses and research questions play in ethnographic research?
4. What are the main data sources in ethnographic research?
5. Through what procedures are data usually obtained in ethnographic research?
6. What is the role of the investigator in obtaining data?
7. In what form are ethnographic data usually compiled?
8. How are the data analyzed in ethnographic research?
9. How are findings reported in ethnographic research?

The Nature of Ethnographic Research

Research
Navigator.com
ethnography

Ethnography (*ethno-* refers to human cultures; *-graphy* means description of) is a research process used in the scientific study of human interactions in social settings. Long a predominant research procedure in anthropology, ethnography has in recent years become increasingly popular in educational research, where it is used to illuminate in detail the conditions and interactions of individuals and groups as they function within the schools and larger society (Wiersma, 2000).

Ethnography is essentially a descriptive approach, but is placed in a category of its own because (1) it is unique in focusing on social behavior within natural settings; (2) it relies on qualitative data, usually in the form of narrative descriptions made by an observer of, or participant in, the group being studied; (3) its perspective is **holistic**—observations and interpretations are made within the context of the *totality* of human interactions; (4) hypotheses and research questions may emerge *after* data collection is well underway, rather than being stated at the beginning of the investigation; and (5) its procedures of data analysis involve **contextualization,** where research findings are interpreted with reference to the particular group, setting, or event being observed.

Ethnographic research can thus be described concisely as follows:

1. *Purpose:* to describe and explain a facet or segment of group social life as it relates to education.
2. *Hypotheses and questions:* begin as broad statements about the purpose of the research, then are allowed to emerge more specifically as data are amassed.
3. *Data:* verbal descriptions of people, interactions, settings, objects, and phenomena within the context being studied.
4. *Data sources:* the people, settings, and relevant objects being observed.
5. *Data collection:* done by the researcher through observation, sometimes combined with interview.
6. *Data treatment and analysis:* presentation of verbal descriptions and/or logical analysis of information to discover salient patterns and themes.

Topics in Ethnographic Research

Because ethnographic research studies people in small or large groups in an attempt to understand the groups and how they function, the range of topics in ethnographic research is quite broad. The following topics hint at the range of possibilities:

- Faculty interactions in the lounge and workroom
- Kindergartners' behavior on the playground
- The daily regimens of administrative personnel
- Korean American students' lives at school and work
- The lifestyles of top student athletes
- The coping behaviors of students who consider themselves oppressed

The list could go on and on. Virtually any topic involving social behavior that impinges on education can be approached through ethnographic methods.

Procedures in Ethnographic Research

The following general procedures are followed when conducting ethnographic research:

1. A question or concern worthy of research is formalized.
2. A group is identified for use in studying the concern. The group may be very small, consisting of two or three people, or quite large, consisting of hundreds of individuals.
3. The investigator introduces the proposed research to the group and obtains their agreement for involvement.
4. The investigator may function as a **privileged observer** (also known as a *nonparticipant observer*) of the group, who does not participate in its activities, or as a **participant observer,** participating actively as a regular member in all group activities.

Research
Navigator.c✦m
participant
observer

5. The researcher's method is to watch and listen attentively, a procedure called **naturalistic observation,** and to record as faithfully as possible all pertinent information. (Note the qualifier *pertinent*—even though the ethnographic approach is holistic, no one can record every detail of events, interactions, objects, settings, etc. The investigator must exercise quick judgment in deciding what is and is not worth recording.) Although such watching, notetaking, and sometimes audio and video recording are done as the behaviors occur, ethnographers also use informants, whom they interview systematically.

6. The duration of ethnographic research may be as short as a week or two or as long as several years. In educational research done by graduate students, the duration should be adequate to obtain detailed information but usually should not stretch out over more than two months.

7. These observations and their recordings produce vast quantities of written notes, which comprise the data obtained in the study.

8. Data analysis, which often requires as much time as does data collection, involves primarily verbal analysis and interpretation. As we have seen, qualitative data do not lend themselves to statistical treatments. Investigators must look instead for patterns of language and behavior that provide insight into the group's concerns and functions. These patterns, once identified, are to be described carefully. Patton (2001) considers this descriptive aspect crucial, believing that if descriptions are good enough, readers can make their own interpretations. However, researchers are also obliged to interpret and explain the findings of their investigation. Reflecting on the following questions may help in formulating interpretations:

    a. What commonalities tie group members together? Did those commonalities or other factors make this group deserving of study?

    b. What seems to be the key life perspectives of this group? Do members feel isolated, put upon, prejudiced against, overworked, misunderstood? Do they feel superior in identifiable ways? Do they seem unusually able to exercise control over their fate?

    c. How do these perspectives, if identified, seem to cause the group to react to opportunity and threat? Do they tend to be aggressive, antagonistic, submissive, escapist? Do they complain, blame, and scapegoat? Do they reach out for greater challenges? Do they attempt to control or dominate?

    d. How does the group attempt to solve or otherwise deal with problems, expectations held for them, or demands made on them? What are the results of their efforts?

    e. What language patterns are associated with identified perspectives and behaviors? What special terms are used and with what meanings?

    f. What are the group's preferred activities? Is there evident linkage between activities and life perspectives?

    g. Which objects within the setting receive major attention (e.g., automobiles, electronic equipment, clothing, printed materials, weapons, sports paraphernalia)?

    h. What patterns of leadership, friendship, dominance, and submission are noted within the group? What are the effects of those patterns? What special words or terms are associated with them? What activities, events, or routines seem to strengthen the bonds that hold the group together?

For those who are interested in learning more about the process of conducting ethnographic research, students are directed to several books written by Harry F. Wolcott (1994, 1995, 1999, 2001), a longtime and leading expert on the topic of ethnographic methods. These books address such topics as how to collect data in the field, how to analyze and interpret ethnographic data, and how to write up the results of ethnographic research studies.

The Richness of Ethnographic Research

A major appeal of ethnographic research is that it can construct, better than any other type of research, a richly detailed picture of human life—a picture that is interesting, informative, and potentially filled with implications. This quality is evident in the following excerpt from the writing of Horacio Ulibarrí (1958), who decades ago described the cultural patterns of Spanish American groups in New Mexico and Colorado (where Spain established settlements in the 1600s that today still retain individual identities and customs). Ulibarrí remembered the fiesta of his boyhood thus:

> The Fiesta was probably the most colorful event of the year in any community. The Fiesta usually took place on the village's Patron Saint's Day. The celebration started with the singing of vespers the night before. All of these were sung in Latin, of course. At certain intervals when the choir would sing, *"Per omnia saecula saeculorum,"* a man at the rear of the church would beat a drum. When this happened, another man or two would fire a volley outside the church.
>
> When vespers were over, the procession took place. The men had built luminarias out of peachwood around the village, and these would be lit for the procession. The people filed out of the church, men on one side and women on the other. The choir took its place in the middle of the procession, followed by the priest and the Patron Saint which was carried on the shoulders of the Mayordomos (persons who had taken care of the church, sweeping and cleaning it for the past year). The procession wound through the plaza singing the rosary. The men sang the first part of the Hail Mary and the women answered; or the choir sang the first part and all answered. It was a very colorful picture to behold—with the luminarias blazing away, the people dressed in their finest, the strains of a singing procession, an occasional beating of a drum and the shattering of the night silence by volleys of gunfire. (p. 84)

With regard to the effects of education among Spanish Americans in 1958, Ulibarrí wrote:

> There are in New Mexico a great number of unacculturated Spanish Americans [Ulibarrí meant unacculturated to Anglo ways]. There are a great number of old people that do not speak the English language. Among the young there are many who stopped their formal education early and as a result, do not speak the English language fluently and do not begin to understand the Anglo folkways and mores. Along the continuum of acculturation, there are a number of people that exist in a half-Spanish half-Anglo world. They have accepted some of the folkways and mores of the Anglo but still retain the Spanish values. Still others… have lost all the Spanish values, practically speaking. About the only contact they have with their (traditional) culture is the language and the food. At the same time it is possible to find Spanish Americans highly acculturated in one or two fields but still quite traditional in others. The whole situation is very complex and almost impossible to measure. (pp. 48–49)

Strengths and Concerns in Ethnographic Research

Much of the popularity of ethnographic research in education stems from its holistic nature. Educational practitioners have long expressed dissatisfaction with research findings obtained from investigations that focus on minute aspects of education or personal behavior—findings that appear isolated and unrealistic outside their normal context. Ethnography helps satisfy this concern by presenting what educators consider to be realistic pictures of group behavior. Educators often feel they can derive better insights from those realistic portrayals than from traditional research, with the result that they become able to work more profitably with students under their guidance.

But concerns also exist about ethnography, principally about the reliability of data and hence, the validity of research conclusions. A major problem is that frequently only a single observer records the descriptions that comprise the data, leaving the research open to questions concerning expertise, consistency, and bias. Take Ulibarrí's excerpt for example. He wrote decades ago and in his writings often recalled events that he had experienced years earlier. Did Ulibarrí know what he was talking about? Was he unbiased? Was his memory good? Were his descriptions accurate? We cannot, without corroboration from other sources, answer those questions. That exemplifies a major concern about the validity of ethnographic findings. It is difficult to resolve that concern, even today when two or more observers collect data as a check against one another. An additional problem with ethnographic research has to do with the generalizability of its findings. In far too many cases, it is clear that conclusions drawn from ethnographic research, even though they illuminate the group being studied, do not seem to be applicable to other groups and settings. As you can see, this limits the practical value of the research.

An Example of Ethnographic Research

The following is a report of an investigation of teachers who frequented a particular bar, what they discussed, and the things about which they were concerned.

Exercise 10.1

As you read the following article, see if you can answer the following questions about it:

1. *Problem:* What was the focus and intent of the study?
2. *Time:* Over what length of time was the study conducted?
3. *Subjects or participants:* Who was involved?
4. *Design:* What, specifically, was done to gain access to pertinent data?
5. *Data collection:* What kinds of data were obtained?
6. *Data analysis:* How were the data analyzed, if at all?
7. *Findings and conclusions:* What did the investigators find and conclude?

Teachers in Bars: From Professional to Personal Self

Edward F. Pajak and Joseph J. Blase
University of Georgia

This article reports findings from a study that investigated the interaction among public-school teachers in a barroom over a three-month period. Research questions focused on the relationship between this setting and the job of teaching and on the meaning of the barroom setting for teachers. Data were collected through participant observation and unstructured tape-recorded interviews. The data suggest that teachers dichotomized their professional and personal identities and that barroom interaction facilitated the transition from a restricted professional self to a more spontaneous personal self.

[Information that typically appears in an abstract]

The study of saloons has a fairly long tradition in the United States. At the turn of the century, for example, Moore (1897) and Melendy (1900) recognized the social functions that saloons served for a typically working-class clientele in Chicago. More recently, in an extensive study of approximately 100 settings in San Francisco, Cavan (1966) developed a typology of bars based on the interactions among customers—convenience, nightspot, marketplace, and home territory. LeMasters (1975) examined the values, beliefs, and lives of the patrons of a single saloon in a working-class neighborhood; and Anderson (1978) intensively studied interactions among black customers in a barroom on the south side of Chicago. In the LeMasters study and particularly, the Anderson study, interaction among patrons was intensive and ongoing, allowing for the development of a social structure similar to that of a primary group, which exhibits a high degree of personal investment of self and where opportunities for firmly establishing one's personal identity occur.

The research reported here is part of a more comprehensive ethnographic study of public-school teachers in a barroom setting. In some ways the events, and the meanings teachers attached to these events, differed little from what may be observed in any other barroom. Teachers used the barroom to unwind from the disciplined involvement of the work setting, as do other saloon patrons, in an atmosphere of unseriousness, openness, and mild licentiousness

that is characteristic of drinking establishments generally (Cavan, 1966).

Like LeMasters (1975), we focused our study on a homogeneous occupational group. But unlike LeMasters's study, which focused on the relationship of the bar to the personal lives of construction workers, our inquiry was directed toward understanding the relationship of the bar to the professional lives of teachers.

The phenomenon we studied was also somewhat unique because teachers utilized the barroom quite differently than did working-class (LeMasters, 1975) and lower-class (Anderson, 1978) saloon patrons. We found that the setting represented only a temporary system for teachers, and involvement of the self was fairly limited in that the barroom functioned primarily as a transitional setting where teachers moved from a professional self to a personal self.

The findings reported represent teachers' perceptions of their professional role and its relationship to other persons and to self. Essentially, the data suggest that the teachers studied tended to dichotomize their professional and personal identities. It was discovered that the barroom served three major functions related to this dichotomization. First, the barroom provided an opportunity for teachers to discuss problems encountered at school, thus reducing the adverse impact of work-related problems on their private lives. Second, the barroom setting compensated for the impersonal character of schools and the lack of opportunity for the expression of the teacher's personal self while on the job. Finally, barroom interaction permitted movement from the restrictiveness associated with the professional role to a more spontaneous expression of the personal self. Broadly, schools as bureaucracies and the bureaucratically defined role of teacher seemed to precipitate a distinction between professional and personal self and a compartmentalization that kept these identities separate. We concluded that the barroom served specific functions related directly to the teacher's work setting. Essentially, the teachers appropriated a public drinking place for several hours each

[Summary of findings]

week in order to separate themselves from the contrastingly serious, restrictive, and moralistic social reality of schools.

Method

The larger field study that provided the data base for this article involved five researchers who observed and interviewed teachers in a single barroom over a three-month period. The researchers had learned that 200 to 300 teachers were congregating at a particular bar called O'Keefe's every Friday after school, and it seemed possible that this setting might provide some interesting insights into the teaching occupation. An initial phase of data collection was limited to two general questions: (1) Who are the

> Initial guiding research questions

teachers who go to O'Keefe's? and (2) What do they do there?

The preliminary data, collected through observation and 15 unstructured interviews, satisfied the

> Data collected through observations and interviews

researchers that the phenomenon at O'Keefe's was probably related in

more than a superficial way to the job of teaching and was worthy of further investigation. Two more specific questions emerged, which served as the focus for a second phase of data collection: (1) Do the partici-

> Preliminary data collection and revised questions

pants themselves view the setting as relating in any way to the job of being a

teacher? and (2) What meaning does the setting at O'Keefe's have for the participants? This phase of data collection involved tape-recorded interviews with 42 teachers. Data were transcribed and analyzed according to general qualitative research criteria developed by Bogdan and Taylor (1975) and specific guidelines for grounded-theory inquiry described in Glaser and Strauss (1967) and Glaser (1978). Thus, the categories discussed in this article are supported by substantial data. The quotes included are not exhaustive, but are used to illustrate the categories identified. It should be noted that the respondents comprise a limited sample; consequently, their particular adjustments to the role of teacher are not necessarily representative of the larger population.

The Setting

O'Keefe's is situated approximately in the center of a small shopping plaza in an urban middle-class resi-

dential neighborhood that is part of a metropolitan area with a population in excess of 250,000. At the time, the plaza was comprised of 14 businesses, including a bank, 2 supermarkets (one of which was vacant), a drugstore, a hardware store, and various clothing and gift shops. During the day, O'Keefe's provided a convenience function, according to Cavan's (1966) typology, serving lunches and drinks to shoppers and business people. Most evenings it took on qualities of the home-territory saloon, catering to a small clientele of local residents, some of whom were graduate students at a nearby university.

At 3:15 P.M. on Fridays, however, O'Keefe's prepared for a different group of customers. The lights would dim and contemporary music was piped over the sound system. A bar 75

> Very detailed description of the setting

feet in length stretched along almost the entire wall on the right. Approximately 20 high round tables were strung along the opposite wall, which was punctuated by shallow alcoves. Wooden barstools, temporarily neatly arranged along the bar and around each of the tables, awaited the teachers, who began to arrive singly and in small groups about ten minutes later.

The earliest arrivals from schools nearby often staked out tables for themselves in the alcoves opposite the bar, which provided a semblance of privacy and a focal point of activity later in the evening for larger groups that would spill out onto the wide floor between the tables and the bar. Later arrivals tended to cluster at the bar, and again, groups extended into the open space down the center of the room. Clusters that formed in this open area tended to gravitate toward one side or the other, although there was considerable milling about. By 4 P.M., five bartenders and two waitresses busily served two-for-the-price-of-one drinks to several hundred teachers who came from schools as far as 20 miles away.

O'Keefe's emerged as a teacher's bar for a variety of reasons. Teachers cited the inexpensive drinks, adequate parking, and a respectable atmosphere, but they also described a process of selection in which faculties from different schools informally scouted various bars at the beginning of the school year, finally settling on a particular bar on the basis of a spontaneously developed reputation as one that other teachers frequented. Some suggested the possibility that faculties from larger schools made the final determination and the smaller schools followed their lead.

By mid-year, in any case, 200 to 300 teachers were regularly meeting at O'Keefe's every Friday afternoon.

Teachers expressed enjoyment over the unpredictability of the selection process and expressed doubts that O'Keefe's would be the place to go next year. Most teachers were able to name a bar from the previous year that had declined in popularity because of difficulties with parking. A few teachers felt that O'Keefe's had already peaked in popularity and had begun a new search. A noticeable decline in the number of patrons did not become evident, however, until local competing merchants complained to police about the overflow parking at O'Keefe's and a few cars were towed away.

Interviews and observations indicated that most of the teachers frequenting O'Keefe's were under age 35, and considerably more than half were single. Older married teachers stopped by but not as regularly, and when they did appear they did not stay long, citing family responsibilities as the reason for leaving. Sometimes younger administrators showed up for a single drink, perhaps buying a round for their faculties. Part of the folklore of the setting was that an administrator from a large nearby school district had come to O'Keefe's and mingled with the teachers for the first and only time several days before he was publicly named to the superintendent's post by the school board.

Individuals were fully aware that most of the other people at O'Keefe's were also teachers who had stopped in after work. With few exceptions, teachers reported that teaching kept them busy most weeknights and that Friday was the only night they went out to a bar. Some said that they came to O'Keefe's only on special occasions, such as before or after vacations or to celebrate a birthday, which was confirmed for a small group through observation. The majority of teachers, however, saw stopping at O'Keefe's as a regular prelude to the weekend:

> example of "raw" data   I don't get out all week, so I stay home, I do my lessons plans, I do my research, whatever I have to do, my grading. And when it comes to Friday, it's time to forget it all and just have a good time.

The Job of Teaching

The responses of teachers to the question "Is being here tonight in any way related to your job as a teacher?" were recorded, transcribed, and classified into four major categories according to the predominant content of the response:

Intensity of Teaching	5
Self/Role Conflict	8
Relationship to Students	14
Relationship to Adults	15
Total	42

A small number of teachers (5) said that the organization of the school required uninterrupted activity and contact with students. Having no respite from the intensity of classroom interaction, these teachers viewed O'Keefe's mainly as an opportunity to relax at the end of the week:

> I wasn't one who felt this tired when I've worked in other jobs. I am physically exhausted and I'm mentally exhausted. I think it's never having that break. You've got a half hour for lunch. I've got 6 classes a day. I've got 30 new kids coming in every 35 minutes. Know their names, be able to relate to them, be able to teach them something. Unless you teach, I don't think you can understand the pressures of teaching, because kids bring in their problems.

Another teacher stated,

> When you're in school you're working under a set of rules, a schedule that you have to follow very strictly because you're depended on by students and by other people in the building. You don't have to be on constantly [at O'Keefe's] like you do when you're teaching. You don't have to be anywhere.

A slightly larger number of teachers (8) spoke of a need to cope with the conflict they experienced between their personal and professional identities:

> I have to shed my school. I just have to get rid of it. It's not that you don't like it. You just—You want a little life a little bit.

The barroom was clearly recognized as a setting where teachers were off stage and could be safely out of role. Socializing with colleagues made the transition from professional role to private life a little easier. If they didn't stop at O'Keefe's, in fact, a few of the teachers in this category reported experiencing something of a temporary void on Friday:

Before I came to O'Keefe's—I'm not much on drinking, actually I can't drink—but I used to go home, turn off all the lights and turn on the stereo, and lie down and force myself to relax. But this is just another way.

Another teacher said,

We get out of school so early that sometimes you just go home and you kind of don't do anything. You could just sit yourself down in front of a television set and become a nonentity, and become nothing. And this way, at least you're interacting with people.

The majority of responses involved references to interpersonal relationships at school. Approximately half of these (14) referred specifically to students. Both male and female teachers defined effectiveness with students as being able to relate to kids:

…being able to relate to children, giving them successful experiences, if they feel good when they're leaving, after forty-five minutes, that they've done something well.

Teachers with several years of experience occasionally expressed a fear and sometimes a feeling of no longer being able to relate to students and closing them off. They suggested that at that point a teacher ought to leave the occupation.

Despite this emphasis on the importance of relating to students, most teachers perceived their role as requiring them to maintain distance from students:

When you're in the classroom you can't get too personal with them. You can't tell them where you live or things like that, because then they have an edge. You have to be so professional, you know.

An example of a theme beginning to emerge during data collection and analysis

Largely, the practice of distancing themselves from students was related to the problem of keeping control and discipline. This difficulty was a regular theme in our interviews:

It's not just necessarily teaching. It's dealing with kids. I had to go from a very easy-going personality

to a very hard, strict personality only to make my life a little easier.

One teacher felt helpless and felt the need to suppress her emotions in response to students' impoverished homes. This made her "feel a hundred years older" since she began teaching that year.

Distancing also resulted from a belief that it was part of the role of the teacher to represent an image or model of superior morality to students. Such models were difficult to follow in practice.

You have to stand up there and say, "You kids shouldn't smoke, you shouldn't drink, you shouldn't smoke dope." And yet teachers do.

Both the disciplinarian pose and the morality pose seem to be derived from a concern with restrictive control—control of students on one hand and of oneself on the other. Generally, teachers did not seem comfortable with either and reported that they occasionally let the role slip if for some reason they identified particularly strongly with a student. One teacher, for example, said that he had inadvertently caught a student smoking in the lavatory and had overlooked the incident, despite school policy, because he remembered smoking in the lavatory himself when he was young. Typically, however, teachers maintained their detachment by disciplining students and appearing respectable until the end of the week when they went to O'Keefe's.

You have to uphold an image of being a responsible adult. "We're not going to fool around. We're very serious about what we're doing." So when Friday comes, "let's go out and—" I'm pretty young and I can relate to the kids' problems, and you almost feel you are this model. When you go out with your friends you can be more yourself.

Being at O'Keefe's represented an opportunity to escape from the responsibility of being an adult among children.

During the week I restrict myself. I'm very straight, restricted, whatever it is you want to call it. And Friday night, whether I do anything wild or not, it's just getting out. It's nice. It's getting away from— Like I said to Sandy once when we were out—I think we were here one night and some little kids were running around and I said, "Good-night! You can't even go out, and they're here."

The teachers who were primarily concerned about their relationships with students were uneasy about a particular aspect of the teaching role. This was the perceived requirement to take the rules and practices of the school seriously when in fact they regarded them as artificial and the image they upheld as an illusion. The illusion, furthermore, was constantly threatened from one side by students' non-conforming behavior and personal problems and from the other side by the teachers' desire to relate as human beings.

Limitations on genuine interpersonal interaction while in school, however, were not confined solely to student-teacher relationships. In fact, the largest number of teachers (15) were mostly concerned about difficulties they encountered in communicating with other teachers while at school:

> Often these are various people you wouldn't even talk to at all in school. You just wave to them. So I find being at the bar to be a good thing.

Another teacher suggested,

> In school they're real strict, powerful people; but as soon as they come here, the front drops.

Teachers thus portrayed the school as a place where the role of teacher is rarely if ever dropped, in sharp contrast to the atmosphere at O'Keefe's, where people could talk and get to know each other on more than a superficial level:

> They sort of work themselves into their role of being a teacher, which is what it really is. You do get into that role. And you come in here, the only person you can be is yourself. You can be the teacher for the first ten, fifteen minutes, but after that you have to let yourself go....

In the amicable climate at O'Keefe's a young woman said she felt free to ask people to go skiing or shopping with her, something which she felt unable to do at work. She also believed that having a good time off the job "helps to establish trust" and makes working together at school easier.

A student teacher described the teachers at O'Keefe's as "a lot freer, a lot looser" and said that "they show you themselves." She did not find this to be true at school and was frankly surprised to "see teachers as people." With respect to one male colleague who became slightly inebriated and suddenly affectionate, she said, "I was surprised. I thought he was, you know, a real teacher." Letting the role drop in front of colleagues was clearly temporary, however, a once-a-week occurrence. The professional role was resumed on Monday morning:

> It's almost always a school-centered conversation, but it's things you'd never talk about in school. The more they drink, the looser they get, and the more you let your frustrations and complaints come out. And I think it's a good thing. Then you can get to school on Monday and that same person does not talk to you at all about those things.

In summary, teachers described the classroom as a demanding, yet fragile, reality that is continuously imperiled not only by student misbehavior but also by internal conflicts involving (1) identification with students' behaviors, (2) empathy with students' problems, and (3) conflict between the teachers' conception of their professional role and their personal identities. These conflicts are apparently dealt with by drawing a clear distinction between the professional self and the personal self, between being "on" and being "off":

> Basically, this is my escape. I just let it all hang out. That's the reason I come here. I'm so professional where I am that when I come here, I feel relaxed. You know, I can mingle with people, talk to someone, and I don't have to put on a front.

Being a professional for these teachers, thus, represents the capacity to successfully maintain working relationships, and that means remaining essentially aloof and emotionally uninvolved. This professional role seems to be further subdivided into an all-good "model of morality" pose and a mean and nasty "disciplinarian" pose; one or the other sometimes predominates in certain individuals. This splitting of the teacher's identity is apparently activated by an attempt to protect the artificial social realities of the classroom and school from intrusions of the outside world. Not surprisingly, this manner of dealing with the situation seems to affect the teacher's perception of self and relationships with other teachers. Interaction with colleagues at O'Keefe's, a setting that in many ways represents a polar opposite of the school organization (Blumberg and Kleinke, 1980), evidently helped teachers to maintain these conflicting self images and made the transition from the professional role to the personal self somewhat easier.

The Meaning of the Setting

In some ways, the events that occurred in O'Keefe's on a Friday evening differ little from what goes on in any barroom setting, and it is not surprising that the meanings teachers attached to such events are very similar to the meanings attributed to events in other barrooms. Cavan (1966), for example, found that saloons are used as places to unwind by people who have recently left another setting, such as work, that requires them to sustain "disciplined involvement or a particular pitch of excitement" (1966:149). The descriptions of schools as work settings suggest that such is the case for teachers.

Slightly over 25 percent of the teachers talked about tensions and pressure accumulating during the week when asked, "What does it mean for you to be here tonight?" One male teacher described the feeling of being at O'Keefe's as "just a chance to take your coat off and go, 'ahhh'."

> You come to O'Keefe's, you have a few drinks, and you loosen up. You release everything that's been bothering you all week. You forget about it. You have a good time. If you just stayed in, it would be bottled up.

Fridays at O'Keefe's also very clearly represented what Cavan (1966) describes as an inconsequential time-out from the seriousness of everyday life. The restraint and reserve required of teachers was temporarily relaxed and the real self exposed. This contrasts with other reports that teachers rarely if ever let down their protective masks of emotional detachment in front of colleagues even outside of school (McPherson, 1972). At O'Keefe's, however, like all saloon patrons, teachers held each other temporarily less accountable for what might be said or done, and by simply entering the establishment, they signaled to everyone present that they were now available for open conversation (Cavan, 1966):

> I look for people who work where I work. When I see somebody who comes through this door from where I work, I like that. That means something.

Fully half of the teachers interviewed mentioned friendship and camaraderie as the primary meaning of the setting for them. The following four examples are typical:

> There's a kind of camaraderie. You meet people and they're from other schools. You really have the same thing in common with them.

> I'm more tempted to come here than any other bar because I know more teachers will be here.

> Once in a while you bump into somebody at the bar or whatever, and you find out that you're both teachers, and all of a sudden you've got an instant camaraderie.

> There are a lot of people here who I know from the job. When I come here I want to see some friends. If I didn't know the people who were going to be here, I wouldn't come.

This ambience of informal collegiality apparently served as an ideal environment for the induction of new teachers into the faculty group and into the larger network of teachers in the area. As in the case of personal friendship, membership in the faculty group was seen as difficult to establish, but going to O'Keefe's facilitated both:

> You know when you're in a new place, it was hard for me at the beginning because I didn't know what kind of a staff they were. But within a week I found out. I mean they were coming up to me, and I felt I was part of the whole staff because they would say, "Hey, we're going to O'Keefe's on Friday. Why don't you come along?" I thought, "Hey, they're pretty nice."

Another teacher stated,

> I'm new in the area and to me it's an opportunity to get out and to know people in the area. I have no other opportunities to meet people.

The setting at O'Keefe's also provided a safe, supportive atmosphere of understanding among adults who share the same meanings and beliefs about the job of teaching. Teachers reported the importance of this understanding to them and clearly felt that such sympathy was unavailable from the people outside the profession:

> Because they work in the same environment, the same place as you, they understand your grievances. They know the day-to-day hassles, they know what the administration that you work under is like, the working conditions and all. And for that reason, you can relate to the people around you, more so than if you were to go out with someone you didn't work with.

In some cases, even spouses were apparently unable to provide the understanding that teachers occasionally needed at the end of the week:

> If you come here and you talk about it and you get it out, then you don't go home having to talk about it with other people who really don't understand what you're talking about. Talking about things that really bug you at school, like the kids, or the administration, or things like that—The best way you can talk about those kind of things are with other teachers when you're not in school. And I found it a better means for me to get it out, and I won't go home and complain about it all the time. If I do it now, you know, I get it out and over with.

A few teachers reported that they used other teachers at O'Keefe's as sounding boards to get justification for actions they had taken or planned to take. Others derived justification from learning that their colleagues had similar problems and from being told that what they are doing is acceptable to others. The overall result was agreement that things are in fact manageable, that there is only so much one person can do, that no one's problems are unique, and that one must keep trying:

> It gives you incentive to go back and keep plugging. It does me some good. Perhaps the other people had the same problems, and you could discuss them and say that the kids were worth it. You know, take it easy with them, be firm, be strong. Just knowing other people have the same problems, and saying you'll go back and try another approach.

Conversations such as those reported above appeared to occur more frequently, however, at the beginning than at the end of an interaction among teachers. One teacher claimed that there were definite limits to the length of time anyone could talk about or would listen to school-related subjects. If someone continued to talk about students beyond this limit, he said that people would just walk away. A male teacher suggested that it was primarily the less-experienced teachers who talked about students and that the older teachers mainly listened. A female teacher said that she considered talking about students at O'Keefe's to be unprofessional. Thus, although many of the teachers at least initially engaged in dialogue with other teachers about their relationships with students, this type of conversation was most pronounced and acceptable at the beginning of an interaction, was viewed as a somewhat disagreeable necessity tolerated for a short time, and was considered by some as an indication of inexperience.

To summarize, the meaning of the setting at O'Keefe's for teachers appears to be similar to the meaning most other patrons attribute to barroom settings. Yet the phenomenon of hundreds of teachers spontaneously gathering at a particular time and place cannot be dismissed entirely as typical. The setting at O'Keefe's provided an opportunity for interaction with other adults, but specifically with adults who shared the same experience of working with children. As important as casual interaction was in itself, it also established common interpretations and understandings of school experiences. This closed off the week's work and prepared teachers to pursue private weekend lives without residual affect.

Although unseriousness, openness, and mild licentiousness are characteristic of all saloons (Cavan, 1966), on a Friday afternoon at O'Keefe's these qualities of the setting made it possible for the teachers involved to separate themselves from the contrastingly serious, restrictive, and moralistic social reality of the school. Thus, for several hours the teachers appropriated a public drinking place, along with its attendant meanings, for their own collective purpose.

Theoretical Implications

Some fifty years ago, Waller (1932) addressed the issue of what teaching does to teachers. He described teaching as an occupation that systematically limited the emotional and intellectual development of its incumbents through strict conservative community norms governing teacher behavior and through more subtle psychological influences inherent in the teaching role itself. These forces led to a social distance, which teachers experienced between themselves and both students and community members. This, in turn, resulted in social isolation from normal interpersonal relationships, which Waller believed interfered with teachers' psychosocial growth. He argued that this stunting of the teacher as a person was ultimately harmful to the personality development of students as well and presented a major obstacle to humanistic reform of the schools.

Implications of this study for previous work on topic of the work of teachers...

Although he considered it unlikely, Waller believed that the teacher stereotype should be dissolved and that the community should accept teachers as normal human beings entitled to minor vices and lapses of decorum without subjecting them to unusually harsh public censure. That the present study was conducted in a barroom indicates that teachers have considerably more freedom today to develop and express a private life than was possible in Waller's time. This freedom did not come about, however, because of a sudden unified rebellion by teachers, but rather is the result of gradual changes in the values and norms of society. Particularly in metropolitan areas, where greater tolerance and anonymity prevail, teachers are far less subject to the community's critical vigilance, rumor mill, and sanctions.

Ironically, this unheralded and accidental liberation of teachers from the constraints of parochial attitudes does not seem to have significantly altered teachers' enactments of the role. Much of their behavior and many of the feelings and concerns about their work that teachers expressed at O'Keefe's are in fact very similar to those described by Waller a half century ago. Waller (1932) noted the existence in many towns of informal fellowships of "young, well-educated, mostly unmarried, transient, and discontented" teachers who, not unlike the participants at O'Keefe's, offered each other a unique opportunity to "be spontaneous and relatively unreserved" (1932: 56). Then, as now, the restrictions and formality of the work situation prevented teachers from experiencing intimate relationships with their colleagues while at school. In their contacts with other teachers off the job, teachers of the 1930s typically talked shop and talked particularly about their relationships with students. As in the present study, such interaction provided teachers with sympathy and understanding, was instrumental in the socialization of beginning teachers, and gave subgroup sanction to teacher interpretations and attitudes toward students and events at school.

It would seem that the adjustment of the teacher to students and colleagues has changed little in the past fifty years despite fewer community constraints on teacher behavior. While in school, at least, the image of the teacher as an unrelenting bastion of firmness, certainty, and morality evidently still flourishes in the hearts and minds of those studied, even though it is sometimes compromised in practice and may have already gone out of vogue in the general community.

Professional to Personal Self

The findings of the study reported here can be interpreted in terms of self theory. Within this framework, Turner (1976) suggests a distinction between a self identified with institutional prescriptions (e.g., norms and rules) and a self emanating from the person (e.g., values and feelings). Turner argues that a general societal trend away from a self anchored in institutions and toward a self located in impulse has accelerated in recent decades. When our data are compared with Waller's, it appears that such a shift in locus of self is evidenced among teachers.

...and on the topic of transition from professional to personal lives...

The teacher Waller described fifty years ago exhibited a fuller merging of the personal self and the professional role, a tendency encouraged by community expectations that the teacher represent a moral exemplar as defined by the community, even when outside of school. Our data suggest that today the personal self and the professional role of the teacher are more likely to coexist independently. That is, teachers tend to define their personal selves *outside* the role of teacher. The absence of person-role merger (Turner, 1978) can be seen both in teachers' greater unwillingness to maintain their professional roles in the community and in the inconsistencies between their privately held attitudes and beliefs and those required by their professional role.

Interaction in the bar on Friday afternoons apparently served several distinct functions related to this professional-personal self dichotomy. First, the barroom interaction allowed some discussion of official role-related problems. By talking over difficulties encountered during the work week, teachers were able to resolve problems and express feelings, which helped them avoid continued preoccupation with these problems. Thus, barroom talk buffered the teacher's private life from possible intrusions of school-related issues.

Second, barroom interaction actually facilitated the transition of the teacher from a professional to a personal status. We observed patterned movement from institutional talk to personal talk within the bar, which mirrored the real-time movement of the teacher from institution to person. Furthermore, neophyte teachers were taught to talk less about their official role and experiences with students. This suggests not only their socialization into the bar setting but also socialization into the specific subcultural understanding among teachers that a natural division does and should exist within individuals between the institutional actor and the personal actor.

Finally, the barroom seemed to function as a setting that compensated for the impersonal character of schools. The bar gave teachers an opportunity to present personal dimensions of self and view each other in alternative and even contradictory ways. Such opportunities to see behind the teacher's professional facade or mask sensitize us to the distinction between the person and the professional role and to the motives and values of the individual behind the role (Turner, 1978). In effect, teachers communicated to colleagues the message, "I am a real person. I am not the 'other' you see in school." The experience of talking in the barroom as *people* about job-related problems and interacting with each other informally was, to some extent, carried back to school. The impersonal professional role was resumed on Monday, but the distance and some of the problems associated with this role appear to have been ameliorated by Friday's opportunity to interact as private individuals.

Teacher–Student Interaction

The most troubling finding of our study is that schools continue to seriously restrict authentic contact between teachers and their students. The image of school, as described by teachers, is that of a rather flat, humorless setting where distancing from the professional role and expressions of personal self are considered inappropriate. This finding contrasts with the popular assumption among educators that teachers, to be effective, ought to integrate their personal selves with their professional selves. This notion is consistent with Turner's (1978:15) proposi-

...and on the topic of teacher–student interactions

tion that roles involving the socialization of others are especially likely to be merged with the person. Some of the distancing between teachers and students, of course, may be interpreted at least partially as an accommodation to the inevitably conflicting expectations of teaching.

Several studies (e.g., Lortie, 1975; Jackson, 1968; Waller, 1932) pointed out the inherent difficulties of maintaining a professional stance with regard to the control and discipline of students. Jackson discussed a "fundamental ambiguity in the teacher's role" (1968:154) that involved conflicting allegiances to the school as an institution and to the students as individuals. Although institutional definitions of responsibility, authority, and tradition generally prevailed in their enactments of the role, the teachers Jackson studied favored and cultivated a teaching style considerably less formal than their conception of traditional teacher behavior. In fact, teachers helped to "soften the impact" (p. 152) on students of the impersonal and regimented institution of school through their humanness, feelings of uncertainty, and zealous idealism (Jackson, 1968).

In contrast, among the teachers we studied, professionalism was reported to predominate in school to such an extent that closeness to both self and students was by and large disallowed. Our teachers actually seemed to define professionalism as a depersonalized enactment of the role. Although the personal self occasionally broke through in empathic responses to students, such occasions were perceived as awkward. Clearly, in the perceptions of these teachers, the personal self was not considered legitimate within the school. When it did appear (for example, in giving students special consideration), the self was viewed as breaking the rules. Our data thus suggest that conflicts and tensions experienced by teachers at school between professional role demands and personal needs and values were dealt with primarily through compartmentalization, a mechanism which distances teachers from self as well as students as they attempt to keep their personal and professional lives separate.

Several factors may contribute to the kind of depersonalized interaction between teachers and students reflected in our data. Lortie (1975) pointed out that the traditional structure of the occupation is such that "people with limited commitment can get into and stay in teaching" (p. 95). Consequently, teaching may never have required a high degree of commitment as long as an individual could enact a reasonable performance of the role. But we believe that several relatively recent developments not only permit voluntary disengagement of the self but actually discourage investment of one's self in teaching.

The continuing bureaucratization of schools, for example, along with the emphasis on prescribed technique, external evaluation, and legalistic definitions (what Wise [1979] calls the "hyperrationalization" of education), may be working to severely limit opportunities for self-expression by teachers. An unintended outcome of such administrative attempts at efficiency and quality control may have been the expulsion of the true self of the teacher from the classroom. The constant psychological and behavioral changes required of teachers in adjusting to externally imposed demands also may have contributed to an alienation of the teacher by undermining the self-determined continuity and predictability of the classroom required for a merging of the personal self with professional responsibilities. Finally, while the anonymity of metropolitan areas (such as the one in which the present study was conducted) frees teachers to develop a personal self outside of school, to a considerable extent this means decreased contact with students and their parents. Such circumstances, we believe, substantially increase the likelihood that teachers will treat students more as clients than as individuals.

References

Anderson E. (1978). *A place on the corner.* Chicago: University of Chicago Press.

Blumberg, A., & Kleinke, D. (1980). *Factors associated with frequenting a teacher bar.* Paper presented at the Annual Meeting of the American Educational Research Association, Boston.

Bogdan, R. C., & Taylor, S. J. (1975). *Introduction to qualitative research methods: A phenomenological approach to the social sciences.* New York: Wiley.

Cavan, S. (1966). *Liquor license.* Chicago: Aldine.

Glaser, B. G. (1978). *Theoretical sensitivity: Advances in the methodology of grounded theory.* Mill Valley, CA: The Sociology Press.

Glaser, B. G., & Strauss, A. L. (1967). *The discovery of grounded theory: Strategies for qualitative research.* Chicago: Aldine.

Jackson, P. W. (1968). *Life in classrooms.* New York: Holt, Rinehart and Winston.

LeMasters, E. E. (1975). *Blue-collar aristocrats.* Madison: University of Wisconsin Press.

Lortie, D. (1975). *Schoolteacher.* Chicago: University of Chicago Press.

McPherson, G. H. (1972). *Small town teacher.* Cambridge, MA: Harvard University Press.

Melendy, R. (1900). The saloon in Chicago. *American Journal of Sociology 6,* 289–306; Part II: 443–464.

Moore, C. (1897). The social value of the saloon. *American Journal of Sociology 3,* 1–12.

Turner, R. (1976). The real self: From institution to impulse. *American Journal of Sociology 81,* 989–1016.

Turner, R. (1978). The role and the person. *American Journal of Sociology 84,* 1–23.

Waller, W. (1932). *The sociology of teaching.* New York: Wiley.

Wise, A. (1979). *Legislated learning: The Bureaucratization of the American classroom.* Berkeley: University of California Press.

"Teachers in Bars: From Professional to Personal Self," by Edward F. Pajak and Joseph J. Blase, *Sociology of Education,* vol. 57, pp. 164–173, 1984. Reprinted with permission of the authors and the American Sociological Association.

Address correspondence to the authors at the Department of Curriculum and Supervision, Aderhold Hall, Room 124, University of Georgia, Athens, GA 30602.

Organizing for Ethnographic Research

Elmwood Lincoln High School has in attendance a specific group of students whose record of effort and achievement is very poor. With some exceptions, most of those students seem to relate adequately with others and they cause relatively few disruptions in class. Despite making little or no effort to learn, they continue attending school. Testing has failed to show, for 20 of those students, any psychological or learning problems that would account for a lack of effort and learning. Among those 20 students is a group of six

> ## 📚 A D D I T I O N A L   E X A M P L E S   O F
> ## P U B L I S H E D   E T H N O G R A P H I C   S T U D I E S
>
> In order to better understand a particular research methodology, it is often beneficial to examine additional examples of published research that utilizes that specific methodology. Several such examples of ethnographic research have been identified for you, through the use of *Research Navigator*™, available on the Web at www.researchnavigator.com. The following list consists of published research articles available free of charge in full-text format via *Research Navigator*™. These articles are available in either HTML and/or PDF formats and are easily located by searching the database by *article number* (abbreviated "**AN**"), which has been provided for each citation.
>
> Duncan, D. M. (2000). The socialisation of mature women student teachers: The importance of ethnographic accounts to educational research. *Teaching in Higher Education, 5*(4), 459–475. **[AN: 3888284]**
>
> Kugelmass, J. W. (2001). Collaboration and compromise in creating and sustaining an inclusive school. *International Journal of Inclusive Education, 5*(1). **[AN: 3990417]**
>
> Lahelma, E. (2002). Gendered conflicts in secondary school: Fun or enactment of power? *Gender & Education, 14*(3), 295–306. **[AN: 7484690]**
>
> MacFarlane, B. (2002). Dealing with Dave's dilemmas: Exploring the ethics of pedagogic practice. *Teaching in Higher Education, 7*(2), 167–178. **[AN: 6576220]**
>
> Nespor, J. (2000). School field trips and the curriculum of public spaces. *Journal of Curriculum Studies, 32*(1), 25–43. **[AN: 3811748]**
>
> Nilan, P. (2000). "You're hopeless I swear to God": Shifting masculinities in classroom talk. *Gender & Education, 12*(1), 53–68. **[AN: 2969132]**
>
> Scott, T. J. (1998). Thai exchange students' encounters with ethnocentrism. *Social Studies, 89*(4), 177–181. **[AN: 861040]**
>
> Talburt, S. (1999). Open secrets and problems of queer ethnography: Readings from a religious studies classroom. *International Journal of Qualitative Studies in Education (QSE), 12*(5), 525–540. **[AN: 2489488]**
>
> Tsouroufli, M. (2002). Gender and teachers' classroom practice in a secondary school in Greece. *Gender & Education, 14*(2), 135–147. **[AN: 6886168]**
>
> Weis, L., & Fine, M. (2001). Extraordinary conversations in public schools. *International Journal of Qualitative Studies in Education (QSE), 14*(4). **[AN: 5171614]**

Applying Technology: **More about Qualitative Research**

In this chapter, you read about ethnographic research, which is classified as a type of qualitative research. In our text, we barely "brush the surface" of the details of qualitative research. Here, however, we have provided several on-line resources which provide additional information—and even more resources—for you to investigate in an effort to learn more about qualitative research methods. Please keep in mind that this is by no means an exhaustive list, but it will provide you with valuable resource information. A sampling of Web sites addressing issues related to qualitative research includes:

- An Introduction to Qualitative Research
  (www.uea.ac.uk/care/elu/Issues/Research/Res1Cont.html)—an online qualitative research text developed by Dr. John Schostak of East Anglia University (UK); as stated on the page itself, the guide has been used as an introductory text for master's level courses aimed at teachers, health professionals and business consultants; provides an excellent overview of the qualitative approach to conducting research.

- Qualitative Measures
  (http://trochim.human.cornell.edu/kb/qual.htm)—Dr. Trochim's introductory and overview discussion of qualitative research.

- Qualitative Approaches
  (http://trochim.human.cornell.edu/kb/qualapp.htm)—Dr. Trochim introduces the four major approaches to conducting qualitative research (i.e., ethnography, phenomenology, field research, and grounded theory).

- Qualitative Methods
  (http://trochim.human.cornell.edu/kb/qualmeth.htm)—a discussion of the more commonly used methods of qualitative measurement (i.e., participant observation, direct observation, unstructured interviewing, and case studies).

- Qualitative Validity
  (http://trochim.human.cornell.edu/kb/qualval.htm)—alternative criteria for judging the validity of qualitative research (i.e., credibility, transferability, dependability, and confirmability) are presented and discussed.

- Qualitative Research Resources on the Internet
  (www.nova.edu/ssss/QR/qualres.html)—a page of qualitative research resource sites on the Internet maintained by Ron Chenail of Nova Southeastern University; includes a link to an extensive alphabetical listing of qualitative research websites, as well as links to individual qualitative research papers, research journals, and research conferences (including the Annual Conference on Ethnographic and Qualitative Research in Education and the Annual Midwest Qualitative Research Conference).

(continued)

Applying Technology: **More about Qualitative Research**   *Continued*

- QSR (Qualitative Solutions and Research) Home Page (www.qsr.com.au)—the home page for a company who produces software for qualitative data analysis; specifically, the software program is called NUD*IST (be careful…the name is the acronym for "Non-Numerical Unstructured Data Indexing Searching and Theorizing"!); the site includes a free, downloadable demo version of NUD*IST (simply point your browser to www.qsr.com.au/DemoReg/DemoReg1.asp).

- Research Proposal Evaluation Form: Qualitative Methodology (www.gslis.utexas.edu/~marylynn/qreval.html)—an online proposal evaluation form maintained by Mary Lynn Rice-Lively; summarizes 10 essential criteria for developing or evaluating qualitative research proposals.

that socializes together on and off campus. Suppose you are asked to conduct research with those six students as participants, in order to determine what structures their lives, orients their outlooks, and motivates their activities. The students and their parents grant permission for you to conduct the research.

Exercise 10.2

1. Formulate three main questions that you judge you would ultimately need to answer.
2. Formulate three subquestions for each of the main questions.
3. Within which situations and settings, in school and out, would you hope to obtain data?
4. What role would you attempt to assume when collecting data from the group of students—privileged observer? participant? interviewer?
5. What might you do to encourage students to behave and speak as if you were not present?
6. If the study were supposed to begin in mid-January and end by mid-May, make a preliminary time line (calendar) you would follow in data collection, analysis, and summary of findings and conclusions.

Chapter Summary

Ethnographic research is used to gain an understanding of particular groups of people as they function within given settings and conditions. This type of research may have a variety of focuses, such as behaviors, language patterns, preferred activities, means of coping, reactions to threats and opportunity, routines for strengthening personal bonds, the phenomena of the settings within which the group functions, and the various objects that play important roles in the individuals' lives.

Ethnographic research is often organized in terms of research questions. It is common for new research questions to emerge as data are being collected and analyzed. Data consist of written and recorded descriptions of what the investigator observes or of what the informants reveal. Data are rarely subjected to statistical analysis. In some research, it is sufficient merely to present the data, with little further analysis, but in most ethnographic research data are analyzed verbally and logically, to identify recurring patterns and themes that can illuminate and help explain the participants' behavior. Ethnographic research can present vivid, detailed descriptions but is usually open to questions concerning observer expertise and bias, as well as the generalizability of the resultant findings.

L I S T   O F   I M P O R T A N T   T E R M S

contextualization	naturalistic observation	privileged observer
holistic	participant observer	

A C T I V I T I E S   F O R   T H O U G H T   A N D   D I S C U S S I O N

1. Here are the focusing questions presented at the beginning of the chapter. How well can you answer them?

   a. What is the main purpose of ethnographic research?

   b. What distinctive characteristics set ethnographic research apart from other types of research?

   c. What roles do hypotheses and research questions play in ethnographic research?

   d. What are the main data sources in ethnographic research?

   e. Through what procedures are data usually obtained in ethnographic research?

   f. What is the role of the investigator in obtaining data?

   g. In what form are ethnographic data usually compiled?

   h. How are the data analyzed in ethnographic research?

   i. How are findings reported in ethnographic research?

2. Strengths of ethnographic research were given as richness, contextualization, and implications for educational improvement. Concerns were expressed about reliability, validity, and generalizability. Generally speaking, to what extent do you judge that the stated strengths and concerns are evident in the Pajak and Blase article that was presented in the chapter?

3. Suppose you wish to conduct a study of the family lives of five parents who volunteer their services as aides in Cutter Elementary School. Explain why ethnography would, or would not, be an appropriate type of research for your purpose.

4. Suppose you decided to conduct the study mentioned in activity 3 and you felt the study could best be oriented by research questions. Formulate a main research question and at least five subquestions related to it to provide a beginning framework for your study.

ANSWERS TO CHAPTER EXERCISES

Because multiple correct answers are possible for the chapter exercises, no list of "correct" answers is provided here. It is suggested that responses to exercises be made a topic of class discussion.

REFERENCES AND RECOMMENDED READINGS

Bogdan, R., & Biklin, S. (2003). *Qualitative Research in Education: An Introduction to Theory and Methods* (4th ed.). Boston: Allyn and Bacon.

Gay, L., & Airasian, P. (2003). *Educational Research: Competencies for Analysis and Application* (7th ed.). Upper Saddle River, NJ: Merrill.

Lancy, D. (1993). *Qualitative Research in Education*. White Plains, NY: Longman.

Lincoln, Y., & Guba, E. (1985). *Naturalistic Inquiry*. Newbury Park, CA: Sage.

Pajak, E., & Blase, J. (1984). Teachers in bars: From professional to personal self. *Sociology of Education, 57,* 164–173.

Patton, M. (2001). *Qualitative Research and Evaluation Methods* (3rd ed.). Newbury Park, CA: Sage.

Ulibarrí, H. (1958). The effect of cultural difference in the education of Spanish Americans (Research monograph). Albuquerque, NM: University of New Mexico, College of Education.

Vierra, A., & Pollock, J. (1988). *Reading Educational Research*. Scottsdale, AZ: Gorsuch Scarisbrick.

Wiersma, W. (2000). *Research Methods in Education: An Introduction* (7th ed.). Boston: Allyn and Bacon.

Wolcott, H. F. (1994). *Transforming Qualitative Data: Description, Analysis, and Interpretation*. Thousand Oaks, CA: Sage.

Wolcott, H. F. (1995). *The Art of Fieldwork*. Walnut Creek, CA: AltaMira.

Wolcott, H. F. (1999). *Ethnography: A Way of Seeing*. Walnut Creek, CA: AltaMira.

Wolcott, H. F. (2001). *Writing Up Qualitative Research* (2nd ed.). Thousand Oaks, CA: Sage.

CHAPTER

11 Action Research and Evaluation Research

Preview

In this chapter we consider two types of educational research that have much in common:

- Action research

and

- Evaluation research

Action research is done by educational practitioners, usually at the local level, to resolve matters of concern in their particular setting.

Evaluation research is typically done by school districts to determine the effectiveness of given products, procedures, programs, or curricula.

Similarities between the two types of research include:

- Done by educators rather than professional researchers
- Accomplished in the local school setting
- Intended to resolve local school concerns or questions
- Not intended to be generalized to other groups or settings

Differences usually, but not always, seen between the two types:

- Action research develops something new.
- Evaluation research appraises quality.
- Action research tends to be smaller in scope than evaluation research.
- Action research is for isolated application.
- Evaluation research is for broader application.

Targeted Learnings

This chapter explores two types of research that have much in common—action research and evaluation research. Action research is typically done by teachers or other educational practitioners. It is related to the local setting, such as a classroom, gymnasium, library, or shop, and is intended to resolve a problem for that locale only. Evaluation research, on the

245

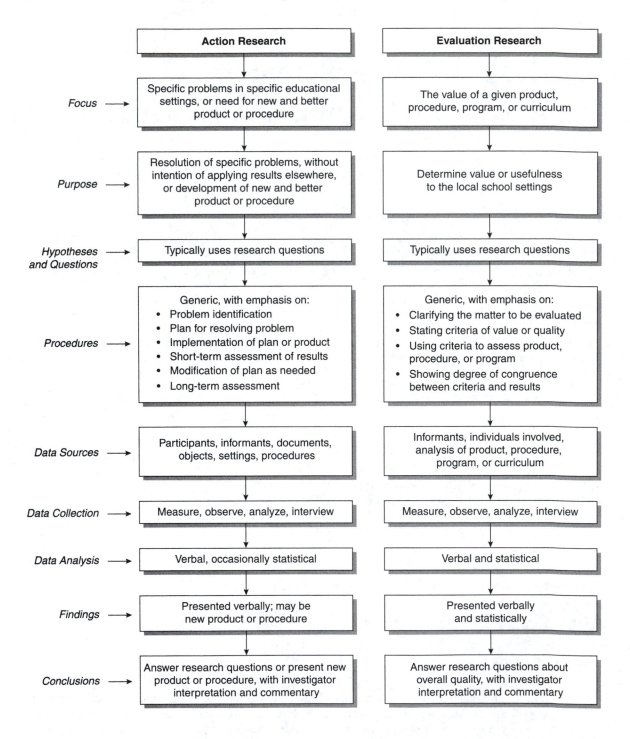

	Action Research	**Evaluation Research**
Focus	Specific problems in specific educational settings, or need for new and better product or procedure	The value of a given product, procedure, program, or curriculum
Purpose	Resolution of specific problems, without intention of applying results elsewhere, or development of new and better product or procedure	Determine value or usefulness to the local school settings
Hypotheses and Questions	Typically uses research questions	Typically uses research questions
Procedures	Generic, with emphasis on: • Problem identification • Plan for resolving problem • Implementation of plan or product • Short-term assessment of results • Modification of plan as needed • Long-term assessment	Generic, with emphasis on: • Clarifying the matter to be evaluated • Stating criteria of value or quality • Using criteria to assess product, procedure, or program • Showing degree of congruence between criteria and results
Data Sources	Participants, informants, documents, objects, settings, procedures	Informants, individuals involved, analysis of product, procedure, program, or curriculum
Data Collection	Measure, observe, analyze, interview	Measure, observe, analyze, interview
Data Analysis	Verbal, occasionally statistical	Verbal and statistical
Findings	Presented verbally; may be new product or procedure	Presented verbally and statistically
Conclusions	Answer research questions or present new product or procedure, with investigator interpretation and commentary	Answer research questions about overall quality, with investigator interpretation and commentary

other hand, is typically done by school district personnel. Its purpose is to evaluate the quality of school programs, materials, curricula, and the like. As you read this chapter, look especially for information related to the following:

1. Of what value is action research to educational practitioners?
2. What sorts of topics are best approached through action research?
3. What distinguishes action research from other types of research?
4. What are the procedures by which action research is carried out?
5. What is the purpose of evaluation research?
6. What sorts of topics are best approached through evaluation research?
7. What distinguishes evaluation research from other types of research?
8. What are the procedures by which evaluation research is carried out?

Action Research

Action research is a catchall label for research done by teachers, administrators, and other on-site educators to resolve problems at the local level. Mills (2003) has formally defined action research as "any systematic inquiry conducted by teacher researchers, principals, school counselors, or other stakeholders in the teaching/learning environment to gather information about how their particular schools operate, how they teach, and how well their students learn" (p. 5). Its purpose is to develop reflective practice so that educators can effect positive change within their own educational environments; simply put, action research is research done *by* teachers *for* themselves.

Action research usually focuses on the development, implementation, and testing of a new product, plan, or procedure. A team of teachers might wish, for example, to develop and implement a new discipline plan for Elmwood high school or a new creative writing program for the sixth grade in Cutter Elementary School. The research designs for these projects would not be sophisticated. Although there would be little hesitation in sharing the results of these investigations with others, any report that did so would explain that the project was illustrative of *one* school's efforts with little certainty that the procedures would produce the same results elsewhere (i.e., that the results would be generalizable). It is important to note that the focus of action research does *not* lie in its ability to generate results and conclusions that are generalizable to other settings or populations. On the contrary, action research focuses only on the immediate setting (e.g., classroom, school building, school district, etc.) and seeks to find answers to immediate problems or questions therein.

The Importance of Action Research

Due to the fact that it is considerably applied in nature, action research has the potential to make a substantial impact on the process of teaching and learning. Action research is a methodological technique that truly connects research to practice. Mills (2003) lists several important means by which action research can impact the practice of education. His list includes the following:

■ *Action research is persuasive and authoritative.* Data collected during action research are persuasive and influential because teachers are invested in the legitimacy and careful collection of those data. Therefore, the findings and recommendations are meaningful since they are not put forward by "experts"—the teachers *are* the experts in their own classrooms.

■ *Action research is relevant.* Often, teachers express concern over the relevance of published research to what actually occurs in their classrooms and schools (i.e., a problem of generalizability). Research conducted by teachers or other educators in the actual settings in which they work and with the individuals with whom they work results in findings that are directly applicable to those settings and individuals.

■ *Action research allows teachers access to research findings.* Another problem with published research is the lack of accessibility to it. Educators must be familiar with and have access to research databases and libraries that house the countless numbers of volumes of academic journals in which published research of interest may appear. Action research provides findings that are meaningful to practitioner researchers because *they* have identified the area of focus. In addition, instead of simply reading a study and becoming informed of its results (which typically does not result in positive changes to classroom practices), educators are directly responsible for and have direct access to those findings that are most meaningful—those which have provided insight into *their* problems.

■ *Action research is not a fad.* Good teaching has always involved systematically examining the instructional process and its effects on student learning. Teachers are always looking for ways to improve instructional practice, whether it be a new approach, new supplemental activities, or new techniques for reinforcement. Educators have seldom referred to this process of reflection, revision, and improvement as *research*, but that is exactly what it is.

■ *Action research can become an integral part of the daily process of teaching.* Once educators become aware of the proportion of time in their professional day that is spent doing this kind of reflection and revision, it becomes more obvious that this investment of time and effort is worth the potential outcomes. By integrating action research into daily teaching practices, educators feel the positive impact on both their personal and professional lives. This idea of reflective practice is part of what it means to be an educational professional.

Characteristics of Action Research

Although a fairly straightforward process, action research is sometimes misunderstood by practitioners in the field of education. There are many aspects of action research that characterize its uniqueness as an approach to conducting research. The following is a partial list of characteristics that describe what action research is (Carson, Connors, Smits, & Ripley, 1989).

- Action research is a process that improves education by change.
- Action research is educators working together to improve their own practices.

- Action research is developing reflection about our teaching.
- Action research is collaborative; that is, it is educators talking and working with other educators in empowering relationships.
- Action research is a systematic learning process.
- Action research is a process that requires that we "test" our ideas about education.
- Action research is open-minded.
- Action research is a critical analysis of our places of work.
- Action research is an emphasis on the particular.
- Action research is a cycle of planning, acting, observing, and reflecting.
- Action research is a justification of our teaching practices.

Although it is important to understand what action research is, it is also important to understand what it is *not*. The following list has also been adapted from Carson et al. (1989).

- Action research is not the *usual* thing that teachers do when thinking about teaching. It is more systematic and more collaborative.
- Action research is not simply problem solving. Again, it is more systematic and involves the specification of a problem, the development of something new (in most cases), and reflection on its effectiveness.
- Action research is not done "to" or "by" other people. Action research is research by particular educators on their *own* work.
- Action research is not a way to implement predetermined answers to educational questions. Action research explores, discovers, and works to create contextually specific solutions to educational problems.

At this point, you may be asking yourself an important question: "Why should I become involved in an action research project, especially with all the demands and responsibilities placed on me as an educator today?" There are several important reasons to consider involvement in such a project (Carson et al., 1989; Dick, 1993). Remember that action research deals with your problems, not someone else's. Second, action research is very timely; it can start now—or whenever you are ready—and provides immediate results. Third, action research provides educators with opportunities to better understand and, therefore, improve their educational practices. Fourth, as a process, action research can also promote the building of stronger relationships among colleagues with whom we work. Finally, and possibly most importantly, action research provides educators with alternative ways of viewing and approaching educational questions and problems and with new ways of examining our own educational practices.

These answers may have prompted yet another question in your mind: "Why doesn't everyone do action research?" First, although its popularity has increased over the past decade, action research is still relatively unknown when compared to more traditional forms of conducting research. Second, although it may not seem the case, action research is more difficult to conduct than traditional approaches to research. Educators themselves are not only responsible for implementing the resultant changes but also for conducting the research. Third, action research does not conform to many of the requirements of conventional research with which you may be familiar—it is, therefore, less structured and more difficult to conduct. Finally, because of the lack of fit between standard research requirements and the process of conducting action research, you may find it more difficult to write up your results.

An Example

Action research need not be conducted on a schoolwide basis. In fact, it is regularly carried out by classroom teachers singly or in groups and is usually conducted in an informal way. Such is illustrated in teacher Carol Huckaby's attempt to improve her sixth-grade students' library skills. Here is an accounting of Huckaby's action research:

The Need.   Mrs. Huckaby was well liked by her students. After they had completed sixth grade and gone on to junior high, they often returned to visit her. She always asked them how they were doing in school, and after a while she began to see that something important to their academic success was not being accomplished in elementary school. The problem as she saw it was that the students were not learning skills for using the library, which they were expected to have in junior high school when preparing term papers and other projects.

Obtaining Information.   To determine whether the need she identified was widespread, Mrs. Huckaby contacted a number of her former students. They suggested that they did in fact need better preparation in library skills. Huckaby spoke with junior high English teachers who confirmed the students' opinion. Those teachers agreed that their incoming students knew very little about the purposes of various parts of books or how to locate materials in the library. The teachers also said the students needed more experience in completing written projects of the kind expected in junior high.

This need was further substantiated in the Public Information Report distributed in Huckaby's district. That report showed that the district's seventh-grade students were below the national average in their ability to locate information in books, encyclopedias, and newspapers. Given this information, Huckaby decided to organize and implement a corrective program in her sixth-grade class. She told her fellow grade-level teachers of her idea, and they asked to be included. In planning the program, Huckaby listed objectives, planned activities, prepared and collected materials, and developed the following procedures:

Project Objectives.   As objectives for the project, Huckaby specified student knowledge of and competence in the following:

For Books, the Ability to Use

1. Table of contents and index
2. Preview page, foreword, and introduction
3. Glossary
4. Chapter titles

For the Library, Knowledge of

1. The system by which books are shelved
2. The organization of the library

3. Use of the *Reader's Guide to Periodical Literature*
4. How encyclopedias and other reference books are shelved, organized, and used

For Finished Written Products, the Ability to

1. Provide sequence organization
2. Use illustrations
3. Cite references
4. Select good titles
5. Make a table of contents

Project Activities, Materials, and Procedures.   Huckaby decided to help students achieve the objectives by having them produce an end product—a photo-essay by each student on individually chosen topics. The specific activities, materials, and procedures she provided were

1. A pretest covering library skills and the purposes of various sections of books
2. An introduction to the photo-essay project
3. A guide to help students complete all aspects of the project
4. A model of a completed photo-essay for student reference
5. Instructions to help students select topics and take appropriate photographs (Parents gave their support with cameras, film, and processing.)
6. Informative talks by the school librarian on how books are shelved, how the Library of Congress system works, and how the books are catalogued
7. Instructive sessions on using the *Reader's Guide to Periodical Literature*
8. Note-taking lessons on how to record bibliographical information, how to write exact quotations, and how to paraphrase and condense
9. Activities in which students practice organizing note cards into a bibliography
10. Student development of rough drafts of their essays to accompany their photographs
11. Individual conferences between teacher and student to determine needs concerning writing, references, and photography
12. Completion of final drafts of photo-essays, to be bound attractively and arranged in a display for parents
13. A posttest covering library skills and the various components of books

Ongoing Monitoring.   Huckaby kept a close watch for student difficulties and errors. She helped students and corrected their work appropriately, either by redirecting students or by reexplaining or restructuring activities.

Evaluation.   To evaluate the project and its effectiveness, Mrs. Huckaby did the following:

1. Analyzed pretest and posttest scores to determine student growth
2. Analyzed photo-essay projects to determine how well they reflected improvement in stated objectives
3. Asked parents to respond to the following four-item questionnaire (using a five-level rating scale):

     a. How would you rate your child's interest in the photo-essay project?

     b. How would you rate the value of this project?

     c. How difficult do you consider this project to be for your child?

     d. To what degree do you feel positively about the demands the project placed on your own time and resources?

The Action Research Process

The generic research process, which you have seen stated repeatedly, includes a problem statement, hypotheses or research questions, selection of a sample, design for data collection, analysis of data, presentation of findings, and statement of conclusions. But for action research aimed at the development of new products or procedures, a somewhat different process is used, as was evident in Carol Huckaby's research. She identified a problem, envisioned a way to resolve it, planned and implemented the solution envisioned, monitored student reactions, identified project strengths and shortcomings, made needed revisions, and assessed the program's overall effectiveness. As exemplified by Huckaby's efforts, the action research and development process can be outlined as follows:

1. Identify a problem or need
2. Collect information and resources
3. Prepare the project
   a. Formulate objectives
   b. Select activities
   c. Assemble and prepare materials
   d. Plan procedures
4. Introduce and implement the project
5. Monitor procedures and reactions
6. Identify strengths and shortcomings of the project
7. Correct errors, difficulties, and omissions
8. Appraise the project's ongoing and long-term results

    This eight-step process can be simplified into a four-stage procedure, which would fit any type of action research project. Steps 1, 2, and 3 comprise the preparation for the project (the *planning* stage); step 4 involves the actual application or implementation of the project (the *acting* stage); step 5 requires the collection of data and other forms of information (the *observing* stage); and steps 6, 7, and 8 provide the opportunity to examine the effects of the projects and to develop appropriate revisions (the *reflecting* stage).

    Furthermore, the process of action research is not linear; it has historically been viewed as a *cyclical* process. That is to say, whereas action research has a clear beginning, it does not have a clearly defined endpoint. For example, after Carol Huckaby developed and implemented her project, she monitored and evaluated its effectiveness and then made revisions to the program. She would likely implement her program again (perhaps with

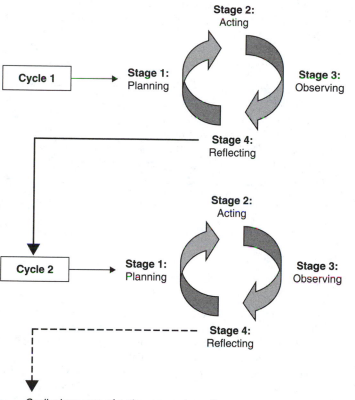

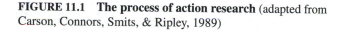

Cyclical process of action research continues...

FIGURE 11.1   The process of action research (adapted from
Carson, Connors, Smits, & Ripley, 1989)

next year's students), again monitoring and evaluating its effectiveness, followed by the
consideration of appropriate revisions and improvements to be implemented next time.
One should be able to quickly see that her project may *never* have a clear end—she may
continue to go through subsequent cycles of implementation, evaluation, and revision,
spiraling from one year to the next. This process of action research, with its cyclical and
spiraling nature, has been depicted in Figure 11.1.

A Published Example of Action Research

The illustrative examples presented up to this point in the chapter are from unpublished
projects completed by teachers pursuing graduate studies in education. The following is an

action research report published in the journal *Educational Leadership*. Note that the headings included in the body of the report do not correspond to the elements of action research previously listed.

Exercise 11.1

Indicate by paragraph and page where the elements of the action research and development process could be used as headings in the report "Designing an Authentic Assessment." The paragraphs in this article are numbered at the ends of paragraphs for easy reference.

Designing an Authentic Assessment

Sandra Schnitzer

As a high school science teacher, I often posed exam questions that required application of the many facts that students learned. Usually I finished grading the exams feeling quite frus- Identification of the problem trated. The students didn't seem able to use what they had learned in any novel way or new situation. Why couldn't they do tasks that required them to see relationships, compare, or make decisions? [1]

The answer came to me when I began working with the authentic task assessment model that the Mid-Continent Regional Educational Laboratory (McREL) developed for the Aurora Public Schools. What students had learned was missing a crucial piece. I had not taught them the thinking processes that they needed in order to use the knowledge that they had acquired. [2]

The McREL assessment model identifies 14 complex thinking processes: comparison, classification, structural analysis, supported induction, supported deduction, error analysis, constructing support, extending, decision making, investigation, systems analysis, problem solving, experimental inquiry, and invention. These complex thinking tasks can be integrated into a range of authentic tasks and assessments of performance on those tasks. [3]

The timing of my discovery was opportune. The Aurora school district, like many others across the country, had been looking for ways to restructure the curriculum so that it would present more challenging and engaging tasks to the students. Fortunately, the district was able to provide funds to underwrite time for teachers to plan and work collaboratively. Pairs of science teachers at Gateway High School were released from the classroom for two days to design authentic tasks and assessments in their content areas. [4]

My partner, Bob Legge, and I worked together to design an assessment task that would integrate one of the McREL thinking processes into Bob's advanced biology class. Since the class was ready to begin studying the uses and regulation of biotechnology, we set out to design a task that would allow students to demonstrate their biotechnological knowledge and simultaneously incorporate a complex thinking process. [5]

Decision making seemed to be the most appropriate thinking process to concentrate on, because it Further specification of the problem is a way to resolve complex issues that have no clear-cut answer, the very kind of task encountered in determining the uses, possibilities, and limitations of biotechnological applications. [6]

Bob and I recognized that students should be given opportunities to practice with the form of an assessment before it is used. In other words, they need time to practice the decision-making process without also having to attend to content. Consequently, we had students practice making and using a decision matrix that would determine what to do about a hypothetical American hostage situation in Iran (Iozzi and Bastardo, 1990). The students were to advise the President on a course of action that would best resolve a situation in which passengers on an airliner were seized as hostages. [7]

A decision-making task requires students to evaluate a list of alternatives that are scored using carefully weighted criteria. In our practice run, students' choice of alternatives (that is, their decision) was based on the alternatives and criteria that we provided. The alternatives to be considered included military action, economic sanctions, a blockade, doing nothing, giving in, and diplomatic intervention. [8]

The selection criteria included hostages' safety, public opinion, world opinion, economic repercussions, potential for war, and more kidnapping (Iozzi and Bastardo, 1990). With

Preparation for the project

teacher guidance, the students determined the weighting factors by deciding which of the criteria were most important to a good decision (the weighting factors are proportions of 100 percent; they add up to 1). Students also give each alternative a score, based on the extent to which each choice possessed each criterion. Each score was then multiplied by the weighting factor to obtain a final total score for each alternative. The alternative with the highest total is the decision. These scores were based on previous student knowledge (but, in later assessments, on their research and reading). [9]

The students then began developing the matrix that would determine the best advice to give the President. The first decision reached was to do nothing. The students were very surprised. [10]

After much discussion, the students decided that the original weight that they had assigned to the world opinion criterion was not heavy enough. A change in the weight of that criteria resulted in a decision to use military action. The students' alteration illustrates an interesting feature of making decisions by using a matrix, and that is that by changing the weights assigned

to the chosen criteria, students can see the immediate effect on the decision. [11]

Once familiar with the process, the students were ready to apply their decision-making model to the content in biology. In preparation for this authentic task, the class read and discussed material on genetic engineering and biotechnology, including the late Judge John Sirica's decision to prohibit experiments that would release engineered organisms into the environment. The issue presented to the students was, who should regulate and monitor biotechnology—society or the scientific community (Iozzi and Bastardo, 1990)? [12]

Working in cooperative groups, the students determined the alternatives, the criteria, the weighting factors, and the final decision scores. A decision was generated, and as a group, students shared

Description and implementation of the project

their decisions orally with the rest of the class. [13]

Now that the students had practiced on two types of decisions, they were ready to begin the authentic assessment. It would allow them to demonstrate their decision-making skills and their ability to integrate and apply these skills in new situations. Students were allowed to choose among several controversial issues in biology. The issues included *in vitro* fertilization, alternatives to animal experimentation, and organ donation. [14]

We provided students with initial background information on each issue (the data were taken from *Taking Sides: Clashing Views on Controversial Bio-Ethical Issues,* Levine 1990). Students cooperated in gathering further information about their issue. We encouraged them to seek information from a variety of sources. [15]

In the assessment, students were to develop a decision-making matrix using criteria, alternatives, and weighting factors to generate scores based on the information that they had gathered. We also asked the students to prepare a visual representation of their decision. It was to be used as groups presented their issue and decision to the class. [16]

To help students develop their representation, we showed them how to change their decision matrix into a Microsoftworks computer spreadsheet. A student-generated spreadsheet on the issue of organ donation lists the alternatives considered: (1) leave the laws as they are currently written (do nothing), (2) harvest organs only with prior permission, and (3) stop harvesting organs entirely. The criteria for making the decision were: (1) improvement of lives, (2) prevention of deaths, and (3) ethical beliefs. [17]

The students' conclusion was interesting and noteworthy. They decided to let the laws governing the removal of organs stand as they are presently written. [18]

We also instructed the students on the computer procedure for converting spreadsheet information into a graph. Once the spreadsheet and graph data were entered, students were able to print both the spreadsheet and graph on a transparency. The students thus created a professional-looking visual aid to help them lead the class discussion about their issue. [19]

The Assessment of Decision Making

From the outset of this series of activities, students knew that their performance would be assessed according to a model developed by McREL for each of the 14 complex thinking processes. Each of the processes has assessment criteria, which describe the characteristics of someone who uses the thinking process effectively. We changed McREL's wording about decision makers to make the criteria more specific to the task. Our three assessment criteria ultimately were:

Criteria used to assess the project (i.e., identify its strengths and weaknesses)

Did the students' final recommended decision match their chosen criteria?

Did the students apply accurate and important biological information to the process of decision making?

Did the students select appropriate and important criteria with which to assess the alternatives? [20]

The McREL assessment model also specifies a four-step rubric. It describes observable characteristics by which student performance can be gauged against each of the assessment criteria (Redding, 1992). For example, our final criterion for the process of decision making read, "Did the student select appropriate and important criteria with which to assess the alternatives?" The rubric for this criterion reads:

Level 4: The student clearly and completely identified the criteria by which the alternatives

were assessed. The criteria were presented in detail and reflected an unusually thorough understanding and concern for the repercussions of the decision.

Level 3: The student clearly identified the alternatives to be assessed. With no significant exceptions, the criteria were appropriate to the alternatives and important to the decision task.

Level 2: The student correctly identified the principal criteria by which the alternatives would be assessed. Some criteria might be omitted, or included criteria might not be important factors for consideration or entirely appropriate for the decision.

Level 1: The student specified criteria that were not appropriate for the selected alternatives or of importance to the decision. [21]

Our students knew that level 3 is the standard, and all work is expected to reach that quality. Level 4 is exemplary work, and we encouraged students to make that their goal. Both Bob and I assessed the results, but students also used the McREL rubrics to assess their own performances. [22]

What Is the Difference?

This authentic task and the assessment of it was an excellent way for students to both learn information and grasp the relationships among the data. Instead of just collecting and sharing factual information with their classmates, students needed to synthesize what they had learned, integrate it into the form of a decision, and then justify that decision to others. The students also learned a great deal about the process of making decisions with no clear-cut answers. [23]

Authors identify several strengths—but no weaknesses—of the project; since no weaknesses are identified, no recommendations for future cycles of the project are offered

The conversations that took place during cooperative learning were lively. They engaged every student. Furthermore, students took responsibility for some of their own learning, especially when they orchestrated the class discussion. [24]

The preparation for the assessment seemed to work very well. The preassessment activities provided students with all the skills and experiences needed to perform successfully in the assessment.

Students also knew all of the assessment criteria right from the start, so they had a clear, stationary target to aim at. [25]

Students were able to transfer their learning, too. A few days after the student presentations, a representative from the Aurora Water Department was a guest speaker in the class. She presented material on how water was delivered to the city. Then she asked the students what they thought her real purpose was in visiting the class that day. Confidently, a student answered, "To talk about making decisions about water use." The surprise on the face of the guest speaker was apparent. [26]

The animation of the students was even more unmistakable. Eagerly, they helped the guest speaker generate a list of alternate ways to supply Aurora's growing demand for water and a list of criteria by which to judge the appropriateness of each alternative. [27]

Finally, this assessment procedure exposed students to a new way to use technology, namely creating a high-quality product to use in a classroom presentation. Though many students knew about word processing programs, none were familiar with either the spreadsheet or graphing applications. [28]

In short, we think that authentic tasks and assessments, one such as we have described, will help our students graduate better equipped to handle the complexities and uncertainties of the 21st century. [29]

References

Iozzi, Louis A., & Bastardo, Peter J. (1990). *Decisions for Today and Tomorrow.* Longmont, Colo.: Sopris West, Inc.

Levine, Carol. (1984). *Taking Sides: Clashing Views on Controversial Bio-Ethical Issues.* Guilford, Conn.: The Dushkin Publishing Group, Inc.

Redding, Nora. (May 1992). "Assessing the Big Outcomes." *Educational Leadership 49* (8): 49–53.

Review of Action Research

In most cases, the purpose of research is to discover new information that can be generalized to other settings. But you have seen that the purpose of action research is not to make generalizable discoveries. It originates with a strongly felt need in a particular situation or setting—usually associated with a difficulty or dissatisfaction—and is carried out in order to resolve the concern. Although its results may prove to be useful in other settings, they are particular to the situation where the concern exists and are not intended to be generalized.

Organizing for Action Research

Action research is planned along the following lines:

1. Identify a problem or need
2. Collect information and resources
3. Prepare the project
   a. Formulate objectives
   b. Select activities
   c. Assemble and prepare materials
   d. Plan procedures

ADDITIONAL EXAMPLES OF PUBLISHED ACTION RESEARCH STUDIES

In order to better understand a particular research methodology, it is often beneficial to examine additional examples of published research that utilizes that specific methodology. Several such examples of action research have been identified for you through the use of *Research Navigator*™, available on the Web at www.researchnavigator.com. The following list consists of published research articles available free of charge in full-text format via *Research Navigator*™. These articles are available in either HTML and/or PDF formats and are easily located by searching the database by *article number* (abbreviated "**AN**"), which has been provided for each citation.

Angelides, P. (2002). A collaborative approach for teachers' in-service training. *Journal of Education for Teaching, 28*(1), 81–82. [AN: **6410433**]

Auger, W., & Wideman, R. (2000). Using action research to open the door to life-long professional learning. *Education, 121*(1), 120–127. [AN: **3726884**]

Ballantyne, R., Hughes, K., & Mylonas, A. (2002). Developing procedures for implementing peer assessment in large classes using an action research process. *Assessment & Evaluation in Higher Education, 27*(5), 427–441. [AN: **7287807**]

Burchell, H., & Higgs, T. (1999). Assessment of competence in radiography education. *Assessment & Evaluation in Higher Education, 24*(3), 315–326. [AN: **2333440**]

Carless, D. R. (2002). The "mini-viva" as a tool to enhance assessment for learning. *Assessment & Evaluation in Higher Education, 27*(4), 353–363. [AN: **7067084**]

McCall, A. L. (2002). That's not fair! Fourth graders' responses to multicultural state history. *Social Studies, 93*(2), 85–91. [AN: **7095900**]

Pereira, M. A. (1999). My reflective practice as research. *Teaching in Higher Education, 4*(3), 339–354. [AN: **2274775**]

Spilkova, V. (2001). Professional development of teachers and student teachers through reflection on practice. *European Journal of Teacher Education, 24*(1), 59–65. [AN: **4645442**]

Winsor, P., Butt, R. L., & Reeves, H. (1999). Portraying professional development in pre-service teacher education: Can portfolios do the job? *Teachers & Teaching, 5*(1), 9–31. [AN: **6831982**]

4. Introduce and implement the project
5. Monitor procedures and reactions
6. Identify strengths and shortcomings of the project
7. Correct errors, difficulties, and omissions
8. Appraise the project's ongoing and long-term results

The following illustrations are presented to help clarify this process:

The Problem. The statement of the problem in action research takes a form such as the following:

> *The purpose of this research was to design an authentic assessment procedure for use in science programs in Aurora school district.*

The problem statement alone may provide adequate orientation. Hypotheses are sometimes used, but a series of questions is usually more helpful, such as:

> *What is authentic assessment, and what does it involve?*
>
> *What do educators, particularly teachers, say about the value and practicality of authentic assessment?*
>
> *In what situations is authentic assessment being used successfully?*
>
> *Can authentic assessment be used in evaluating student progress in science classes?*
>
> *What procedures and materials are needed for authentic assessment in science?*
>
> *Will Aurora district science teachers accept and make use of authentic assessment?*

Desired Outcomes. The outcomes one hopes to achieve through action research are shown in the problem statement and questions. Occasionally, desired outcomes take the form of objectives, as in the Huckaby library skills project.

Information and Resources. Whereas other types of research are often designed to obtain and analyze original data to help answer questions or test hypotheses, existing resources are used in action research to put together a procedure or product that will resolve the problem at hand. For example, most of the questions used in developing a program of authentic assessment can be answered by consulting the literature, and the resources the program might require probably already exist as well. The creative aspect of action research and development lies in the organization, implementation, refinement, and evaluation of the new product or procedure.

Sequence of Research Activities. It is helpful to lay out an anticipated sequence of activities to be undertaken in the course of the project. A calendar should be used to assign dates for completing each activity, and a budget should be prepared, if appropriate.

Refining the Product or Procedure. As the project develops, preliminary field-testing should be done. Here, one tries out the project on a limited scale with real participants, the purposes being to identify what works well and what does not and to gauge participants' reactions. Needed modifications can then be made before the project is implemented on a wider scale.

Evaluating the Product or Procedure.   Once refinements have been made, the project is implemented and subsequently evaluated in terms of effects, practicality, and degree of acceptance by participants. The data used for making evaluative judgments about the project may be qualitative or quantitative.

Strengths and Cautions in Action Research

Action research provides benefits not often encountered in other types of research. It resolves an immediate problem. It can produce a tangible product or useful procedure. It has great potential for bringing about improvements in teaching and learning. It is relatively easy to carry out, and it can help make classroom experiences more enjoyable for students and teachers alike.

But keep in mind certain negative realities. Of all types of educational research, action research is the least precise and most subject to errors of bias, reliability, and validity. The findings are limited to the setting where the research was done; if they are applied elsewhere it must be understood that the results may well be different.

Exercise 11.2

You are made director of a project to improve teacher morale in your school district. Following the elements of the action research process, list the steps you would take. Illustrate each step with a specific example of what you would do or give attention to.

Evaluation Research

Evaluation research is done to determine the relative merits of various products and approaches used in education. Teachers and administrators often conduct this type of research, especially for formally assessing products and processes developed in action research. Gall, Gall, and Borg (1999) identify six aspects of education in which evaluation research is often seen:

- instructional methods
- curriculum materials
- programs (e.g., social science programs)
- organizations (e.g., teachers' organizations)
- educators
- students

The first three areas can be especially fruitful for research by graduate students, as educators are always concerned about which methods, materials, or programs best meet their needs. On the other hand, teachers should approach evaluative studies of organizations, teachers, or students with caution. Research into those topics can stir up a great deal of emotional controversy and often raise questions of ethics. Unless those cautions can be dealt with adequately, research into such topics should be left to highly trained researchers.

Evaluating Methods, Materials, and Programs

Methods, materials, and programs can be evaluated in various ways. The following methods of evaluation are common and are completed most satisfactorily when the researcher can set forth explicit criteria for making judgments.

1. *Comparative content analysis.* The components of a given method, material, or program are identified and analyzed to determine how well they correspond to stated curricular goals, which are clarified as criteria. Those criteria are used in judging the value of the method, material, or program. Evaluation of textbooks, tests, and instructional programs usually involves this process.

2. *Analysis of theoretical, philosophical, or moral tenets.* Methods, materials, and programs are increasingly being scrutinized as to their theoretical, philosophical, and moral underpinnings. Textbooks and programs, especially in natural science, mathematics, language, and social science, can reflect various theoretical views, such as those having to do with the nature and process of science, the procedure of thinking mathematically, the psycholinguistic parameters of language acquisition, and a variety of social values and lifestyles. They also may reflect philosophical views concerning gender equity, racial equity, or cultural understanding and cooperation. Evaluation research is useful in addressing such concerns. Again, it requires stating explicit criteria of quality or worth, scrutinizing materials or curricula, and compiling and analyzing data obtained from that scrutiny, usually qualitatively.

3. *Teacher acceptance.* The extent to which new curricula, materials, and programs will be implemented depends largely on teachers' favorable or unfavorable reactions. If teachers do not buy into innovations—if they find fault with them or for any other reason resist their use—the innovations have little chance of success. Therefore, it is very important that teacher reactions be evaluated early and regularly as new programs or materials are introduced into schools. Criteria for such evaluation studies tend to be somewhat nebulous, but generally resemble the following:

   - The innovation is educationally sound.
   - The innovation shows promise of improving learning, teaching, or relationships.
   - The innovation can be incorporated into the ongoing program.
   - The innovation will not add unduly to the burdens teachers already carry.

   Data are obtained from teachers or others involved directly with delivering the innovation.

4. *Changes produced in teachers.* Many innovative programs that districts attempt to put into place require that teachers undergo in-service training. It is especially

important in those cases to ascertain whether the training effects are being carried over into classroom practice. Even if teachers profess to espouse a new method or set of materials, they may not change their ways of teaching accordingly. Whether or not they make desired changes can be determined through evaluation research. Data can be obtained either by asking teachers what they do differently when using the innovation or by observing and noting their behaviors as they teach. Asking the teachers is by far the easier procedure, but the information obtained may be unreliable. Observing the teachers may yield better data, but such observations may be very difficult for graduate students to arrange, even if they are practicing educators. Whether teachers are interviewed or observed, behaviors relevant to the innovation must be identified and made explicit. Those behaviors might have to do with preparation, delivery of instructions, feedback to students, use of questions to stimulate thought, and procedures of assessing student performance.

For making judgments in this evaluative approach, teacher behavior prior to the innovation can be established as baseline performance. For example, in research into equal opportunity for students to participate in class discussions, an observer could note which students a teacher calls on during discussions over a period of a week. After receiving equal-participation training, that same teacher could again be observed and his or her behavior compared to the baseline behavior. Differences between baseline and subsequent behavior are then explored.

5. *Student acceptance and involvement.* Just as teachers must accept innovations if those innovations are to be successful, so must students accept them and participate willingly. Student reactions to innovations are not difficult to obtain, as students not under threat are usually willing to express their opinions freely. It is also possible to document student behavior in given classes or subject areas before and after the innovation is introduced. Again, appropriate criteria are stated; behavior prior to the innovation establishes a baseline, and behavior subsequent to the innovation allows one to determine the results of the innovation.

6. *Resultant student achievement or behavior.* Changes in achievement and behavior are prime criteria for judging the value of an innovation, but changes in student attitude are important, too. If achievement gains are seen to result from the innovation, the investigator must make sure that the gains have not occurred at the expense of other learnings that would otherwise have taken place. Some innovations consume more time than did the activities they replaced, so that less instructional time is left for other areas of the curriculum. Achievement in those other areas may suffer as a result.

An Example of Evaluation Research

The following article reports large-scale evaluation research done in Tennessee over a period of years. The primary changes implemented in the schools were mandated by the state legislature. This research helps determine whether those changes have served their intended purpose.

Exercise 11.3

See if you can answer these questions about "Class Size Does Make a Difference."

1. What is being evaluated?
2. What is the main criterion of effectiveness?
3. What quantitative data figure prominently in the study?
4. What do the quantitative data lead investigators to conclude?
5. What qualitative data figure prominently in the study?
6. What do the qualitative data lead investigators to conclude?
7. What additional questions does the research seem to raise?
8. How are those questions explored, and what are the answers determined to be?
9. What are identified as lessons learned from the STAR study?

Class Size Does Make a Difference

Helen Pate-Bain, C. M. Achilles, Jayne Boyd-Zaharias, and Bernard McKenna

Dissatisfied with earlier research and wishing to have conclusive results, Tennessee's state legislature funded a $12 million, four-year study of class size. Project STAR (Student/Teacher Achievement Ratio) analyzed student achievement and development in three types of classes:

Summary of purposes and major findings of the original evaluation study of STAR

small classes (13–17 students per teacher), medium classes (18–21 students per teacher), and regular classes (22–25 students) with a teacher and a full-time teacher aide. An important characteristic of the study was its longitudinal nature: Project STAR followed students from kindergarten in 1985–86 through third grade in 1988–89. In order to assess the effects of class size in different school locations, the project included 17 inner-city, 16 suburban, eight urban, and 39 rural schools. Students and teachers were randomly assigned to class types.

The main focus of the study was on student achievement as measured by three devices: appropriate forms of the Stanford Achievement Test (K–3), STAR's Basic Skills First Criterion Tests (grades 1–2), and Tennessee's Basic Skills Criterion Tests (grade 3). The study's most important finding was that students in the small classes made higher scores (the difference in scores was both statistically and educationally significant) on the Stanford Achievement Test and on the Basic Skills First (BSF) Test in all four years (K–3) and in all locales (rural, suburban, urban, inner city). Other relevant findings include the following:

The greatest gains on the Stanford were made in inner-city small classes.

The highest scores on the Stanford and BSF were made in rural small classes.

The only consistent positive effect in regular classes with a full-time aide occurred in first grade.

Teachers reported that they preferred small classes in order to identify student needs and to provide more individual attention, as well as to cover more material effectively.

The importance of the economic background of students was underscored by the finding that, in every situation, those students who were not economically eligible for the free lunch program always out-performed those students who were in the free lunch program.[1]

Benefits of Small Classes

To determine whether small classes had a cumulative effect, the top 10% of STAR classes for each year were categorized by class type. The number of small classes in the top 10% increased each year from kindergarten through third grade. In kindergarten, small classes made up 55% of the top-scoring 10% of STAR classes. By third grade, small classes made up 78% of the top 10%. This finding strongly suggests a cumulative and positive effect of small classes on student achievement in grades K–3.

During the course of the study more than 1,000 teachers participated in year-end interviews. Their comments revealed a number of ways that instruction benefited from small class size.

1. Basic instruction was completed more quickly, providing increased time for covering additional material.
2. There was more use of supplemental texts and enrichment activities.
3. There was more in-depth teaching of the basic content.
4. There were more frequent opportunities for children to engage in firsthand learning activities using concrete materials.
5. There was increased use of learning centers.
6. There was increased use of practices shown to be effective in the primary grades.

A common benefit cited by teachers in small and regular-plus-aide classes was that they were better able to individualize instruction. These teachers reported increased monitoring of student behavior and learning, opportunities for more immediate and more individualized reteaching, more enrichment, more frequent interactions with each child, a better match between each child's ability and the instructional opportunities pro-

vided, a more detailed knowledge of each child's needs as a learner, and more time to meet individual learners' needs using a variety of instructional approaches.

Further Questions

Jeremy Finn and C. M. Achilles noted: "This research (STAR) leaves no doubt that small classes have an advantage over larger classes in reading and mathematics in the early primary grades." They also pointed out that, "although this experiment yields an unambiguous answer to the question, 'Is there a class-size effect?,' other questions remain unanswered."[2] In this article, we take a first look at some additional questions, such as, Do the benefits of small-class participation continue in later grades?

> Conclusions drawn from original study, which led to further questions (subsequently investigated in this study)

Lasting Benefits Study

Project STAR proved that reduced class size in grades K–3 significantly enhanced student achievement. To determine if those positive benefits continue for the STAR students as they progress through the higher grades, the Tennessee State Department of Education appointed the Center of Excellence for Research in Basic Skills at Tennessee State University to conduct a Lasting Benefits Study (LBS).

> Current evaluation extended the longitudinal nature of original study

All students who participated in Project STAR third-grade classes were eligible for LBS observation in the fourth grade. The LBS fourth-grade sample contained 4,230 students in 216 classes. Although all students had participated in STAR during the third grade, they may not have been STAR participants in previous grades.

For consistency in statistical analysis, the LBS fourth-grade sample was categorized by the location of the school the students had attended in third grade. Academic achievement of LBS fourth-grade students was measured by the Tennessee Comprehensive Assessment Program (TCAP) test battery. Since 17 schools that had participated in Project STAR did not administer the TCAP test battery during the 1989–90 school year, students from these schools could not be LBS fourth-grade participants.

The TCAP includes both a norm-referenced test (NRT) and a criterion-referenced test (CRT). The

Comprehensive Test of Basic Skills (CTBS/4), published by CTB/McGraw-Hill and nationally normed in 1988, constituted the NRT component, which indicates students' proficiencies in reading, language, mathematics, study skills, science, and social science. The CRT component was "customized" for Tennessee to assess skill levels attained from the state's mathematics and language arts curriculum. The CRT component indicates students' mastery levels (mastery, partial mastery, or nonmastery) in language arts and mathematics content.

The LBS analysis yielded clear and consistent results from both the NRT and the CRT test scores.

> Significantly greater achievement for students previously enrolled in smaller classes

Students who had previously been in small STAR classes demonstrated significant advantages on every achievement measure over students who had attended regular classes. Further, these results favoring small classes were found to be consistent across all school locations. The positive effects of involvement in small classes are pervasive one full year after students return to regular-size classes.[3]

Effective Teachers

In order for educators to make the best use of class-size reductions, they must be aware of what constitutes effective teaching.

> Further evaluation based on effectiveness of instruction

The Project STAR "within-school" design, which required each participating school to contain at least one class of each type (small, regular, regular-plus-aide), reduced major sources of variation in student achievement attributable to school effects. The class was the unit of measurement, not the individual student. This design made it possible to identify the effects of teachers and of classroom instruction on student achievement.

In order to determine the characteristics and instructional styles of effective teachers, STAR researchers observed and interviewed 49 first-grade teachers whose classes had made the greatest gains. The teachers selected for observation and interviews were those whose classes scored in the top 15% of scaled-score average gains in reading and math for each of the four school types.

These teachers consistently displayed similar affective behaviors and characteristics. Their enthusiasm was obvious as they engaged in "acting," demonstrating, and role-playing activities. The teachers frequently expressed positive attitudes toward children, emphasized positive behavior, praised success, and used humor to promote learning and to motivate students. A love of children seemed to permeate their professional repertoires.

The most effective teachers engaged their students through the use of creative writing, hands-on experiences, learning centers, and math manipulatives. They provided immediate feedback. They practiced Lee Canter's assertive discipline or some variation of it and made it clear that they had high expectations for their students. They maintained good communication with parents.

In addition to these common behaviors and characteristics, class size appeared to have been a contributing factor to the success of the most effective teachers. Only eight of the 49 (16%) taught regular classes of 22–25 students. Twenty-three (46%) taught small classes of 13–17; seven (14%) taught classes of 18–21; and 12 (24%) had full-time instructional aides in regular-sized classes. The 22–25 class size may be smaller than the norm in many states. If so, these results are conservative.

Two of the teachers in the STAR program, one from a rural school and the other from an inner-city school, provide concrete illustrations of what constitutes effective teaching. Pat McAndrews is a first-grade teacher in a rural school.

> Illustrations of the effective instruction portion of the evaluation study

Her classroom is a beehive of purposeful activities. She wants children to enjoy school, and she challenges them with motivational games, films, stories, and puppets. She encourages peer tutoring as a way to help students master difficult concepts. For one of her creative writing assignments, which called for students to write a story about a magic hat, she made hats out of styrofoam cups and gave one to each student to decorate. Her 250 teacher-made games, available for use in the learning centers, show her creative and organizational skills. She edited all the first-grade educational television lessons to fit her curriculum.

McAndrews keeps up regular communication with the families of her students. At the beginning of each six weeks, she sends home a letter to explain the material to be covered. Each week students take home a folder of their work to be signed and returned. She telephones family members to discuss good as well as poor behavior. If there is no phone in the home, she visits. She capitalizes on an advantage enjoyed by rural teachers, which is that they know most of the families of their students through informal community and social activities.

Helen Dortch teaches at an inner-city school in Memphis. She works hard to build a good self-concept in her students, many of whom come from poor and broken homes. She gives each student a plaque that reads, "No one can make YOU feel inferior without your consent."

To release tension Dortch has her students "break dance" while holding on to the backs of their chairs. She rewards correct answers by saying, "You're smart!" and leading the class in a round of applause. Vocabulary lessons are a daily ritual. Dortch uses auditory, visual, comprehension, and context exercises. She believes that every child can succeed and is willing to work with each student individually until a task is mastered.

Dortch maintains communication with the home through individualized notes, telephone calls, and home visits. She gives parents her home phone number. She sends home deficiency forms before each report card to enable parents to help students catch up. She enlists family volunteers to accompany her on selected Saturdays when she takes the entire class to cultural events such as plays and concerts at nearby LeMoyne University or visits to Beale Street, a local historic area.

Lessons from the STAR Study

Project STAR and the LBS established that there are benefits to be gained in small classes. Project STAR also found that these bene- | Conclusions and discussion | fits are greater when the teachers possess certain characteristics and use certain instructional styles.

In spite of claims by some policy makers that America doesn't need to spend more money on education, studies such as STAR and the LBS continue to point up the fact that additional funds are needed to attain high-quality education in this country. It takes | Implication and recommendations for policy development | money to cut down on the number of students per teacher and to enable teachers to develop particular characteristics and learn to use effective instructional strategies. It is short-sighted to attack class-size

research mainly on the ground that classes smaller than the normal will be costlier than larger classes. Research continues to be needed to help identify appropriate sizes, mixes, or organization of classes for achieving various purposes and outcomes of education. The class-size debate should continue, as we believe that educators still do not know all the answers to the class-size questions.

Some critics contend that class-size reduction is no more than a means for education associations to placate (or increase) their memberships or to make teachers' work less demanding. Other views are that class-size reduction is too expensive for the results achieved and that other procedures are more "cost effective."[4] Such arguments, frequently replete with policy implications but seldom based on sound research or theory, apparently assume that class-size research is "intended" to reduce class size to some number that has been mystically set as "correct." This line of reasoning appears to begin with the idea that education is a mass-production, industrial-age enterprise, best conducted in assembly-line fashion with large numbers of relatively passive children who are fed specified "facts" and molded for economic purposes.

We have a different premise. We view education not as a mass-production effort, but as a personal and individual experience. The model is not the factory. | Recommendations to continue the research on class size | The focus is on serving clients. Class-size research is not an attempt to reduce class size; at its best it is an effort to find appropriate casework loads, because much of sound educational practice consists of individual instruction, coaching, mentoring, and tutoring. The challenge has been well-stated by Benjamin Bloom: "Can researchers and teachers devise teaching/learning conditions that will enable the majority of students under group instruction to attain levels of achievement that can at present be reached only under good tutoring conditions?"[5] Class-size studies attempt to find an economical alternative to one-to-one instruction.

One of the biggest questions that remains is how best to share the expertise of those teachers who are recognized as being effective. Communication among classroom teachers is one of the weakest links in our education system. How can we make improvements in this area? How can we provide more in-service programs that will allow teachers who have never experienced small classes to spend time observing and consulting with effective teachers of small classes?

How will teacher preparation programs be different if typical class size moves from 25–30 students to 15–18 students?

Providing teachers with an appropriate student load will make possible the individualized and personalized instruction that is the basis of sound education. However, if this reduction in student load is to be educationally effective, finances must be provided for all present and future teachers to be adequately trained in small-group instruction.

[1]Elizabeth R. Word et al., *The State of Tennessee's Student/Teacher Achievement Ratio (STAR) Project: Technical Report* (Nashville: Tennessee State Department of Education, 1990). Copies of the report can be obtained from the Center of Excellence for Research in Basic Skills, Tennessee State University, 330 10th Ave. N., Nashville, TN 37203-3401.

[2]Jeremy D. Finn and C. M. Achilles, "Answers and Questions About Class Size: A Statewide Experiment," *American Educational Research Journal,* Fall 1990, pp. 573–574.

[3]Barbara A. Nye et al., *The Lasting Benefits Study: Fourth Grade Technical Report* (Nashville: Center of Excellence for Research in Basic Skills, Tennessee State University, 1991). Copies of the report can be obtained from the Center of Excellence for Research in Basic Skills, at the address given in note 1.

[4]Tommy Tomlinson, "Class Size and Public Policy: The Plot Thickens," *Contemporary Education,* Fall 1990, pp. 17–23.

[5]Benjamin S. Bloom, "The 2 Sigma Problem: The Search for Methods of Group Interaction as Effective as One-to-One Tutoring," *Educational Researcher,* June/July 1984, pp. 4–16.

"Class size does make a difference" by Helen Pate-Bain, C. M. Achilles, Jayne Boyd-Zaharias, and Bernard McKenna. *Phi Delta Kappan, 74, 3,* pp. 253–256, November 1992. Reprinted with permission.

Organizing for Evaluation Research

We have seen that evaluation research is used to determine the worth of a product, procedure, program, or curriculum that has been put into place to serve a particular purpose, or that is being considered for use. *Products* are tangible objects such as series of textbooks or manipulatives for mathematics instruction. *Procedures* are ways of doing things, such as communicating with parents, assigning student grades, or attempting to equalize attention given to individuals in a classroom. *Programs* are organized efforts of broad scope that constitute components of the overall education plan offered by schools. Examples are the social science program, the athletics program, and the music program, each of which is described by its purpose and the classes it includes. *Curricula* are the specifics of instructional programs, including objectives and activities of individual courses and groups of courses. Examples are the biology curriculum, the natural science curriculum, the fifth-grade curriculum, or the middle-school curriculum.

Problem. As in other research, the problem statement indicates the purpose of the research:

> *The purpose of this investigation is to determine the degree of correspondence between the contents of the Silver Medal Language Series textbooks and the items included on three standardized achievement tests used in Elmwood school district.*

Questions or Hypotheses. In evaluation studies, research questions are most often used to guide the investigation. The main research question might parallel the problem statement:

ADDITIONAL EXAMPLES OF PUBLISHED EVALUATION RESEARCH STUDIES

In order to better understand a particular research methodology, it is often beneficial to examine additional examples of published research that utilizes that specific methodology. Several such examples of evaluation research have been identified for you through the use of *Research Navigator™,* available on the Web at www.researchnavigator.com. The following list consists of published research articles available free of charge in full-text format via *Research Navigator™.* These articles are available in either HTML and/or PDF formats and are easily located by searching the database by *article number* (abbreviated "**AN**"), which has been provided for each citation.

Carter, D. S. G. (1999). A whole-school approach to adolescent peer-leader development for affective learning in health-related curricula. *Research Papers in Education, 14*(3), 295–319. **[AN: 6698638]**

Forrester-Jones, R. (2003). Students' perceptions of teaching: The research is alive and well. *Assessment & Evaluation in Higher Education, 28*(1), 59–69. **[AN: 9259426]**

Frey, K. S., Hirschstein, M. K. & Guzzo, B. A. (2000). Second step: Preventing aggression by promoting social competence. *Journal of Emotional & Behavioral Disorders, 8*(2), 102–112. **[AN: 3183611]**

Gardner, N. (2002). Evaluating flexible delivery across a tertiary institution. *Open Learning, 17*(1), 11–22. **[AN: 6087921]**

Hall, E. (2001). Babies, books and "impact": Problems and possibilities in the evaluation of a Bookstart project. *Educational Review, 53*(1), 57–64. **[AN: 4230093]**

Hill, J., & Woodland, W. (2002). An evaluation of foreign fieldwork in promoting deep learning: A preliminary investigation. *Assessment & Evaluation in Higher Education, 27*(6), 539–555. **[AN: 7584450]**

Matthews, J. (2002). An evaluation of educational psychologists' interventions at Stage 3 of the Code of Practice. *Educational Psychology in Practice, 18*(2), 139–156. **[AN: 6736171]**

Nelson, J. R., Martella, R. M., & Marchand-Martella, N. (2002). Maximizing student learning: The effects of a comprehensive school-based program for preventing problem behaviors. *Journal of Emotional & Behavioral Disorders, 10*(3), 136–148. **[AN: 7313580]**

Traynor, P. L. (2002). A scientific evaluation of five different strategies teachers use to maintain order. *Education, 122*(3), 493–510. **[AN: 6763548]**

To what degree do the contents of the Silver Medal Language Series textbooks correspond to the contents of the three standardized achievement tests used in Elmwood schools?

This main research question will ordinarily be followed by a number of subquestions:

Regarding Vocabulary Development
1. *How much overlap exists between vocabulary development in the textbooks and vocabulary knowledge on the tests?*
2. *To what extent do textbook activities include the same vocabulary words as do the standardized tests?*

Regarding Sentence Structure
1. *How much overlap exists between textbook activities on sentence structure and test items involving sentence structure?*
2. *(and so forth)*

However, it is certainly possible to guide the research through hypotheses rather than questions if one so desires. For example, in evaluating student achievement in language arts, one could use a hypothesis such as:

The mean language achievement of Elmwood Middle School students does not differ from the mean language achievement of middle school students nationwide.

Design for Obtaining Data.   Evaluation research is designed, first, to determine the contents, status, or results of whatever is being evaluated, and second, to compare that assessment against a set of criteria that indicates desired traits. The degree of correspondence between assessment and criteria is used to indicate the worth of whatever is being assessed, and the resultant information is used for making decisions or changes.

Criteria.   Criteria are specific indicators of quality. They might have to do with contents or traits or end results. For example, one might evaluate a series of textbooks to determine whether their contents correspond to curriculum objectives and items on standardized tests. Or one might assess student learning occurring in the language arts program. The criteria (or criterion) may be a single factor, such as student achievement. (School districts often evaluate their programs at least partly in terms of how their students stand, on average, in comparison to national achievement norms.) Normally, however, the list of criteria for evaluation studies will include a number of specific elements. For example, criteria used in evaluating a new schoolwide system of discipline might include specific indicators such as:

The Discipline System
- *Specifies what constitutes misbehavior*
- *Emphasizes steps for preventing misbehavior*
- *Indicates clearly what teachers should and should not say and do when correcting misbehavior*

Applying Technology: **More about Action and Evaluation Research**

In this chapter, you learned about action and evaluation research. These two research methodologies have many valuable applications in school settings. By pointing your Web browser to the following sites, you can learn even more about action research and evaluation research.

Action Research
"Creating Possibilities—An Action Research Handbook"
(www.epsb.ca/pd/pegasus/creatingcont.htm)—Terry Carson, Bryan Connors, Hans Smits, and Dale Ripley of the Edmonton Public Schools (Edmonton, Canada) have developed this electronic handbook consisting of eight chapters. Included in their handbook are chapters on such issues as suitable topics for action research, the action research process, school and university perspectives on action research, and ethics in action research. It is a very comprehensive manual.

"You Want to Do an Action Research Thesis?"
(www.scu.edu.au/schools/gcm/ar/art/arthesis.html)—Bob Dick of Southern Cross University in New South Wales, Australia, maintains this site, in which he walks the student through the process of conducting and reporting action research. Although very thorough in his approach, the author has developed a manual that is truly a beginner's guide.

"Research to Practice: Guidelines for Planning Action Research Projects"
(http://literacy.kent.edu/Oasis/Pubs/0200-08.htm)—This site includes guidelines to help in the planning of action research projects. Nancy Padak and Gary Padak discuss the four stages of the action research process: identifying questions to guide the research, collecting information to answer the questions, analyzing the information that has been collected, and sharing the results with others.

"Classroom Action Research"
(www.madison.k12.wi.us/sod/car/carhomepage.html)—This site contains several links that provide assistance in planning and conducting classroom-based action research. Included are links to such topics as what action research is and is not, what teacher researchers do, and guidelines for developing questions, gathering data, analyzing data, and formally writing the results.

Introduction to Evaluation
(http://trochim.human.cornell.edu/kb/intreval.htm)—Dr. Trochim, in his online research methods textbook, provides a thorough introductory discussion of evaluation research. He discusses various definitions of evaluation, goals for evaluation studies, strategies and types of evaluation, as well as highlighting several types of questions that can appropriately be asked as part of an evaluation. Also included is a link to another page, titled The Planning-Evaluation Cycle (http://trochim.human.cornell.edu/kb/pecycle.htm), which allows the student to see the "big picture" of the relationship of evaluation to the implementation of the larger project.

■ *Contains strategies for student motivation and harmonious relationships*
■ *Can stop misbehavior immediately*
■ *Can redirect misbehaving students appropriately*
■ *Contains provisions for fostering goodwill between teacher and students*
■ *Emphasizes the development of student responsibility and self-control*

Data. Data may be obtained by testing or interviewing students, teachers, other educators, and parents. They may also be gathered by analyzing tangible objects such as books and materials, or analyzing documents that describe programs, procedures, and curricula, or by observing and noting procedures as they are implemented. Some of the data, such as test scores and ratings, will be numerical. Other data, such as notations, interview responses, and written descriptions, will be largely verbal.

Data Analysis. Data are analyzed either statistically or qualitatively, using procedures that facilitate comparison of data to criteria.

TABLE 11.1 Elements and Descriptions of the Research

Generic	Action Research	Evaluation Research
Problem topic	Specific concerns in local settings; often develops new product or procedure; no intent to generalize; done by educational practitioners	Quality of products, programs, procedures, curricula; uses lists of criteria
Orientation	By questions; rarely hypotheses	By questions; sometimes hypotheses
Data sources	Any source appropriate for the type of research used	Characteristics of products, programs, procedures, or curricula; students and other persons involved in the topic under investigation
Data collection	Various, as appropriate for type of research being done	Analysis, testing, observation, and recording
Key attributes	Emphasizes product or procedure development, implementation, in-process valuation, modification, long-term evaluation	Focuses on existent materials or on programs already in place, to determine present or potential quality
Data analysis	Usually qualitative; may be in part statistical	Sometimes qualitative, sometimes statistical, often both
Findings/conclusions	Presentation of new product or procedure; investigator commentary on development and effectiveness	Judgments made against criteria, stated verbally, supported by statistics

Findings.   Findings report the results of data analysis—what is discovered about the products, procedures, programs, or curricula being investigated.

Conclusions.   Here the investigator compares findings with the stated criteria used in the study, makes judgments concerning the degree of correspondence between the two, and reports his or her considered opinion concerning meanings and implications.

Chapter Summary

The chapter is summarized in Table 11.1, which shows a comparison of generic, action, and evaluation research processes.

ACTIVITIES FOR THOUGHT AND DISCUSSION

1. For Ms. Matheson's spelling program, a description of which follows, see if you can answer these questions:
   a. What is the problem?
   b. What type of research is Ms. Matheson attempting to conduct?
   c. What would you expect might be her main criterion regarding learning?
   d. Do you think she would list a criterion that does not have to do directly with spelling achievement?
   e. Based on the criteria you gave in (c) and (d), what conclusions might Ms. Matheson draw from her study?

Ms. Matheson is dissatisfied with the spelling program used in her fifth-grade class. Students do not like spelling, and Ms. Matheson does not enjoy teaching the lessons. She believes the program would be more enjoyable and more effective if it were built around the words her students are dealing with in their reading programs. She confers with her principal and receives permission to develop and use a spelling program of the type she envisions for a three-month trial period. She begins by compiling lists of words from the students' reading program. She incorporates the word list into instructional units enhanced with cartoons, rhymes, puzzles, vignettes, and high-interest worksheets.

When preparations are completed, Ms. Matheson introduces the program to her class. She observes carefully to see how students react to the activities. She finds that the students are interested in the cartoons and rhymes but have difficulty interpreting the special messages she has tried to build into the vignettes. She begins at once to correct the problem. Before long she realizes that she should build into her lists certain service words such as *danger, poison,* and *flammable.*

As time passes, Ms. Matheson finds that her students seem to enjoy the activities and no longer groan when she tells them it is time for spelling. She finds, too, that students learn to spell their words with little difficulty and remember how to do so. As a check on their progress, she administers two spelling tests from the regular program. Student performance is average on the tests even though they have not had specific instruction on at least half of the words included in the tests.

2. Here are the questions listed with the targeted learnings at the beginning of the chapter. See if you can answer them without looking back in the chapter.
   a. Of what value is action research to educational practitioners?
   b. What sorts of topics are best approached through action research?
   c. What distinguishes action research from other types of research?

d. What are the procedures by which action research is carried out?

e. What is the purpose of evaluation research?

f. What sorts of topics are best approached through evaluation research?

g. What distinguishes evaluation research from other types of research?

h. What are the procedures by which evaluation research is carried out?

3. Here are summaries of action research and evaluation research. See if you can supply the missing parts that are indicated by blanks.

Action Research

Characteristics

Research carried out by _____ at _____ to resolve _____.

Distinguishing traits are low level of _____, intended to resolve problem, with no intent to _____.

Procedure

Problem identification

Plan for resolving problem

Development and implementation of plan

Short-term _____ of plan

Long-term _____ of effectiveness

Evaluation Research

Characteristics

Used to determine the _____ of a given product, procedure, program, or curriculum.

_____ are obtained from product, procedure, _____ and _____; and from testing, interviewing, and observing students, educators, and others involved.

Procedure

Clarify the matter to be evaluated

Clearly state desired _____ that indicate value or quality

In terms of those _____, assess the _____, procedure, program, or curriculum

Compare assessment results against criteria; show degree of _____; present interpretations of _____ and _____

ANSWERS TO CHAPTER EXERCISES

11.1. 1. paragraph 2   2. paragraph 3   3a. paragraph 5
3b. paragraph 7   3c. paragraph 7
3d. paragraph 5   4. paragraph 10
5. paragraph 12   6. paragraph 27   7. none
8. paragraph 28

11.2. Discuss in class.

11.3. 1. Class size
2. Achievement
3. Class enrollment, test scores, number of participants
4. Smaller class size produces higher student achievement.

5. Teacher interview responses
6. Answers found under article heading "Benefits of Small Classes."
7. Do benefits last? What do effective teachers do?
8. Benefits last over time. Effective teachers were found to be affective, enthusiastic, positive, motivating.
9. Smaller classes are better and should be funded. The focus of teaching should be on serving clients (students).

REFERENCES AND RECOMMENDED READINGS

Brandt, R. (1991). The reflective educator [Special issue emphasizing action research]. *Educational Leadership, 48*(6).

Brown, D. (1991). Secondary teacher's participation in action research. *The High School Journal, 75*(1): 48–58.

Carson, T., Connors, B., Smits, H., & Ripley, D. (1989). *Creating Possibilities—An Action Research Handbook.* Available online at www.epsb.ca/pd/pegasus/creatingcont.htm

Dick, B. (1993). *You want to do an action research thesis?* Available online at www.scu.edu.au/schools/gcm/ar/art/arthesis.html

Gall, J., Gall, M., & Borg, W. (1999). *Applying Educational Research: A Practical Guide* (4th ed.). White Plains, NY: Longman.

Mills, G. E. (2003). *Action Research: A Guide for the Teacher Researcher* (2nd ed.). Upper Saddle River, NJ: Merrill.

Pate-Bain, H., Achilles, C., Boyd-Zaharias, J., & Mckenna, B. (1992). Class size does make a difference. *Phi Delta Kappan, 74,* 253–256.

Santa, C., Isaacson, L., & Manning, G. (1987). Changing content instruction through action research. *The Reading Teacher, 40,* 434–438.

Schnitzer, S. (1993). Designing an authentic assessment. *Educational Leadership, 50*(7): 32–35.

12 Descriptive Research and Historical Research

Preview

In this chapter we undertake a closer examination of two similar types of research:

- Descriptive research

and

- Historical research

Both types focus on depicting and interpreting

- Settings
- Conditions
- Events

The two types of research frequently use the same or similar

- Sources of data: informants, documents, objects, environments
- Means of collecting data: measuring, observing, analyzing, interviewing
- Data analysis: verbal, and sometimes statistical

The two types differ primarily in

- Time orientation (present versus past)
- Use of participants (only occasionally involved in historical research)
- Amenability to measurement (more likely with descriptive research than with historical research)

The case study, descriptive or historical, is used to conduct research based on a single individual, product, or process.

Targeted Learnings

As you read this chapter, look especially for information needed to answer these questions:

1. For what kinds of research topics are descriptive and historical research used?
2. What is the general research procedure used in the two types of research?
3. What are the similarities and differences between descriptive and historical research?
4. How would you organize research to describe the early history of the school you first attended?

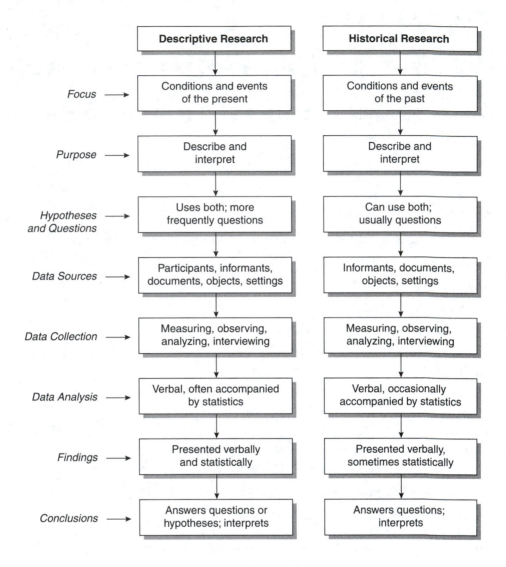

	Descriptive Research	Historical Research
Focus →	Conditions and events of the present	Conditions and events of the past
Purpose →	Describe and interpret	Describe and interpret
Hypotheses and Questions →	Uses both; more frequently questions	Can use both; usually questions
Data Sources →	Participants, informants, documents, objects, settings	Informants, documents, objects, settings
Data Collection →	Measuring, observing, analyzing, interviewing	Measuring, observing, analyzing, interviewing
Data Analysis →	Verbal, often accompanied by statistics	Verbal, occasionally accompanied by statistics
Findings →	Presented verbally and statistically	Presented verbally, sometimes statistically
Conclusions →	Answers questions or hypotheses; interprets	Answers questions; interprets

5. How would you organize research to describe the current status of the school you first attended (presuming that it still exists)?
6. How would you organize a case study of a beginning teacher's experiences during the first year of teaching?

This chapter discusses the nature and procedures of descriptive and historical research and explains how both are organized and carried out. To illustrate the types, two reprinted articles are included—one that reports descriptive research and another that reports historical research. In the descriptive research report you will see qualitative data supplemented with a small amount of quantitative data. In the historical research report you will see qualitative data used with little further analysis to answer the research questions.

The Nature of Descriptive Research and Historical Research

Descriptive research and historical research have much in common with regard to design, procedures, and methods of analyzing data. To describe these commonalities and show how both types of research are organized and conducted, we will give attention to their purpose and topics, questions and hypotheses, design, data collection, data analysis, findings, and conclusions.

Purpose and Topics

The purpose of both types of research is to show status by first describing and then, to the extent possible, interpreting present and past situations, conditions, behaviors, interactions, events, and trends. This information sometimes serves no end except to satisfy a desire to gain increased knowledge about the phenomenon of interest; additionally, it may frequently provide a basis for decision making.

Topics of descriptive and historical research can include any people, places, situations, conditions, procedures, interactions, and undertakings about which we wish to know more.

Hypotheses and Questions

In descriptive and historical research, questions are more frequently used than hypotheses, but hypotheses are sometimes seen in descriptive research, especially where traits or performances of two or more groups are compared.

Data Sources and Collection

Data needed for answering questions and testing hypotheses are obtained in the form of measurements, descriptions, and statements. Consider the following excerpt, in which informant Joe Morgan provides information about a small Appalachian country school, Hickory Grove, that he attended as a small boy. Morgan's information came in response to questions contained on an interview guide that paralleled subquestions in the research. Those questions were:

Main Question (which was not asked of informants):

How does Hickory Grove School today compare with the school as it was 60 years ago?

Subquestions (which were asked of Morgan and other informants):

1. What was the community of Hickory Grove like in 1935, and what is it like now?
2. What were the school's physical facilities like when you were a student there?
3. What do you remember of the curriculum—the subjects you studied?
4. How large was the student body?
5. What was the ethnic makeup of the student body?
6. What role did the school play in the community?
7. How would you rate the quality of the school and teachers when you attended?

Morgan was able to answer most, but not all, of the questions. The following comprise portions of his responses:

I started first grade in 1935 in the village of Hickory Grove, which still exists and looks to me to be about the same size now as it was then. I remember real clearly the two-story brick building that housed all the grades, with its great big doors and windows. On one side of the building was a playground for little kids, and on the other side were playing fields for the big kids. Standing apart was a small gymnasium, made by the WPA I think, I'm not sure, that was used for basketball games, plays, concerts, community meetings, and whatever else might have been needed. They were real proud of that gym. Directly behind the main school building was a large outhouse, one side for the boys and the other side for the girls. There were no flush toilets, but there was a water tank and wash basin and towel for washing your hands. On the kids' playground were a set of seesaws that I rode pretending I was driving my dad's green pickup, and some swings on which I pretended to fly an open-cockpit biplane, like in the movies they showed in the gym on Friday afternoons for five cents.

About the curriculum I don't remember much. I know I learned to read in first grade, but don't recall it. I think we used those Dick and Jane readers with a dog named Spot. I liked art better than anything else we studied. We were always drawing airplanes. For some reason we put the wings, one over and one under the fuselage, parallel with the length of the plane instead of across it. We knew the difference, but that was the way we drew them. I guess we had good teachers. We learned as well as anybody. I don't know if I liked school there or not. I know I didn't enjoy school very much later on. I remember wrestling with Helmut Guttman every day. I took my lunch in a metal lard bucket with bail and lid, and all the young boys went barefoot until it began to frost. Wearing shoes was unpleasant for us.

The school was the most important thing in the community. Like I said, everything revolved around it. The school put on plays and concerts and other kinds of performances and they held lots of community events there. I think I remember grownups having parts in the plays and two or three of them playing instruments in the school band, too.

How large was the student body? I don't know. Eighty or a hundred in the entire school, I'd guess. Ethnic makeup? Never thought about it. All the kids were white, I think. I can't remember for sure.

Hickory Grove was at that time an important place where the highway crossed the railroad. Automobiles couldn't travel far without stopping for gasoline, radiator water, or tire repair. Most of the roads were graveled. There were lots of service stations along the road and some had small restaurants with them. My father operated such a place in Hickory Grove. There was another service station there, a post office, and a general hardware, mercantile, and feed store. There were 40 or 50 homes there, scattered across the hill among oak trees, not on streets like we have now. We lived in one of the few painted houses. It was yellow, beside the highway about 50 yards from the service station.

We moved away when I was in third grade. In 1990 I returned with my wife and two grandchildren to show them where I started school. I could still recognize the place. Our old station and café buildings were there, but boarded up. We asked someone about the place and they said it had been closed for several years and, no, they didn't remember my dad's name. Our old house was there, too, but abandoned, beside the ramshackle garage on whose pitted concrete floor I learned to roller-skate in a tight circle.

We went up to the school. Same brick building, same gymnasium, same playgrounds. It was summer, and the school was locked. I've wondered about that place a lot. In these changing times, how could it have remained so much the same? What had happened to the kids I knew, Helmut Guttman and Arnold Stowater? I wondered if the stage curtain in the gymnasium still displayed advertisements for village businesses.

Seven data sources play prominent roles in descriptive and historical research. They are participants, procedures, settings, objects, records, documents, and informants. Primary sources among them are

Participants: individuals presently involved in a study

Informants: people (such as Morgan) who were participants in or eyewitnesses to the situations being studied

Settings: the physical locale (such as Hickory Grove community) being studied

Records: notations from school registers, grade files, tax rolls, and the like

Objects: the physical things now present or once present in the setting

Documents: written accounts such as minutes, transcripts, policy statements, and curriculum guides

Secondary data sources are

Informants: persons not directly involved in the event being studied, but who have close knowledge of it, such as relatives, community members, scholars, and other experts

Newspaper accounts: reconstructed descriptions of people and occurrences

Reference book accounts: descriptions given by scholars who have studied and interpreted primary data

Tools for Obtaining Data

Data useful in descriptive and historical research include descriptions, analyses, opinions, scores, and other measurements. Those data are obtained through the use of tools that include interview guides, questionnaires, analysis criteria, tests, and other measuring devices.

Interview guides are used when researchers seek data by talking directly with informants, such as Joe Morgan, who spoke about Hickory Grove School. The properly conducted interview is not a chat but is organized to obtain useful information in a short amount of time. For example, the researcher, trying to put together a picture of a typical school day in Hickory Grove, tells the informant the purpose of the interview and then asks for help in answering predetermined questions, such as:

```
How did the school children dress?
How did children get to and from school?
What was the classroom like?
What do you remember about the teacher?
What subjects do you remember studying?
What did you especially like and dislike about school?
```

Several informants might be interviewed and asked the same questions, which would bring breadth of information and also provide *cross-checking* for data reliability. Though the interview guide is prestructured, the interviewer remains alert for other important information the informant might offer.

Questionnaires are used to obtain information from informants who cannot be interviewed personally because of distance and/or time constraints. Like the interview guide, the questionnaire is structured to parallel research subquestions and may call on the informant to select among answers provided, give short answers, or compose longer answers to open-ended questions. Here is an example of *answer selection,* which the informant simply checks:

```
What do you recall about the strictness of teachers at Hickory
Grove School?
____ They were all quite strict.
____ Some were strict and some were not.
____ Most were strict but were understanding as well.
____ They were not very strict.
____ I don't recall.
```

Here is an example of an *open-ended question* to which the informant must compose an answer:

```
What do you recall about the relative strictness or leniency of
teachers at Hickory Grove School?
```

(Space is left or blank lines are included on which informant writes response.)

Analysis criteria are used to help obtain information when one analyzes objects and written accounts. The criteria help the investigator remain focused on information that is needed. An example of analysis criteria used in studying the 1935 Hickory Grove curriculum guide might be that the guide does the following:

- Specifies subject areas to be covered, and the time allotted to each
- Indicates amount of time to be spent in silent reading
- Indicates amount of time to be spent in group activities
- Names textbooks and other instructional materials to be used
- Suggests frequency and types of tests

Standardized tests and other measuring instruments are often used in descriptive research. The measurements desired might be test scores in academic areas, indicators of preference, physical measurements, timed events, and measures of aptitude and personality. Descriptive research may involve the administration of tests to participants or the use of test results recently obtained by the school. Test results from years past can frequently be found in school records.

For historical research, one must rely on records and documents for such information.

Treatment and Analysis of Data

Data in descriptive and historical studies are treated or analyzed in one or more of the following ways:

1. *Presentation.* Often, studies merely present data in an organized manner without further analysis. A typical school day in Hickory Grove, for example, might be depicted verbally, as described by informants. The information answers the question posed; no further analysis is needed.

2. *Data Conversion.* Some data are more clearly understood if converted to numbers or representations that can be compared directly. For example, if information were presented on the degree of community involvement in Hickory Grove School, past and present, raw numbers might not present an accurate picture, especially if the community population had increased or decreased. One could make the numbers comparable by converting them to percentages or presenting them in graphs.

3. *Further Statistical Treatment.* It is often sufficient in descriptive and historical research simply to present the raw verbal or numerical data. When comparing two or more groups, however, statistical treatment is often required. Chi-square analysis, *t* test for the difference between means, and analysis of variance (treatments described in Chapter 8 and in Appendix A) are used for this purpose.

An Example of Descriptive Research

The following descriptive research report was published in the November/December 1992 issue of the *Journal of Educational Research.* Note its excellent abstract and section headings that facilitate reading.

Exercise 12.1

As you read the report, indicate what you find concerning the following research elements:

1. Problem
2. Research questions
3. Research design
4. Data collection
5. Data analysis
6. Findings
7. Conclusions

Urban Teachers Who Quit: Why They Leave and What They Do

Martin Haberman
University of Wisconsin–Milwaukee

William H. Rickards
Public Policy Forum

Why do teachers leave urban schools? Do they quit teaching altogether or just shift to other teaching jobs? Nationally, approximately one-half of beginning teachers leave teaching in the first six years. In urban districts this turnover occurs in five years. In a few urban districts one-half of the beginners leave in a three- to four-year period. This level of turnover leads to many urban classrooms having several teachers in one school year. It also indicates a high level of waste. Since it takes approximately three years to become competent in an urban classroom, urban schools may be losing teachers at the very point they are becoming effective professionals. In the study that follows there was no attempt to determine the competence of the leavers; the focus was on teachers' perceptions of their problems and their subsequent activities.

> Research questions appear first

> Purpose of the study

Background

In 1989, teachers nationally stated their biggest problems as

1. Lack of parental support
2. Lack of financial support for public schools
3. Pupils' lack of interest
4. Lack of discipline (Elam, 1989)

While these are the same problems teachers cited five years earlier (1984), these perceptions do not agree with the perceptions of the public in general. The public's top four problems are

> Brief literature review

1. Use of drugs
2. Lack of discipline
3. Lack of financial support for public schools
4. Difficulty of getting good teachers

The public agrees with teachers about the lack of finances and discipline but feels that drugs and poor teachers are greater problems than teachers do.

In 1989, the reasons teachers nationally cited for leaving the profession were

1. Low salaries
2. Lack of public financial support for education
3. Low status of teaching
4. Discipline
5. Unmotivated, uninterested students

These reasons, except for lack of public financial support, remain unchanged from the same survey five years earlier. The public's view of why teachers leave teaching is comparable, except that the public regards lack of parental support as more important than the low status of teaching. The parents' ranking of why teachers leave is

1. Discipline
2. Low salaries
3. Unmotivated, uninterested students
4. Parents' lack of support
5. Lack of public financial support for public education

In an effort to learn more about why urban teachers leave, we decided to study a sample of teachers in Milwaukee, Wisconsin.

The Sample

Names of Milwaukee teachers who resigned, retired, or terminated their contracts between January 1988 and December 1988 were taken from monthly reports compiled by the school system. One hundred twenty-four names were gathered in this way. A questionnaire was sent to these individuals. Forty written responses were received. Ten others were interviewed by telephone.

> Description of sample; nonprobability judgment sampling used

> Many other details about methodology are missing

Findings

Table 1 summarizes the reasons teachers give for leaving. These reasons should be considered in relationship to what teachers are now doing.

TABLE 1   Reasons for Leaving the Milwaukee Public Schools

Reason	Number
Other employment	17
Residency requirement	12
Personal reasons	11
Moving from area	7
Retirement	2
Further education	1
Total	50

> Due to lack of information about methods, not sure how these data were collected or analyzed

TABLE 2   Current Employment Status of Former Milwaukee Teachers

Status	Number
Teacher	36[a]
Professional staff in school	1
Other employment	6
Retired	4
Unknown	3
Total	50

[a]Four are substitute teaching.

TABLE 3   Problems Perceived by Urban Teachers (Milwaukee, 1988)

	Ranking at Time of Resignation	Ranking before Teaching
Discipline	1	2
Inadequate support from administrators and supervisors	2	5
Heavy load—inadequate preparation time	3	9.5
Lack of parental support	4	3.5
Underachieving students	5	1
Clerical burden	6	9.5
Dealing with students' different cultural backgrounds	7	3.5
Inadequate support staff	8	9.5
Inadequate resources and supplies	9	6.5
Salary	10	6.5
Communication with staff of different cultural backgrounds	11	9.5
Class size	12	12

> Again, not sure how data were collected or analyzed

Table 2 reveals the current work status of these teachers. Except for the seven who moved from the area, all are still in the greater Milwaukee metropolitan area. It is clear from a comparison of the two figures that almost all of the individuals who leave for "other employment," "the residency requirement," or "personal reasons" are still teaching (thirty-six of forty-two).

Problems perceived by teachers were separated into those they perceived before beginning to teach and those perceived at the time they resigned. Table 3 compares the rank order of these anticipated and real problems.

There is some degree of correspondence between these sets of teacher perceptions. The last five items show some degree of correspondence, although salary, lack of resources and supplies, and communi-

cation with staff of different cultural backgrounds seem to be problems that become less important for teachers as they gain experience.

Greater divergence between anticipated and real problems occurs in the top five rankings. While discipline and lack of parental support seem fairly constant, the other three items show a discrepancy between anticipation and reality. Before teaching, there seems to be greater anticipation that underachieving students will be a greater problem than they prove to be. On the other hand, before teaching there seems to be a downplaying of the issues of heavy load and inadequate support from administrators. Both of these problems increase in intensity with actual experience.

It is interesting to note that before teaching, there is a greater expectation that dealing with students of different cultural backgrounds will be a greater problem than it proves to be in practice.

Discussion and Implications

These findings deal with teacher perceptions and do not attempt to verify reality factors externally. Nevertheless, it is interesting to note some counterintuitive findings and raise questions about their explanations. In urban teaching it is commonly assumed that teachers will be overwhelmed by low-achieving students and by students of cultural backgrounds different from their own. These expectations are reflected in the high ranking (1 and 3.5) given these problems before teaching. After teaching, these problems are ranked lower (5 and 7). One explanation is that, with experience, teachers "adjust" to low achievement and cultural differences by improving their effectiveness or by lowering their expectations. Another explanation, however, is that problems unforeseen by beginning teachers become more critical with experience, that is, heavy work loads and inadequate support from administrators.

From these data there is no way to determine whether those leaving the Milwaukee Public Schools are the "better" or the "poorer" teachers. It is, however, reasonable to assume that teachers who leave Milwaukee Public Schools and are hired elsewhere must still be interested in teaching. It also seems reasonable to assume that since neighboring systems can select teachers from large candidate pools, these teachers must be, or appear to be, more highly qualified than other applicants.

Note the tentative nature of the commentary

Discounting the teachers who actually move out of the Milwaukee area or retire, 90 percent of the leavers in this sample sought and were able to secure teaching jobs. It seems clear that active teachers, not those leaving the profession entirely, are quitting the Milwaukee Public Schools. In an urban system that desperately needs teachers, the loss of experienced professionals seems to be a dreadful waste. While the residency requirement was an important factor in teachers' decisions to leave, it was cited less frequently than other employment.

Since there is a continuing need for urban teachers, it might be wise for urban districts to conduct exit interviews with those leaving the system. Information from such interviews should not be limited to personnel officers but might be shared with school officials who bear responsibility for the conditions under which teachers work. Although it is not a common practice, it might be wise not only to listen to the leavers but to seek to ameliorate some of the conditions about which they complain. It might also be appropriate, although it is not common practice in urban schools, for "important" school officials to meet with classroom teachers and even encourage them to stay. The reactions of urban school leavers make it quite clear that the isolation, anonymity, and low esteem they perceive is justified when no one in "the system" communicates with them in any manner when they resign. They expressed the belief that after working someplace for years, even decades, there ought to be someone to say "so long." It seems strange policy formation for an urban school district to try to solve its teacher shortage by recruitment only and simultaneously to ignore the retention of experienced teachers—teachers considered desirable by surrounding suburbs.

Recommendations begin here

Finally, if we consider the twelve problems perceived by urban teachers, there are three that are amenable to improved teacher education: discipline, underachieving students, and working with students of various cultural backgrounds. These are areas in which teacher education should be held accountable for doing a better job. But the other nine problems are essentially the conditions under which teachers work. If an urban school system were interested in decreasing the number of urban teachers who leave, improving the conditions of work would seem to be the best way to do it.

References

Elam, S. M. (1989). The second Phi Delta Kappa poll of teachers' attitudes toward public schools. *Phi Delta Kappan, 70,* (June), 785–798.

Haberman, M., and Richards, W. H., *Urban Education,* Volume 25, Number 3, pp. 297–303. Copyright 1990 by Sage Publications, Inc. Reprinted by permission of Sage Publications, Inc.

ADDITIONAL EXAMPLES OF PUBLISHED DESCRIPTIVE STUDIES

In order to better understand a particular research methodology, it is often beneficial to examine additional examples of published research that utilizes that specific methodology. Several such examples of descriptive research have been identified for you, through the use of *Research Navigator*™, available on the Web at www.researchnavigator.com. The following list consists of published research articles available free of charge in full-text format via *Research Navigator*™. These articles are available in either HTML and/or PDF formats and are easily located by searching the database by *article number* (abbreviated "**AN**"), which has been provided for each citation.

Brinkman, F. G., & Van Rens, E. M. M. (1999). Student teachers' research skills as experienced in their educational training. *European Journal of Teacher Education, 22*(1), 115–125. **[AN: 6641731]**

Chanock, K. (2000). Comments on essays: Do students understand what tutors write? *Teaching in Higher Education, 5*(1), 95–105. **[AN: 2900643]**

Hannay, L. M., Erb, C. S., & Ross, J. A. (2001). To the barricades: The relationship between secondary school organizational structure and the implementation of policy initiatives. *International Journal of Leadership in Education, 4*(2), 97–113. **[AN: 4499609]**

Klecker, B. M., & Loadman, W. (1999). Measuring principals' openness to change on three dimensions: Affective, cognitive and behavioral. *Journal of Instructional Psychology, 26*(4), 213–226. **[AN: 2656277]**

Lorentsen, A. (2001). The impact of ICT on staff development. *European Journal of Engineering Education, 26*(4), 351–359. **[AN: 5522992]**

McQuarie, N., & Zarry, L. (1999). Examining the actual duties of resource teachers. *Education, 120*(2), 378–386. **[AN: 2809144]**

Sweeting, H., & West, P. (2001). Being different: Correlates of the experience of teasing and bullying at age 11. *Research Papers in Education, 16*(3), 225–246. **[AN: 5425318]**

An Example of Historical Research

The following is a short report of an investigation into the history of grading, published in the Spring 1993 issue of *The Educational Forum.* Although the research elements are not identified with headings, you should be able to find the information called for in Exercise 12.2.

Exercise 12.2

As you read the article on the history of grading, find the following information:

1. *Problem:* The purpose of study
2. Research questions
3. *Research design:* What did the investigator do to gain access to needed data?
4. *Data collection:* In what form were data obtained?
5. *Data analysis:* What data analysis, if any, was done?
6. Findings
7. Conclusions

An A Is Not an A Is Not an A: A History of Grading

Mark W. Durm

"Is that information going to be on the test?" This question is one teachers often hear from students. When instructors hear this, they should realize those particular students probably consider grades a higher priority than learning. It seems, for some, that securing a higher grade point average takes precedence over knowledge, learning career-related skills, and other aspects needed to compete in today's world. This fact, coupled with the realization that many college students will, if given a choice, opt for the "easy teacher" rather than one from whom they may learn more, should make teachers reexamine the current system of grading.

Measuring Progress

Why do most schools use the A, B, C, D, and F marking system? What happened to E? Why divisions of grades? Why not three, four, seven, or eight for that matter? I. E. Finkelstein (1913), concerned with these questions, offered the following:

> Poses some interesting questions

When we consider the practically universal use in all educational institutions of a system of marks, whether numbers or letters, to indicate scholastic attainment of the pupils or students in these institutions, and when we remember how very great stress is laid by teachers and pupils alike upon these marks as real measures or indicators of attainment, we can but be astonished at the blind faith that has been felt in the reliability of the marking system. School administrators have been using with confidence an absolutely uncalibrated instrument.... What faults appear in the marking systems that we are now using, and how can these be avoided or minimized?

Finkelstein wrote this in 1913! Can we better answer these questions today? Is our grading system still uncalibrated?

Finkelstein further wrote:

> ...[V]ariability in the marks given for the same subject and to the same pupils by different instructors is so great as frequently to work real injustice to the students.... Nor may anyone seek refuge in the assertion that the marks of the students are of little real importance. The evidence is clear that marks constitute a very real and a very strong inducement to work, that they are accepted as real and fairly exact measurements of ability or of performance. Moreover, they not infrequently are determiners of the student's career.

Because of the truthfulness of Finkelstein's assumptions, academe may have created its own nightmare. By looking back to the original sources of

Purpose of the paper

grading in this country, we may find answers to the questions raised above about the present state of college grading systems. A brief study of the origin of grades appears to have merit.

There is no doubt that colleges from the very beginning had some method of student evaluation, but there was no standard. Differentiating between students in the very earliest days of American colleges and universities seemed to center around social class. For example, in the early years of Harvard, students were not arranged alphabetically but were listed according to the social position of their families (Eliot, 1923).

In addition, there was apparently no standard process for the selection of the valedictorian. Ezra Stiles, the president of Yale in the late eighteenth century, had an interesting statement in his diary concerning the valedictory oration in Latin for July of 1781. The valedictorian was elected by the class. Stiles wrote: "The Seniors presented me their Election of Gridly for Valedictory Orator, whom I approved…" (Stiles, 1901).

Note the variety of data sources used, including books, diaries, published articles, and university documents

Yale Beginnings

The history of grading in American colleges was eloquently detailed by Mary Lovett Smallwood (1935). She related that marking, or grading, to differentiate students was first used at Yale. The scale was made up of descriptive adjectives and was included as a footnote to Stiles's 1785 diary.

President Stiles wrote that 58 students were present at an examination, and they were graded as follows: "Twenty Optimi, sixteen second Optimi, 12 Inferiores (Boni), ten Pejores" (Stiles, 1901, vol. 3). In all probability, these may have been the very first collegiate "grades" given in the United States.

Yale took the initiative in formulating a scale. Smallwood quoted the following from the *Book of Averages—Yale College*:

"Record of Examinations," 1813–1839: Rules respecting this Book and its records, 1. This book shall be kept with the Senior Tutor of the College, whose duty it shall (be) to see that the following rules are carried into effect. 2. The average result of the examination of every student in each class shall be recorded in this book by the Senior Tutor of the class.

Also this very same book from Yale gives a reference to marking on a scale of 4. In all probability, this was the origin of the 4.0 system used by so many colleges and universities today. There was, however, still no connection to letter grades. For example, an A was not a 4.0, for at this point in time, there was no A.

The gap of 28 years between President Stiles's remarks of 1785 and Yale's in 1813 is also interesting. It is hard to imagine there were not any records or statements concerning grading written during this time, but apparently none have been found.

After 1813 the records show a variety of attempts to evaluate and grade students. Smallwood noted that in the William and Mary Faculty Reports of July 16, 1817, the following classification of students was used: No. 1. (Names listed) The first in their respective classes; No. 2. Orderly, correct, and attentive; No. 3. They have made very little improvement; No. 4. They have learnt little or nothing.

The first numerical scale used at Harvard was dated 1830 and employed a scale of 20, not 4, and was used in an examination in rhetoric. In 1837 at Harvard, mathematical and philosophical professors used a scale of 100 (Smallwood, 1935). Yale, which had used the 4.0 scale starting in 1813, apparently changed later to a 9.0 scale. In 1832 the faculty records report a desire of the faculty to return to the 4.0 system, and apparently the institution did so (Smallwood, 1935).

There is no record that William and Mary had ever used a numerical scale until 1850. Before 1850, teachers used expressive adjectives in reports that were sent to parents (Smallwood, 1935). The University of Michigan was an example of an aggressive institution trying to find a workable grading system. It first used the numerical system, then opted for a pass–no pass system in 1851. In 1852 an examination book recorded a plus sign to indicate if the student passed. By 1860 Michigan added a "condit" (abbreviation for conditional) grade in addition to the plus sign. Shortly after 1860, they reinstituted the 100 scale numerical system. By 1867 they had adopted a P for passing, a C for conditioned, or A for absent (Smallwood, 1935). Apparently Michigan believed in the adage "try and try again."

Letter Grades at Harvard

Evidently such experimentation with grading systems at universities was the norm. As Smallwood wrote, "Before 1850 descriptive adjectives and various numerical systems of evaluation had been tried. Through the next fifty years, several new scales of merit and demerit were devised." The following (Smallwood, 1935, 50–52) is a chronological list of those scales:

1. 1877—Harvard faculty started classifying students in six divisions, based on a 100 percent basis. The following is taken from the Harvard Faculty Records, April 2, 1877:

   1. Students shall be ranked in each study in divisions according to merit.

      Division 1–90 or more on a scale of 100
      Division 2–89 to 75
      Division 3–74 to 60
      Division 4–59 to 50
      Division 5–49 to 40
      Division 6–below 40

2. 1883—At Harvard there is a reference to a student making a B. This apparently was the first use of a letter for a grade that can be found.

3. 1884—The Annual Report of the President of Harvard, 1885 stated: "The Faculty last year did away with the minute percentage system of marking, and substituted a classification of the students in each course of study in five groups, the lowest of which includes those who have failed in the course."

4. 1886—The Harvard Faculty Records, February 2, 1886, reported:

   1. Classes I, II, III (corresponding approximately to the nineties, eighties, and seventies of the present percentage scale). Those students who have passed with distinction, and are worthy of a place on the rank list.

   2. Class IV (corresponding to that part of the present scale which lies between the lower limit of the rank list and the minimum mark for passing). Those who have passed without distinction.

   3. Class V. Those who have failed to pass.

5. 1895—Harvard adopted three classifications for merit—"Failed," "Passed," and "Passed with Distinction."

6. 1895—Michigan adopted the following: Moved and carried that there shall be 5 marks on Examination: Passed—Incomplete—Conditioned—Not Passed—Absent.

7. 1896—Yale related to its students that they must have a standing of 225 for the previous term or half term in order to continue. Thus, the decimal point at Yale must have been dropped.

8. 1897—This year should be a red letter year in the annals of college grading. It was this year that Mount Holyoke adopted letters for marking students. The following was used:

   A Excellent, equivalent to percents 95–100

   B Good, equivalent to percents 85–94 (inclusive)

   C Fair, equivalent to percents 76–84 (inclusive)

   D Passed (barely), equivalent to percent 75

   E Failed (below 75)

Mount Holyoke in 1897 was using a marking [What happened to "E"?] system that combined the three types of grading: descriptive adjectives, letters, and percentages. In 1898 they again changed the scale in a minor fashion to read: A—95–100; B—90–94; C—85–89; D—80–84; E—75–79; F—Failed.

Therefore, what Mount Holyoke adopted in 1897 became the cornerstone for college grading. Some colleges and universities have altered this standard in different ways. In addition, at most colleges and universities, the letter grade also denotes the early point scale: A for 4.0, B for 3.0, C for 2.0, and D for a 1.0.

As the record reveals, the history of grading in schools in the United States is replete with trial and error. Is it the best we can accomplish? Probably not. [Somewhat abrupt end to the paper]

References

Eliot, C. W. (1923). *Harvard Memories*. Cambridge: Harvard University Press.

Finkelstein, I. E. (1913). The marking system in theory and practice. *Educational Psychology Monographs 10*.

Smallwood, M. L. (1935). *Examinations and Grading Systems in Early American Universities.* Cambridge: Harvard University Press.

Stiles, E. (1901). *The Literary Diary of Ezra Stiles. Vol. 2. 1776–1781.* New York: Charles Scribner's Sons.

Stiles, E. (1901). *The Literary Diary of Ezra Stiles. Vol. 3. 1782–1795.* New York: Charles Scribner's Sons.

ADDITIONAL EXAMPLES OF PUBLISHED HISTORICAL STUDIES

In order to better understand a particular research methodology, it is often beneficial to examine additional examples of published research that utilizes that specific methodology. Several such examples of historical research have been identified for you through the use of *Research Navigator*™, available on the Web at www.researchnavigator.com. The following list consists of published research articles available free of charge in full-text format via *Research Navigator*™. These articles are available in either HTML and/or PDF formats and are easily located by searching the database by *article number* (abbreviated "**AN**"), which has been provided for each citation.

Andrada, M. (2001). The privatization of education in Argentina. *Journal of Education Policy, 16*(6), 585–595. [AN: 5655617]

Johnson-Bailey, J. (2001). The road less walked: A retrospective of race and ethnicity in adult education. *International Journal of Lifelong Education, 20*(1/2). [AN: 4394492]

LeMelle, T. J. (2002). The HBCU: Yesterday, today, and tomorrow. *Education, 123*(1), 190–196. [AN: 7717422]

Pascoe, R. (1999). Admission to Australian universities. *Journal of Higher Education Policy & Management, 21*(1), 17–30. [AN: 2157045]

Pave, D. M., Inglebret, E., & Banks, S. R. (2001). Tribal colleges and universities in an era of dynamic development. *PJE: Peabody Journal of Education, 76*(1), 50–72. [AN: 5877950]

Phillips, R. (1999). History teaching, nationhood and politics in England and Wales in the late twentieth century: A historical comparison. *History of Education, 28*(3), 351–363. [AN: 3640384]

Reschly, D. J. (2002). Change dynamics in special education assessment: Historical and contemporary patterns. *PJE: Peabody Journal of Education, 77*(2), 117–136. [AN: 9228570]

Wachtel, H. K. (1998). Student evaluation of college teaching effectiveness: A brief review. *Assessment & Evaluation in Higher Education, 23*(2), 191–211. [AN: 852923]

Weiner, G. (2000). Harriet Martineau and her contemporaries: Past studies and methodological questions on historical surveys of women. *History of Education, 29*(5), 389–404. [AN: 3613503]

Organizing for Descriptive Research and Historical Research

As you have seen, descriptive and historical research have much in common. They often use the same data sources and data treatments. Both can at times be entirely qualitative, whereas at other times both can be at least partially quantitative.

Generally, however, of the two types, historical research tends more toward qualitative data and analysis. It is guided more frequently by research questions than by hypotheses, and the data are more often compiled and analyzed verbally than statistically. In both types of research, if the raw data answer the research questions, no further analysis is needed. However, if one group is compared to another, statistical analysis may be helpful.

Let us now consider how to organize historical research. Here we use the generic elements of educational research—problem, hypothesis/questions, design, data collection, data analysis, findings, and conclusions—as a structure to assist in organizing a research project concerning the history of Cutter school, the oldest elementary school remaining in Elmwood.

Suppose you were asked by the Elmwood school board to prepare a brief history of Cutter Elementary School's first five years, 1933 to 1938.

Exercise 12.3

1. *Problem.* State the problem ("The purpose of this study is to…").
2. *Questions.* Structure a main research question and five subquestions.

Exercise 12.4

1. *Research design.* Briefly indicate the plan you will use to obtain data to answer your five subquestions. Mention three primary and three secondary data sources you anticipate consulting.
2. *Data.* What kinds of data do you expect to obtain?
3. *Cautions.* What cautions will you keep in mind concerning external criticism (authenticity of information) and internal criticism (accuracy of the information obtained)?

Exercise 12.5

1. *Data analysis.* What data analysis do you think will be required, if any?
2. How will the data be used in answering the research subquestions?
3. *Findings and conclusions.* What distinction will you make between your findings and your conclusions? Give an example that differentiates the two.

Let us suppose that you completed the historical research project you just outlined. The school district was so pleased with your work that they asked you to undertake a descriptive study of Cutter school as it is today.

Case Study

Research Navigator.com
case study

At times, one may wish to make a close study, either descriptive or historical, of a particular person, group, produce, or process—what Gall, Borg, and Gall (1996) call a particular *phenomenon* within a larger setting. For instance, a researcher might be interested in exploring certain aspects of a school's program for gifted and talented students, as that program affects a particular student. Rather than placing emphasis on the program itself, the researcher studies the selected student, as he or she is affected by the program. Focusing closely on a particular instance such as this is called a **case study.**

Purposes of a Case Study

Case studies are usually done for one of the following three reasons:

To Provide Vivid Descriptions.   It is often helpful to obtain vividly descriptive pictures of a particular person or instance, such as what happens to student James within the program for gifted and talented students, or the personal dynamics that occur between

Applying Technology: More about Descriptive and Historical Research

Since both descriptive and historical research studies are predominated by qualitative data, the reader is advised to revisit *Applying Technology:* More about Qualitative Research, which was presented in Chapter 10. Recall that a sampling of websites addressing issues related to qualitative research methods—including various approaches of qualitative research, qualitative measures, and qualitative research resources on the Internet—was presented in this section. Many of these resources are also applicable to descriptive and historical research studies.

The reader is also referred back to Chapter 7—specifically the section titled *Applying Technology:* Survey Construction. The information provided in that section concerns various elements involved in and considerations to be made when developing a survey as a means of collecting data. The methods, techniques, and considerations presented and discussed may be extremely appropriate in certain types of descriptive research studies—especially those which may include or rely entirely on quantitative data, as well as data resulting from open-ended questions.

coauthors Samuels and Levine as they produce an illustrated book for young readers. In such an investigation, the researcher would strive to put together what anthropologists call a *thick description,* a detailed re-creation of contexts, meanings, and intentions. Such research can yield information not ordinarily available, since what happens to particular individuals within groups is usually obscured when research explores a larger group as a unit.

To Provide Explanations.   At times, descriptions, however vivid, are not sufficient in themselves. Instead of merely knowing *about* someone or something, one wishes to know *why* the situation is as it is, or why the individual behaves as observed. A case study can help provide such understanding by seeking out identifiable patterns in behavior and procedures. The researcher attempts to learn which phenomena are associated with which others—whether, for example, James's giftedness coincides with a particular lifestyle of his family, or whether coauthoring an illustrated children's book seems to be best facilitated by single-minded intention, fortuitous happenstance, cooperation, or give and take. Two types of patterns can be investigated: *relational patterns,* which simply indicate that two or more events or traits seem to occur together—James is attending a special class and he says he is not enjoying it—and *causal patterns,* in which it is determined, for example, that a certain aspect of the program James attends is making him feel unhappy.

To Provide Evaluations.   A third purpose of a case study is to evaluate programs, individuals, and settings. In studying James's behavior as a student in the gifted program, one makes judgments concerning how well the program serves his interests. Such research will probably identify program strengths and shortcomings, and will lead to suggested modifications. It may also make evaluations of James himself, as regards his efforts, behavior, attitude, and self-control.

Organizing and Conducting the Case Study

A case study is organized and conducted as indicated in the following steps:

1. The purpose of the study is clearly stated. For example: "The purpose of this study is to determine, based upon one individual student's perspective, the qualities and limitations of Cutter school's program for gifted and talented learners." A number of research questions are listed to guide the acquisition of data, as shown in the following examples:

   - Which parts of the program does the student like best, and why?
   - Which parts of the program does the student dislike, and why?
   - What do the student's parents think of the program?

2. The case is selected. The case may be a person, a group of people, a procedure, a document, or the like—any individual element or phenomenon that figures importantly in a program or setting. In the example noted, the case is a student named James.

3. Access is obtained to the case and to the site. In order to gain such access one must

   - Determine who must be contacted for site access (site meaning school, classroom, home, office, and the like)

- Decide what language—questions, requests, tone, phrasing—should be used in approaching case individuals and site personnel
- Make sure to point out the benefits that will accrue from the research
- Determine which method of contact with cases and personnel is preferable—personal visit, telephone, formal letter
- Anticipate questions, concerns, and objections that might be raised when the requests are made and decide how they can best be addressed or assuaged

4. The research begins and data are obtained. In case studies, most of the data are gathered directly by the researcher through close contact with the case individual. Testing, questioning, and analysis may be involved, but much of the data are obtained from direct observations made by the researcher. These data are usually taken in the form of notations and recordings. As with ethnographic research, the investigator typically involves himself or herself closely with the individuals being studied, and similarly, new questions will arise during the course of the investigation.

5. Data are analyzed. Some data obtained in case studies are quantitative in nature and can be analyzed statistically or merely reported. Most data, however, are qualitative in nature—statements describing observations, judgments, interpretations, and so on—and are, therefore, analyzed logically, as described for ethnographic research in Chapter 10, a process that involves identifying themes and patterns evident within the data and then making interpretations from those patterns.

6. Findings are listed and interpretations are made. Once data have been analyzed, factual findings are stated. The researcher uses intuition and judgment in setting forth findings that accurately portray the phenomenon under scrutiny, such as, "James does not like working in cooperative groups that were emphasized in the Cutter program." The investigator presents that and other conclusions together with the evidence that supports them.

7. Conclusions are stated. Here the investigator states the conclusions that seem warranted by the findings. The list of conclusions might be extensive. Examples might be: "Cutter school students would be better served if the program directors for gifted and talented education identified which students enjoyed and profited from cooperative group work and which did not."

Certainly the processes of presenting findings, making interpretations, and presenting conclusions are subjective, and the results are therefore likely to be questioned. Researchers prepare for this eventuality by using strong logic and by identifying questions critics are likely to raise. In so doing, they can reassure themselves as well as answer criticisms of their work.

Chapter Summary

The purpose of both descriptive research and historical research is to describe and make interpretations about objects, settings, conditions, and events. Both types of research can be guided by hypotheses but are much more frequently structured by research questions.

Research design in both cases consists of identifying who or what is to be described, selecting available sources of information, and then obtaining pertinent data from sources deemed to be reliable. The data thus obtained are often subjected to verbal analysis. Sometimes, they are used with little further analysis in answering the research questions. When two or more groups are being compared, statistical treatment may be needed. Findings are presented as answers to subquestions. Conclusions are presented as answers to the main research questions and usually include the investigator's commentary concerning implications or need for further research.

A C T I V I T I E S   F O R   T H O U G H T   A N D   D I S C U S S I O N

1. Try your hand at answering these questions, which were presented at the beginning of the chapter.
   a. For what kinds of topics are descriptive and historical research used?
   b. What is the general research procedure used in the two types of research?
   c. What are the similarities and differences between descriptive and historical research?
   d. How would you organize research to describe the early history of the school you first attended?
   e. How would you organize research to describe the current status of the school you first attended (presuming that it still exists)?
   f. How would you organize a case study of a beginning teacher's experiences during the first year of teaching?

2. Suppose you want to research the motives that caused fellow students to pursue graduate studies. State the problem, research questions, and procedures of data collection and analysis.

3. Suppose you wished to research the educational backgrounds of the parents of your fellow students. How would you structure the study? How would you resolve possible concerns about external criticism and internal criticism?

4. Compare and contrast the two articles reprinted in this chapter regarding (a) readability, (b) organization, (c) data analysis, and (d) conclusions.

A N S W E R S   T O   C H A P T E R   E X E R C I S E S

Responses to the chapter exercises can vary and still be correct for individual respondents. It is suggested that responses be discussed and evaluated as group activities.

R E F E R E N C E S   A N D   R E C O M M E N D E D   R E A D I N G S

Durm, M. (1993). An A is not an A is not an A: A history of grading. *The Educational Forum, 57,* 294–297.

Gall, M., Borg, W., & Gall, J. (2003). *Educational Research: An Introduction* (7th ed.). Boston: Allyn and Bacon.

Gay, L., & Airasian, P. (2003). *Educational Research: Competencies for Analysis and Application* (7th ed.). Upper Saddle River, NJ: Merrill.

Haberman, M., & Rickards, W. (1990). Urban teachers who quit: Why they leave and what they do. *Urban Education 25*(3): 297–303.

Wiersma, W. (2000). *Research Methods in Education: An Introduction* (7th ed.). Boston: Allyn and Bacon.

13 Correlational Research

P R E V I E W

This chapter explains the nature and procedures of

- Correlational research

which is used to explore

- Covarying relationships between two or more variables (such as between motivation and academic achievement)

The purposes of exploring such correlations are

- To identify variables that relate to each other in this fashion
- To make predictions of one variable trait from the other (such as to predict academic achievement from level of motivation), and/or
- To examine the possible existence of causation (such as the influence motivation might be exerting on academic achievement)

Various kinds of measures that can be correlated include:

- Two or more sets of numerical scores
- Two or more sets of rankings (first, second, third…)
- One set of scores and one dichotomy (either–or; yes–no…)
- Two dichotomies

Targeted Learnings

This chapter explains the purposes and methods of correlational research and provides exercises to help you organize and conduct correlational research. Included is a reprinted article that exemplifies correlational research. As you read the material and complete the exercises, look especially for information related to the following:

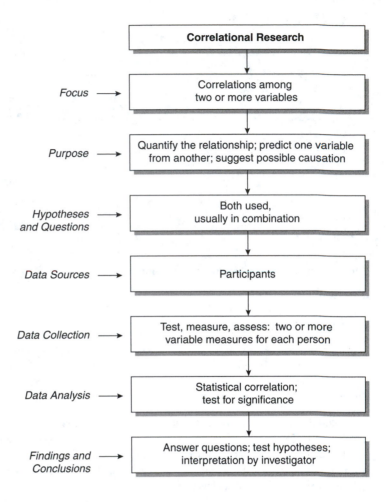

1. What differentiates correlational research from other types of research?
2. What can correlational research accomplish, and what are its limitations?
3. What elements comprise the method of correlational research?
4. What is meant by *criterion variable* and *predictor variable?*
5. What are some of the different methods of computing coefficients of correlation, and what kinds of data are used in each?
6. How do coefficients of correlation help answer research questions or test hypotheses?

Weather and the Process of Education

Most of us make several observations of the weather every day and exchange comments about it. You would think that after a while we would understand weather, at least well enough to predict wind or rain. But even after a lifetime of observation, commentary, and in some cases advanced study in meteorology, no one can explain much about what "causes" weather.

The process of education is somewhat like weather in that regard. After a lifetime of study, educators can hardly say what causes a person to become educated. They can of course describe conditions that are associated with education, but those particular conditions may or may not produce an educated person, and we know that it is possible to become educated without exposure to the usual trappings of schooling.

These facts are perplexing and sometimes frustrating. The human mind wants to *know*—not only know about things but also to know how and why they function as they do. We would like to know not just that there are clouds in the sky and that it is raining but also what causes clouds to form and precipitation to occur and pressure to change. In a similar sense, we would like to know not only that learning is occurring among seventh-grade students but also what is causing the learning to occur, and why it occurs for some students and not for others.

These questions may or may not be answerable through normal thought processes. Human logical thinking tends to be linear: If X happens, then Y will result; if we drop an apple, it will fall to earth; if the night gets cold, frost will form; if Joshua is taught his number facts, he will be able to do arithmetic. Such linear thinking serves fairly well in hard sciences such as physics and chemistry, but less well in the softer sciences of psychology, learning, and meteorology. If we drop an apple, it will almost certainly fall toward earth (except when weightless in space), but just as cold nights do not always produce frost, neither does teaching number facts always result in arithmetic competence.

Despite our desire to know what causes what, the best we can do in explaining most aspects of weather or education or human behavior in general is to determine what is related to what—to say with some certainty that X (teaching of number facts) is related to Y (competence in arithmetic), or that X and Y (humidity and temperature) are related to Z (precipitation). "Related" simply means that certain conditions occur together and change together. Most of the time, being taught and becoming competent go hand in hand, as do precipitation and humidity and temperature. Scientifically, we can only say that the variables are associated, that they tend to be present together and to covary with each other.

Correlations

Research Navigator.com
correlations

Although clear cause–effect patterns may not be always evident in education, we nevertheless can identify numerous related phenomena—numerous conditions, materials, interventions, teaching methods, and styles of communication that have to do with when, how much, and under what conditions people learn. Searching for such relationships, such *correlations,* is the purpose of correlational research. When correlations among variables are discovered, it becomes possible to predict one of the variables from the other. For example, if we know that vocabulary competence and school learning are correlated, we can predict that students with better vocabularies will usually learn more than will students with limited vocabularies. Correlations also raise questions about whether one of the related variables may be causing the other to occur and, therefore, suggest fertile areas for experimental research. If we learn that a correlation exists between vocabulary and achievement, we might wish to follow our correlational study with an experimental study in which vocabulary training is provided, to see if higher school achievement occurs as a result.

Educators would be delighted to discover reliable cause–effect relationships in education. But for the most part, education occurs too chaotically to be explained in terms of cause and effect. Therefore, educators rely on correlational evidence for much of what they know about conditions and practices that affect education.

The Nature of Correlational Research

The purpose of correlational research is to discover relationships between two or more variables. *Relationship* means that an individual's status on one variable tends to reflect his or her status on the other. Correlational research in education seeks out traits, abilities, or conditions that covary, or correlate, with each other. As we have noted, correlations help us

- Understand certain related events, conditions, and behaviors
- Predict future conditions or behaviors in one variable from what we presently know of another variable
- Sometimes obtain strong suggestions that one variable is "causing" the other

For example, we know that high school grade point average is correlated with subsequent student success in college. The correlation is far from perfect; indeed, perfect correlations are virtually never discovered in education. Nevertheless, we can predict, albeit imperfectly, a person's future college success by the grades he or she earns in high school.

Cautions Concerning Cause and Effect

Correlations show the extent to which variables are related to each other. It has been explained that correlations do not, in themselves, show that one of the variables causes the other—a conclusion toward which the intellect automatically turns, though often erroneously. For example, certain Native American tribes once believed that toads could call forth rain. That seemed plausible, for the rainy season began at the same time toads went into a frenzy of mating, egg laying, and ceaseless croaking. More rain followed predictably as the toads continued to croak. It could certainly seem that the croaking brought forth rain. But that is an example of the **post hoc fallacy**—*post hoc ergo propter hoc*—in other words, "after the fact, therefore because of the fact." The fallacy lies in concluding that because it rained after the toads croaked, it therefore rained because the toads croaked. One could as logically, or more logically, say that the rain was causing the toads to croak. Sometimes when we find correlated variables, one of the two does in fact turn out to be the cause and the other the effect.

Such may well be the case in the correlation that medical researchers have found between smoking and lung disease, which is in the news at times and is the scientific basis for recent lawsuits of magnitude. But statistical correlations do not demonstrate cause and effect. It is only through experimental research that causal relationships can be demonstrated convincingly, where purposeful manipulations of independent variables are consistently followed by corresponding changes in dependent variables. In this illustration, you see the advantage correlational research has over experimentation; we would hardly force people to smoke heavily for years on end to see whether or not smoking causes them to have lung disease.

Topics for Correlational Research

Six categories of topics are especially amenable to correlational research in education:

1. Suspected relationships between certain human traits (X) and learning or other school behavior (Y)
2. Suspected relationships between classroom environment or organizational schemes (X) and learning or attitude (Y)
3. Suspected relationships between various teaching practices and instructional materials (X) and learning (Y)
4. Conditions or practices (X) that are suspected of interfering with learning or optimal performance (Y)
5. Predicting from a given variable X (e.g., self-concept) some other variable Y (e.g., the future success, adjustment, or difficulties of students, teachers, and other professionals)
6. Establishment of validity and reliability of tests and other diagnostic and assessment instruments

Hypotheses and Questions in Correlational Research

Correlational research may be oriented by either research questions or hypotheses, or both. If you wanted to explore a possible relationship between students' overall evaluation of the classes they are taking and the amount of homework assigned in those classes, you might pose a question such as:

> *What degree of relationship exists between high school students' evaluation of their classes and the amount of homework assigned in those classes?*

If you decided to guide your study with hypotheses, you might state a hypothesis that contends

> *High school students give lower evaluations to classes in which larger amounts of homework are assigned.*

For statistical testing you might state the hypothesis in the null form:

No relationship exists between (1) the evaluations high school students give to classes and (2) the amount of homework assigned in those classes.

You would then collect data that answer the question or test the hypothesis.

Of course, an actual correlational study would likely be larger in scope than suggested by this example. A genuine study into a topic of this sort might be guided by a main research question such as:

What coursework factors do high school students believe to be most closely related to the quality of their classes?

Several subquestions might then be put forth. Some of those questions might be approached through testing null hypotheses, as shown in the following examples:

No relationship exists between students' appraisal of the quality of classes and their liking for the teachers.

And

No relationship exists between students' evaluation of the quality of their classes and their appraisal of the fairness of discipline regulations.

Correlational Research Design

Correlational research design is relatively simple, and its procedures are uncomplicated. In essence, correlational research is designed as follows:

1. Variables whose relationship is to be explored are identified and clarified.
2. Questions or hypotheses are stated.
3. A sample is selected—with a minimum sample size of 30 individuals.
4. Measurements are obtained from sample members on each of the variables being explored.
5. Correlations between and among variables are computed to determine degrees of relationship.

Suppose you read a report of an investigation into the relationship between carbohydrate intake and the performance of high school cross-country runners. You would find included in the report (1) either questions or hypotheses, (2) a sample of runners selected for inclusion in the study, (3) two measures obtained from each subject—one for carbohydrate intake and the other for running performance, and (4) a coefficient of correlation that has been calculated to show the degree of relationship between carbohydrate intake and running performance.

You can see from this design that data are obtained by testing, measuring, or making judgments and are compiled so as to pair the measures obtained for each individual. The data are analyzed statistically and the results show the size of the correlation and its direction (whether positive or negative). The coefficient of correlation is then tested for statistical significance.

Data Sources and Collection

Correlational research relies on relatively few sources of data. Those sources are usually individuals in the study sample, from each of whom at least two measures are obtained. Those two measures are paired, as pairs of test scores, pairs of ratings, pairs of measures, pairs of dichotomies, or combinations thereof.

The data are collected either by directly measuring the participants (to determine physical characteristics), by sorting participants on the basis of certain criteria (to group them into categories), or by having them respond to tests and rating scales (to obtain sets of scores). Instruments frequently used in data collection include standardized tests, rating scales, and devices or indexes that gauge height, weight, frequency, and the like.

Although in most cases data for correlational studies are obtained through measurement, at times they come from judgments made by researchers, teachers, or other qualified persons. For example, suppose you wanted to explore the relationship between student cooperation and scholastic achievement. You could measure each subject's level of achievement objectively, but participants' degrees of cooperation would have to be determined by qualified judges, such as teachers.

Subjective judgments invariably raise questions about data reliability. When judgment must be used, researchers should be meticulous in spelling out the criteria on which judgments are based. For example, in a study to explore the relationship between personal attractiveness and social acceptance (both of which would have to be determined subjectively), the researcher should express very explicitly the criteria by which attractiveness and acceptance (both nominal data) are to be determined. This is not to suggest that all nominal data present difficulties. It is easy to assign numerical values to certain dichotomies, such as "boy–girl," "tall–short," "pass–fail," and "correct–incorrect." But in cases where gradations exist, as in "adjustment to the group" or "level of attention," clear criteria are especially needed.

What Can Be Correlated and How

Several kinds of variable data can be correlated. As indicated, you must have two measures or ratings for each individual in the sample. (Please remember that computer statistical software calculates all these correlations for you and tests their significance.)

Research
Navigator.c⊕m
product-moment
correlation

Product-Moment Correlation

Most commonly, correlational studies explore the relationship between variables expressed in continuous interval data, such as numerical test scores or numerical measures of physical performance. The **Pearson product-moment correlation**—often called "Pearson r" or simply "r"—is used to correlate such data.

Biserial Correlation and Point-Biserial Correlation

At times, one variable can be expressed as continuous interval data while the other variable is expressed as a *dichotomy*—either an **artificial dichotomy** (a dichotomy to which participants are arbitrarily assigned, such as "happy–sad") or a **natural dichotomy** (a dichotomy that occurs naturally, such as "left-handed–right-handed").

A **biserial correlation** is used to explore the relationship between a continuous variable and an artificial dichotomy. For example, "school achievement," a continuous interval variable, could be correlated with "poverty-level" versus "nonpoverty family income," an artificial dichotomy.

A **point-biserial correlation** is used when one variable is continuous and the other variable is a natural dichotomy.

For example, "school achievement," a continuous variable, could be correlated with the "number of parents resident in the family" (either one or two—a natural dichotomy).

Phi Correlation and Tetrachoric Correlation

Some research explores relationships in which both variables are expressed as dichotomies. If the dichotomies are both natural—for example, "handedness" (left–right) and "varsity sports participation" (yes–no)—a **phi correlation** is used. If both variables are artificial dichotomies—for example, "class participation" (high–low) and "family income" (poverty–nonpoverty)—a **tetrachoric correlation** is the appropriate procedure.

Correlations from Rankings

Data organized into **rankings,** such as "best to worst" or "quietest to loudest," can be correlated through two different procedures—the **Spearman rho** and the **Kendall tau.** Spearman rho is preferable for larger samples; the Kendall tau is preferable for samples smaller than ten.

Multivariate Correlations

The types of correlations discussed to this point have been **bivariate correlations**—that is, correlations involving only two sets of scores. Some studies, however, call for explorations of relationships among three or more variables, calling for **multivariate correlations.** Multivariate procedures that investigate correlations include partial correlation, multiple regression, discriminant analysis, and factor analysis.

Partial Correlation

Often it is found that the correlation between two variables is affected strongly by a third variable. An example is the high correlation between scores on reading tests and on vocabulary tests, where both of these variables are highly related to intelligence. To explore the relationship between reading ability and vocabulary per se, with the influence of intelligence removed, it is necessary to use a procedure that "partials out" the effects of intelligence. This is accomplished by means of the procedure called **partial correlation,** whose coefficient is called *partial r.*

Research
Navigator.c⊕m
partial correlation

multiple
regression

Multiple Regression

Multiple regression is used to determine the degree of correlation between a continuous criterion variable (*Z*) and a combination of two or more predictor variables (*X* and *Y*, etc.). This procedure might be used, for example, in exploring the relationship between school achievement (*Z*, the *criterion variable*) and a combination of intelligence (*X*) and motivation (*Y*), two *predictor variables.*

Research
Navigator.c⊕m
discriminant
analysis

Discriminant Analysis

Discriminant analysis is analogous to multiple regression, except that the *Z* or criterion variable consists of two or more categories rather than a continuous range of values. An example might be an exploration of the relationship between class participation (*Z*, categorized as "above average" and "below average") and a combination of self-concept (*X*) and grade point average (*Y*).

Research
Navigator.c⊕m
factor analysis

Factor Analysis

The procedure called **factor analysis** is often used when a large number of correlations have been explored in a given study; it is a means of grouping into clusters, or *factors,* certain variables that are moderately to highly correlated with each other. In studies of intelligence, for example, numerous variables may be explored, and those that are found to be highly correlated with each other are clustered into factors such as verbal ability, numerical ability, spatial orientation, and problem solving.

An Example of Correlational Research

The following is a reprinted research report that makes extensive use of correlations.

Exercise 13.1

As you read the report, identify the following:

1. Question or hypothesis
2. Variables whose possible relationship is being explored
3. Sample
4. Data collection
5. Results

Relationship of Computer Science Aptitude with Selected Achievement Measures among Junior High Students

Linda Coates
St. Margaret Mary School
Omaha, Nebraska

Larry Stephens
University of Nebraska at Omaha

Computer science aptitude was measured for 69 students at the junior high level by the Konvalina, Stephens, and Wileman Computer Science Aptitude Test (KSW). These aptitude scores were correlated with the following: (a) the composite score of the Survey of Basic Skills Test (published by Science Research Associates), (b) the mathematics subtest result of the composite Basic Skills Test score, (c) the first and second semester mathematics achievement scores for students in a mathematics course which utilized computer assisted instruction, and (d) programming achievement scores for students in the same courses.

The relationship between computer science aptitude and all five achievement measures was strong for both seventh and eighth graders with the eighth graders demonstrating a stronger relationship than the seventh graders for all five measures. The *r*-squared values ranged from 40–50% for eighth graders and from 15–35% for seventh graders. In addition, computer science aptitude was compared for males and females and no significant difference was found.

> First paragraph is actually the article's abstract…entire study is summarized.

Recent surveys indicate that over 60% of teachers in the United States are using computers for instruction (Riccobono, 1984). The use of computer-based instruction (CBI) ranges from drill-and-practice programs for reading readiness in kindergarten to graduate degrees in some disciplines. Following this trend, the number of research studies investigating computer science aptitude has been increasing.

The purpose of this study was to examine the relationship between computer science aptitude and achievement at the junior high level. Specifically, the objectives were: (a) to determine the correlation between computer science aptitude and general achievement, mathematical achievement, and achievement in courses using CAI,

> Purpose of the study and objectives (research questions stated in different format)

and (b) to investigate for differences in aptitude based on sex.

Research at the college level has shown that mathematical achievement, competency, and background are related to computer science aptitude and achievement (Alspaugh, 1972; Konvalina, Wileman, & Stephens, 1983; Peterson & Howe, 1979; Wileman, Konvalina, & Stephens, 1981). With the appearance in recent years of magnet schools at both the junior and senior high level, where computer science is stressed in all subjects, there is a need to investigate the same relationships with younger students. Recently Hearne, Poplin, and Lasley (1987), using junior high participants, found a significant correlation between mathematical achievement on the SAT math subscales and computer aptitude, as measured by the Computer Aptitude Literacy and Interest Profile (CALIP). Further, in keeping with earlier findings among college students (Stephens, Wileman, & Konvalina, 1981), this research also found no difference in aptitude due to the sex of participants.

> Limited literature review

Method

The participants for this study were seventh-and-eighth-grade upper middle-class students from a private metropolitan junior high school. Ages ranged from 11 to 14 years. Of the 69 students, 35 were male and 34 were female. Students in the eighth grade had had programming experience in the seventh grade, and all students had had some type of CAI prior to seventh grade.

> Description of sample and validity and reliability of instrumentation

The Konvalina, Stephens, and Wileman Computer Science Placement Test (KSW) was used as the computer science aptitude measure in the correlation research. Validity and reliability of the KSW as a predictor of achievement in computer classes has been demonstrated in several studies (Konvalina, Wileman,

& Stephens, 1983; Stephens, Wileman, Konvalina, & Teodoro, 1985; Wileman et al., 1981). In Wileman et al. (1981), the instrument was reported to have a Kuder-Richardson #20 measure of reliability equal to 0.76 and an overall correlation of 0.46 with a final exam. Point biserial correlation coefficients were computed for all 25 questions and average values were reported for the five component parts of the test; these ranged from 0.25 to 0.60. Similar reliability and validity measures have been obtained in further studies of the instrument as well as in the current study. The test consists of 25 questions with 5 items covering each of the following participants: number and letter sequences, logical reasoning, operation of a hypothetical calculator, algorithmic execution, and algebraic word problems.

The following is a description of the achievement variables used and the coding for each:

| Narrative descriptions of dependent (achievement variables) |

1. SRAC—The Science Research Associates Survey of Basic Skills Test composite score, based on three subtest results: reading, mathematics, and language.
2. SRAM—The mathematics subtest result of the composite SRAC score.
3. MATH1—The students' first semester math grade. For both seventh and eighth grade, this score was the average of three subtotals: chapter tests, quizzes, and graded assignments. All students had the same instructor and grading method. The math curriculum for both grade levels involves programming in BASIC and LOGO. Drill-and-practice software programs and tutorials, such as *Math Blaster* (Davidson & Eckert, 1983) and *Introductory Algebra* (Joesten, 1982), were also included in the course work.
4. MATH2—The second semester math grade, obtained in the same manner as MATH1.
5. PROG—The final first semester exam score for the programming work done in BASIC.

The students in the study were arranged into three groups and coded as follows: WHOLE—entire population, 8ALL—eighth-grade students, and 7ALL—seventh-grade students. To measure the relationship between the KSW

| Data collection design and analyses |

computer science aptitude scores and the achievement factors for each group, the Pearson correlation coefficient was calculated by means of SPPSX (Nie, Hul, Jenkins, Steinbrenner, & Bent, 1983). The 2-sample *t* test was used to test for differences in computer science aptitude for males and females.

Results

Table 1 shows a high positive correlation between KSW performance and each of the achievement factors for all groups. The *r*-squared values ranged from 40–50% for eighth graders and from 15–35% for seventh graders, indicating a strong relationship. The SRA composite and math subtest scores generally showed the strongest relationships to computer science aptitude in all three groups. For all variables, the eighth grade evidenced a higher correlation between aptitude and achievement than did the seventh grade.

Results of correlational analysis

TABLE 1   Correlations of Computer Science Aptitude (KSW) Scores with Achievement Variables by Groups

	SRAC	SRAM	MATH1	MATH2	PROG
WHOLE ($n = 69$)	.62**	.59**	.50**	.51**	.52**
8ALL ($n = 34$)	.71**	.67**	.68**	.63**	.63**
7ALL ($n = 35$)	.59**	.52**	.39**	.39**	.45**

**$p < .01$

Table 2 shows the results for the *t* test for KSW scores and sex of subject. The findings indicate no difference in computer science aptitude test scores for males and females.

Discussion

The findings in this research show a strong relationship between computer science aptitude and general achievement (as measured by the SRA Composite score) and mathematical achievement (as measured by the SRA math subtest and achievement scores made in a mathematics course) among junior high students.

With the appearance in recent years of magnet schools at both junior and senior high levels, where

Results of group comparison analysis

TABLE 2   Comparisons of the KSW Scores for Sex

	Sex	Mean	T-Value	2-Tail Probability
KSW	M	8.83	1.59	.116
	F	10.29		

(n_{male} = 35)
(n_{female} = 34)

computer science is stressed in all subjects, there will be a continuing need for accurate methods of placing students on the basis of computer science aptitude. The

Significance of the study

KSW test can be useful in assuring proper placement.

As this study supports prior research indicating no difference in computer science aptitude based on sex, even in younger students, it is suggested that suc-

Recommendations

cess for women in computer science depends on the development of a positive attitude and an interest in the area. Instructors at the junior high level and below can assist in this process by developing computer-assisted instruction that appeals to all students and by encouraging any student indicating interest or ability in the subject.

References

Alspaugh, C. (1972). Identification of some components of computer programming aptitude. *Journal for Research in Mathematics Education 18,* 89–94.

Davidson, J., & Eckert, R., Jr. (1983). Math blaster [Computer program]. Torrance, CA: Davidson and Associates.

Hearne, J. D., Poplin, M. S., & Lasley, J. (1987). Predicting mathematics achievement from measures of computer aptitude in junior high students. *Educational Research Quarterly, 10,* 18–24.

Joesten, V. (1982). Introductory algebra [Computer program]. Eugene: Avant-Garde.

Konvalina, I., Wileman, S. A., & Stephens, L. J. (1983). Math proficiency: A key to success for computer science students. *Communications of the ACM, 26,* 377–380.

Nie, N. H., Hul, C. H., Jenkins, J. G., Steinbrenner, I., & Bent, K. H. (1983). *Statistical package for the social sciences.* New York: McGraw-Hill.

Peterson, C. G., & Howe, T. G. (1979). Predicting academic success in introduction to computers. *Association for Educational Data Systems Journal, 12,* 182–191.

Riccobono, J. A. (1984). *Availability use and support of instructional media 1982–83.* Washington, DC: National Center for Educational Statistics.

Stephens, L. J., Wileman, S., & Konvalina, J. (1981). Group differences in computer science aptitude. *Association for Educational Data Systems Journal, 11,* 84–95.

Stephens, L. J., Wileman, S., Konvalina, J., & Teodoro, E. V. (1985). Procedures for improving student placement in computer science. *Journal of Computers in Mathematics and Science Teaching, 4,* 46–49.

Wileman, S., Konvalina, I., & Stephens, L. J. (1981). Factors influencing success in beginning computer science courses. *Journal of Educational Research, 74,* 223–226.

Coates, L., & Stephens, L. (1990). Relationship of computer science aptitude with selected achievement measures among junior high students. *Journal of Research and Development in Education, 23*(3), 162–164. Reprinted with permission.

Organizing for Correlational Research

As evident in the foregoing report, you must, when planning and conducting correlational research, give attention to the following:

1. Identification of variables to be explored
2. Hypotheses or questions
3. Means by which variables will be measured or assigned
4. Selection of a sample

ADDITIONAL EXAMPLES OF PUBLISHED CORRELATIONAL STUDIES

In order to better understand a particular research methodology, it is often beneficial to examine additional examples of published research that utilizes that specific methodology. Several such examples of correlational research have been identified for you through the use of *Research Navigator™*, available on the Web at www.researchnavigator.com. The following list consists of published research articles available free of charge in full-text format via *Research Navigator™*. These articles are available in either HTML and/or PDF formats and are easily located by searching the database by *article number* (abbreviated "**AN**"), which has been provided for each citation.

Brookhart, S. M., & DeVoge, J. G. (1999). Testing a theory about the role of classroom assessment in student motivation and achievement. *Applied Measurement in Education, 12*(3), 409–425. [**AN: 3344488**]

Donlan, C., & Masters, J. (2000). Correlates of social development in children with communication disorders: The concurrent predictive value of verbal short-term memory span. *International Journal of Language & Communication Disorders, 35*(2), 211–226. [**AN: 3860997**]

Heffler, B. (2001). Individual learning style and the Learning Style Inventory. *Educational Studies, 27*(3). [**AN: 5253808**]

Kidder-Ashley, P., Deni, J. R., Azar, K. R., & Anderton, J. B. (2000). Comparison of 40 states' procedures for identifying students with serious educational problems. *Education, 120*(3), 558–569. [**AN: 2990147**]

Klecker, B. M., & Loadman, W. (1999). Measuring principals' openness to change on three dimensions: Affective, cognitive and behavioral. *Journal of Instructional Psychology, 26*(4), 213–226. [**AN: 2656277**]

Lewis, V., Boucher, J., Lupton, L., & Watson, S. (2000). Relationships between symbolic play, functional play, verbal and non-verbal ability in young children. *International Journal of Language & Communication Disorders, 35*(1). [**AN: 3860963**]

Okpala, C. O., Smith, F., Jones, E., & Ellis, R. (2000). A clear link between school and teacher characteristics, student demographics, and student achievement. *Education, 120*(3), 487–494. [**AN: 2990115**]

Warash, B. G., & Markstrom, C. A. (2001). Parental perceptions of parenting styles in relation to academic self-esteem of preschoolers. *Education, 121*(3), 485–493. [**AN: 4434335**]

5. Collection of data
6. Analysis of data

You will find these tasks illustrated and further clarified as you move through the following set of exercises on planning correlational research.

Suppose you wish to identify factors that predict how successful new teachers are likely to be during their first year in the classroom. You call your investigation "Predictors of Success in First-Year Teaching."

Selecting the Variables

**Research
Navigator.c⊕m**

criterion variable

predictor variable

In prediction studies such as are reflected in this series of exercises, the variable to be predicted is called the **criterion variable,** which in this case is success in the first year of teaching. The other variable is called the **predictor variable** and designates the trait or condition that one hopes will predict first-year teaching success.

The variables to be explored in correlational research are suggested by the problem being investigated. In relationship studies whose main purpose is to describe, you can identify for consideration any two or more variables whose possible correlations you wish to explore, such as reading ability and writing ability. In relationship studies whose main purpose is to predict, the criterion variable is established in the research topic (e.g., success in first-year teaching). The predictive variable is then selected logically and on the basis of previous research—you use knowledge and judgment to identify one or more traits or conditions that seem likely to predict the criterion variable.

To repeat, for the exercises that follow, the tentative criterion variable is success in first-year teaching. As stated, however, this variable is vague. You need a criterion variable that can be measured, ranked, or otherwise objectively observed. You might consider such variables as student learning, good evaluations from the principal, popularity with students, popularity with fellow teachers, favorable comments from parents, special contributions to the school program, unusual accomplishments, and the like. The predictor variable(s) can be any measurable or observable trait, behavior, or experience that you believe can forecast success in first-year teaching, such as personality traits, grade point average in college, teacher training background, communication skills, poise, and so forth.

Exercise 13.2

1. Specify a measurable or observable trait or quality that you believe evidences success in first-year teaching.
2. Once you have clarified the criterion variable, identify one or more variables that you believe might predict the criterion variable. As you do so, be sure that your predictor variables can be quantified, ranked, or dichotomized. A possible variable that is easy to quantify would be college grade point average. A possible variable easy to dichotomize would be gender. A variable that might be ranked is teacher popularity with students. In contrast, a variable that would be difficult to quantify, rank, or dichotomize would be an understanding of children.

Stating Questions or Hypotheses

Once the criterion variable and predictor variable(s) have been clarified, research questions and/or hypotheses are stated as appropriate. A suitable form for an overall research question is

> *Example 1: Can degree of success in first-year teaching be reliably predicted?*

If only a single predictor variable is involved, a suitable form would be

> *Example 2: To what degree can success in first-year teaching be predicted from the basis of evaluations earned in student teaching?*

If more than one predictor variable is involved, a main research question can be posed as in Example 1, followed by a subordinate question for each predictor variable, as shown in Example 2.

Hypotheses, if used, are stated differently. Recall that hypotheses may be stated in the research form or the null form, but you would not use an overall research hypothesis unless exploring a single predictor variable. Instead, you would state a null hypothesis of relationship between X and Y for each of the predictor variables, as shown in this example:

> *No predictive relationship exists between success in first-year teaching and evaluations previously earned in student teaching.*

Exercise 13.3

Select a predictor variable that you identified in Exercise 13.2 and use it to

1. Formulate a research question.
2. Formulate a research hypothesis.
3. State a null hypothesis.

Assessing and Quantifying the Variables

Both the criterion variable and the predictor variables must either be assigned scores, placed into rankings, or placed into dichotomies such as gender, handedness, or high–low. It is preferable, when possible, that all variables be measurable, so they yield continuous interval data that indicate a wide degree of quality or accomplishment. When such measurement is not feasible, *and only then,* should variables be ranked or dichotomized.

If one of the predictors is scores made on initial interviews, existing numerical data are available. If one of the predictors is evaluation by administrators, you will need to decide how such evaluations can be assigned numerical equivalents, dichotomized, or ranked. If one of the predictors is popularity with students, you will have to devise a means of measuring, ranking, or dichotomizing popularity.

Exercise 13.4

1. Indicate how the criterion variable you described in Exercise 13.2 could be quantified. If not quantifiable, indicate how it could be ranked or dichotomized.
2. Indicate how one of the predictor variables you named in Exercise 13.2 could be quantified. If not quantifiable, indicate how it can be ranked or how it can be dichotomized naturally (e.g., on the basis of gender), or artificially (e.g., high–low).

Selecting a Sample

In the research we have been considering, a sample of teachers must be selected from whom to obtain data. Because the criterion is success in first-year teaching, it is preferable that the teachers be assessed at the end of their first year or early in their second year of teaching. For the sample's correlations to be safely generalizable to the population, the sample should include at least 30 teachers, selected at random. In actual practice such a sample would be difficult to obtain except in costly, large-scale research. In most cases, a convenience sample would have to suffice, one consisting perhaps of second-year teachers from various school districts.

Collecting Data

Data are obtained from members of the sample, who are tested or otherwise assessed in accordance with the criterion and predictor variables. At least two scores are obtained for each person in the sample—one for the criterion variable and one for each of the predictor variables. Those scores are paired thus:

Person	Predictor	Criterion
Gary	32	47
Ruth	29	43
Sean	33	46

Analyzing the Data

Correlations between predictor and criterion variables are calculated using the correlational procedure appropriate for the type of data obtained, as described earlier.

As discussed, one of the main uses of correlations is making predictions of criterion variable scores from predictor variable scores. The process of predicting a given person's unknown (Y) score from his or her known (X) score is rather involved, but computer software does the task very quickly.

Almost all variables, even those that seem completely unrelated, such as teaching success and number of dental fillings, will show a slight positive or negative coefficient when correlated. Such results may or may not have occurred by chance. Correlations are

Applying Technology: **More about Correlational Research**

Dr. Ann Maria Rousey of Cankdeska Cikana Community College (an American Indian Tribal College located in Ft. Totten, ND) has included in her online course in developmental psychology a couple of pages that describe correlational research, and what it does and does not do. The first page, titled Correlational Research (www.fractaldomains.com/devpsych/corr.htm), provides a thorough discussion of exactly what correlational research is and incorporates several graphical displays. A sample screen from Dr. Rousey's page follows:

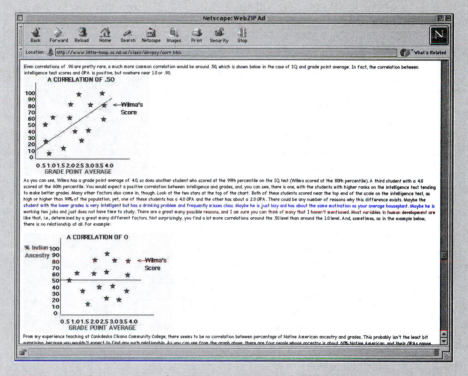

A second page (www.fractaldomains.com/devpsych/corr2.htm) presents an extremely appropriate discussion—especially to the novice researcher—of what a correlation can tell you and what it cannot tell you, specifically focusing on the issue of implying causation from correlational research. Included is a wonderful example of the positive correlation between shoe size and reading achievement in elementary school students.

tested for significance in order to determine whether the observed correlation is likely to have occurred due to errors in selecting the sample. If the correlation is found to be statistically significant, we may rule out sampling error and deem the finding real for the population. Computer software will help you select the appropriate analytical approach, will perform the calculations, and will test the results for significance.

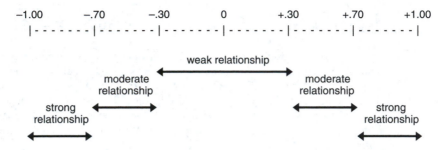

FIGURE 13.1   General rule of thumb for interpreting correlation coefficients

The highest possible coefficient of correlation is 1.0, either positive or negative. From such perfect correlations perfect predictions can be made. That is, if you know Tom's score on the predictor variable plus the range of scores possible on the criterion variable, you can predict the exact score he will make on the criterion variable. However, this level of predictive precision is virtually impossible because perfect correlations are almost never seen in education and the social sciences.

As described earlier, coefficients of correlation are generally considered to be high if ±.70 or above, moderate if between ±.40 and ±.60, and low if below ±.20 (see Figure 13.1). The lower the correlation (i.e., the closer it is to zero), the less accurate are the predictions of one variable from the other. The degree of predictive accuracy for correlations is determined by calculating the standard error of estimate, which your statistical software will do for you. The standard error of estimate indicates the range of likely error inherent in predicting one variable from the other. If you know the correlation between X and Y and know Tom's score on the X variable, with your computer you can predict his score on the Y variable. The higher the correlation between X and Y, the lower the standard error of estimate; hence, the more accurate the prediction is likely to be.

Chapter Summary

Most relationships among variables of interest in education cannot be explained persuasively in terms of cause and effect, because of the cumulative influence of countless unidentified variables combined with sources of error endemic to research involving human participants. Nevertheless, a great deal about education can, and has, been learned through investigating relationships in which one variable is found to be correlated with a second.

Such investigations are carried out through correlational research, used when one wishes to explore descriptive or predictive relationships among two or more variables. Descriptive relationships, such as might be conducted to show a relationship between gender and physical coordination, contribute to educational knowledge but have limited practical value. Predictive relationships, such as between preschool experience and later academic success, can have considerable value as an underlying rationale for programmatic change, even though the correlation itself does not "prove" that early experiences cause later achievement. Although correlational research cannot, technically, demonstrate cause and effect, it may suggest such relationships strongly and offer grounds for subsequent experimental research.

Correlational research is comparatively easy to conduct. It involves identifying and clarifying variables whose possible relationship is to be explored, stating research questions or hypotheses, selecting a sample from which to obtain data, collecting the data, analyzing the data, presenting findings, and making interpretations. The coefficients of correlation obtained in data analysis are used to help answer research questions or test hypotheses.

LIST OF IMPORTANT TERMS

artificial dichotomy
biserial correlation
bivariate correlation
criterion variable
discriminant analysis
factor analysis
Kendall tau

multiple regression
multivariate correlation
natural dichotomy
partial correlation
Pearson product-moment
   correlation
phi correlation

point-biserial correlation
post hoc fallacy
predictor variable
ranking
Spearman rho
tetrachoric correlation

ACTIVITIES FOR THOUGHT AND DISCUSSION

1. Here are the questions presented at the beginning of the chapter. See if you can answer them without looking back.
   a. What differentiates correlational research from other types of research?
   b. What can correlational research accomplish, and what are its limitations?
   c. What elements comprise the method of correlational research?
   d. What is meant by *criterion variable* and *predictor variable?*
   e. What are some of the different methods of computing coefficients of correlation, and what kinds of data are used in each?
   f. How do coefficients of correlation help answer research questions or test hypotheses?

2. Suppose you wanted to plan research into a possible relationship between superstition and scientific knowledge among eighth-grade students. Outline the steps you would take and the considerations you would keep in mind.

3. Suppose you worked for two years in developing a short vocabulary test that you believed would be as good as a long and expensive vocabulary test that you have used with your students. You hope to show that your quick test can accurately predict student performance on the long test. How would you determine whether your test could do what you hope?

ANSWERS TO CHAPTER EXERCISES

Because the chapter exercises call for personal responses, unequivocal answers are not possible. It is suggested that answers to exercises be made a topic of class discussion.

REFERENCES AND RECOMMENDED READINGS

Bruning, J., & Kintz, B. (1987). *Computational Handbook of Statistics* (3rd ed.). Glenview, IL: Scott, Foresman.

Coates, L., & Stephens, L. (1990). Relationship of computer science aptitude with selected achievement measures among junior high students. *Journal of Research and Development in Education, 23*(3): 162–164.

Coleman, J., & Dover, G. (1993). The RISK screening test: Using kindergarten teachers' ratings to predict future placement in resource rooms. *Exceptional Children, 59,* 468–477.

Friedman, I., & Farber, B. (1992). Professional self-concept as a predictor of teacher burnout. *Journal of Educational Research, 86*(1): 28–35.

Gall, J., Gall, M., & Borg, W. (1999). *Applying Educational Research: A Practical Guide* (4th ed.). White Plains, NY: Longman.

Gall, M., Borg, W., & Gall, J. (2003). *Educational Research: An Introduction* (7th ed.). Boston: Allyn and Bacon.

Mertler, C. A., & Vannatta, R. A. (2001). *Advanced and Multivariate Statistical Methods: Practical Application and Interpretation* (2nd ed.). Los Angeles, CA: Pyrczak.

Rousey, A. M. (2000). *Correlational Research.* Available at www.fractaldomains.com/devpsych

Vierra, A., & Pollock, J. (1988). *Reading Educational Research.* Scottsdale, AZ: Gorsuch Scarisbrick.

14 Experimental, Quasi-Experimental, and Causal-Comparative Research

PREVIEW

This chapter examines three closely related types of research:

- Experimental research
- Quasi-experimental research
- Causal-comparative research

The three types are very similar in the following ways:

- All are used to show cause and effect.
- All have an independent variable (cause) linked to a dependent variable (effect).
- In all three, differences that exist or occur in the independent variable are said to cause (produce, bring about) differences in the dependent variable.

Experimental research can convincingly demonstrate cause–effect relationships; it manipulates (makes changes in) an independent variable, possibly producing corresponding changes in the dependent variable.

Quasi-experimental research shows cause and effect, just as does experimental research, but less convincingly because the participants involved have not been selected at random, thus leaving doubt as to whether the sample properly reflects the population.

Causal-comparative research strongly suggests cause and effect but even less convincingly because the independent variable is fixed and cannot be, or is not, manipulated.

Targeted Learnings

Experimental and quasi-experimental research have a unique ability to demonstrate cause–effect relationships, where changes in the independent variable produce resultant changes in the dependent variable. Quasi-experimental research differs from experimental research only in that participants are not randomly assigned to treatments as they are in experimental research. Closely related is causal-comparative research, used to explore the possibility of cause and effect when independent variables cannot be manipulated. Because of the power that cause–effect relationships provide in helping us control events, experimental research is highly valued.

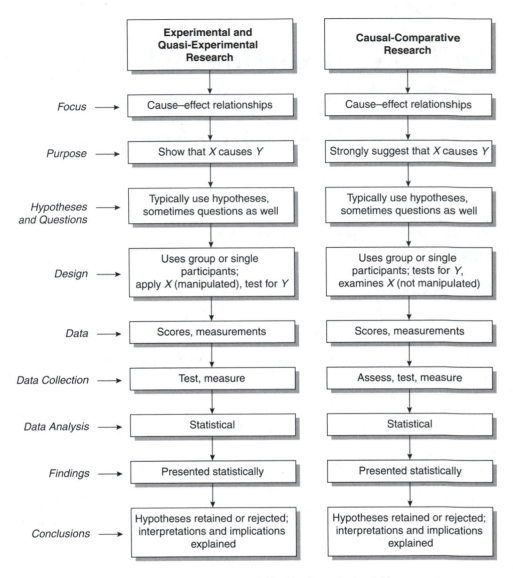

	Experimental and Quasi-Experimental Research	Causal-Comparative Research
Focus →	Cause–effect relationships	Cause–effect relationships
Purpose →	Show that *X* causes *Y*	Strongly suggest that *X* causes *Y*
Hypotheses and Questions →	Typically use hypotheses, sometimes questions as well	Typically use hypotheses, sometimes questions as well
Design →	Uses group or single participants; apply *X* (manipulated), test for *Y*	Uses group or single participants; tests for *Y*, examines *X* (not manipulated)
Data →	Scores, measurements	Scores, measurements
Data Collection →	Test, measure	Assess, test, measure
Data Analysis →	Statistical	Statistical
Findings →	Presented statistically	Presented statistically
Conclusions →	Hypotheses retained or rejected; interpretations and implications explained	Hypotheses retained or rejected; interpretations and implications explained

Note: *X* = independent variable; *Y* = dependent variable

As you read this chapter, look especially for information related to the following questions:

1. What sets experimental research apart from all other types of research?
2. What is the difference between experimental research and quasi-experimental research?
3. What research designs are most frequently used in experimental research?

4. What research designs are most frequently used in quasi-experimental research?
5. What are the main threats to internal and external validity in experimental research and quasi-experimental research?
6. What do experimental and causal-comparative research have in common, and how do they differ?
7. Why cannot causal-comparative research convincingly demonstrate cause and effect?
8. What are the principal data sources in experimental and causal-comparative research?
9. Which data analysis procedures are most often used in experimental and causal-comparative research?
10. Why is it said that causal-comparative research begins by considering the effect, before considering the cause?

The Search for Causation

Researchers are usually delighted when they are able to discover that one thing causes another. Such knowledge, not easy to come by but perhaps the most powerful element in science, provides not only increased understanding of phenomena but also the ability to manipulate conditions to produce changes for the better. Is there a teacher who would not change teaching methods if shown that a new method, just as easily used, could substantially increase student learning? Or one who would not adopt a new discipline system if convincing evidence showed the new system improved student behavior and work habits?

Other types of research do not have the power to demonstrate this prized cause–effect relationship. Correlational, action, and evaluation research suggests such a relationship but fail to supply compelling evidence, which is brought forth only when an independent variable can be shown to influence a dependent variable. If we measure how much people in a given group smoke and also measure their overall cardiovascular health, we can very likely find a correlation between smoking and health, which makes us want to say that smoking causes poor health. We have noted, of course, that the correlation itself simply shows that the two are related, not that one causes the other, though we may certainly make inferences about causation. But frequently we look too eagerly and recklessly and believe we see a causative relationship where there is no evidence to show that one in fact exists. Or we may even confuse cause with effect, as did early Native Americans who believed that toads called forth rain.

Experimental Research

Research
Navigator.com
experimental
design

As noted, **experimental research** can demonstrate cause and effect convincingly. Why, then, are correlational, action, evaluation, and causal-comparative research ever used in relation to questions of cause and effect? The answer lies in what experimental research requires, which usually includes the following components of **experimental design.**

- A sample of participants randomly selected and randomly assigned to experimental group(s) and control group(s)

- An independent variable (i.e., **treatment condition**) that can be applied to the experimental group
- A dependent variable that can be measured in all groups

If we wanted to conduct an experiment on sixth-grade classroom discipline, for example, we would need to randomly select and assign sixth-grade students to two or more classes, at least one of which would receive the experimental treatment while another, serving as a **comparison group,** or control group, would not. The experimental treatment (the manipulated independent variable) is a new system of discipline. The dependent variable (which will be measured) is the incidence and severity of student misbehavior. The control group receives no experimental treatment. If, after the new discipline system has been in effect for a while, the experimental group exhibits behavior significantly different from that of the control group, a cause–effect relationship has been discovered—provided that threats to validity have been accounted for. It can then be said with some confidence that the discipline system has caused better (or perhaps worse) student behavior.

Quasi-Experimental Research

We have seen that experimental research requires random assignment of participants to experimental and control groups. However, researchers, despite their wishes, cannot always make random assignments to groups. This is particularly true in school settings. When random assignment cannot be made, true experimental research cannot be done. In its place, **quasi-experimental research** is used, which embodies the characteristics of experimental research except for random assignment of participants. The label *quasi-experimental* indicates that this type of research is otherwise very much like experimental research.

Causal-Comparative Research

Causal-comparative research is used to explore the possibility of cause and effect when neither experimental nor quasi-experimental research can be done. Causal-comparative research does not convincingly demonstrate cause and effect but can strongly suggest it. Such research might be used by medical researchers trying to establish the possibility that smoking is causing heart disease. They could not do experimental research because they could not ethically select a group of people and make them smoke heavily to see what happens to their health. They could, however, randomly select groups of heavy smokers and groups of nonsmokers and then assess the groups for incidence of heart disease. If heavy smokers were found to have a higher rate of heart disease, that would be a strong indication, though still not absolute proof, that the disease was being "caused" by smoking.

As another illustration, one might hypothesize that "female-ness," compared to "male-ness," causes better student achievement in certain curriculum areas. If researched, achievement would be the dependent variable (*Y* **variable**) and gender the independent variable (*X* **variable**). Obviously, gender cannot be manipulated. However, if differences are found in the dependent variable (achievement), it might be inferred that gender is somehow causing those differences. Logic is used to help establish the direction of cause and effect; in this case there can be no confusion—higher or lower achievement could not possibly affect one's gender. Causal-comparative research might, therefore, strongly suggest a cause–effect relationship between gender and achievement in certain areas but could not demonstrate such a relationship unequivocally.

Fundamentals of Experimental and Quasi-Experimental Research

Research Navigator.com
cause and effect

Cause and Effect

When a cause–effect linkage is suspected, *cause* is a condition or event that exists or occurs prior to the effect. *Effect* is a condition or event that occurs subsequent to the cause.

$$\text{Cause exists} \;\rightarrow\; \text{then} \;\rightarrow\; \text{Effect occurs as a result}$$

The linkage between the two is intellectual: Based on evidence, one concludes that had it not been for the causal condition or event (e.g., new discipline system), the second condition or event (e.g., better student behavior) would not have occurred. The cause–effect connection is demonstrated when, by manipulating the independent variable, a resultant change occurs in the dependent variable.

Research Navigator.com
random assignment

Random Selection and Assignment

Random selection of samples and **random assignment** of sample members to experimental and control groups are essential and distinguishing features of experimental design. The only exception occurs in single-participant experiments, usually conducted on an individual diagnosed as having significant personal problems—for example, obsessive eating or uncontrolled outbursts. Random selection and assignment help ensure equivalence of groups and control for many extraneous variables that might otherwise contaminate the results of the investigation. When it is not possible to draw a randomly selected sample of participants (one usually cannot randomly select for research conducted in school settings), one must, if possible, randomly assign students to experimental and control groups. When random assignment cannot be done, what one has is quasi-experimental rather than experimental research.

Use of Experimental Research

We have seen that experimental research is done to show that event or condition X (an independent variable) can cause or modify event or condition Y (a dependent variable). If you supply enough heat (X), you can make water boil (Y). If you ask your students certain kinds of questions (X), you can cause them to give more thoughtful and complete answers (Y).

You would, therefore, use experimental research when

- You strongly suspect that a cause–effect relationship exists between two conditions or events
- At least one randomly assigned group is available to participate in the study
- The independent (causal) variable can be introduced to the participants and modified, regulated, or otherwise manipulated
- The resulting dependent (effect) variable can be measured in the participants

Under ideal circumstances, experimental research would involve at least two groups of participants randomly assigned from the sample. The experimental group would receive the experimental treatment—that is, an independent variable would be introduced or modified—while the control group would proceed as usual, that is, would receive no treatment. After a time, the two groups would be tested to see if differences had appeared in the dependent variable.

Experimental Designs

Several different designs are used in experimental research. The following five are the most common. In addition to describing them in narrative fashion, we will present them in standard experimental design notation, using the following symbols:

X_1 = Unusual or new treatment condition
X_2 = Control condition
O = Observation (pretest or posttest)
R = Random assignment

1. *Single-Group Pretest-Treatment-Posttest Design.* This design, though included here, is technically a "preexperimental design" because it makes use of only a single group of students. Suppose that Mrs. Simpkins believes students learn more when they have to explain their learnings to others. She decides to conduct an experiment in which sixth-grade students explain to their parents or guardians selected mathematics concepts and algorithms learned in school. Her principal agrees at the beginning of the year to assign students to Mrs. Simpkins's classroom randomly from among all sixth-graders at the school. After several weeks of instruction, Mrs. Simpkins tests her class to determine their level of knowledge. She then asks the students to explain what they have learned to adults at home, over a week's time. She provides no new math instruction during that week. She then retests her class to see if their level of knowledge has increased. The design can be diagrammed as follows:

Assigned Group $\rightarrow$ given a Pretest, then $\rightarrow$ receives Treatment, then $\rightarrow$ given a Posttest

Using experimental design notation, this design would appear as:

R O X_1 O

This design is sometimes used by graduate students in education, but it is not a strong design, for three reasons: first, it has no control group against which to make comparisons, second, the pretest may actually instruct students so that they make higher scores on the post-test, and third, the learning effects might be attributable to a trait peculiar to Mrs. Simpkins. There is, therefore, no way to be sure that changes in student knowledge would not have occurred anyway, even without the home teaching.

2. *Two-Group Treatment-Posttest-Only Design.* This design uses two groups, an **experimental group** and a **control group,** with participants randomly assigned to the groups. An independent variable treatment is given to the experimental group, while none is given to the control group. Later, both groups are tested on the dependent variable. This design is illustrated as follows:

Group 1 is given the $\rightarrow$ Experimental Treatment and later is given a $\rightarrow$ Posttest

Group 2 $\rightarrow$ (no special treatment) $\rightarrow$ Posttest

Using experimental design notation, this design would appear as:

Group 1   R X_1 O
Group 2   R X_2 O

This was the design Mrs. Simpkins used the following year when she enlarged her study to include Mrs. Almira's next-door sixth-grade class, also randomly assigned, as a control group. She and Mrs. Almira coordinated their teaching so that both classes were taught the same content, but Mrs. Almira's students were not asked to explain the learnings at home. Later, both classes were tested on what they had been taught. This experimental design is sometimes used by graduate students in education, but despite the random assignment, it leaves some question as to whether the two groups are initially equivalent. If they are not, differences that show up on the posttest cannot be attributed with certainty to the effects of the experimental treatment.

3. *Two-Group Pretest-Treatment-Posttest Design.* To establish initial equivalence of the two groups, Mrs. Simpkins next refined her design to include the same pretest for both her class and Mrs. Almira's class. The design can be illustrated as follows:

Group 1 is given a $\rightarrow$ Pretest, then the $\rightarrow$ Experimental Treatment, and then a $\rightarrow$ Posttest

Group 2 is given the $\rightarrow$ Pretest $\rightarrow$ (no experimental treatment) $\rightarrow$ Posttest

Again, using standard notation, this design would be:

Group 1   R   O X_1 O
Group 2   R   O X_2 O

This design is popular among graduate students in education. The design is strong because potential sources of error have been reduced.

4. *Factorial Designs.* Up to this point the examples of research designs have included only a single independent variable. At times, two or more independent variables and two or more dependent variables may be included simultaneously in the experimental design. (The variables are in this case referred to as *factors,* hence, the name *factorial design.*) This design enables one to determine differential effects, that is, to see if the treatments have different effects on participants according to, for example, their IQ, ethnic origin, or gender. Mrs. Simpkins might decide to explore the effects of two independent variables—students' reteaching to adults versus in-class review—and, further, to determine if the two treatments produce different effects for higher-achieving versus lower-achieving students. To do this, she would enlist the cooperation of Mr. Mohl, the other sixth-grade teacher in her school. She would identify lower-achieving and higher-achieving students in all three classes, use the reteaching treatment in her class while having Mrs. Almira use the review treatment, and use Mr. Mohl's class as the control group. Her 2 × 3 factorial design, with Mr. Mohl's class serving as the control group, might be diagramed as in Table 14.1:

TABLE 14.1

	Reteaching Group	Review Group	Control Group
Higher achievers Lower achievers	Mrs. Simpkins's "	Mrs. Almira's "	Mr. Mohl's "

Her procedure would be as follows:

Simpkins's class: Pretest → Reteaching Treatment → Posttest

Almira's class: Pretest → Review Treatment → Posttest

Mohl's class: Pretest → (no treatment) → Posttest

Using standard notation, this factorial design would be:

Group 1 (Simpkin)	R	O	Y_1	X_1	O
	R	O	Y_2	X_1	O
Group 2 (Almira)	R	O	Y_1	X_2	O
	R	O	Y_2	X_2	O
Group 3 (Mohl)	R	O	Y_1	X_3	O
	R	O	Y_2	X_3	O

where Y_1 are high achievers and Y_2 are low achievers.

Mrs. Simpkins would compare the posttest performance of students initially identified as higher and lower achieving and would be able to examine the comparative effects of reteaching and in-class review on learning by students of different ability levels. She would have a control group against which to compare the results. An obvious source of potential error is that each treatment is given by a different teacher, which does not control for differences in teacher skill or personality. The pretest would enable Mrs. Simpkins to deal with the question of initial group differences.

5. *Single-Participant Measurement-Treatment-Measurement Design.* Most experimental research is accomplished through the use of groups but as we noted may at times involve only a single participant. Such research is seen in studies of exceptional students, where it would be inappropriate to administer experimental treatment to participants other than those with special needs. Suppose Mr. Mohl has a student, Jonathan, who chronically misbehaves and does not respond to the disciplinary techniques Mr. Mohl uses with his other students. Mr. Mohl may decide to conduct a single-participant experiment to see if he can improve Jonathan's behavior.

In such a study, Mr. Mohl would need to make accurate measurements of Jonathan's behavior before applying the experimental treatment. Mr. Mohl would prepare a chart of misbehaviors and ask an aide to record, over a period of a week or two, the number of times that Jonathan exhibits those misbehaviors, such as shouting out, getting up and wandering about the room, provoking confrontations with other students, and refusing to comply with Mr. Mohl's directions. These notations would serve as a baseline measurement against which to compare Jonathan's behavior during and after receiving the experimental treatment.

Mr. Mohl would then implement the experimental treatment, perhaps a special system of behavior modification. At a designated time, Jonathan's misbehaviors would again be recorded over several days. This process might be repeated several times. Mr. Mohl's single-participant experimental design could be diagrammed as follows:

Participant (Jonathan) $\rightarrow$ Baseline Measurement $\rightarrow$ Experimental Treatment $\rightarrow$ Measurement Repeated $\rightarrow$ Entire Process Repeated

In standard notation, this design is:

$$O \quad O \quad O \quad O \quad X_1 \quad X_1 \quad X_1 \quad O \quad O \quad O \quad O$$

In this process, the baseline measurements should accurately reflect Jonathan's typical behavior. Jonathan should be carefully observed two or three different times before the experiment is begun. When applying the treatment, Mr. Mohl must be very careful to limit himself to what he intends to do and say, so as to keep the treatment consistent. Even when these conditions are met, the results of single-participant experiments can only be generalized with great caution. When groups are used, individual differences among participants tend to cancel one another out. This is not the case in single-participant experimentation. What works for Jonathan may not work for Christopher, a chronically misbehaving student in another class.

Quasi-Experimental Designs

As mentioned earlier, quasi-experimental research is just like experimental research, except that participants are not randomly assigned to treatments. Three research designs commonly used in quasi-experimental research are (1) posttest only with nonequivalent groups, (2) pretest-posttest with nonequivalent groups, and (3) time series design with a single group.

1. *Posttest Only with Nonequivalent Groups.* This design uses two groups of participants from the same population (such as two established classrooms in the same school system). One group is given the experimental treatment, and then both groups are given the posttest to see if the groups show differences in the criterion variable. This design can be diagrammed as follows:

> Group 1 $\rightarrow$ Experimental Treatment $\rightarrow$ Posttest
>
> Group 2 $\rightarrow$ (no treatment) $\rightarrow$ Posttest

Using the standard notational symbols, this design would be:

> *Group 1* X_1 O
>
> *Group 2* X_2 O

This is not a strong design because it leaves doubt as to whether the groups are equivalent before the experimental treatment is introduced.

2. *Pretest-Posttest with Nonequivalent Groups.* In this design two groups of participants are used, as in the previous example. The difference is that the groups are given a pretest to help establish their equivalency, prior to introducing the experimental treatment. This is a stronger design and can be diagrammed as follows:

> Group 1 $\rightarrow$ Pretest $\rightarrow$ Experimental Treatment $\rightarrow$ Posttest
>
> Group 2 $\rightarrow$ Pretest $\rightarrow$ (no treatment) $\rightarrow$ Posttest

Again, using standard notation, this design would be:

> *Group 1* O X_1 O
>
> *Group 2* O X_2 O

3. *Time Series Design.* This design uses a single group of participants. The group is measured over a period of days or weeks. In an interval between two of the measurements, the experimental treatment is introduced. If a noticeable change occurs after introduction of the experimental treatment, that treatment may be judged to have caused the change. This design can be diagrammed as follows:

> O O O X_1 O O O

The Commonality of Experimental and Quasi-Experimental Designs

The experimental and quasi-experimental designs described in the preceding paragraphs share the following characteristics.

- A cause–effect relationship is hypothesized, which stipulates that trait or condition *X* will produce, bring about, or cause trait or condition *Y*.
- Participants are selected for the experiment. In experimental designs, participants or classrooms are randomly assigned to experimental and control groups. Occasionally,

only a single participant is used. In quasi-experimental designs, participants and class-rooms are not randomly assigned to treatments.

- The experimental treatment is applied. The treatment is an introduction of a new in-dependent variable or else a modification of an existing one—something is added or changed.
- After the experimental treatment has been completed, all participants are measured to determine the effects, if any, of the experimental treatment.
- Data are usually obtained in the form of scores made on the posttest. (Single-participant experiments sometimes use qualitative data.) Data analysis includes test-ing for significance of differences observed in the dependent variable. If a significant difference is found, and if possible errors can be satisfactorily accounted for, the treatment can be said to have caused the observed difference.

Threats to Internal and External Validity

Research Navigator.c⊛m
internal validity

Validity of research refers to the degree to which research conclusions can be considered accurate and generalizable. Both experimental research and quasi-experimental research are subject to **threats to validity,** both internally and externally. These threats must be con-trolled or otherwise accounted for so that the potential error they might introduce does not put research conclusions into question.

Internal validity has to do with conditions present in the participants or their envi-ronment while the experiment is in progress. Threats to internal validity may include the following (Campbell & Stanley, 1966):

1. *Differential selection of participants.* Participants for the groups are not selected or assigned randomly. (This threat is always inherent in quasi-experimental research.)
2. *History.* When experimental treatments extend over longer periods, such as a semes-ter or year, factors other than the experimental treatment have time to exert influence on the results.
3. *Maturation.* If treatments extend over longer periods of time, participants may un-dergo physiological changes that produce differential effects in the criterion variable. For example, they may become stronger, better coordinated, better able to do ab-stract thinking, and have better endurance than before.
4. *Testing.* If pretests and posttests are used, participants may learn enough from the pretest to improve performance on the posttest, even when the experimental treat-ment has no effect. If equivalent forms of a test are used, despite their being consid-ered equal, one form may in fact be easier than the other.
5. *Attrition.* While the experiment is in progress, there may be a loss of participants for reasons such as illnesses, dropping out, or moving elsewhere.

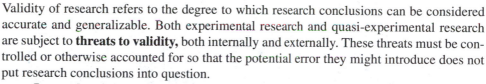

Research Navigator.c⊛m
external validity

External validity of research refers to the extent to which results can be generalized to other groups or settings. It is well known that what works in one setting may not work in another. Considerations about the external validity of research (see Bracht & Glass, 1968) include the following:

1. *Population validity.* This refers to the degree of similarity among (1) the sample used in a study, (2) the population from which it was drawn, and (3) the target population to which results are to be generalized. The greater the degree of similarity among the three, the greater one's confidence in generalizing research findings.

2. *Personological variables.* A given research finding can apply well to some people and poorly to others. Individuals differ in what they find acceptable, comfortable, and useful. Self-directed learning is an example. Some students prefer to work on their own and can do so effectively. Other equally intelligent students require guidance from a teacher and desire the companionship of their peers.

3. *Ecological validity.* This refers to the situation, physical or emotional, that exists during the experiment. An experimental situation may be quite different from a new setting where results are to be applied. For example, some groups of participants, especially when involved in innovations, develop a group spirit that motivates high achievement. Such groups' results may be quite different from results seen in groups that lack a similar group spirit.

Exercise 14.1

Mr. Smith and Mr. Jones have very different ideas about how civics should be taught. They decide to conduct a semesterlong experiment to determine which of the two teachers' procedures produces higher student achievement. Indicate what you would suggest they do in their experiment about the following:

1. Selecting and assigning students to be involved as participants.
2. Clarifying the experimental treatments (methods and materials) that each intends to use, including equalizing the time commitments for homework expected of students.
3. Measuring achievement at the end of the semester.
4. Controlling error that might be associated with the teachers—that is, effects attributable to teacher personality and skill, as distinct from the methods and materials in the experimental treatment.

An Example of Experimental Research

The following is a reprinted report of an experimental study published in *Action in Teacher Education* (1993).

Exercise 14.2

As you read the study, be sure to note the following:

1. Focus of the study (what it is about)
2. Research questions, if any
3. Hypotheses, stated or implied

Exercise 14.2 *Continued*

4. Selection of participants
5. Assignment of participants to control and experimental groups
6. The independent (treatment) variable(s) and the dependent (result or criteria) variable(s)
7. Instrument(s) used for measurement
8. Application of the experimental treatment(s) (i.e., introduction or manipulation of an independent variable)
9. Procedures by which data are obtained and analyzed
10. Findings
11. Conclusions

The Development of a Positive Self-Concept in Preservice Teachers

Marcia M. Meyer, Malcolm E. Linville, and Gilbert Rees
University of Missouri

(Note: The term "subjects" is used in this report to refer to "participants.")

Introduction

In 1990 a state-supported task force in California recommended that all teachers in the state have training in the development of a positive self-esteem, both to improve their own teaching skills and to be able to help their students in this area (California Task Force, 1990). Educators such as Canter (Canter & Canter, 1976) have for some years been stressing the importance of a positive self-concept for teachers, reflected in an assertive style of teaching and communicating. Canter stated that many educators felt "overwhelmed and powerless" when coping with behavior problems in schools and in interacting with parents and administrators (Canter & Canter, 1976, p. vi).

Introduction provides the background literature review

This emphasis on self-esteem reflects a major concern of many psychologists. Zimbardo, a social psychologist, has stated that self-conceptions influence relationships with others, the individual's sense of autonomy, and what he called "the quality of our private emotional life" (Zimbardo, 1975, p. 434). Torrance, who has done extensive research in the field of creativity, also saw a relationship between self-esteem and the individual's sense of autonomy. Referring to students, he stated that those lacking in self-esteem were vulnerable to pressures toward group conformity (Torrance, 1965). Other influential psychologists, such as Rogers (1969) and Maslow (1954), saw a positive self-esteem as basic to the development of desirable personality traits and a state of good mental health.

Psychologists may see a positive self-esteem as a desirable trait in teachers and others in the helping professions who serve as role models. Yet ways to increase self-esteem have generally been presented in rather vague, abstract terms, using language that is prescriptive in nature. The limited research in the area has used adolescents or community college students as subjects. The present study was made with a different group, preservice teachers who were juniors and seniors in a university and were in their first year of a teacher-training program.

In the present study, an effort was made to increase the positive self-esteem of preservice teachers through a brief course in assertion training. This method was chosen because several psychologists have directly related self-esteem to assertive behaviors. The behavioral psychologists Hilgard, R. C. Atkinson, and

R. L. Atkinson stated that a well-adjusted person appreciates his self-worth and feels accepted by others, but "at the same time, he does not always feel obligated to subjugate his opinion to those of others" (Hilgard et al., 1975, p. 455). Zimbardo (1975) also stressed the relationship between self-esteem and a sense of autonomy. In addition, research studies by Waksman (1984a, 1984b) have indicated that assertion training could increase the self-esteem of adolescents.

Therefore, a training program was developed for the present study in which the skills of assertive behaviors were taught in the broader concept of effective communication skills. Positive self-acceptance and self-esteem were stressed as basic to behaving in a desirable assertive way.

> Description of training program developed for study

This study was designed to investigate the following questions:

1. Will a brief course in assertion training increase the positive self-esteem of preservice teachers?
2. How many hours of assertion training are needed to increase the positive self-esteem of preservice teachers?
3. What would be the effects of three hours of assertion training; of six hours; of nine hours?

> Research questions

Methodology

Participants

The study was conducted with students in their first year of teacher education in a large Midwestern urban university. The majority of the subjects were college juniors. The students had previously taken foundation courses in educational psychology and the social and philosophical foundations of education. They had not yet had curriculum or methods courses.

The students were asked to volunteer for a study of the effects of assertion training. Of the 97 students contacted, 93 volunteered to participate in the study. Four did not, stating they thought more work would be required of those participating in the study.

> Students volunteered…not really random selection

The 93 volunteers were randomly assigned to three experimental groups and a control group. Experimental Group I received three hours of assertion training; Experimental Group II received six hours; and Experimental Group III received nine hours. The control group received no assertion training. The varying amounts of training were designed to answer questions concerning the relationship of the time spent in such programs to changes in self-esteem.

> Description of random assignment to treatment and control groups

Eleven students did not complete the study, leaving 47 students in the three experimental groups and 35 in the control group.

Instruments

The dependent variable of self-esteem was measured by the *Berger Self-Acceptance Scale* (SA). This standardized instrument has 36 items, each of which is answered on a five-point scale. The scale progresses from "not at all true" to "completely true." Berger's (1952) initial scale consisted of 47 items. The 36 items which best discriminated between those who scored high and low on the scale were retained. The SA was based upon the premise that acceptance of self and acceptance of others are positively related.

> Study utilized existing instruments, although no information provided for validity/reliability

The dependent variable of self-concept was measured by the *Tennessee Self-Concept Scale* (TSCS) (Clinical and Research Form), a widely used standardized instrument. This instrument consists of 100 self-descriptive statements that respondents use to portray their own self-pictures. The scale progresses from "completely false" to "completely true." The scale is self-administering for either individuals or groups. It can be used with individuals aged 12 or older who can read at approximately a fourth-grade level or higher.

Participants in the experimental and control groups experienced the same procedure in the first session. The investigator stated that the students were to take part in a research study designed to be of help to teachers, counselors, and mental health therapists. She stressed that participants would be anonymous and would use code numbers based on the last four digits of their social security numbers. Then all four groups were given the *Berger Self-Acceptance Scale* and the *Tennessee Self-Concept Scale.*

In the next session, the three experimental groups began the assertive training program. Subjects in the training sessions experienced a combination of didactic presentations, films, and role-playing interaction, with feedback from both peers and instructors. During the two-week period between class activities, subjects practiced specific behaviors and recorded them in a behavior journal.

The control group attended classes which dealt with materials not related to assertiveness training or effective communications. They experienced activities concerning current problems in education.

An outline of three sample training sessions is given below.

Session One

Lecture. What assertiveness is (at both the verbal and nonverbal levels). The distinction between nonasser-tiveness, assertiveness, and aggression and hostility.

> Nice overview of training provided for the reader

Demonstration. When to be assertive. Three styles of dealing with students who do not do assigned work: nonassertion, assertion, hostility (verbal and nonverbal approaches).

Class Exercise. Students will divide into pairs and practice the distinction between assertive and nonassertive behaviors, using an exercise developed by Lee Canter.

Lecture. Lee Canter's Assertive Discipline: Stating your wants and needs assertively.

Class Exercise. Developing a list of five behaviors you want to see in students.

Assignment. Describe the journal students are to keep.

Journal Assignment. Personal experiences. Estimate the percentages of your teachers who have been assertive, nonassertive, or hostile. Describe specific teachers with whom you have had or are having difficulties. Specify the difficulties. Describe how you reacted to that individual. Did you do anything to improve the situation? Describe your feelings. ("I felt weak as though I was a helpless victim of circumstances," etc.) Describe how you might have stated your needs, wants, and feelings assertively to the teacher.

Session Two

Lecture. Lee Canter's Assertive Discipline: Setting consequences when students do not meet your wants

and needs. Dealing with individual students: The broken-record technique (keeping students on the subject). Fogging technique (saying "no" without giving offense).

Film. *Assertive Discipline* with Lee Canter.

Lecture. Lee Canter's Assertive Discipline: Creating a positive classroom climate as the basis for assertion. Individual and group reinforcement at the elementary and secondary levels.

Class Activity. Distribute sheets listing 99 ways to express approval. Students in pairs practice selected items from this list on each other.

Assignment. Use Robert Alberti's journal outline for an analysis of individual behaviors, feelings, and attitudes (Alberti, R., *Learner's Manual for Making Yourself Heard.* New York: Guilford Publications, 1986, p. 9).

Journal Activity. Involves completing the Rathus Assertiveness Grid, which deals with willingness to use assertive behavior in specific situations and with a variety of individuals.

Session Four

Lecture. Models of assertive communication. Presentation of the Jack Gibb Defensive Communication Model, Faber's Responsive Listening Model, and Thomas Gordon's I-Language.

Film. *Image and Self-Projection* (dealing with nonverbal skills).

Class Activity. Role-playing of supportive verbal behaviors, active listening, and I-Messages.

Film. *Thomas Gordon's Teacher Effectiveness Training.*

Assignment. Journal work—Practice at least ten times using Gordon's supportive model, active listening responses, and Gordon's I-Messages. Record in the journal what you did, how it was perceived, and your own feelings and reactions.

At the conclusion of the training program the participants were given the *Berger Self-Acceptance Scale* and the *Tennessee Self-Concept Scale* as posttests.

Results

The data were analyzed using an Analysis of Variance. There was no significant difference found between the total experimental group and the control group on the

TABLE 1   Comparison of Mean Change Scores on the *Berger Self-Acceptance Scale* between Experimental Group III and the Control Group

Group	N	Pretest		Posttest		Mean Dif.
		M	SD	M	SD	
Control	35	138.29	19.26	138.20	17.57	–.09
Experimental	13	123.15	27.89	137.85	23.09	14.70*

*p < .05

TABLE 2   Comparison of Mean Change Scores on the *Tennessee Self-Concept Scale* between the Total Experimental Group and the Control Group

Group	N	Pretest		Posttest		Mean Dif.
		M	SD	M	SD	
Control	35	297.11	14.10	293.06	21.14	–4.05
Experimental	47	291.79	13.71	298.19	15.53	6.40*

*p < .01

Berger Self-Acceptance Scale. However, there was significant difference found on the Berger Scale between Experimental Group III, which received the most training in assertive behavior, and the control group. (See Table 1.)

Brief discussion of results; good reference to tables

A highly significant difference, beyond the .01 level, was found between the total experimental group and the control group in mean change scores on the *Tennessee Self-Concept Scale.* (See Table 2.)

Discussion

Several psychologists have assumed a relationship between self-concept and a willingness to assert oneself (Hilgard et al., 1975; Zimbardo, 1977). The research studies which have measured self-esteem as an outcome of assertion training have not supported this assumption consistently.

However, the present study found a significant increase in self-acceptance and self-concept after assertion training. The significant increases were found in scores on both *Berger's Self-Acceptance Scale* and the

Tennessee Self-Concept Scale. The significant difference in mean change scores on the Berger Scale was found between Experimental Group III, which had nine hours of training, and the control group. Apparently the longer training period affected the change in self-acceptance.

It might be noted that three of the four studies in which there was a significant increase in self-concept were all done with students younger than those in the present study. Three were done with students at the secondary level. The fourth study was done with community college students and, though no data on age are available, it is likely that the mean age of this group would be less than that of the subjects used in the present study. All of the latter group were in their junior year of college and beyond; some had reentered college after a period in other occupations. Data obtained in the present study indicated that there can be changes in the self-acceptance and self-concepts of adults even though their personality patterns might be more firmly estab-

Comparison of results of present study to existing literature

lished than the personality elements of younger subjects. It is possible that those wishing to increase self-acceptance and positive self-concept might use the kind of assertion training program developed for this study as a basis for change.

The training program developed for the present study presented assertiveness behaviors in the broader context of communication skills. Positive self-acceptance and self-concept were stressed as basic to behaving in an assertive way. We have only limited information on the content of other training programs. It may be that some programs did not emphasize the relationship of self-acceptance and self-concept to assertiveness behaviors. This may explain the differences in findings in this area.

It is worth noting that two standard measures of self-acceptance and self-concept (*Berger's Self-Acceptance Scale* and the *Tennessee Self-Concept Scale*) yielded significant results. The data obtained from them would indicate that the assertiveness training program used in this study did affect the self-acceptance and self-concepts of subjects who participated in the training program.

This is supported by self-report statements of these subjects when they were asked to evaluate the effectiveness of their training in an open-ended questionnaire. Samples from their responses, which were almost all positive, would also provide evidence that assertion training can increase the willingness to implement what was presented in the training sessions:

I feel more in control of my action, thoughts, and feelings. I guess I'm saying I'm just more in control of the things in my life that were out of control before. I think the training will help me when I become a teacher, and I hope I will remember the important keys to effective assertiveness.

My quest for assertiveness had helped me realize that I have carried a lot of personal "baggage" and I needed to be more sensitive and responsive to the feelings of those around me. Perhaps the most significant discovery that I have made is that in my quest to be more sensitive and responsive to others, I find less stress in myself.

I realize that I have strong feelings which I do not communicate to others. If at home, I tend to get more and more upset, but keep my feelings in until I blow up and yell. Outside of my home, again I kept my feelings and wants pent up and then am really frustrated and talk about the person I am having a problem with. Being assertive has really helped me communicate my feelings and wants in an acceptable

way, relieving my feelings and needs. I do not feel guilt, but I have not lost my temper or been two-faced. It is hard to change old ways, but this assertiveness training has really helped me in my daily life, and I'm sure it will help me in teaching.

I'm learning more about myself in these past months than I ever expected to. All my life I've carried a lot of defensiveness and smoldering anger that kept me from being effective with people—but I didn't know what to do about it. Now I'm beginning to know. I'd always identified assertiveness with aggressive or coldly manipulative people. Now I realize assertiveness isn't so much about getting something from others as it is just being comfortable within myself, whether or not others make changes. It doesn't always seem quite so important that people do things my way anymore, as long as I can tell them what I really wanted instead of just getting angry. Being assertive is a wonderful alternative to constantly complaining about an uncomfortable situation as I have always done in the past. Even when being assertive doesn't actually accomplish any more than just getting uncomfortable feelings off my chest, it leaves me with a relief from having vented those feelings in a non-threatening manner. I find myself maybe liking myself a little more—at least being more comfortable with myself.

Both the empirical results and the subjects' comments would indicate that the assertion-training program described above might be a means to help a teacher assume a greater role in policy-making and the development of curricula in the teacher's own school, one of the goals of the movement for empowerment of teachers. Beane has seen this movement as "expanding the meaning of the very concepts that support personal and social efficacy" (Beane, 1990, p. 167). Expanding such concepts was a major goal of this study.

Nelson, Palonsky, and Carlson have stated that teachers "must have the authority to make essential decisions about how to teach, how to pace instruction, and how to interact with students" (Nelson et al., 1990, p. 223). A major movement in education at the present time is toward giving teaching such empowerment. To wield effectively such power, a teacher would need to be properly assertive and to have positive feelings about who I am and what I am capable of doing. The training program developed for this study could represent a major step in preparing teachers for the increasing power that may soon be theirs.

Recommendations for practice

In conclusion, the kind of program described above did significantly increase the self-concepts of young adults as measured by two standardized instruments. Such an assertion-training program may be one of the best ways to increase self-esteem through direct training over a short period of time. The comments of several of the students involved may be of special significance, as they indicated that changes at some depth had occurred.

References

Beane, J. A. (1990). *Affect in the curriculum: Toward democracy, dignity, and diversity.* New York: Teachers College, Columbia University.

Berger, E. M. (1952). The relation between expressed acceptance of self and expressed acceptance of others. *Journal of Abnormal Psychology, 47,* 778–782.

California Task Force (1990). *Toward a state of esteem.* Sacramento, CA: California State Department of Education.

Canter, L. with Canter, M. (1976). *Assertive discipline: A take charge approach for today's educator.* Los Angeles: Canter and Associates.

Hilgard, E. R., Atkinson, R. C., & Atkinson, R. L. (1975). *Introduction to psychology* (6th ed.). New York: Harcourt Brace Jovanovich.

Maslow, A. H. (1954). *Motivation and personality.* New York: Harper and Row.

Nelson, J. L., Palonsky, S. B., & Carlson, K. (1990). *Critical issues in education.* New York: McGraw-Hill.

Rogers, C. R. (1969). *Freedom to learn.* Columbus, OH: Merrill.

Torrance, E. P. (1965). *Gifted children in the classroom.* New York: Macmillan.

Waksman, S. A. (1984a). Assertion training with adolescents. *Adolescence, 19,* 123–130.

Waksman, S. A. (1984b). A controlled evaluation of assertion training with adolescents. *Adolescence, 19,* 277–282.

Zimbardo, P. G. (1977). *Psychology and life* (9th ed.). Glenview, IL: Scott Foresman.

"The development of a positive self-concept in preservice teachers" by Marcia M. Meyer, Malcolm E. Linville, and Gilbert Rees. *Action in Teacher Education, XV,* no. 1, pp. 30–35, Spring 1993. Reprinted by permission of the Association of Teacher Educators.

ADDITIONAL EXAMPLES OF PUBLISHED EXPERIMENTAL STUDIES

In order to better understand a particular research methodology, it is often beneficial to examine additional examples of published research that utilizes that specific methodology. Several such examples of experimental and quasi-experimental research have been identified for you through the use of *Research Navigator*™, available on the Web at www.researchnavigator.com. The list following consists of published research articles available free of charge in full-text format via *Research Navigator*™. These articles are available in either HTML and/or PDF formats and are easily located by searching the database by *article number* (abbreviated "**AN**"), which has been provided for each citation.

Frankenberger, W., & Cannon, C. (1999). Effects of Ritalin on academic achievement from first to fifth grade. *International Journal of Disability, Development & Education, 46*(2). **[AN: 4106082]**

Hancock, D. R. (2002). Influencing graduate students' classroom achievement, homework habits and motivation to learn with verbal praise. *Educational Research, 44*(1), 83–95. **[AN: 6411043]**

Knapp, J. L., & Stubblefield, P. (1998). Assessing student's knowledge of the aging process. *Education, 119*(1), 135–141. **[AN: 1271274]**

Oladunni, M. O. (1998). An experimental study on the effectiveness of metacognitive and heuristic problem solving techniques on computational performance of students in mathematics. *International Journal of Mathematical Education in Science & Technology, 29*(6), 867–874. [**AN: 1446330**]

Reason, R., & Morfidi, E. (2001). Literacy difficulties and single-case experimental design. *Educational Psychology in Practice, 17*(3). [**AN: 5066646**]

Sluijsmans, D. M. A., Brand-Gruwel, S., & van Merriënboer, J. J. G. (2002). Peer assessment training in teacher education: Effects on performance and perceptions. *Assessment & Evaluation in Higher Education, 27*(5), 443–454. [**AN: 7287806**]

Yu, M., Darch, C., & Rabren, K. (2002). Use of precorrection strategies to enhance reading performance of students with learning and behavior problems. *Journal of Instructional Psychology, 29*(3), 162–174. [**AN: 7355607**]

Causal-Comparative Research

The Nature of Causal-Comparative Research

Causal-comparative research is done to explore possible cause and effect, though it cannot demonstrate cause and effect as does experimental research. Its concern is similar to that of experimental and quasi-experimental research, but it differs from them in the following regards:

- In causal-comparative research the independent variable is not manipulated, either because manipulation is impossible or because it is impractical or unethical.
- Of necessity, causal-comparative research focuses first on the effect and then attempts to determine the cause of the observed effect. The basic question it explores is "What is causing this effect that I observe?"

The nature of causal-comparative research might be outlined as follows:

1. First one focuses on the effect; for example, differences in ethnic group achievement.
2. Then one hypothesizes a cause; for example, differences in stability of home life.
3. Finally, make a logical connection that persuasively suggests that the observed effect is being influenced by the hypothesized cause.

You can see in these steps that the independent variable, stability of home life, cannot be manipulated as would be required in experimental research.

You may see causal-comparative research referred to as *ex post facto* **research.** *Ex post facto* means "after the fact" and simply indicates that one is exploring a suspected "cause" of a condition that already exists. This kind of research can again be illustrated by cardiovascular disease and smoking. One identifies a sample of 70-year-old people who have advanced cardiovascular disease and asks, "What has caused these people to have this disease?" One might hypothesize that the cause is heavy cigarette smoking over a period of years. To explore that hypothesis, one selects another sample of 70-year-old people who do not have cardiovascular disease and investigates both groups' histories of cigarette smoking. This reveals that some individuals with cardiovascular disease have never smoked; some who have smoked heavily all their lives have no cardiovascular disease; many with the disease have smoked heavily for decades; and many without the disease have smoked little if any during their lifetimes.

One examines these findings and applies careful logical thinking to the hypothesis and in so doing perhaps concludes that prolonged heavy smoking does probably tend to cause cardiovascular disease. But because the independent variable (amount of smoking over a long time) cannot be manipulated experimentally, the hypothesis that smoking causes the disease remains open to debate. Indeed, cigarette manufacturing companies for many years claimed that no linkage between smoking and disease could be shown.

Further, because the independent variable cannot be manipulated, some question exists concerning which is cause and which is effect. Could it not be that whatever condition predisposes people to cardiovascular disease might also make them want to smoke? This question shows that the cause-effect linkage explored in causal-comparative research must be argued very persuasively.

How does one make such arguments?

1. You provide examples showing that without the first condition (smoking), the second condition (disease) does not occur, or else occurs differently or less frequently. The first (causal) condition, therefore, must be shown to precede the second (effect) condition.
2. You consider carefully whether the cause you have hypothesized is sufficient in itself or in combination with other factors to have produced the effect.
3. You seriously explore whether there are other conditions or events that might be equally plausible as causes.

Consider how these three elements of persuasive argument would come into play in a study exploring the hypothesis that, with intelligence held constant, family wealth produces higher student achievement.

1. You identify the Elmwood high school students whose family income is in the upper 10 percent. You determine the students' achievement levels. You find that several are high achievers, but that many are average and a few are low achievers. You then make a search of the records for other high-achieving students who are not from wealthy families. You find that many are from middle-income families and that many others are from low-income families. But you see that a certain level of family income is present in the majority of high-achieving students.
2. You now probe the hypothesized cause—wealth—to see if it seems to be sufficient in itself to produce high achievement. You have already found high-achieving students from poor families and lower-achieving students from wealthy families. This causes you to wonder whether you can support your hypothesis, although you continue to believe that wealth is probably one of the causes of higher achievement.

3. You now seriously explore whether there might be other causes of high achievement as important or more important than family wealth. Because you have used statistical procedures to hold intelligence constant, you explore other potential causative factors such as family stability, language skills, family belief in the value of education, and individual motivation to excel in school. After considering these possibilities, you may decide that you cannot make a strongly persuasive argument for wealth as the main causative factor in school achievement, even though you still believe it plays a role.

Exercise 14.3

1. Suppose you have noted that girls are more likely than boys to raise their hands before speaking in class discussion
   a. Hypothesize two possible causes for that difference.
   b. Support each cause with two arguments.
   c. Is there any way you can demonstrate cause and effect for this phenomenon? (To do so you will have to manipulate the independent variable you hypothesize as the cause.)
2. Mr. Simmons claims that students who smoke a great deal are less responsible and considerate than those who do not. He says smoking causes students to lose self-respect. Would you agree or disagree with that assertion? What arguments would you present to support your views?

Conducting Causal-Comparative Research

Chapter 3 described a graduate student, Jan, who believed that students who entered kindergarten at age 4 tended to experience social and learning difficulties to a greater degree in later years than did students who entered kindergarten at age 5. To explore her hypothesis, she selected from among sixth-grade students a sample that had begun school at age 4 and a second sample that had begun school at age 5. She used stratified samples to make sure the groups were equivalent in gender, ethnicity, and socioeconomic status. She then examined records and interviewed teachers to compare the achievement levels and social adjustment patterns of the two groups.

Jan's study is an example of causal-comparative research. She was aware of learning and social problems that certain schoolchildren experienced; she believed the cause of their difficulties was immaturity, attributable to age of entry into kindergarten. As indicated for causal-comparative research (Gay & Airasian, 2003), Jan did the following:

1. Identified the dependent variable (social, emotional, and academic difficulties)
2. Defined the independent variable (early age entry into kindergarten), which she hypothesized to be the cause of the problems associated with the dependent variable
3. Selected for comparison two groups that were as similar as possible except for the independent variable
4. Measured both groups to ascertain the level or degree of the dependent variable

5. Analyzed the differences between the groups' dependent variable data
6. Built a logical case to support the hypothesis that early age entry to kindergarten contributed to later difficulties socially, emotionally, and academically

Jan's conclusions were not airtight. No research conclusions ever are, and any cause–effect linkage suspected in causal-comparative research is always open to question. Although Jan believed a relationship was present between the independent and dependent variables in her study, it is possible that the relationship was not causative. Certainly many early entry students do well throughout their school careers, with no unusual problems. Some other unidentified factor might have brought about the difficulties that drew Jan's attention, such as family makeup, parental strife, nutritional patterns, or presence of younger or older siblings. In Jan's logical analysis of the data, however, she was unable to identify any other causes that in her mind could account for the student problems observed.

Exercise 14.4

Suppose you conducted a causal-comparative study in which your dependent variable was artistic ability and your independent variable was handedness. In the study you confirmed that left-handed students, on average, tended to be significantly more artistic than right-handed students. Would you, therefore, contend that left-handedness caused artistic ability? Explain. Is it possible that a third factor might be causing both handedness and artistic ability? What other causal variable might you identify?

An Example of Causal-Comparative Research

The following is a causal-comparative study published in *Gifted Child Quarterly* (1993).

Exercise 14.5

As you read through the report, "The Relation of Gender and Academic Achievement to Career Self-Efficacy and Interests," identify the following:

1. Focus of the study—what it is about. (You can find a definition of self-efficacy in the third paragraph of the report.)
2. The dependent variables are self-efficacy and interests. What independent variables are considered?
3. Three hypotheses are stated in the study. What are they?
4. Were the data and data analyses mainly quantitative or qualitative?
5. Did the data support or fail to support the hypotheses?
6. What cautions did the investigator advise regarding the conclusions of the study?

The Relation of Gender and Academic Achievement to Career Self-Efficacy and Interests

Kevin R. Kelly
Purdue University

The career development of gifted young women is of great concern in the field of gifted education. It is evident to even casual observers that talented young women have not fully realized their talents in the occupational world. This observation is not new to readers of this journal. Previous GCQ articles have described career underachievement by women (Reis, 1987) and identified barriers to their career development (Hollinger & Fleming, 1984; Schwartz, 1980).

> Significance of the topic

Gifted educators have become more sensitive to issues relating to the career development and achievement of women. However, Reis and Callahan (1989) questioned how much this heightened sensitivity has affected the career achievement of gifted women. They found little comfort in the trend for young women to enroll in more math and science courses in high school. Reis and Callahan (1989) issue a challenge for educators to determine how far we have come in enabling gifted women to realize their talents in careers and derive the benefits of outstanding career achievement.

Researchers who have examined the constricting effects of gender socialization on career development have found Bandura's (1977, 1982) social learning theory a productive guide. A central construct in social learning theory is self-efficacy. According to Bandura (1977), self-efficacy is the expectation that one has the ability to complete a given task or goal. Strength of self-efficacy determines whether a behavior will be initiated, the amount of effort devoted to pursuing a goal, and the degree of goal persistence in the face of barriers. An individual with high career efficacy expectations is likely to initiate progress toward a career, expend the appropriate amount of effort to prepare for and enter the career, and persist in the face of obstacles (Lent & Hackett, 1987). The purpose of this study is to compare the relative strength of gender and academic achievement as predictors of career self-efficacy and career interest.

Gender and Career Self-Efficacy

Betz and Hackett (1981) were the first to investigate career self-efficacy, which is the strength of one's expectation that one can prepare for and enter particular careers successfully. They found that the efficacy expectations of college men were similar for traditionally male (e.g., drafter, engineer) and female (art teacher, physical therapist) occupations. College women, in contrast, had higher efficacy expectations for traditionally female than traditionally male occupations. Further, young women expressed high interest in careers for which they had high efficacy expectations and low interest in careers in which they did not think they could succeed. The lack of interest by young women in male occupations was related to their low career self-efficacy expectations for male fields of work. For women, career self-efficacy was a much stronger predictor of perceived career options than academic ability.

> Review of related literature, separated into two subheadings, corresponding to the two independent variables and their relation to the dependent variable

Subsequent investigations have indicated that career self-efficacy is related to career preparation and development. Betz and Hackett (1983) found math self-efficacy to be positively related to choice of science majors in college. The men in this study, who had significantly higher math self-efficacy than women, were more likely to have selected science majors than women. Math self-efficacy was a more powerful predictor of college major choice than math aptitude. Post-Kammer and Smith (1985) found that both self-efficacy and career interests were related to range of perceived career options for female adolescents while only career interests were predictive of range of career options for male adolescents. For women, career self-efficacy seems to have a greater influence on perceived career options than academic achievement or career interests.

Career self-efficacy also has been predictive of academic persistence and success in studies of college science majors. In a study by Lent, Brown, and Larkin (1984), students with high science efficacy expectations tended to attain high grades in science courses and remain in science majors. Self-efficacy explained more of the variance in academic success and persistence than career interests for both women and men. This same pattern of findings was replicated in two studies (Lent, Brown, & Larkin, 1986, 1987). Notably, there were not marked gender differences in the career self-efficacy expectations of the college women and men in these studies. Perhaps women have developed more robust career efficacy expectations since the Betz and Hackett (1981) investigation.

Academic Achievement and Career Self-Efficacy

The empirical evidence regarding the relation between academic achievement and career self-efficacy is not clear. Ayres (1980) did not find academic achievement to be related to career self-efficacy. Betz and Hackett (1981) found small correlations between academic achievement and career self-efficacy. Lent et al. (1984) found moderate correlations between math achievement and self-efficacy for science careers. The current strength of academic achievement as a predictor of career self-efficacy remains to be established.

The line of research regarding gender and career self-efficacy is of vital importance to those seeking to promote the career development of talented women. Career self-efficacy is a key variable because it is a stronger predictor than career interests or academic progress and success in college and career entry. Research findings indicate that even gifted young women give greater weight to the gender appropriateness of careers than they do to their abilities and interests in career decision making.

There is a need, however, for further study of the interrelations of gender, academic achievement, and career self-efficacy. First, there are signs that gender differences in career self-efficacy have diminished over time. The most recent studies have not evidenced the striking gender differences in career self-efficacy documented by Betz and Hackett (1981). The current strength of the influence of gender on career self-efficacy should be assessed. Second, the relation of academic achievement to career self-efficacy seems to be more substantial in more recent investigations. A

current assessment of the relation of achievement to self-efficacy is warranted.

The purpose of the current study was to explore the relative strength of gender and academic achievement as predictors of self-efficacy for and interest in female, male, and sex-balanced careers. If gender accounts for little of the variance in career self-efficacy, then it can be considered that young women have made real progress in reducing the influence of gender stereotypes on their career development. If gender continues to be a stronger predictor of career self-efficacy than achievement, greater urgency will be given to the call for action sounded by Reis and Callahan (1989). Whatever the particular pattern of results, these findings can be used by educators and counselors to develop appropriate career education programs for talented young women.

Purpose of the present study

Significance of the present study

Based on previous research findings, the following hypotheses were tested:

1. Girls will have lower career self-efficacy expectations for male careers than boys. It was anticipated that gender would not influence career self-efficacy ratings for female or sex-balanced careers.
2. Girls will express greater interest in female occupations and less interest in male occupations than boys. Gender will not influence interest in sex-balanced occupations.
3. Academic achievement will be positively related to career self-efficacy for female, male, and sex-balanced occupations.

Three stated hypotheses

Method

Participants

The participants were 186 9th- and 11th-grade students from an urban high school in a midwestern state. Ten intact classes were included in the study. Four of the classes were for gifted students, including honors sections of algebra, trigonometry, language arts, and modern literature courses. Two of these classes were at the 9th-grade and two were at the 11th-grade level. Students scoring above the 95th percentile on the math subtest of the most recent achievement test were included in the honors math courses. Students scoring above the 95th percentile on the verbal subtest of the most recent achievement test were included in the honors sections of the language arts courses. The remaining six classes, three 9th-grade and three 11th-grade, were regular curriculum offerings of math and language arts courses.

There were 56 girls and 33 boys in the 9th-grade classes and 45 girls and 52 boys in the 11th-grade classes. The average age for this sample was 15.6 years with a range of 14 to 18 years.

Students' achievement test scores were recorded from school records. The composite achievement score was used as an independent variable. The overall mean achievement composite percentile was 72.2. The achievement composite percentile was 92.9 for the gifted students and 56.5 for the regular curriculum students.

Measures

Participants were required to make self-efficacy and interest ratings of the 20 occupations studied in the original career self-efficacy study by Betz and Hackett (1981). Ten of the occupations were defined by Betz and Hackett (1981) as "female" because at the time of their study at least 70 percent of the workers in these occupations were women (U.S. Women's Bureau, 1975). The female occupations were: art teacher, dental hygienist, home economist, medical technician, physical therapist, secretary, social worker, travel agent, and radiological technician. The 10 male occupations were those in which at least 70% of the workers were men. These occupations were: accountant, drafter, engineer, highway patrol officer, lawyer, mathematician, physician, probation officer, sales manager, and school administrator.

> Researchers adapted an existing "instrument," so to speak

Since that time, there have been significant changes in the proportions of female and male workers in some of these 20 occupations. The same 20 occupations were studied in this investigation but classified into three categories. Female occupations are those in which, according to latest U.S. Department of Labor (1989) statistics, at least 70% of the workers are female. These occupations are: art teacher, dental hygienist, elementary teacher, home economist, medical technologist, physical therapist, radiological technician, and secretary. Male occupations are those in which at least 70% of the workers

are male, including: drafter, engineer, highway patrol officer, lawyer, physician, and probation officer. Sex-balanced occupations are those in which at least 30% of the workers are women and at least 30% of the workers are men. These occupations are: accountant, mathematician, sales manager, school administrator, social worker, and travel agent.

Participants were asked two questions in regard to each of these 20 occupations. The first question was: How confident are you that you could successfully complete the educational and training requirements necessary to enter these occupations? Participants used a 10-point scale (1 = not confident at all, 10 = totally confident) to respond to each occupation. These responses provided a measure of self-efficacy for educational requirements for each of the 20 occupations. The individual self-efficacy scores for the 8 female occupations were averaged to derive an overall score for self-efficacy for completing educational requirements for female occupations (SEF). The individual self-efficacy scores for the 6 male occupations and 6 sex-balanced occupations also were averaged to derive overall self-efficacy scores for the male (SEM) and sex-balanced occupations (SESB).

Response to the second question, "How seriously have you considered entering each of these occupations?," provided three measures of occupational interest. The interest scores for each of the female occupations were averaged to create a composite score of interest in female occupations (INTF). Composite scores for interest in male occupations (INTM) and sex-balanced occupations (INTSB) were also calculated. In total, 26 dependent measures were derived for each of the participants.

Data indicate that the composite scores in this study are reliable. The alpha coefficients for the SEF, SEM, and SESB variables were .71, .70, and .72. The alpha coefficients for INTF,

> Reasonable values for reliability

INTM, and INTSB were .76, .73, and .77. These measures had acceptable levels of internal consistency. There is no reliability data for the SE measures for the 20 individual occupations.

There is substantial evidence for the validity of the self-efficacy measures used in this study. Self-efficacy ratings have been found to

> Good discussion of validity of measures

be related to perceived career options, academic success, and choice of college major. College students were found to consider careers as viable alternatives when they expressed high efficacy expectations for those careers (Betz & Hackett, 1981). Self-efficacy has been found to be positively related to consideration of occupational alternatives for economically disadvantaged populations (Post-Kammer & Smith, 1986). Career self-efficacy was predictive of academic achievement and persistence by college science and engineering majors in two studies (Lent et al., 1984, 1986). Career self-efficacy was demonstrated to be a better predictor of academic performance in college than either theme congruence or decisional consequences, two other theoretical constructs in vocational psychology (Lent et al., 1987). Finally, math self-efficacy was found to predict choice of math or science majors in college (Betz & Hackett, 1983). Self-efficacy, as operationalized by the SE measures, seems to be a valid construct.

It should be acknowledged that these career self-efficacy measures share the limitations of other self-report indices. It is relatively easy for the gifted student to make the so-cially desirable response and overstate career self-efficacy in all areas. Results should be interpreted in light of this possibility. However, self-reports of career self-efficacy have been found to be more closely related to career development behaviors, such as college major choice and academic achievement, than other self-report measures of career development such as career interests.

Limitations of self-report data

Results

Multiple regression procedures were used to analyze the data. The independent variables were achievement and gender. The interactive effect of achievement and gender on the dependent variables was also analyzed. The dependent variables were: individual SE scores for the 20 occupations; summary SE scores for the female (SEF), male (SEM), and sex-balanced (SESB) occupations; and summary interest scores for the female (INTF), male (INTM), and sex-balanced (INTSB) occupations. The independent variables were entered into regression analyses with the stepwise technique. Because numerous analyses were completed, a conservative level of statistical significance was used ($p < .01$). Descriptive

Good review of variables involved

TABLE 1   Descriptive Data for Self-Efficacy and Interest Ratings

Female occupations	M	SD
Art Teacher	4.66	3.35
Dental Hygienist	4.59	3.06
Elementary Teacher	7.15	3.03
Home Economist	5.67	3.09
Medical Technician	4.54	3.17
Physical Therapist	5.04	3.15
Secretary	6.51	3.18
Radiological Technician	5.41	3.38
SEF	5.44	2.24
INTF	2.68	1.47
Male occupations		
Drafter	4.91	3.57
Engineer	4.78	3.34
Highway Patrol Officer	6.40	3.22
Lawyer	5.27	3.36
Physician	4.47	3.28
Probation Officer	6.07	3.18
SEM	5.32	2.14
INTM	3.58	2.97
Sex-balanced occupations		
Accountant	5.70	3.08
Mathematician	4.82	3.32
Sales Manager	6.94	3.04
School Administrator	5.95	3.37
Social Worker	6.40	3.13
Travel Agent	7.29	2.95
SESB	6.18	2.27
INTSB	3.22	1.95

data are summarized in Table 1. Summaries of the regression analyses can be found in Table 2.

Female Occupations

Gender accounted for a significant portion of variance in only three of the eight occupations: elementary teacher, home economist, and secretary. In each case, female participants expressed greater efficacy expectations than male participants. Gender did not account for a significant amount of the variance in INTF, $R^2 = .017, p = .09$.

Achievement was related to the SE ratings of six of the eight female occupations. Overall, nearly 14% of the variance in the SEF score was accounted for by achievement. Higher achievers tended to express greater efficacy expectations than lower achievers. Self-efficacy for art teacher and home economist were the only variables not related to achievement.

Achievement was also related to INTF, $R^2 = .103$. Higher achievers expressed less interest in traditionally female careers than low achievers. High achievers tended to have high efficacy expectations for female careers but be less interested in pursuing these careers than lower achievers were.

Male Occupations

Gender accounted for a significant portion of the variance in the SE ratings of three of the six male occupations: drafter, engineer, and highway patrol officer. In each occupation, male participants expressed higher self-efficacy than female participants. Gender did not account for any of the variance in INTM.

Achievement was related significantly to SE ratings for all of the male occupations. Again, higher achievers tended to express greater efficacy expectations for male occupations than lower achievers. Achievement did not account for any variance in INTM.

Sex-Balanced Occupations

Gender did not account for any variance in the self-efficacy ratings for the sex-balanced occupations. Gender did account for a small amount of variance in INTSB. Female participants expressed higher interest in sex-balanced occupations than male participants.

Achievement was related to self-efficacy ratings for five of the six sex-balanced occupations. Only self-efficacy ratings for sales manager were unrelated to achievement. Achievement was unrelated to interest in sex-balanced occupations.

The Gender X Achievement interaction was not related to any of the self-efficacy or interest ratings of the female, male, or sex-balanced occupations.

Discussion

There was partial support for the first hypothesis. As anticipated, gender influenced the self-efficacy ratings for three of the six male occupations: drafter, engineer,

> Discussion of results is tied directly back to three original hypotheses

TABLE 2 Summary of Regression Analyses

Female occupations	Gender Partial R^2	Achievement Partial R^2	Model R^2
Art Teacher	.000	.025	.025
Dental Hygienist	.005	.188**	.193**
Elementary Teacher	.118**	.054*	.172**
Home Economist	.053*	.030	.083*
Medical Technician	.000	.108**	.108**
Physical Therapist	.022	.042*	.064*
Secretary	.078**	.050*	.128**
Radiological Technician	.000	.091**	.091**
SEF	.032	.139**	.171**
INTF	.017	.103**	.119**

Male occupations	Gender Partial R^2	Achievement Partial R^2	Model R^2
Drafter	.089**	.087**	.176**
Engineer	.117**	.069**	.182**
Highway Patrol Officer	.129**	.052*	.181**
Lawyer	.000	.050*	.051*
Physician	.002	.098**	.100**
Probation Officer	.004	.042*	.046*
SEM	.067**	.124**	.191**
INTM	.032	.001	.033

Sex-balanced occupations	Gender Partial R^2	Achievement Partial R^2	Model R^2
Accountant	.001	.099**	.100**
Mathematician	.001	.099**	.101**
Sales Manager	.000	.027	.027
School Administrator	.000	.173**	.173**
Social Worker	.030	.062*	.092*
Travel Agent	.007	.053*	.060*
SESB	.002	.166**	.167
INTSB	.069**	.006	.075

*$p < .01$
**$p < .001$

and highway patrol officer. Boys tended to have higher efficacy expectations than girls for the ability to complete the educational requirements necessary to pursue each of these occupations. Contrary to expectations, gender also influenced self-efficacy ratings for the following female occupations: elementary teacher, home economist, and secretary. Girls expressed higher efficacy expectations for success in these occupations than boys.

Examination of Table 2 will indicate, however, that gender did not account for a large amount of the variance in self-efficacy. Further, gender accounted for virtually none of the variance in the self-efficacy ratings for lawyer, physician, probation officer, and the sex-balanced careers. Gender does influence expectations of success in preparation for some "traditionally female" and "traditionally male" occupations, but this influence is not nearly as strong as it was in the Betz and Hackett (1981) study a decade ago.

The second hypothesis was that girls would express greater interest in female occupations and less interest in male occupations than boys. This hypothesis was not substantiated. Gender did not account for any variance in interest in the female or male occupations. The young women did tend to express more interest in the sex-balanced careers than the male participants. These findings are dramatically different from the original finding by Betz and Hackett (1981) that college women were much more interested in female careers and much less interested in male careers than college men. It is heartening to see how little influence gender had on the occupational interest measures used in this study.

The third hypothesis was firmly supported. Achievement accounted for significant amounts of variance in the self-efficacy ratings of six of the eight female occupations, all of the male occupations, and five of the six sex-balanced occupations. It should be acknowledged that achievement explained a relatively modest amount of variance in these variables. Nonetheless, achievement was a stronger predictor of career self-efficacy than gender in this study. These results stand in stark contrast to the findings of Betz and Hackett (1981) and Ayres (1980) that academic achievement was unrelated to career self-efficacy.

Gifted students are likely to have high efficacy expectations for a number of careers. These expectations for success should be validated by educators. At the same time, talented students should be encouraged

to discover the types of skills and training that are required to enter the careers they are considering as occupational options.

It should be noted that achievement was inversely related to interest in traditionally female careers. Both female and male students at higher achievement levels tended to express less interest in traditionally female careers than students of more modest achievement. This is the first empirical evidence that high achievers are disinterested in careers that may limit their professional growth, creative expression, and personal financial rewards. It appears that gifted girls may be developing occupational interests based more on the actual work of careers than on the gender appropriateness of careers.

Caution is warranted in the interpretation of these results for the following reasons. As stated earlier, self-report measures are subject to social desirability effects. Participants may have given the socially desirable response to the self-efficacy measures rather than their most honest assessment of their personal efficacy expectations. This may be particularly true for gifted girls. Another limiting factor is the homogeneous population used in this study. All participants attended the same school. These findings remain to be replicated with a more heterogeneous group. Finally, readers should recall that career self-efficacy was not used to predict college major choice or academic success. The influence of career self-efficacy on actual career development behaviors such as choice of major and career achievement for gifted students remains to be documented.

> Concern for the previously stated limitation is reiterated

Given these cautions, the findings of this study still provide important information relative to the call by Reis and Callahan (1989) to assess how much progress has been made in promoting the career achievement of gifted women. Although gender still influences career self-efficacy, it is considerably less influential than academic achievement. Real progress has been made by young women in surmounting the repressive effects of gender socialization on occupational self-efficacy and interest.

> Discussion of results, in light of limitations

This progress should not be attributed too quickly to the educational efforts of teachers and counselors promoting gender equity in career choice and preparation. Note that gender was least influential in determining self-efficacy for sex-balanced careers. It is likely that young women believe they can successfully prepare to become accountants, mathematicians, and school administrators because they actually know women pursuing these occupations. The fact that significant numbers of women have entered these occupations over the past decade means that there are many more successful women to serve as models for young women than there were a generation ago. Vicarious observation by young women of the rewards professional women have received in these occupations is likely to have raised personal efficacy expectations. Young women are likely to believe they can do something if they see it done by women.

This is not to say that counselors and educators

Recommendations for practice

are relieved of their responsibility to empower young women to succeed in traditionally male occupations. Empowerment can be achieved by building efficacy expectations for success in nontraditional careers. Gifted women are not likely to express interest in careers for which their efficacy expectations are low. Interests develop after efficacy expectations have become reasonably high. Perhaps the best way to build self-efficacy for de-

More recommendations for practice

manding occupations is to challenge and counsel talented young women to complete rigorous academic programs. The findings of this study inspire optimism that progress is being made toward the goal of enabling talented young women to develop their talents more fully in the world of work.

References

Ayres, A. L. (1980). Self-efficacy theory: Implications for the career development of women. Unpublished doctoral dissertation, Ohio State University.

Bandura, A. (1977). Self-efficacy: Toward a unifying theory of behavioral change. *Psychological Review, 84,* 191–215.

Bandura, A. (1982). Self-efficacy theory in human agency. *American Psychologist, 37,* 122–147.

Betz, N. E., & Hackett, G. (1981). The relationship of career-related self-efficacy expectations to perceived career options in college women and men. *Journal of Counseling Psychology, 28,* 399–410.

Betz, N. E., & Hackett, G. (1983). The relationship of mathematics self-efficacy expectations to the selec-

tion of science-based college majors. *Journal of Vocational Behavior, 23,* 329–345.

Hollinger, C. L., & Fleming, F. S. (1984). Internal barriers to the realization of potential: Correlates and interrelationships among gifted and talented female adolescents. *Gifted Child Quarterly, 24,* 113–117.

Lent, R. W., Brown, S. D., & Larkin, K. C. (1984). Relation of self-efficacy expectations to academic achievement and persistence. *Journal of Counseling Psychology, 31,* 356–363.

Lent, R. W., Brown, S. D., & Larkin, K. C. (1986). Self-efficacy in the prediction of academic performance and perceived career options. *Journal of Counseling Psychology, 33,* 265–269.

Lent, R. W., Brown, S. D., & Larkin, K. C. (1987). Comparison of three theoretically derived variables in predicting career and academic behavior: Self-efficacy, interest congruence, and consequence thinking. *Journal of Counseling Psychology, 34,* 293–298.

Lent, R. W., & Hackett, G. (1987). Career self-efficacy: Empirical status and future directions. *Journal of Vocational Behavior, 30,* 347–382.

Post-Kammer, P., & Smith, P. L. (1985). Sex differences in career self-efficacy, consideration, and interests of eighth and ninth graders. *Journal of Counseling Psychology, 32,* 551–559.

Post-Kammer, P., & Smith, P. L. (1986). Sex differences in math and science self-efficacy measures among disadvantaged students. *Journal of Vocational Behavior, 29,* 89–101.

Reis, S. M. (1987). We can't change what we don't recognize: Understanding the special needs of gifted females. *Gifted Child Quarterly, 31,* 83, 89.

Reis, S. M., & Callahan, C. M. (1989). Gifted females: They've come a long way—or have they? *Journal of the Education of the Gifted, 12,* 99–117.

Schwartz, L. L. (1980). Advocacy for the neglected gifted: Females. *Gifted Child Quarterly, 24,* 113–117.

U.S. Department of Labor. (1989). *Handbook of labor statistics.* Washington, DC: U.S. Government Printing Office.

U.S. Women's Bureau. (1975). *Handbook on women workers.* Washington, DC: U.S. Government Printing Office.

📚 **A D D I T I O N A L   E X A M P L E S   O F   P U B L I S H E D
C A U S A L - C O M P A R A T I V E   S T U D I E S**

In order to better understand a particular research methodology, it is often beneficial to examine additional examples of published research that utilizes that specific methodology. Several such examples of causal-comparative research have been identified for you through the use of *Research Navigator™*, available on the Web at www.researchnavigator.com. The following list consists of published research articles available free of charge in full-text format via *Research Navigator™*. These articles are available in either HTML and/or PDF formats and are easily located by searching the database by *article number* (abbreviated "**AN**"), which has been provided for each citation.

Bisset, J. D., Borja, M. E., Brassard, D. E., Reohr, J. R., O'Neill, K., & Kosky, R. (1999). Assessing the importance of educational goals: A comparison of students, parents, and faculty. *Assessment & Evaluation in Higher Education, 24*(4), 391–398. [**AN: 2984074**]

Lee, A. M., Fredenburg, K., Belcher, D., & Cleveland, N. (1999). Gender differences in children's conceptions of competence and motivation in physical education. *Sport, Education & Society, 4*(2), 161–174. [**AN: 2596665**]

Mota, J., & Silva, G. (1999). Adolescent's physical activity: Association with socio-economic status and parental participation among a Portuguese sample. *Sport, Education & Society, 4*(2), 193–199. [**AN: 2596667**]

Pomplun, M., & Sundbye, N. (1999). Gender differences in constructed response reading items. *Applied Measurement in Education, 12*(1), 95–109. [**AN: 3348898**]

Reid, R., Riccio, C. A., Kessler, R. H., DuPaul, G. J., Power, T. J., Anastopoulos, A. D., Rogers-Adkinson, D., & Noll, M. (2000). Gender and ethnic differences in ADHD as assessed by behavior ratings. *Journal of Emotional & Behavioral Disorders, 8*(1), 38–48. [**AN: 2856206**]

Taplin, M., & Jegede, O. (2001). Gender differences in factors influencing achievement of distance education students. *Open Learning, 16*(2). [**AN: 4499411**]

Chapter Summary

This chapter has explained the nature and procedures of experimental research, quasi-experimental research, and causal-comparative research. Experimental research is used to identify cause–effect relationships, in which changes in a prior condition or event (X = the independent variable) produce changes in a subsequent condition or event (Y = the dependent variable). The independent variable is considered to be the cause, the dependent variable the effect, and in experimental and quasi-experimental research, the independent variable is manipulated to determine whether, and how, it influences the dependent variable.

Applying Technology: **More about Experimental and Quasi-Experimental Research Designs**

Dr. William Trochim has again provided an extremely thorough discussion of experimental and quasi-experimental research designs. His material on these topics spans several Web pages. Initially, in Experimental Designs (http://trochim.human.cornell.edu/kb/desexper. htm), Dr. Trochim presents an overview of experimental research designs, focusing on the relationship of internal and external validity to those designs. Probably more importantly, however, are his links to pages that present discussion of specific types of designs. These pages contain not only narrative information about the various designs but also incorporate wonderful graphic images that strongly support his discussions. Included in his text are the following designs:

- Two-Group Experimental Designs (http://trochim.human.cornell.edu/kb/expsimp.htm)
- Factorial Designs (http://trochim.human.cornell.edu/kb/expfact.htm)
- Randomized Block Designs (http://trochim.human.cornell.edu/kb/expblock.htm)
- Covariance Designs (http://trochim.human.cornell.edu/kb/expcov.htm)
- Hybrid Experimental Designs (http://trochim.human.cornell.edu/kb/exphybrd.htm)

He has also included pages that examine quasi-experimentation (http://trochim. human.cornell.edu/kb/quasiexp.htm). Specific discussions include the following:

- The Nonequivalent Control Group Design (http://trochim.human.cornell.edu/kb/quasnegd.htm), and
- Other Quasi-Experimental Designs (http://trochim.human.cornell.edu/kb/quasioth. htm).

Closely related to experimental research is quasi-experimental research, which follows the same procedures except that for any number of reasons the researchers are not able to assign participants randomly to treatment groups.

Several factors are known to affect the internal validity (accuracy of results) and external validity (generalizability) of experimental and quasi-experimental research. Referred to as "threats to validity," those factors must be accounted for satisfactorily if the research is to have credibility and usefulness.

Causal-comparative research is also aimed at exploring possible cause–effect relationships, though it cannot demonstrate cause and effect as can experimental and quasi-experimental research. Procedurally, causal-comparative research differs from experimental research in that the independent variable cannot be manipulated, for one of three reasons: (1) the independent variable is fixed (e.g., gender, handedness), (2) manipulation of the independent variable would be unethical (e.g., having students drink in order to test alcohol's effect on test performance), or (3) manipulating the independent variable would be impractical (e.g., giving students large sums of money to see how newly acquired wealth affects their school behavior). Causal-comparative research proceeds as follows: It focuses on the effect (Y = the dependent variable); it then asks what might be causing that effect (X = the independent variable); and it attempts to identify and substantiate a plausible connection between the effect and its cause. The cause–effect linkage must be made logically because it cannot be demonstrated by manipulating the independent variable, as is done in experimental research.

LIST OF IMPORTANT TERMS

comparison group	*ex post facto* research	threats to validity
control group	external validity	treatment condition
experimental design	internal validity	X variable
experimental group	quasi-experimental research	Y variable
experimental research	random assignment	

ACTIVITIES FOR THOUGHT AND DISCUSSION

1. Here are the questions posed at the beginning of the chapter. How would you answer the questions now?

   a. What sets experimental research apart from all other types of research?

   b. What is the difference between experimental research and quasi-experimental research?

   c. What research designs are most frequently used in experimental research?

   d. What research designs are most frequently used in quasi-experimental research?

   e. What are the main threats to internal and external validity in experimental research and quasi-experimental research?

   f. What do experimental and causal-comparative research have in common, and how do they differ?

   g. Why cannot causal-comparative research convincingly demonstrate cause and effect?

   h. What are the principal data sources in experimental and causal-comparative research?

   i. Which data analysis procedures are most often used in experimental and causal-comparative research?

   j. Why is it said that causal-comparative research begins by considering the effect before considering the cause?

2. Explain why a researcher might decide to conduct causal-comparative research rather than experimental research.

3. Suppose educational researchers wanted to try to identify the causes of the behavior pattern typically known as attention deficit disorder (ADD) syndrome. Which type of research would be indicated: experimental, quasi-experimental, or causal-comparative? Would the most appropriate design include groups or be limited to single participants?

4. Suppose medical researchers wished to study the effects of a new medication to deal with attention deficit disorder syndrome in primary-grade children. Which type of research is indicated: experimental, quasi-experimental, or causal-comparative? Of the experimental designs described in this chapter, which would seem most appropriate for this research?

ANSWERS TO CHAPTER EXERCISES

14.1. **1.** If a true experiment, ask to have students randomly assigned to the two classes. If a quasi-experiment, use existing class enrollments. If desired, pretest the groups to ensure equivalency. Consider using a fellow teacher's class as a control group.

2. Write out what they intend to do. Agree to a certain amount of homework and allow the teachers to satisfy themselves that the agreement is being adhered to.

3. The same test, preferably a standardized test, should be given to all groups involved at the end of the experiment.

4. The teacher personality and skill variables probably cannot be adequately controlled in this study.

14.2. Answers are found in the article. Discuss the answers in class.

14.3. Your responses should be presented to other members of the class for discussion.

14.4. You would be hard-pressed to make a convincing argument that handedness affects artistic ability. A more plausible explanation (if this effect is found) is that some other factor is responsible for both handedness and artistic ability. Right-brain dominance might be one possibility.

14.5. Answers to all questions except question 4 are found in the article. The answer to 4 is "quantitative." Discuss your answers in class to ensure understanding.

REFERENCES AND RECOMMENDED READINGS

Bracht, G., & Glass, G. (1968). The external validity of experiments. *American Educational Research Journal, 5,* 437–474.

Brown, S., & Walberg, H. (1993). Motivational effects on test scores of elementary students. *Journal of Educational Research, 86,* 133–136.

Campbell, D., & Stanley, J. (1966). *Experimental and Quasi-Experimental Designs for Research.* Chicago: Rand McNally.

Crowl, T. (1993). *Fundamentals of Educational Research.* Dubuque, IA: WCB Brown & Benchmark.

Gall, M., Borg, W., & Gall, J. (2003). *Educational Research: An Introduction* (7th ed.). Boston: Allyn and Bacon.

Gay, L. & Airasian, P. (2003). *Educational Research: Competencies for Analysis and Application* (7th ed.). Upper Saddle River, NJ: Merrill.

Kelly, K. (1993). The relation of gender and academic achievement to career self- efficacy and interests. *Gifted Child Quarterly, 37,* 59–64.

Meyer, M., Linville, M., & Rees, G. (1993). The development of a positive self-concept in preservice teachers. *Action in Teacher Education, 15*(1), 30–35.

APPENDIX A

Overview of Statistical Concepts and Procedures

Statistical concepts and procedures were introduced as needed in various chapters. Here they are brought together in an expanded presentation that permits consideration and practice in greater detail, should one desire. Some of the material on the following pages is repetitious of earlier presentations.

Here we will consider the following:

- The nature and uses of statistics
- The relationship of statistics to populations and samples
- The difference between parametric and nonparametric statistics
- The calculation and interpretation of descriptive statistics
- The relationship of statistics to the normal probability curve
- Relative standings associated with the normal curve
- The calculation and interpretation of inferential statistics
- Chi-square, its use, calculation, and interpretation
- Calculating and interpreting standard error and confidence limits
- Testing for significance
- Type I and Type II errors

The Nature and Uses of Statistics

Statistics are used to describe and analyze numerical data. As pointed out previously, the term *statistics* has two widely used meanings. One refers to summary statements resulting from data analysis, such as mean, median, standard deviation, and coefficient of correlation. The other refers to the procedures by which data are analyzed mathematically. We begin this review by considering the ways statistical analysis is typically used:

- *To summarize data and reveal what is typical and atypical within a group*. Research often yields hundreds or thousands of items of numerical data that, until summarized, cannot be interpreted meaningfully. Researchers are especially interested in learning what is typical of the group being studied, as well as what individuals do that is atypical.
- *To show relative standing of individuals in a group*. Statistics can show where an individual stands for a given measurement in relation to all other individuals being

studied. Such standings are shown through percentile rankings, grade equivalents, age equivalents, z scores, T scores, and stanines, all discussed later.

- *To show relationships among variables.* Investigators are often interested in determining whether correlations exist among variables—for instance, between students' family backgrounds and their success in school. Such relationships can be described by means of statistical correlations.

- *To show similarities and differences among groups.* Researchers are often interested in ascertaining the degree to which groups are similar to or different from each other. For example, in experimental research they need to establish that the two or more groups involved at the beginning of the experiment are approximately equal in the trait being investigated. Then later they need to determine whether the groups have become different from each other, possibly due to the experimental treatment that has been given to one or more of the groups.

- *To estimate error that may have occurred in sample selection.* Samples almost always differ to some extent from the population from which they are drawn. This difference introduces a degree of error into research, so that one can never be precisely sure that a statistical finding is also correct for the population. Error refers to an estimate of disparity that may exist between a given statistic and its corresponding parameter value—that is, between what is measured in a sample and what exists in the population. Statistical procedures enable one to determine a value called **standard error**—of measurements, means, correlations, and differences between means. When the standard error is known, it is possible to specify the "confidence levels" for a particular value or finding. For example, if we find a sample mean of 6.2 and then determine its standard error, we can conclude with confidence that the population mean lies somewhere within a given range, such as between 7.1 and 5.3.

- *To test for **significance** of findings.* When researchers discover apparent correlations between variables or differences between means, they apply statistical tests of significance. These tests help determine whether their findings might be due to chance errors that occurred when the sample was selected, which could result in the sample's not reflecting the population. If the finding is sufficiently large to override sampling error, the researcher will call the finding significant. Significance permits one to conclude that a particular finding is probably real for the population rather than a result of sampling error.

Research Navigator.com
standard error

Populations and Samples

As we proceed into consideration of statistics and their calculation and interpretation, let us acknowledge again the relationships among population, sample, parameters, and statistics. *Population* refers to the totality of individuals or objects that correspond to a particular description. The following are examples of populations:

- All the females in North America
- All the girls in Cutter Elementary School

- All the boys in Cutter Elementary School who qualify for the honor society
- All the sixth-grade mathematics textbooks published during the past 20 years

Parameters are numerical descriptions of populations. Parameters include such descriptions as:

- The number of individuals in the population
- The mean (arithmetic average) of various measures made of population members, such as height, weight, or IQ
- The median (midpoint) in a set of measurements of a particular trait, such as height
- The standard deviation (an indicator of variability) of various measures made on population members
- The range of difference between the highest and lowest measures of a particular trait

Samples are smaller groups selected from populations. Samples are used in research when it is not feasible to study the entire population. Since the sample is intended to reflect the characteristics of the population, special care is taken in its selection. Members of the sample are usually selected randomly from the population, a procedure that usually, but not always, yields a sample representative of the population. The following are examples of samples:

- 1,000 females selected at random from all the females in North America
- 50 girls selected from among all the girls in Cutter Elementary School
- Each fifth title from an alphabetized list of all titles of sixth-grade mathematics textbooks published during the past 20 years

Statistics are numerical descriptions of samples. They are the same as parameters, except that they refer to samples rather than populations. The following are examples of statistical descriptions:

- The number of individuals in the sample
- The mean (arithmetic average) of various measures made of sample members, such as height, weight, or IQ
- The median (midpoint) in a set of sample measurements of a particular trait, such as height, weight, or IQ
- The standard deviation (an indicator of variability) of various measures taken from sample members
- The range of difference between the highest and lowest measures of a particular trait

Parametric Statistics and Nonparametric Statistics

It is important also to distinguish between parametric statistics and nonparametric statistics. Both are useful in research. They are different in that **parametric statistics** are used for analyzing traits that are normally distributed in the population—that is, in a manner

Research
Navigator.c⊛m
nonparametric
statistics

that approximates the normal probability curve, shown later in Figures A.3 and A.4. This curve is also known as the *bell-shaped curve* (from its appearance) and as simply the *normal curve.*

Nonparametric statistics, on the other hand, are used to describe and analyze data that are not assumed to be normally distributed in the population. Examples of such nonparametric data are frequency counts (e.g., the number of blue-eyed participants) and rankings (e.g., the order in which runners finished a race). Several nonparametric statistics have been developed for use in analyzing data; the one you are most likely to encounter is the chi-square test, used to analyze data that are classified into categories. Calculation of chi-square is described later.

The Calculation and Interpretation of Descriptive Statistics

You have seen that statistics are used, among other things, to describe data—to show (1) what is typical of the sample, (2) how diverse or spread out the measures are, (3) the relative standings of individual measures, and (4) relationships among variables being studied. Using a practice set of ten easily handled scores, we will proceed through a few simple exercises to show how these statistical calculations are done. The purpose is to help you develop an understanding of concept and procedure.

Measures of Central Tendency

What is typical for a sample, as concerns any trait being measured, is shown by three statistics referred to as **measures of central tendency.** These three statistics are the mean, the median, and the mode.

The *mean* is the arithmetic average of a set of measures, such as achievement, age, or performance. The mean helps depict what is typical for the group and is a component of many other statistical formulas as well. To calculate the mean, you simply add up the scores and divide the sum by the number of scores. What is the mean of the practice set of scores?

9, 8, 8, 7, 7, 7, 4, 4, 3, 3 (Answer: $\overline{X} = 6$.)

The *median* is a statistic that also indicates typicality. The median is simply the midpoint in an array of scores, determined by counting halfway through an array that has been arranged from highest score to lowest. In other words, the median is the score that separates the distribution or array into two equal halves—with 50 percent of the scores above and 50 percent of the scores below that particular value. If there is an odd number of scores in the array, the median falls on the middle score. For an array with an even number of scores, the median lies halfway between the two middle scores.

What is the median for the practice set of scores?

9, 8, 8, 7, 7, 7, 4, 4, 3, 3 (Answer: *Mdn* = 7.)

The median is sometimes more valuable than the mean in depicting typicality, especially when the distribution contains a few scores that are extremely high or low. The median is normally used to report such things as average personal income and typical cost of homes, because a few extremely high salaries and extremely expensive homes can produce a mean score that is not reflective of the group.

Although *mode* is included here so you will recognize that it indicates the most frequently occurring score or measurement, the concept of mode has no other application in descriptive statistics. What is the mode for this practice set of scores?

9, 8, 8, 7, 7, 7, 4, 4, 3, 3 (Answer: *Mo* = 7.)

Measures of Variability

Measures of variability show how spread out a group of scores is. Researchers want to know to what extent the scores, overall, vary from the mean of the group of scores. Consider the following sets of scores:

Set A: 9, 10, 10, 10, 10, 10, 10, 10, 10, 11

Set B: 1, 3, 5, 7, 9, 11, 13, 15, 17, 19

What are the mean and median of Set A? (Answer: $\overline{X}$ = 10; *Mdn* = 10.)

What are the mean and median of Set B? (Answer: $\overline{X}$ = 10; *Mdn* = 10.)

Which set of scores would you guess shows the greatest dispersion or variability, overall, from the mean? (Answer: Set B.)

To depict the degree to which scores are dispersed in the two sets, three measures of variability are typically used—range, variance, and standard deviation. *Range* shows the distance from highest score through the lowest score and is calculated as R = highest score – lowest score. Thus, the range for scores in Set A is 2: 11 – 9 = 2. The range for Set B is 18. Although range may be of some interest in itself, it does not present an accurate picture of dispersion among scores.

For example, consider the range for the following set of scores:

1, 10, 10, 10, 10, 10, 10, 11, 11, 11

Here the range is 10, but in fact the overall internal dispersion of scores is quite low.

Much more useful indicators of dispersion are variance and standard deviation. Both indicate how much all the scores, when taken into account together, vary from the mean. Both variance and standard deviation are used in formulas for other statistical applications.

Let us calculate the variance and standard deviation of our practice set of scores, using Table A.1, in which $X - \overline{X}$ is the *deviation score* and indicates how much each raw score differs from the mean, and $(X - \overline{X})^2$ shows the deviation squared. Here, the mean ($\overline{X}$) for our scores is 6. If you add up the values by which each score deviates from the mean (second column), what total do you get? The total for this column is always zero. To obtain positive values, each deviation ($X - \overline{X}$) is squared. The sum of those squared values

TABLE A.1 Calculation of Variance and Standard Deviation

Raw Score (X)	($X - \bar{X}$)	($X - \bar{X}$)^2
9	3	9
8	2	4
8	2	4
7	1	1
7	1	1
7	1	1
4	−2	4
4	−2	4
3	−3	9
3	−3	9
sum = 60	?	46 = sum ($X - \bar{X}$)^2
$\bar{X} = 6$	?	S^2 = sum ($X - \bar{X}$)^2/($N - 1$) = 5.11

(known as the *sum of squares*), when divided by the number of scores, gives us the variance (S^2) of scores. If the scores represent a sample, $N - 1$ should be used instead of N in determining the variance.

Variance in the illustration given above is $46 \div 9 = 5.11$, but that still does not tell us much, for there is nothing in practical experience to which most of us can relate this value since it exists on a squared scale. The degree to which the scores are dispersed is made somewhat more understandable by calculating the standard deviation of the scores. The formula for calculating standard deviation is

$$SD = \sqrt{\frac{\Sigma(X - \bar{X})^2}{(N - 1)}}$$

where Σ = the sum of

$(X - \bar{X})^2$ = the square of the amount by which each score differs from the mean

N = the number of scores

Standard deviation is the square root of the sample variance, which we already determined to be 5.11. We simply obtain the square root of 5.11, which gives us a standard deviation of 2.26.

As mentioned, the computer can do all this for you in the blink of an eye. Figure A.1 shows the descriptive statistics for our group of 10 scores, done on the *Statistical Package for the Social Sciences (SPSS)*, version 11.0, a complex but easy-to-use statistical software package—very popular with educational researchers—on which descriptive and inferential statistics can be calculated.

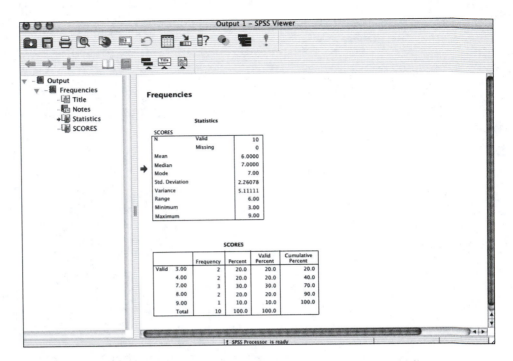

FIGURE A.1   Computer-analyzed descriptive statistics, using *SPSS* (v. 11.0)

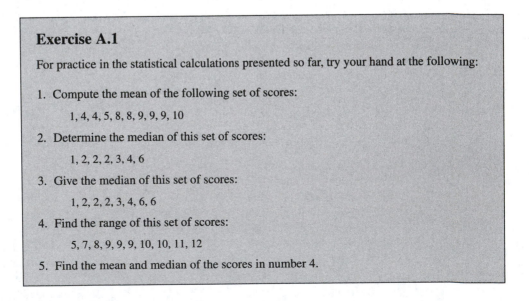

Exercise A.1

For practice in the statistical calculations presented so far, try your hand at the following:

1. Compute the mean of the following set of scores:

    1, 4, 4, 5, 8, 8, 9, 9, 9, 10

2. Determine the median of this set of scores:

    1, 2, 2, 2, 3, 4, 6

3. Give the median of this set of scores:

    1, 2, 2, 2, 3, 4, 6, 6

4. Find the range of this set of scores:

    5, 7, 8, 9, 9, 9, 10, 10, 11, 12

5. Find the mean and median of the scores in number 4.

Descriptive statistics are also used for showing relative position and measures of relationship.

Relative Position

Common statistics that show relative position are percentile rank, stanines, and converted scores.

Percentile rank (%ile or PR) is a ranking assigned to a particular score that shows the percentage of all scores that fall below that particular score.

> Example: *Juan's score fell at the 56th percentile. This means that he equaled or excelled 56 percent of all other students who took the test.*

Stanines are nine bands of scores with values from 1 to 9 (where 5 represents the average), which show where a score stands in relation to others.

> Example: *Mary's score fell in the 6th stanine. This means she was slightly above average among all similar students who took the test.*

Converted scores are values assigned to raw scores, such as the grade-level equivalency that corresponds to the score a student made on a test.

> Example: *Shawn made a score of 46 on the test, which places him at the seventh-grade, sixth-month level.*

Relationships

Relationships are shown statistically through correlations. The numerical value that indicates the degree of covarying relationship between two or more variables is called the *coefficient of correlation*. A coefficient of correlation (the most commonly used correlational procedure—the Pearson product moment—is symbolized by the letter r) is a measure of relationship between two or more sets of scores made by the same group of participants.

> Example: *The correlation between reading ability and achievement test scores was +.32. This means there was a modest positive relationship between the two.*

Research regularly explores relationships between such traits as self-concept and achievement, motivation and achievement, active class participation and achievement, listening ability and achievement, communication and attitude, and so on. The public generally believes that correlations show cause and effect, but as noted previously, such is not the case. The correlation between intake of saturated fat and incidence of heart disease does not, itself, prove that either causes the other. But it is fair to say that correlations often strongly *suggest* cause and effect and can sometimes lead to experimental research that shows that one factor does in fact "cause" another.

Data for correlational research must be obtained in the form of two sets of measures for each individual in the sample. That is, each participant is measured for trait X (perhaps

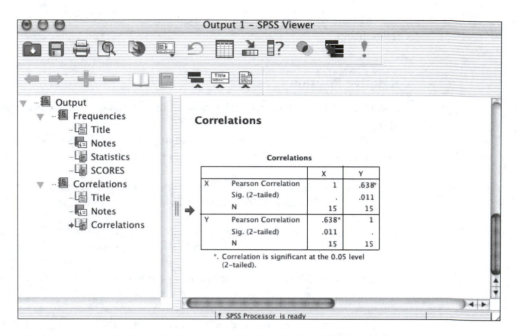

FIGURE A.2   Coefficient of correlation, calculated using *SPSS* (v. 11.0)

attitude toward school) as well as trait *Y* (perhaps grade point average). Then the pairs of measurements are correlated statistically. The resultant coefficient of correlation (*r*) indicates the degree of relationship between the variables, as shown in Figure A.2.

Correlations are most commonly calculated from interval data (such as scores) but can also be computed from nominal data (such as categories) or ordinal data (such as rankings). Computers can instantly calculate coefficients of correlation. For that reason, and because the hand calculation of *r* is laborious to the point of exhaustion, the procedure for deriving *r* is not shown here.

The following should be kept in mind concerning correlations:

1. Correlations vary in magnitude from 0 (absence of relationship) to extremes of ±1.0 (a perfect correlation). Coefficients of 0 and ±1.0 are virtually never encountered in research.
2. Correlations may be either positive or negative. In positive correlations, high marks on one variable tend to accompany high marks on the other variable, average accompany average, and low accompany low. You would expect to find a positive correlation between body weight and caloric intake. In negative correlations, high marks on one variable tend to accompany low marks on the other, average accompany average, and low accompany high. You would expect to find a negative correlation between body weight and frequency of aerobic exercise.
3. Positive and negative correlations have equal value in making predictions.

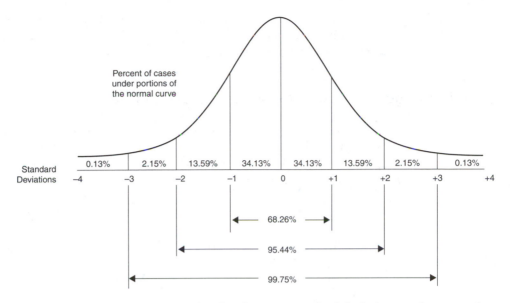

FIGURE A.3   The normal curve, showing the mean, standard deviations, and percent of cases throughout the distribution

4. Correlations discovered in education and the social sciences rarely exceed ±.70. Nonetheless, lower correlations are often useful and enlightening.

Descriptive Statistics and the Normal Probability Curve

Reference has been made to the **normal probability curve,** and parametric statistics were described as related to traits that are normally distributed. At this point, we examine the relationships of statistical concepts to the normal curve.

Note that in Figure A.3 the mean is located at the centermost part of the curve. The curve is deepest there, indicating that more measures fall at that point than anywhere else along the baseline. Progressing along the baseline to the right, where measures are higher than the mean, the frequencies become progressively fewer until none occurs. Similarly, to the left-hand side, which depicts measures lower than the mean, the frequencies again become progressively fewer until there are no more.

Figure A.3 also shows where standard deviations fall in a normal distribution and indicates the proportion of the population bracketed by standard deviations. You see that the area beneath the curve bracketed by the lines at −1 and +1 standard deviations includes 68.26 percent—roughly two-thirds—of all the measures. By going out to −2 to +2 standard deviations, we account for 95.44 percent of all measures, and at −3 to +3 standard deviations, 99.75 percent of the population measures are accounted for.

Be sure to take into account, too, that 95 percent of all the population scores are included in the area bracketed by +1.96 standard deviations down to −1.96 standard deviations.

These areas beneath the curve depict the .05 level used for expressions of confidence and tests of significance—this is the α-level. The area bracketed by +2.58 down to –2.58 standard deviations includes 99 percent of all scores, which equates to the .01 probability level.

Relative Standings Associated with the Normal Curve

Relative standing, which shows the placement of an individual in relation to others measured in the same way, is typically indicated by percentile rankings and occasionally by stanine rankings, which we have explored, and by z scores and T scores as well. These relationships are shown in Figure A.4.

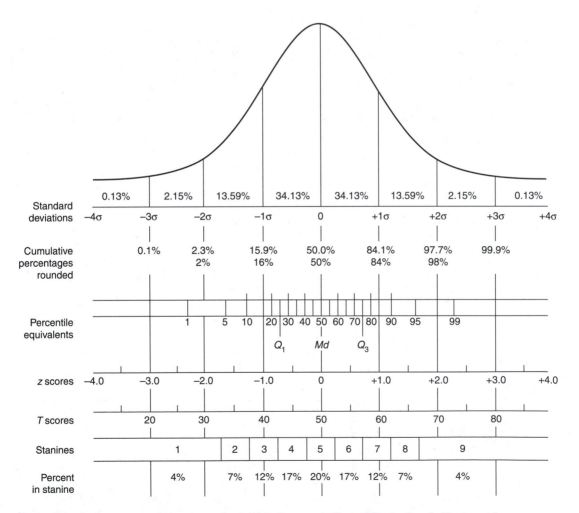

FIGURE A.4   **The relationship of standard deviations, as well as several other indicators of relative position, to the normal curve**

Percentile Rankings

Suppose Steve has taken a science aptitude test and is told his performance places him at the 73rd percentile. This means that Steve's score was as high as, or higher than, 73 percent of all people similar to Steve who had taken the test. This does not mean that Steve responded correctly to 73 percent of the test problems but simply that he performed better than 73 percent of others of his status who have taken the test. Note the words *similar to Steve* and *of his status.* Those qualifiers indicate that Steve, in sixth grade, is not to be compared directly with Frank, who is in eleventh grade. They might have made the same raw score on the test, but Frank might have reached only the 49th percentile, because eleventh-grade students make higher scores than do sixth-grade students. The population that includes Steve is all sixth-grade students. Frank is in a different population—all eleventh-grade students.

As you can see in Figure A.4, percentile rankings range from a low of 1 (1st percentile) to a high of 99 (99th percentile). There is no 0th percentile or 100th percentile; the assumption is made that there could always be a lower or higher score. The mean and the median in a normal distribution both fall at the 50th percentile.

Stanines

Look beneath the curve in Figure A.4 to where stanines are represented. Stanines (as mentioned earlier in the text, the name comes from "standard nine") are bands of scores used for convenience. They begin at the mean, with the middle stanine, the fifth, covering the area from +.25 standard deviation to −.25 standard deviation. Except for the first and the ninth stanines, each stanine covers one-half of a standard deviation, the fourth, third, and second progressively downward, and the sixth, seventh, and eighth progressively upward. The first stanine includes all scores below the second, and the ninth stanine includes all scores above the eighth.

Steve's 73rd percentile ranking falls in the sixth stanine. Notice that his percentile ranking shows his placement more precisely than does his stanine ranking.

Z Scores

Z scores (not shown in Figure A.4) are converted scores that indicate a score's relative position in terms of fractions of standard deviations. If Ann were assigned a z score of +.5, that would mean that her raw score was one-half of a standard deviation above the mean. If Heather were assigned a z score of −.35, that would mean that her raw score was .35 of a standard deviation below the mean. A z score is calculated using the following formula:

$$z = \frac{X - \mu}{\sigma}$$

where X = the individual's original raw score

μ = the population mean

σ = the population standard deviation

T Scores

***T* scores** (another type of converted score, not to be confused with the *t* test) correspond perfectly to *z* scores, except that they begin with an artificial mean of 50, with each standard deviation given a value of 10. *T* scores are direct conversions of *z* scores but with all values being positive. Ann's *z* score of +.5 would convert to a *T* score of 55, whereas Heather's *z* score of −.35 would convert to a *T* score of 46.5. A *T* score is calculated in the following manner:

$$T = 50 + 10z$$

where 50 = the mean of the *T* score scale

10 = the standard deviation of the *T* score scale

z = the individual's *z* score

In practice, *z* scores and *T* scores are not widely used, although they represent relative standings as accurately as do percentile rankings and much more accurately than do stanine rankings.

Calculating and Interpreting Inferential Statistics

Inferential statistics are used to make inferences about the population, based on what has been learned about the sample. They include

1. Error estimates that indicate the range within which a given measure probably lies

   Example: *If the study were repeated many times, the correlation would probably continue to fall between .28 and .36.*

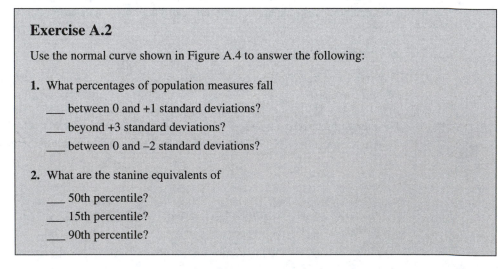

Exercise A.2

Use the normal curve shown in Figure A.4 to answer the following:

1. What percentages of population measures fall

   ____ between 0 and +1 standard deviations?

   ____ beyond +3 standard deviations?

   ____ between 0 and −2 standard deviations?

2. What are the stanine equivalents of

   ____ 50th percentile?

   ____ 15th percentile?

   ____ 90th percentile?

2. Confidence levels that indicate the probability that a population value lies within certain specified boundaries

   Example: *There is 95 percent probability that the population value lies between .22 and .42.*

3. Tests of significance, which indicate whether a finding is sufficiently strong to outweigh the effect of chance errors that might have been made in selecting the sample. Frequently seen tests of significance include:

   ■ Significance of correlation

     Example: *If the study were repeated hundreds of times, errors made in selecting the sample would account for a correlation of this magnitude less than 5 percent of the time. This is symbolized* p < .05.

   ■ Significance of difference between means of small samples (*t* test)

     Example: *If the study were repeated hundreds of times, a difference of this magnitude could be attributed to sampling error in fewer than 5 percent of the cases* (p < .05).

   ■ Significance of difference between or among means (analysis of variance *F* **test**)

     Explanation: Same as for difference between means

   If the test of significance leads us to believe (usually at 95 percent probability or greater) that a particular finding has not occurred because of errors we made in selecting the sample, we call the finding "significant." In this case we may conclude that the finding is probably real for the population. If, on the other hand, the probability level is unacceptably high (usually greater than 5 percent) that our finding might have occurred because of errors we made in selecting the sample, we deem the finding "not significant." In this case we would conclude that the finding is probably not real for the population.

Exercise A.3

Supply the appropriate name for each of the following:

1. The most frequent made score
2. The relationship between two sets of scores made by the same individuals
3. The arithmetic average of the scores
4. The difference between the highest and lowest score in a group
5. A finding is probably real for the population—not attributable to sample error
6. The true measure for the sample probably lies within these boundaries
7. There is a 95 percent probability that the population mean lies within these boundaries
8. Statistics used to make judgments about the population
9. John's score equaled or surpassed 68 percent of all scores
10. Measures that show spread or diversion

Chi-Square—Its Calculation and Interpretation

Chi-square is a nonparametric inferential statistical procedure frequently used in research. The descriptive and inferential statistics discussed to this point have all been parametric procedures, involving variable interval data (e.g., scores) that are presumed to be distributed normally in the population. As you recall, nonparametric statistics such as chi-square are applied to data that are not assumed to be normally distributed in the population. Chi-square is frequently used when data can be placed into categories. To elaborate upon an earlier example, suppose that you wish to determine which of three courses—geometry, English, or biology—Elmwood students consider most valuable in their daily lives. You randomly select from the eleventh-grade Elmwood population a sample of 30 students who took the three courses when in tenth grade. You state a null hypothesis that eleventh-grade students see no differences in value among the geometry, English, and biology courses they took in tenth grade. If the null hypothesis is true, then students will show no pattern of preference; they will choose the three courses equally—perhaps ten selecting geometry, ten selecting English, and ten selecting biology. This equality of choice is what you expect to observe if the null hypothesis is correct.

But suppose that when the 30 students are asked to indicate which of the courses they believe most valuable, they respond as follows: 3 select geometry; 19 select English; and 8 select biology. Those response choices are what you actually do observe.

By statistically comparing what you expect to observe against what you actually do observe, it is possible to determine whether differences between the two are significant. The procedure for calculating and interpreting chi-square is shown as follows.

Using the example figures and the formula for chi-square, we can complete calculations by hand. The formula we use is

$$\chi^2 = \Sigma \frac{(f_o - f_e)^2}{f_e}$$

where χ^2 = chi-square

   Σ = sum of

$(f_o - f_e)^2$ = the square of the difference, for each category, between the observed frequencies and those that were expected. Each square is divided by the appropriate expected frequency, and the results are then summated.

Let us proceed to Table A.2 for a concrete example.

Having obtained a chi-square value of 13.4, we determine its level of significance by consulting a table of critical values for chi-square, presented in Table A.3. The degrees of freedom (df) for our example is 2 (the number of categories minus 1). Check Table A.3 for 2 df and read across to the right. You can see that our 13.4 surpasses the critical value at the .01 level of significance. Based on that, we can reasonably reject the null hypothesis of no difference in course preferences.

TABLE A.2   Calculation of Chi-Square

Course	Observed	Expected	$(f_o - f_e)$	$(f_o - f_e)^2$	$(f_o - f_e)^2/f_e$
Geometry	3	10	−7	49	4.9
English	19	10	9	81	8.1
Biology	8	10	−2	4	.4
					$\chi^2 = 13.4$

TABLE A.3   Table of Critical Values for Chi-Square

df	0.05	0.01	df	0.05	0.01
1	3.841	6.635	16	26.296	32.000
2	5.991	9.210	17	27.587	33.409
3	7.815	11.345	18	28.869	34.805
4	9.488	13.277	19	30.144	36.191
5	11.070	15.086	20	31.410	37.566
6	12.592	16.812	21	32.671	38.932
7	14.067	18.475	22	33.924	40.289
8	15.507	20.090	23	35.172	41.638
9	16.919	21.666	24	36.415	42.980
10	18.307	23.209	25	37.652	44.314
11	19.675	24.725	26	38.885	45.642
12	21.026	26.217	27	40.113	46.963
13	22.362	27.688	28	41.337	48.278
14	23.685	29.141	29	42.557	49.588
15	24.996	30.578	30	43.773	50.892

Source: Adapted from Table IV, p. 47, of Fisher and Yates: *Statistical Tables for Biological, Agricultural and Medical Research,* published by Longman Group Ltd., London (previously published by Oliver and Boyd, Ltd., Edinburgh).

Calculating and Interpreting Standard Error and Confidence Limits

We know that samples are almost never exactly like the populations from which they come. Therefore, we must accept that means, correlations, and other statistical values and findings in the sample are not exactly the same as their parametric counterparts in the population.

In order to estimate how closely a statistic matches its corresponding population parameter, we employ a concept called *standard error.* Standard error can be understood as follows: Suppose we have a population for which we know a parameter. Let us say the population comprises all eleventh-grade students in the state of Kansas, and the parameter that we know is those students' mean grade point average. If we obtained a number of samples from that population and for each sample computed a mean grade point average, we would find that most of the sample means differed somewhat from the population mean, some by tiny amounts and a few by larger amounts. If we plotted those differences we would find that they formed themselves into a distribution shaped like the normal probability curve. In other words, the differences between sample values and their corresponding population values are normally distributed and can, therefore, be analyzed by means of parametric statistics. We can compute a mean of those differences and a standard deviation of those differences, just as if they were raw scores.

Now, let us suppose that we have selected a random sample from a population whose parameters we do not know—let it be a sample of 50 male students from the population of all eleventh-grade male students in the state of Nebraska. This time we measure the heights of those 50 students and calculate a mean and standard deviation. We can obtain a good estimate of how closely this mean approximates that of the population, even though we do not know the population mean. This is done through use of the following formula for determining the standard error of the sample mean:

$$SE_{\bar{X}} = \frac{SD}{\sqrt{N}}$$

where $SE_{\bar{X}}$ = standard error of mean

SD = standard deviation of the sample

N = size of sample

Suppose the mean height for our sample is 69 inches, with a standard deviation of 2 inches. The standard error of our sample mean equals 2 (the sample standard deviation) divided by 7.07 (the square root of 50), which gives a standard error of .28 inches. Now if we say that the real (population) mean does not differ from the sample mean by more than +2.01 standard errors and −2.01 standard errors from the sample mean, we have a 95 percent probability of being correct. In other words, the chances are that if we selected another 1,000 samples from the population, in about 95 percent of those samples the mean height would be between 69.56 inches—our sample mean of 69 inches plus (.28 inches × 2.01)—and 68.44 inches—our sample mean of 69 inches minus (.28 inches × 2.01).

The upper level of 69.56 and the lower level of 68.44 in this case are used to state *confidence limits*. We can "confidently" say that if we repeated the study thousands of times, we would find a mean height between 69.56 inches and 68.44 inches at least 95 percent of the time.

Standard error can be computed for several measures other than the mean, most notably single measurements (e.g., one person's score on a test), differences between means, and correlations. To determine the standard error of a single measurement we must know the reliability coefficient of the measuring scale or test. The formula is

$$SE_M = SD\sqrt{1 - r}$$

where SE_M = standard error of the measurement

SD = standard deviation of test

r = reliability coefficient of test

The result obtained from this calculation is applied just as was the standard error of the mean.

A similar procedure is used to determine the standard error of the difference between means. In studies that involve comparisons, researchers administer a test to two or more groups and then analyze the differences in mean performance of those groups. Suppose we had drawn two 50-student samples from the population of eleventh-grade boys in Nebraska, then given one of the samples two weeks' training in muscle stretching, then tested both groups for the number of chin-ups they could do, and found a difference of .5 chin-ups between the mean of group X and the mean of group Y. We know that if the study were repeated many times, the difference between the means would vary from study to study. Therefore, we wish to find the standard error of the difference between means. However, before we can calculate the standard error, we must first pool the variances of the two samples. This is accomplished through the use of the following formula:

$$ s_p^2 = \frac{SS_X + SS_Y}{df_X + df_Y} $$

where s_p^2 = pooled variance

SS = sums of squares (for each group)

df = degrees of freedom ($n - 1$, for each group)

Once we have calculated the pooled variance, we can use its value and the following formula to calculate the standard error of the difference between means:

$$ SE_{dM} = \sqrt{\frac{s_p^2}{n_X} + \frac{s_p^2}{n_Y}} $$

where SE_{dM} = standard error of the difference between the means

s_p^2 = pooled variance

n = sample size (for each group)

Suppose that the pooled variance for the two groups was equal to 10. Substituting this value into the equation for the standard error would result in a value equal to .63. If this study were repeated hundreds of times, about 95 percent of those repetitions would reveal mean differences within a range of -1.25 and $+1.25$ (i.e., .63 times ± 1.98, which is the critical value for t) from the difference between the means observed in this study.

In all of these cases, you can see that the standard error is inversely proportional to the number of participants in the sample. In other words, the larger the sample, the smaller the standard error. As the sample size approaches that of the population, the standard error shrinks to zero.

Testing for Significance

Findings such as correlations and differences among means are routinely tested for significance. Significance of the coefficient of correlation is determined by consulting a table of critical values for *r*, as presented in Table A.4. You will notice that the table calls

TABLE A.4   Table of Critical Values for Correlation Coefficients (for Both One- and Two-Tailed Tests)

Example: When *N* is 52 and (*N* – 2) is 50, an *r* must be > .273 to be significant at .05 level, and > .354 to be significant at .01 level.

Degrees of Freedom (*N* – 2)	Level of significance for one-tailed test .025	.005	Degrees of Freedom (*N* – 2)	Level of significance for one-tailed test .025	.005
	Level of significance for two-tailed test .05	.01		Level of significance for two-tailed test .05	.01
1	.997	1.000	24	.388	.496
2	.950	.990	25	.381	.487
3	.878	.959	26	.374	.478
4	.811	.917	27	.367	.470
5	.754	.874	28	.361	.463
6	.707	.834	29	.355	.456
7	.666	.798	30	.349	.449
8	.632	.765	35	.325	.418
9	.602	.735	40	.304	.393
10	.576	.708	45	.288	.372
11	.553	.684	50	.273	.354
12	.532	.661	60	.250	.325
13	.514	.641	70	.232	.302
14	.497	.623	80	.217	.283
15	.482	.606	90	.205	.267
16	.468	.590	100	.195	.254
17	.456	.575	125	.174	.228
18	.444	.561	150	.159	.208
19	.433	.549	200	.138	.181
20	.423	.537	300	.113	.148
21	.413	.526	400	.098	.128
22	.404	.515	500	.088	.115
23	.396	.505	1000	.062	.081

Source: From Garrett, Henry E. (1947). *Statistics in Psychology and Education,* Longman, p. 299. Reprinted by permission.

for **degrees of freedom** (*df*). Degrees of freedom in correlational analyses equal the number of pairs of scores minus 2. If you had 50 participants involved in a correlation, you would have 50 pairs of scores. Therefore, $N - 2$ would be 48 degrees of freedom. Suppose you have found a coefficient of correlation of .25 and you had specified an alpha level of .05. Fifty participants were involved in your study. According to Table A.4, does the coefficient of .25 reach the .05 level of significance?

See Figure A.2 for a sample correlation. For an alpha level of .01, check Table A.3 to determine whether or not this correlation is significant ($df = 11$).

Significance of the difference between means, when only two groups are being compared, can be determined by applying a *t* test and then consulting a table of critical values for *t*, as shown in Table A.5.

TABLE A.5   Table of Critical Values for *t* (for Both One- and Two-Tailed Tests)

Degrees of Freedom	Proportion in one tail		Degrees of Freedom	Proportion in one tail	
	.025	.005		0.25	.005
	Proportion in two tails			Proportion in two tails	
	.05	.01		.05	.01
1	$t = 12.71$	$t = 63.66$	20	2.09	2.84
2	4.30	9.92	21	2.08	2.83
3	3.18	5.84	22	2.07	2.82
4	2.78	4.60	23	2.07	2.81
5	2.57	4.03	24	2.06	2.80
6	2.45	3.71	25	2.06	2.79
7	2.36	3.50	26	2.06	2.78
8	2.31	3.36	27	2.05	2.77
9	2.26	3.25	28	2.05	2.76
10	2.23	3.17	29	2.04	2.76
11	2.20	3.11	30	2.04	2.75
12	2.18	3.06	35	2.03	2.72
13	2.16	3.01	40	2.02	2.71
14	2.14	2.98	45	2.02	2.69
15	2.13	2.95	50	2.01	2.68
16	2.12	2.92	60	2.00	2.66
17	2.11	2.90	70	2.00	2.65
18	2.10	2.88	80	1.99	2.64
19	2.09	2.86	90	1.99	2.63

Source: Garret, Henry E. (1947). From *Statistics in Psychology and Education*, Longman, p. 464. Reprinted by permission.

The formula for the t test is

$$t = \frac{\overline{X} - \overline{Y}}{SE_{dM}}$$

where $\overline{X}$ = mean of group X

$\overline{Y}$ = mean of group Y

SE_{dM} = standard error of the difference between means

Suppose you find a difference of 5.0 between two means, with a standard error of the difference between means of 2.0. Degrees of freedom are the total number of participants in both groups, minus 2. Suppose there were 25 participants in each group. Degrees of freedom would, therefore, be 50 minus 2, or 48. Now check Table A.5 at approximately 48 degrees of freedom. Is the difference significant at the .05 level? At the .01 level?

When data from three or more groups are being analyzed for differences among means, analysis of variance (abbreviated ANOVA) should be used. The use of ANOVA is also appropriate in place of a t test when the samples are relatively large and are unequal, provided the discrepancy is not extreme. Earlier you saw the relationship between variance and standard deviation: Variance is the square of standard deviation, and standard deviation the square root of variance.

In analyzing variance to explore difference among means, the variance that exists between groups is compared with the variance that exists within groups. Dividing between-groups variance by within-groups variance, we obtain an F ratio:

$$F = \frac{s^2_{between\text{-}groups}}{s^2_{within\text{-}groups}}$$

The resultant F ratio can be checked manually against a table of critical values of F (not provided here) to determine its significance level, but it is much easier to let the computer do it for you when it calculates analysis of variance.

Type I and Type II Errors

As you know, hypotheses are frequently stated in the null form for greater ease in applying tests of significance. In light of a significance test you have applied, you may reject your null hypothesis and conclude that your finding is real for the population, not due to error made in selecting the sample. Or else you may retain your null hypothesis and conclude that a particular finding is probably due to sampling error and thus is not real for the population. In either case, the statistical procedures you have used make you feel fairly confident about your decision. Still, you never know for sure whether you are right.

Research
Navigator.c⊕m

type I error

It may be that the null hypothesis is correct—that, for example, there is no difference between means or no correlation—but based on your statistical analysis you reject the hypothesis. When you reject a null hypothesis that is in reality true, you are said to have made a **Type I error.** Conversely, if you retain a null hypothesis when it is in reality false, you are said to have made a **Type II error.** To repeat

Type I error: You conclude that there is a correlation or a difference when in actuality there is not. (You wrongly reject the null hypothesis.)

Type II error: You conclude that there is not a correlation or a difference when in reality there is. (You wrongly retain the null hypothesis.)

The likelihood of your making Type I and Type II errors depends on the significance levels you set. Researchers do not wish to make errors of any kind, but generally speaking they would rather make a Type II error than a Type I error—that is, they would rather conclude that no correlation or difference exists (although one does) than to conclude that a correlation or difference exists when it does not. This preference is in keeping with the philosophy of science, which is to require a preponderance of proof before a new finding is accepted.

Review of Statistical Terminology

Descriptive Statistics	Inferential Statistics	Nonparametric Statistics
Central tendency	*Standard error*	*Proportions*
Mean	Of measurement	Chi-square
Median	Of mean	
Mode	Of differences between means	
Variability	*Tests of significance*	
Range	Of correlation	
Variance	Of difference between means	
Standard deviation		
Relative standing	*Analysis of variance*	
Percentile ranking	*Type I error*	
Stanines	*Type II error*	
Grade equivalents		
Age equivalents		

LIST OF IMPORTANT TERMS

degrees of freedom

F test

measures of central tendency

measures of variability

nonparametric statistics

normal probability curve

parametric statistics

significance

standard error

T scores

Type I error

Type II error

z scores

ANSWERS TO EXERCISES

A.1. 1. 6.7 2. 2, yes 3. 2.5 4. 7 5. $\overline{X} = 9$, $Mdn = 9$

A.2. 1. 34.13, .13, 47.72   2. 5, 3, 8

A.3. 1. Mode 2. Correlation 3. Mean 4. Range
   5. Significant 6. Error estimate 7. Confidence
level 8. Inferential statistics 9. Percentile rank
10. Measures of variability, such as range, variance, standard deviation.

A P P E N D I X   B

Using *TakeNote!* to Organize Your Research Reports

Overview

Sometimes the most difficult aspect of developing a research proposal or final research report is actually getting organized and then sitting down to write it. *TakeNote!* (Version 2.0) is an incredibly easy-to-use software program that helps you do just that—*get organized and write.* The program itself installs easily and quickly, regardless of platform (PC or Mac). PC users should be running Windows 95 or higher; Macintosh users can be using any operating system, but installation is easiest on System 7.5 or higher.* One note for Macintosh users who are running OS X: you must start your computer in the Classic (OS 9) environment in order to receive the full benefits of *TakeNote!*.

It is not the intent of the authors to reiterate in this appendix step-by-step procedures, such as those outlined in the *TakeNote!* primer, which is available with the software. In contrast, the focus of this appendix is to provide you with an example of a *TakeNote!* project. This project was developed by the first author of this textbook for a research study recently completed and currently being written up for presentation at a conference and possible publication.

A *TakeNote!* Sample Project

The research study used to develop this example was one that investigated classroom teachers' assessment practices and their knowledge of assessment and measurement terminology, concepts, and standards. I began my *TakeNote!* project by assembling the literature I had collected, consisting primarily of copies of journal articles and conference papers. While in the *Notes* mode, I created the following folders so I could begin categorizing my research notes:

- *Research on Classroom Assessment*
- *Standards for Teacher Competence in the Educational Assessment of Students*
- *What Is "Assessment Literacy"?*
- *Research on Assessment Literacy and/or the Standards*

*As mentioned in the Preface, the *TakeNote!* software is available as an extra value package option; therefore, some students may have received the software package with their copies of this textbook. *TakeNote!* can be ordered through your local sales representative.

Some of these folders also contained subfolders (e.g., the *Research on Classroom Assessment* folder also contained a folder named *Research on Teachers' Assessment Practices*). At the outset, this was my attempt to organize the research I was reviewing. However, little did I realize at the time that it would also later become my literature review outline (i.e., the folders became the major headings for my literature review). This became an incredibly easy way to initially organize—and later revise the organization of—my literature review.

I then began taking notes as I read the literature I had collected. Each note was created through the use of the Card Editor (see Figure B.1). Each note card was titled and categorized. An important feature of *TakeNote!* is that each card includes the reference citation from which the notes were taken. This is a wonderful feature that prevents you from reading something and later forgetting from where it came.

After several hours of reviewing articles and creating and organizing my notes, I had several note cards in each of my original folders (see Figure B.2). My research notes were really beginning to take shape. Note cards can easily be reorganized by simply clicking on them and dragging them to the desired folder.

While taking notes in the *Notes* mode, I simultaneously created new references in order to track my sources and link them to my note cards. I did this using two different techniques. While in the Card Editor window, I could click on the icon immediately to the left of Source and a new box titled Available Sources opens (see Figure B.3). Listed in this box are all the references that I previously created. I could link this new note card to an already existing source by selecting the reference from the list and clicking the Add button. The existing source is now listed in the Source box.

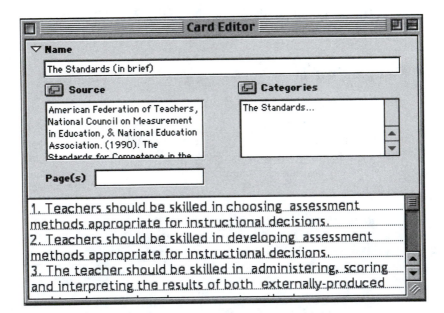

FIGURE B.1   Sample research note created with the Card Editor

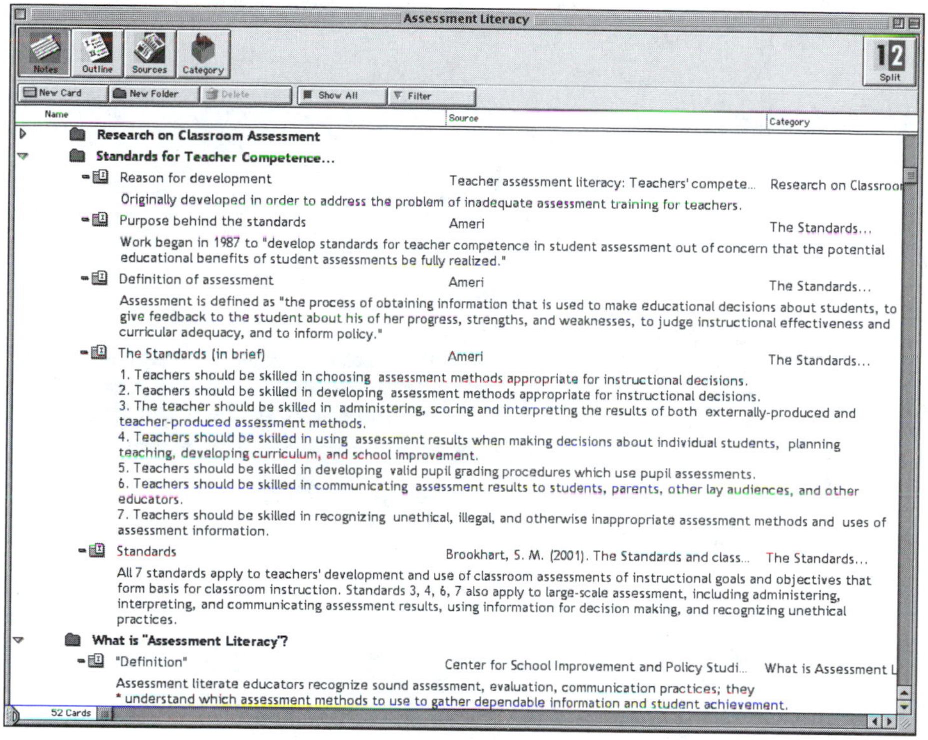

FIGURE B.2   Folders and research note cards, as viewed in the *Notes* mode

If I needed to create a new source, I simply clicked on the New button under Available Sources in the Card Editor and the Source Editor window opened. The alternative technique for creating new references is to click the large button for the *Sources* mode at the top left of the *TakeNote!* window and then click on New Source. When the new generic source appeared in the source list, clicking on the icon to its left would also open the Source Editor window. Creating sources with the Source Editor is quite easy, since it includes 19 predefined Source Types, as well as a Custom style (see Figure B.4). The predefined source formats include books, journal articles, edited works, online discussions, reviews, and World Wide Web sites. When I selected the appropriate source type, *TakeNote!* provided only the necessary fields for the citation that I needed to include.

The Source Editor window also provides the opportunity to view an example citation similar to the one being created (see Figure B.4). Once I finished entering all of the pertinent information for a given source type and for my specific reference (see Figure B.5), I closed the Source Editor window and my newly created source appeared in my reference list (*Sources* mode), in APA (5th edition) format, and in proper alphabetical order (see Figure B.6).

I discovered that *TakeNote!* also offers another method of linking sources to specific note cards through the use of the Split screen feature. I first clicked on the Split button

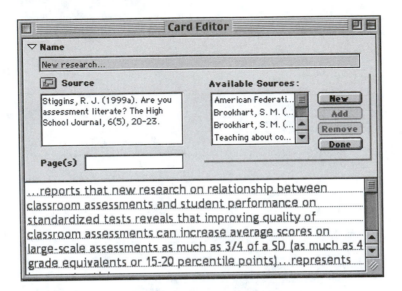

FIGURE B.3   The Card Editor window, highlighting the integration with the *Sources* mode.

Source Editor

Source Type:
- Article in a Journal
- Article in a Magazine
- Article in a Newspaper
- Article in a Reference Work
- Article in an Online Journal
- Article in an Online Magazine
- Article in an Online Newspaper
- Book with Author
- Book with Editor
- Editorial
- Government Document
- Letter to the Editor
- Multi-volume Work
- Online Posting in a Discussion List
- Online Synchronous Communication
- Review
- Translation
- WWW Site
- Work in an Anthology

Custom

Author

Year

Title

Journal

Volume

Issue

Pages

Example:
Wurzbacher, N. Effects of alternative therapies on the mentally ill. *Journal of the American Medical Association*, 12(8), 96-98.

FIGURE B.4   The Source Editor window, highlighting the various predefined Source Types

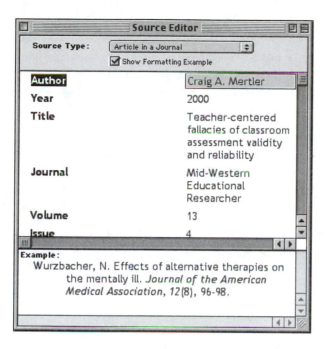

FIGURE B.5   The completed information for a newly
created source in the Source Editor

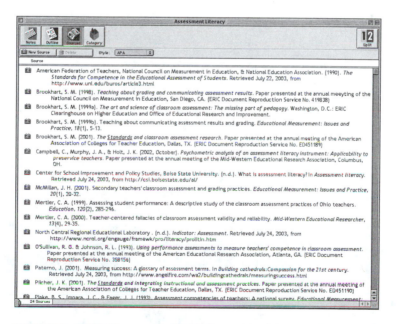

FIGURE B.6   The *Sources* mode window, with alphabetically
arranged source list in APA format

(upper-right corner in the *TakeNote!* window) in order to show two windows. I selected the *Notes* mode in the left window and the *Sources* mode in the right window. If I wanted to change the reference for a specific note card or add a reference if I had forgotten to do so in the Card Editor, I simply clicked on a source in the right window and dragged it to the note card to which I wanted it linked (see Figure B.7).

Once I had completed my review of all of the articles I had located and, therefore, completed my research notes, I was ready to begin preparing the outline for my final research paper. I wanted to work from a complete outline, so, while in the *Notes* mode, I created several additional folders for the following sections (and subsections, where appropriate) that I knew I would also need in my final report (see Figure B.8):

- *Introduction*
- *Methodology* (including subfolders for *Participants, Instrumentation,* and *Data Collection Procedures*)
- *Results* (including subfolders for *Descriptive Results for Preservice Teachers, Descriptive Results for Inservice Teachers,* and *Comparative Results*)
- *Conclusions/Discussion*

Note that, in order to view the entire contents in one screen, I "collapsed" the folders by clicking on the triangles to their left (i.e., I changed the ▼ to ▶).

Developing the outline for the final paper was a couple of simple steps away. I first utilized the Split feature once again, with the *Notes* mode on the left and the *Outline* mode

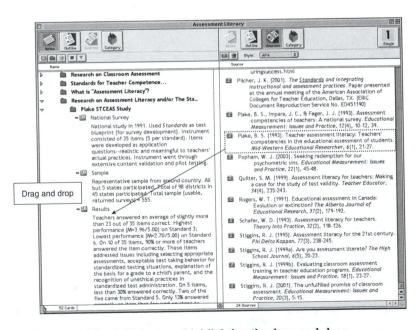

FIGURE B.7   The Split feature, highlighting the drag-and-drop capabilities of *TakeNote!*

FIGURE B.8   The final set of folders and subfolders in preparation for developing the outline for the final paper

on the right. I selected the entire contents of the *Notes* mode window (this can be done by either clicking the mouse once and dragging the arrow over the entire contents or by selecting Edit and Select All from the *TakeNote!* menu bar). I then dragged the entire contents of the *Notes* mode window on the left to the *Outline* mode window on the right (see Figure B.9).

After this dragging-and-dropping procedure, the resulting outline appears on the *Outline* mode window on the right (see Figure B.10). There are several different ways to format an outline in *TakeNote!* through the use of the pop-up menu labeled Format. These formats include plain numeric, alphanumeric, roman, and legal (shown in Figure B.10).

Once I completed my work in *TakeNote!* I needed to either print or export the contents of my project. In the Print dialog, I had options to print my note cards, outline, and/or references. Note cards could be printed in a variety of ways—"standard" (notes are printed one after another in paragraph format), "WYSIWYG" or "What You See Is What You Get" (notes are printed as they appear on the *TakeNote!* screen), "3 × 5 cards" (notes are printed to appear as 3 × 5 index cards), or "4 × 6 cards" (printed to appear as 4 × 6 index cards). Outlines and references are printed in "standard" format.

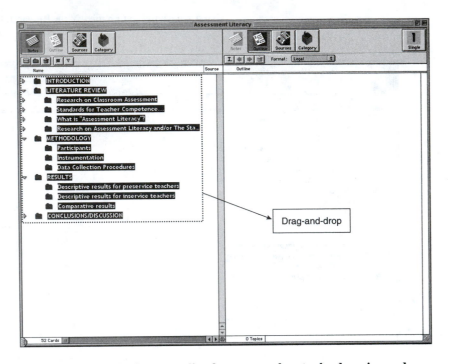

FIGURE B.9   Developing an outline from research notes by dragging and dropping in the Split feature

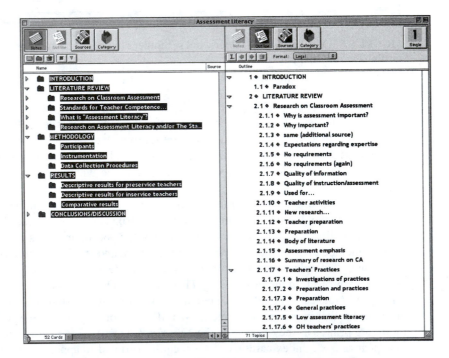

FIGURE B.10   Newly created outline, formatted using legal style

However, since I knew that I would now need to write the complete paper, I decided to export the project file so I could work on it in a word processing program. I selected File and Export from the menu bar; the resulting dialog box shown in Figure B.11 then appeared:

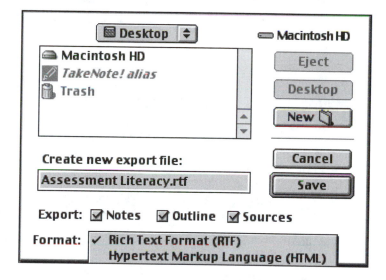

FIGURE B.11   The dialog box for exporting *TakeNote!* projects

I was presented with options to export my notes, outline, and sources by checking the appropriate boxes. I chose to export all three. Next, I chose to export the file in rich text format or "RTF" (this format is "understood" by most word processing software programs). I also had the option of exporting the file in HTML if I had wanted to post the file on a World Wide Web site. Once I clicked Save, a single file containing all three components (i.e., notes, outline, and sources) was saved on my desktop. Since I use Microsoft Word, I could simply double-click on the file icon to open the exported file. Users of other word processing programs may have to start their program and select File and Open in order to view the exported file.

The exported file opened easily and worked perfectly. Figures B.12, B.13, and B.14 show how my notes, outline, and sources looked when I viewed the exported file in Microsoft Word for the first time.

In my estimation, *TakeNote!* is simply the easiest way to organize, develop, and format research papers. Not only did using the program facilitate my organization of the paper, but also it did so in substantially less time than the "old-fashioned" method of taking notes by hand on index cards or on a legal pad. Additionally, the program is very intuitive—it only took working with it for a short while to become comfortable using it.

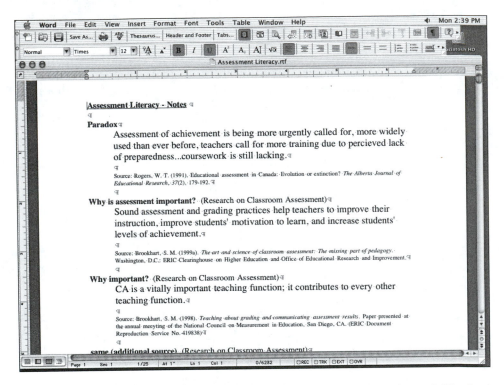

FIGURE B.12   Exported notes from a *TakeNote!* project, as viewed in Microsoft Word

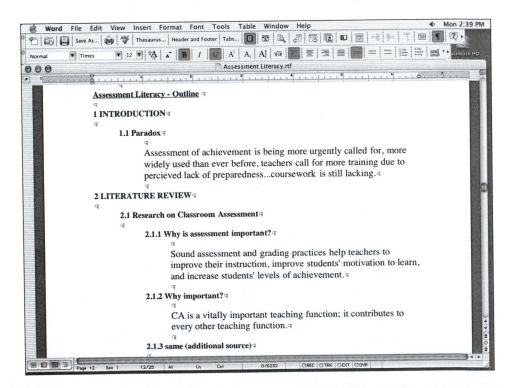

FIGURE B.13   Exported outline from a *TakeNote!* project, as viewed in Microsoft Word

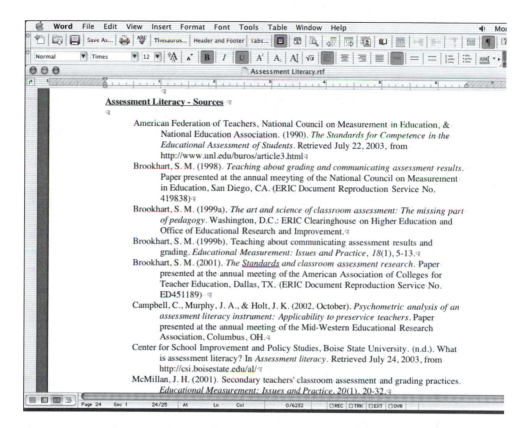

FIGURE B.14 **Exported references from a *TakeNote!* project, as viewed in Microsoft Word**

Finally, for those who are interested, the final version of the research report written from this *TakeNote!* project is available on the Companion Website (www.ablongman.com/mertler5e), in PDF format, under the section titled **Appendix B: Using *TakeNote!* to Organize Your Research Reports.**

GLOSSARY

Abstract A short summary, presented at the beginning of a research report

Action research Research done to develop or improve a product, procedure, or program in a particular setting, with no intention of generalizing the results

Age equivalents Converted scores that indicate the mean raw scores made by persons at different age levels on standardized tests. Example: John's raw score equals eighth year, sixth month

Age norms Values accompanying certain standardized tests that indicate mean performance of subjects at different age levels (*see* age equivalents)

Alpha (α) level The probability level (significance level) that a researcher establishes as acceptable before conducting a test of significance

Amorphous topic A research topic that is too vague; it needs to be clarified, refined, sharpened

Analysis The verbal or statistical treatment of research data to help answer questions and test hypotheses. Also, the process of obtaining information through critical examination of an entity or its various elements

Analysis criteria Guidelines for procedures and points to consider when analyzing processes or products

Analysis of variance (ANOVA) A statistical method for testing the null hypothesis when differences between two or more groups are involved, done by comparing between-groups variance against within-groups variance

Applied research Research done for the express purpose of solving an existing problem

Artificial dichotomy An either–or classification of data, based on judgment (e.g., tall–short; above average–below average)

Assumption Something believed to be true, but not actually verified; important assumptions are usually listed in theses and dissertations

Back material Material placed after the body of a thesis or dissertation, such as bibliography and appendix

Basic research A type of research done merely to gain knowledge, without regard for practical application

Biserial correlation A correlation between variables when one variable is expressed as continuous variable data, such as test scores, and the other as an artificial dichotomy, such as poor–wealthy

Bivariate correlation A correlation that involves two variables

Case study A detailed investigation centered upon a single participant

Causal-comparative research A type of research used to explore possible cause–effect relationships in which the independent (causal) variable cannot be manipulated, as would be the case for gender, handedness, ethnicity, and the like

Cause–effect relationship A relationship between two or more variables where changes in one variable produce changes in a second variable. The first is called the cause, the second the effect.

Central tendency A statistical concept referring to what is typical for a group. Measures of central tendency include mean, median, and mode

Chain sample A sample resulting from initial participants who identify other individuals to participate in a study; see also *snowball sample* and *network sample*

Chi-square A nonparametric statistical procedure used to determine the significance of differences between groups when data are nominal and placed in categories. The procedure compares what is observed against what was expected

CIJE *Current Index to Journals in Education,* an index that lists and summarizes journal articles related to education

Cluster sample A sample consisting of one or more groups already in existence, such as the fourth-grade classes at Cutter Elementary School

Coefficient of correlation The numerical expression of the degree of relationship between two or more variables. It varies in magnitude from 0 (no correlation) to 1.0 (perfect correlation) and may be positive or negative

Comparison group A group, sometimes called a control group, against which an experimental group is compared

Comparison report A general type of research report that compares one or more groups against each other. (Other general types of research reports are status reports and relationship reports.)

Conclusions The investigator's interpretations of research findings

Confounding variable A variable, other than those being explored in a given study, that affects the research outcomes

Constant   A characteristic that is the same for all subjects involved in a study—it might be that all are female or all attend the same school, and so forth.

Continuous variable   A quantitative variable that can assume a large number of different values. Most tests yield continuous variable data

Control group   A group in an experimental study that receives no treatment, and against which the experimental group is compared

Convenience sampling   A procedure of selecting a sample consisting of whomever happens to be conveniently present; example: a group at a playground

Conventions   Agreed-on way of doing things, as procedures in research

Correlation   A covarying relationship between two or more sets of data, as between measures of height and weight

Correlational report   A research report that depicts a covarying relationship between two or more variables

Correlational research   A type of research used to explore correlation between two or more variables, as between IQ and reading ability

Criterion-referenced test   A test whose items are directly linked to specific objectives of instruction

Criterion variable   In prediction studies using correlations, the variable that one attempts to predict

Cross-sectional survey   A survey that obtains data from several different groups of subjects at the same time

DAI   *Dissertation Abstracts International,* a publication that provides abstracts of doctoral dissertations done in the United States and Europe

Data   Basic information obtained in research. The word is traditionally used in its true plural sense (e.g., the data are...) but is increasingly used as if it were singular (e.g., the data is...)

Database   Indexed reference sources and other resources, usually provided for access by computer

Degrees of freedom   The number of observations that are free to vary, used in determining levels of probability

Delimitations   Restrictions that researchers impose in order to narrow the scope of a study

Dependent variable   The "effect" variable in a cause-effect relationship; example: A new method (the independent or causal variable) is being used to improve learning of algebra (the dependent or effect variable)

Description   A means of collecting data by making notations of what is observed

Descriptive research   A type of research used to depict present-day people, conditions, settings, and events

Descriptive statistics   Numerical values that describe subjects and their behavior; also the mathematical procedures used in establishing those values

Descriptor   A term that is used to locate information in the ERIC references or other cataloguing materials

Dichotomous variable   A categorical variable consisting of only two characteristics—either-or

Difference between means   One of the methods used to show the difference between traits or performances of two groups of subjects

Directional research hypothesis   A hypothesis that states what the researcher actually expects to find, as regards both magnitude and direction—e.g., girls will perform better than boys

Discrete variable   A variable that may assume only a limited number of values—for example, ethnic group affiliation

Discriminant analysis   A correlational procedure that predicts, from two or more predictor variables, a criterion variable that is expressed as two separate categories

Educational research   The careful, patient, systematic investigation of topics related to education

ERIC   Educational Resources Information Center, a clearinghouse of information related to education

Ethnographic research   A type of research used to describe group behavior and interactions within social settings

Evaluation research   A type of research used to determine the relative value of products, procedures, and programs

Evidence of validity   Various sources of information used to establish the validity of test data

Experimental design   The plan for research to determine what effect manipulation of an independent variable might have on the dependent variable. There are several different experimental designs

Experimental group   The group in an experiment that receives a new treatment, the effects of which are being explored

Experimental research   A type of research used to explore possible cause-effect relationships. The independent variable is systematically varied to determine the resultant effects on a dependent variable.

***Ex post facto* research**   A name from Latin meaning "that which was done afterward." The effect under investigation has already occurred, but the cause is not clear. Another name for causal-comparative research; the independent variable cannot be manipulated.

External criticism   The careful scrutiny of qualitative data, done to determine authenticity of the source

External validity   The extent to which findings of a particular study can be generalized elsewhere

Extraneous variable   A physical or environmental confounding variable that is usually temporary, such as fatigue, distraction, or nervousness

***F* test**   A test for determining the probability that differences among two or more means occurred by chance

Factor analysis   A process that identifies clusters of correlated variables, referred to as factors, and then correlates those factors with the criterion variable

Findings   The principal discoveries made in research

Front material   Material that is placed before the body of a thesis or dissertation, such as table of contents and list of figures

Grade equivalents   Scores that indicate grade level, converted from mean raw scores made by students at various grade levels

Grade norms   Values accompanying certain standardized tests that indicate mean scores made by students at different grade levels (*see* grade equivalents)

Historical research   A type of research that explores people, events, conditions, and settings of the past

Hypothesis   A testable statement of a predicted relationship or difference among certain variables

Hypothetico-inductive process   A thought process that constructs meaning from data obtained through observation; used in qualitative research. Synonymous with logico-inductive

Independent variable   The causative variable in a cause-effect relationship. The independent variable is intentionally manipulated, when possible, to observe the effects it might bring about in the dependent variable

Inferential statistics   Numerical procedures for determining how closely sample statistics match their corresponding population parameters. Also, the values that result from those procedures

Informant   A person who presents opinion, informed views, or expert testimony used in research

Interim analysis   Data analysis that sometimes occurs in qualitative research, especially ethnographic research, before all the data are collected

Internal criticism   The careful scrutiny of qualitative research data, done to determine accuracy and trustworthiness of the data

Internal validity   The degree to which the effects of extraneous variables have been controlled in a study

Interval scales   Measurement scales expressed in equal numerical units, but not having a true zero point (examples: achievement tests, aptitude tests). Scores made on interval scales can be added and subtracted accurately, but not divided or multiplied

Intervening variable   A variable that alters the relationship that would otherwise exist between certain variables; example: motivation might be an intervening variable between method of teaching and student achievement

Interview   A method of obtaining data from subjects by orally asking them selected questions

Judgmental sampling   A procedure for drawing a sample of only certain segments of the population, such as high achievers or deviant students

Kendall tau   A method of correlating two sets of measures shown as rankings, when the number of pairs is less than ten

Likert scale   A scale used to assess attitude or opinion; subjects respond by indicating how strongly they agree or disagree with the statements provided

Likert-type scale   A scale used to assess items on a continuum other than an agree–disagree scale

Limitations (on research)   Natural conditions that restrict the scope of a study and may affect its outcomes

Logico-inductive analysis   A method of analyzing qualitative data by applying logical thought processes

Longitudinal survey   Research that collects data from the same group of subjects over months or years, usually to document changes that occur over time

Manual search   A library search of the literature, done manually with guides and indexes; contrasts with computer search

Mean   The arithmetic average of a set of scores

Measurement   Obtaining data by using tests, scales, and other measuring devices

Measures of central tendency   Summary numerical values that indicate what is typical for a group of scores

Measures of relationship   Numerical values that indicate the degree of relationships between two or more sets of scores made by the same group of participants

Measures of relative position   Numerical scores that indicate the location of an individual when compared to the population

Measures of variability   Summary numerical values that indicate the internal spread of a group of scores

Median   The midpoint in an array of scores arranged from highest to lowest. If there is an even number of scores, the median is the mean of the two middle scores

Meta-analysis   Research that synthesizes the results of a number of previous studies

Method (of the study)   The procedures followed in planning research and obtaining and analyzing research data

Mode The most frequently occurring test score or measurement

Multiple regression A correlational procedure in which a criterion variable is predicted from a combination of two or more predictor variables

Multivariate correlation A covarying relationship among three or more sets of data

Natural dichotomy An either–or categorization that occurs naturally, such as male–female

Negative correlation A correlation in which high scores on one measure tend to accompany low scores on the other, average tend to accompany average, and low tend to accompany high

Network sample A sample resulting from initial participants who identify other individuals to participate in a study; see also *snowball sample* and *chain sample*

Newspaper Abstracts A database accessible by computer that summarizes articles contained in a number of different newspapers

Nominal scales Measurement scales that classify data into two or more verbal (name) categories, indicating that the data are different but not quantifying the difference

Nondirectional research hypothesis A type of hypothesis that states that a difference or correlation will be found, but makes no further stipulations about the difference or correlation

Nonexperimental research Research that does not involve the manipulation of an independent variable to ascertain its effect on a dependent variable

Nonparametric statistics Statistics, particularly tests of significance, that do not involve variable or ratio data and do not make assumptions about how data are distributed

Nonprobability sampling A sampling procedure in which the researcher cannot specify the probability of individuals in the population being selected for the sample

Normal probability curve The bell-shaped curve to which the frequency of many variable traits corresponds and to which most statistics are related

Norm-referenced test A test that compares individuals' performance against the performance of a great many others

Norms Numerical summaries of test performances of a great many other individuals; norms usually accompany standardized tests

Notation A method of obtaining data by jotting down what is observed

NSSE Yearbooks Reviews of research on selected topics, published annually by the National Society for the Study of Education

Null hypothesis A hypothesis that states that no difference or relationship exists among specified variables

Open-ended questions Questions that leave wide latitude for response, such as "What is your opinion about the quality of today's schools?"

Operating rules of research The ground rules that investigators observe in order to maximize credibility (*see* principles of…)

Ordinal scale A scale that expresses data as rankings, rather than scores

Organismic variable A physical condition (e.g., poor eyesight) that influences a relationship between other variables

$p < .05; p < .01$ Levels of probability (significance) most frequently used by researchers when testing hypotheses. The .05 level indicates a less than 5 percent chance that a finding is occurring because of sampling error; the .01 level indicates a less than 1 percent chance

Parameters Numerical values that describe populations, in the same way that statistics describe samples

Parametric statistics Statistics or statistical tests involving variable or ratio data and based on the assumption that the sample reflects a normal distribution in the population

Partial correlation A covarying relationship that remains after the influence of one or more confounding variables has been removed mathematically (such as the relationship between vocabulary and reading ability, with the effects of intelligence removed)

Participant observer An ethnographic researcher who participates actively and completely in all activities of the group being studied

Pearson product-moment correlation A covarying relationship between sets of measures that are expressed as continuous interval data, such as test scores

Percentile rank A converted score that indicates the percentage of all scores that have been equaled or surpassed by a given performance. Example: Sue's score ranked at the 63rd percentile; she did as well as or better than 63 percent of the people who took the test

Periodical Abstracts A database that provides abstracts of articles from a number of popular magazines

Phi correlation A covarying relationship between sets of data when both sets are expressed as natural dichotomies

Point-biserial correlation A covarying relationship between sets of data when one is expressed as continuous variable data (such as test scores) and the other as a natural dichotomy—for example, male–female

Population The total group, represented by the sample, to whom research findings are to be generalized

Positive correlation A correlation in which high scores on one test tend to accompany high scores on the other, average tend to accompany average, and low tend to accompany low

Post hoc fallacy The unwarranted conclusion that because one event follows another, the first has caused the second

Predictive validity A quality present when one set of data can predict another that occurs at a later time

Predictor variable In correlations, the variable (e.g., motivation) used in attempting to predict the criterion variable (e.g., rate of learning)

Primary data Data that come from direct observation, measurement, eyewitness accounts, or firsthand reports

Primary source Eyewitnesses of events, firsthand accounts by originators of works and behavior, or the books, articles, and documents in which firsthand accounts are reported

Principle of accurate disclosure Individuals participating in research are to be informed accurately about the nature of the research and any unusual procedures or tasks in which they will be involved

Principle of beneficence Research is not done to harm individuals but to promote understanding, opportunity, quality, and improvement

Principle of confidentiality The anonymity of subjects involved in research is to be maintained

Principle of credibility Research must be believable; this is accomplished by following established conventions and giving close attention to data validity and reliability

Principle of generalizability The applicability of research findings to other groups and settings should be as wide as possible

Principle of honesty All research data are to be obtained, analyzed, and reported without bias or omission

Principle of importance The findings of research should likely contribute to human knowledge

Principle of parsimony Other things being equal, the simpler the research design, the better

Principle of probability All research conclusions are considered to be probabilities, not certainties

Principle of protection Research must not subject individuals to physical, mental, or emotional harm

Principle of replicability Proper procedures must be followed, and proper records kept, so that a given study can be repeated by other investigators elsewhere

Principle of researchability Research topics must be approachable through the scientific method and must take into account practical matters such as time, distance, and expenditures

Principle of rival explanations Research conclusions must remain open to, and be judged against, alternative explanations

Privileged observer An ethnograhpic researcher who is allowed to mingle with the group being studied

Probability levels Values that indicate degree of likelihood that a finding has occurred due to chance errors made in selecting a sample that does not reflect the population. Researchers most often use the 0.05 and 0.01 probability levels when testing for significance, values that are also called significance levels and confidence levels

Probability sampling Any sampling procedure that specifies the probability that each member of the population has of being selected for the sample

Problem The topic being investigated, once it has been refined

Problem statement A sentence or paragraph that explains the purpose of a given investigation

Procedures The steps followed in a study to obtain, analyze, and interpret data

Purposive sampling Intentionally selecting, in a nonrandom fashion, subjects who are likely to be able to furnish needed information

Qualitative data analysis The analysis of verbal data through use certain procedures of logical thinking

Qualitative research Research that yields extensive narrative data, which are analyzed verbally

Quantitative data analysis The analysis of numerical data through statistical procedures

Quantitative research Research that explores traits and situations from which numerical data are obtained

Quasi-experimental research A type of research very similar to experimental research, except that subjects are not randomly selected or assigned to groups

Questioning A means of obtaining data from subjects by posing questions that elicit responses

Questionnaire A formal set of written questions to which subjects respond in writing

Quota sample A sample selected to contain exact predetermined numbers (quotas) of people with specific characteristics, such as ethnicity or gender, for example, 20 boys and 20 girls

Random assignment A procedure of assigning subjects to groups so that every subject has an equal chance of being placed in any of the groups

Random sample   A group drawn from the population, with every member of the population having an equal chance of being selected

Range   A statistic defined as highest score in an array minus lowest score; a rough indicator of the spread of scores

Raw score   A test score or numerical measurement that has not been converted in any way

Reject the null hypothesis   Concluding that the evidence obtained does not adequately support the stated hypothesis

Relationship   The tendency for the scores on one variable to reflect the scores on another variable

Relative standing   Where one individual's score or measure stands in relation to those of all other individuals similarly measured

Reliability (of data)   An index of the consistency of data or test results; to be considered reliable, results must be very nearly the same, time after time

Reliability (of research)   An estimate of the consistency of research conditions and procedures

Research   A careful, systematic, patient investigation, using the scientific method, undertaken to discover or verify facts and relationships

Research design   The overall, detailed plan for obtaining, analyzing, and interpreting data

Research hypothesis   A statement of differences or relationships among variables that the investigator expects to discover

Research method   The procedures used to obtain, analyze, and interpret data

Research problem   An educational concern that has been clarified and stated clearly

Research question   The fundamental question or questions that a research project is designed to answer

Retain the hypothesis   Concluding that the evidence one has obtained adequately supports the stated hypothesis

RIE   *Resources in Education,* a publication of ERIC that contains research reports and related documents that have not been published in journals

Sample   A group selected from a much larger population. Usually, it is preferred that the sample distribution be similar to that of the population. Findings made for the sample are often generalized to the population.

Sampling error   Expected chance variations that occur in the selection of samples, which cause the sample to differ somewhat from the population

Scientific method   A procedure commonly used in science that consists of defining a problem, stating the main question or hypothesis, collecting relevant data, and then analyzing those data so as to answer the question or test the hypothesis

Scientific research   A procedure of investigation used to establish facts verifiable through observation and to discover testable relationships among those facts

Secondary data   Information coming not from original sources or eyewitness accounts, but from secondhand reports

Secondary source   Secondhand accounts of events, including scholarly interpretations of work done by others

Semantic differential scale   A scale that presents statements or concepts and calls on respondents to select among seven degrees of difference between pairs of bipolar adjectives such as "effective–ineffective" or "too little–too much"

Semistructured questions   Questions framed to allow respondents some leeway in stating their responses; for example: "How well do you think schools are meeting the needs of diverse ethnic groups?"

Significance level   The odds conventionally used by researchers in tests of significance. Those odds are set at 5 chance recurrences of the finding out of 100 repetitions, on average (the 0.05 probability or significance level), and 1 chance recurrence of the finding out of 100 repetitions, on average (the 0.01 probability or significance level)

Single-theme books   Scholarly books in which the author's original research and commentary are reported

Snowball sample   A sample resulting from initial participants who identify other individuals to participate in a study; see also *chain sample* and *network sample*

Spearman rho   A statistical procedure for determining the correlation between sets of data given in the form of rankings

SSCI   *Social Sciences Citation Index,* an index that lists articles that make reference to specific studies previously done. This indicates importance of the work cited and provides additional literature that investigators might wish to review

Standard deviation   A stable measure of dispersion of scores from the mean. In a normal distribution, 68.26 percent of all scores lie in the area between plus one standard deviation and minus one standard deviation from the mean; 95.40 percent are included between +2 and −2 standard deviations from the mean; and over 99 percent are included between +3 and −3 standard deviations from the mean

Standard error   The standard deviation of the sampling distribution (assuming hundreds of repetitions). Standard error indicates the probable differences between sample measures and their corresponding population values.

Standardized tests Carefully constructed tests accompanied by norms that permit comparisons of individuals

Stanine A conversion of raw scores into nine bands, or stanines, with 5th stanine being average, 9th stanine the highest, and 1st stanine the lowest; the conversion is done to give comparative meanings to raw scores

Statistical significance The very low probability that a particular research finding has occurred because of chance errors made in selecting the sample. Findings that very likely have not occurred by chance are called "significant"

Statistics Numerical values that describe subjects and their behavior or else make inferences about population parameters; also, the mathematical procedures used in making those descriptions and comparisons

Status report A general type of research report that describes people, conditions, and events as they now are, or once were (other general types of reports are difference reports and relationship reports)

Stratified sample A sample selected to reflect accurately the proportions of certain segments of the population, such as gender and ethnic groups. The population segments (strata) are identified, then subjects are randomly selected from them

Structured questions Questions carefully framed to obtain specific information and reduce the diversity among responses; for example: "Do you think today's schools are better, worse, or about the same as they were 20 years ago?"

Style guide A document that explains the style requirements of graduate schools or publishing houses

Subjects A term frequently used to refer to participants in a study, people from whom information is directly obtained

Subquestions Research questions subordinate to the main research question. As subquestions are answered, they contribute to answering the main question.

Survey A procedure that uses interviews or questionnaires to assess opinions, beliefs, and attitudes

Systematic sampling A procedure for obtaining a sample by selecting every nth name from a master list of the population

***T* scores** Conversions made from raw scores that indicate how much a given raw score differs from the mean, in terms of standard deviations; the mean is arbitrarily set at 50 and each standard deviation assigned a value of 10. All T values are, therefore, positive.

***t* test** A statistical procedure used to determine the significance of an observed difference between two means; it compares the difference between means against the standard error of that difference

Tetrachoric correlation A covarying relationship between sets of data when both are expressed as artificial dichotomies

Theory An overall explanation of how large-scale events and relationships probably are, were, or will be, or how and why they came to be as they are

Thesaurus of ERIC Descriptors A publication that lists key terms to facilitate the search of library literature

Threats to validity Conditions or events that may weaken the validity of data. Examples of threats to validity are improper selection of subjects, maturation of subjects over time, and confounding variables that exert undetected influence on the research variables

Treatment condition The independent (X) variable in experimental research. Experimental research determines whether the treatment variable produces an effect in the criterion (Y) variable; also known as *treatment variable*

Type I error Erroneous rejection of the null hypothesis, which leads to the conclusion that a difference or relationship exists among variables when in fact one does not

Type II error Erroneous retention of the null hypothesis, which leads to the conclusion that a difference or relationship does not exist among variables, when in fact one does

UnCover A computer database that displays the tables of contents of journals in all disciplines

Validity (of data) A quality of data that indicates authenticity—that is, the data are in fact what they are purported to be

Validity (of research) A quality of research determined in part by its adherence to conventions that make it easily interpretable, and in part by its generalizability to other groups and settings

Variability The spread that exists within an array of scores or other measurements. Measures of variability include range, standard deviation, and variance

Variable Any characteristic that tends to differ from individual to individual (e.g., height)

***X* variable** The independent (causal, treatment) variable

***Y* variable** The dependent (effect, criterion) variable

***z* scores** Conversions made from raw scores that indicate how much individual raw scores differ from the mean, in terms of standard deviations. Z scores have a mean of zero and a standard deviation of 1 and can, therefore, have positive or negative values

NAME INDEX

Achilles, C., 263–267, 274
Airasian, P., 46, 58, 70, 99, 100, 113, 115, 136, 143, 145, 146, 167, 244, 294, 335, 347
Akers, W., 24
Akey, T., 192
Alkin, M., 91
Allen, J., 136

Babbie, E., 167
Bartz, A., 109, 113, 146, 192
Batt, F., 91
Bauman, J., 136
Best, J., 24, 46, 70, 136, 146, 167, 192
Biklen, S., 167, 244
Blase, J., 230–239, 244
Bogdan, R., 167, 244
Borg, W., 24, 70, 109, 113, 151, 167, 192, 260, 274, 291, 294, 314, 347
Boser, J., 156, 167
Boyd-Zaharias, J., 263–267, 274
Bracht, G., 325, 347
Brandt, R., 46, 274
Broadneck, M., 24
Brown, D., 274
Brown, L., 159, 167
Brown, S., 347
Bruning, J., 314
Bryant, B., 159, 167
Burek, D., 91
Buttlar, L., 91

Campbell, D., 325, 347
Carson, T., 248, 249, 274
Charters, W., 70
Clark, S., 156, 167
Coates, L., 304–306
Cochran-Smith, M., 24, 46
Coleman, J., 314
Connors, B., 248, 249, 274
Cormier, W., 91
Cronk, B., 192
Crowl, T., 46, 136, 347

Dewey, J., 5–6, 24
Dick, B., 249, 274
Donnelly, A., 21, 24
Dover, G., 314
Durm, M., 286–289, 294

Ebert, C., 21, 24
Edyburn, D. L., 46, 52, 70, 91, 113
Eisner, E., 136

Farber, B., 314
Feigl, H., 24
Flake, C., 21, 24
Fleischer, C., 19, 24, 136
Foshay, A., 19, 24
Friedman, I., 314

Gall, J., 24, 70, 109, 113, 151, 167, 192, 260, 274, 291, 294, 314, 347
Gall, M., 24, 70, 109, 113, 151, 167, 192, 260, 274, 291, 294, 314
Gay, L., 46, 58, 70, 99, 100, 113, 115, 136, 143, 145, 146, 167, 244, 294, 335, 347
Ginsburg, A., 49
Glass, G., 136, 325, 347
Glesne, C., 145, 167
Goodson, I., 19, 24
Gravetler, F. J., 105, 113
Green, S., 192
Guba, E., 244
Gullickson, A., 156, 167

Haberman, M., 282–284, 294
Hammill, D., 159, 167
Hopkins, K., 156, 167
Houston, J., 91
Howe, K., 46
Huck, S., 91
Husén, T., 91

Impara, J., 159, 167
Isaacson, L., 274

Jones, F., 38, 46

Kagan, D., 136
Kahn, J., 24, 46, 70, 136, 146, 167, 192
Kelly, K., 337–343, 347
Kounin, J., 38, 46
Krathwohl, D., 24
Kuhs, T., 21, 24
Kutz, E., 113, 136

Lancy, D., 175, 192, 244
Lederman, N., 24, 46
Lesourd, S., 70
Lincoln, Y., 244
Linville, M., 327–332, 347
Lortie, D., 192
Lyne, L. S., 113
Lytle, S., 46

McKenna, B., 263–267, 274
McLaughlin, M., 49
McMillan, J., 24, 59, 136, 159, 167, 192
Mann, T., 70
Manning, G., 274
Mertler, C. A., 159, 167, 192, 314
Meyer, M, 327–332, 347
Mills, G. E., 247, 274

Norusis, M., 192

Ornstein, A., 21, 24

Padak, G., 24, 136
Padak, N., 24, 136
Pajak, E., 230–239, 244
Pajares, M., 113
Pate-Gain, H., 263–267, 274
Patten, M. L., 113
Patton, M., 227, 244
Pearson, J., 21, 24
Peters, R., 24
Piaget, J., 59

Plake, B., 159, 167
Plisko, V., 49
Pollock, J., 113, 151, 167, 192, 244, 314
Postlethwaite, T., 91

Radebaugh, B., 19, 24
Rees, G., 327–332, 347
Reichardt, C., 24
Richardson, V., 19, 24
Rickards, W., 282–284, 294
Ripley, D., 248, 249, 274
Ross, S., 136
Rousey, A. M., 311, 314

Salkind, N., 192
Santa, C., 21, 24, 274
Sawin, E., 46
Schloss, P., 136
Schmidt, T., 46

Schnitzer, S., 254–257, 274
Schubert, W., 24
Schumacher, S., 24, 59
Shaver, J., 109, 110, 113
Shockley, B., 136
Skleder, A., 24
Smith, J., 46
Smith, M., 46, 136
Smits, H., 248, 249, 274
Spies, A., 159, 167
Stanley, J., 325, 347
Stephens, L., 304–306, 314
Stockburger, D. W., 182, 192
Strometz, D., 24

Taylor, D., 99, 113
Thomas, R., 91
Trochim, W. M., 42, 46, 130, 136, 145, 158, 167, 182, 188, 192, 345

Ulibarrí, H., 228, 229, 244

Vannatta, R. A., 192, 314
Vierra, A., 113, 151, 167, 192, 244, 314

Walberg, H., 347
Wallnau, L. B., 105, 113
Wegner, L., 91
Wiersma, W., 115, 116, 136, 225, 244, 294
Winkler, K., 46
Wittrock, M., 91
Wolcott, H. F., 228, 244

Zaharlick, A., 46
Zeuli, J., 113, 136

SUBJECT INDEX

Abstracts, 76, 130, 205
citation of, 100
journals that publish, 78–79
Accessible populations, 145
Accurate disclosure, principle of, 12–13
Action research, 16, 245–260
characteristics of, 246, 248–250, 317
data in, 246, 248
examples of, 250–252, 253–257, 258
focus of, 33, 246, 247–248
organizing for, 246, 257–260
process in, 246, 252–253
strengths and cautions in, 260
topics for, 125
Web site resources for, 258, 270
Age equivalents, 103
Age norms, 103
Alpha level, 109
American Association for Public Opinion Research (AAPOR), 20
American Educational Research Association (AERA), 20, 52, 82, 148
American Psychological Association (APA), 100
Amorphous topic, 56
Analysis, 37–38, 126, 140. *See also* Data analysis
meanings of, 153–154
Analysis criteria, 280
Analysis of Variance (ANOVA), 105–106, 186, 368
Answer selection, 280
Anthropology, 224, 225
APA Manual, 100
Appendix, in reports, 205
Applied research, 29
Articles. *See also* Abstracts
citations for, 96, 97, 100
journal, 205, 208–210

magazine, 73, 75
newspaper, 205, 208–210
Artificial dichotomy, 302
Assumptions, 66
Authenticity, 39–40
Authority, 4

Back material, 205
Basic research, 28
Believability, 39–40
Bell-shaped curve. *See* Normal probability curve
Beneficence, principle of, 11–12, 13
Bias, 18
Bibliography. *See* Citations, bibliography
Bilingual Educationa Database, 80
Bilingualism, 33
Biserial correlation, 302
Bivariate correlation, 302
Books
citations for, 96–97
reference, 73, 76
scholarly, 73, 75
single-theme, 75
style guides, 205–206
Books in Print, 75, 80
Broad topics, 55
Budget, 66, 115, 118

Case studies, 291–293
organizing and conducting, 292–293
purposes of, 291–292
Causal-comparative research, 315, 316, 318–319, 333–336
conducting, 335–336
example of, 336–343
nature of, 333–335
topics for, 33–34, 125
Web site resources for, 344
Cause–effect relationships, 29
cautions concerning, 298–299
correlation and, 107

search for, 5, 297, 298, 317
CD-ROM, 78, 80, 83
Central tendency. *See* Measures of central tendency
Charts, 202
Child Development Abstracts and Bibliography, 78
Chi-square, 104–105, 106, 362–363
Citations
for articles, 96–97, 100
formats for, 100
in literature reviews, 100
Citations, bibliography, 76, 94, 205
Clarifying the topic, 56
Classroom environment, 49
Classroom management, 49
Cluster sampling, 126, 143
Coefficient of correlation, 107, 300, 301, 312, 355
Collection of data. *See* Data collection
Commonsense approach, 4
Communication, effective, 50
Comparative content analysis, 261
Comparison group, 318
Comparison reports, 103–106
Comparisons, 98
Computer assistance, 72
Computer Search, 80
Conclusions, 8, 62, 129, 130, 204–205
identifying the writer's, 95
Conferencing, 50
Confidence intervals, 181
Confidence limits, 363–365
Confidentiality, principle of, 10–11, 13
Confounding variables, 18–19, 28
Consistency, in style, 197
Constants, 26
Consumer's Guide to Tests in Print, A (Hamill et al.), 159
Contextualization, 226
Continuous variables, 26–27

Control group, 321
Convenience sampling, 126, 143
Conventions, 193, 194–195
  of format, 198–205
  of style, 195–198
Converted scores, 102, 180, 355
Correlational reports, 106–108
Correlational research, 32, 295–313
  assessing and quantifying the
    variables, 309–310
  data in, 301, 310, 312, 355–356
  examples of, 303–306, 307
  hypotheses and questions in,
    299–300, 309, 317
  nature of, 298
  organizing for, 306–312
  selecting a sample, 310
  selecting the variables, 308
  topics for, 125, 299
  Web site resources for, 307, 311
Correlational research design,
  300–301
Correlations, 106–107, 182,
  297–298
  among variables, 206, 296,
    297–298, 349
  biserial and point-biserial, 302
  bivarate, 302
  coefficient of, 107–108, 300, 301,
    312, 355
  multivariate, 302–303
  Pearson product-moment, 180,
    301–302
  phi and tetrachoric, 302
  positive and negative, 107, 356
  from rankings, 302
  significance of, 181, 361
Covarying relationships, 98
Credibility
  of data, 151
  principle of, 18
Criteria, 127
Criterion-referenced tests, 158
Criterion variables, 296, 303, 3
  08, 309
Criticism, external and internal,
  39–40, 151
Cronbach's alpha reliability,
  150–151

Cross-sectional survey, 154
*Current Index to Journals in
  Education (CIJE),* 49, 61, 76,
  78, 80, 83, 93, 122, 123

Data, 8. *See also* Data analysis; Data
  collection
  availability of, 17
  credibility of, 151, 182
  identifying needed, 124–126
  non-test, 148
  practicality of, 18
  primary, 35–36
  qualitative and quantitative, 42
  qualities required in, 39–41
  reliability of, 151, 229, 17150
  secondary, 35–36
  sources of, 35–36, 140
  terminology in, 42–44
  test, 148
  treatment and presentation of,
    41–42, 182
Data analysis, 16, 115. *See also
  specific types of research*
  matching to type of research, 170
  procedures for, 18, 115,
    128–129, 169
Databases, 80
Data collection, 138–166. *See also
  specific types of research*
  matching to type of research,
    161–162
  methods and procedures in,
    37–39, 115, 126–127, 151–161
  tools needed for, 127
  validity and reliability in,
    148–151
Data collection profile, 139
Definition of terms, in reports, 199
Degrees of freedom, 367
Delimitations of the study, 66, 118,
  119, 199
Department of Education (ED),
  U.S., 52
Department of Health and Human
  Services, U.S., 20
Dependent variables, 28, 34
Descriptions, 126, 140, 152–153
Descriptive research, 31–32, 276

data in, 277, 279–281
examples of, 278, 281–284,
  285–289
hypotheses and questions in, 277
nature of, 277–281
organizing for, 290–291
purpose in, 277
topics for, 125, 177, 277
Web site resources for, 285
Descriptive statistics, 179–188,
  357–358
  calculation and interpretation in,
    351–357
Descriptors, 80, 122
Deviation score, 352
Dichotomous variables, 26–27
Dichotomy, 302
Difference between means, 105, 106
Digest of Educational Statistics, 79
Direct costs, 66
Directional research hypotheses,
  57, 58
Directories, 72, 123
Discrete variables, 26–27
Discriminant analysis, 303
Discussions, 62, 204–205
Dispersion, terms indicating, 102
*Dissertation Abstracts International
  (DAI),* 78, 80, 123
Dissertations, 204
Diversity, terms indicating, 101–102
Documents, 36, 38, 141
  citation of, 100
Drawings, 202

EBSCO Academic Journal and
  Abstract Database, xxv,
  xxvii–xxviii
Ecological validity, 326
Educational Leadership, 75
Educational research, 3, 9.
  *See also specific types of
  research*
  guiding priciples of, 21–22
  meaning of, 6–7
  orientation to, 1–22
  planning, 115–116, 135
  preliminary skills needed for,
    47–111

procedures for specific types of, 224–344

process of, 7

published, locating, 71–89

rules of operation in, 9–19

sources of data for, 140

types of, 139, 161–162, 163–165

Educational Resources Information Center (ERIC), 76–86

publications of, 76, 77–78, 80

searching Online, 83–86

Education Index, 49, 61, 80

Educators, as researchers, 19–21

Educator's Reference Desk, 83–86

Electronic journals, 82

Electronic References, 100

E-mail communications, 52

citation of, 100

Encyclopedia of Educational Research, 73, 74, 76

EndNote, 100

Equivalent forms method, 150

ERIC. *See* Educational Resources Information Center (ERIC)

ERIC databases, 122

Error

estimation of, 180, 360

standard, 349, 363–365

Type I and Type II, 368–369

Ethical principles, 11–14

Ethics, 20, 54, 118

Ethnographic research, 31, 224–243

appeal of, 228

data in, 163, 173–175, 226, 227

example of, 229–239

nature of, 225–229

organizing for, 239–242

procedures in, 226

strengths and concerns of, 229

topics for, 125, 226, 227

Ethnography, 225

Evaluation, 50

Evaluation research, 245–247, 260–272

data in, 246, 261, 271

example of, 262–267

focus of, 33, 317

methods, materials, and programs in, 261–262

organizing for, 246, 267–272

topics for, 125

Web site resources for, 268, 270

Exceptional Child Education Resources, 80

Experimental designs, 317, 320–323, 324–325

Experimental group, 321

Experimental research, 315

cause and effect in, 315, 316, 317–318, 319

example of, 326–332

fundamentals of, 29, 34, 319–324

random selection and assignment in, 319

topics for, 125

use of, 319–320

Web site resources for, 332–333

Ex post facto research, 333–334

External criticism, 39–40, 149–150

External validity, 325–326

Extraneous variables, 28

Fact, versus truth, 5

Factor analysis, 303

Factorial designs, 321–322

Factors, 322

Family Educational Rights and Privacy Act (Buckley Amendment), 10

Federal Policy for the Protection of Human Subjects, 20

Fifteenth Mental Measurements Yearbook, 159

Figures, 202–203, 205

Findings (results), 62, 128–129, 130, 204–205

presentation of, 8, 188–191, 201, 204–205

significance of, 361, 349

statement of, 201

Formats, report, 61–62, 129–131, 194

conventions of, 198–205, 206

Front material, 205

Full disclosure, 13

Generalizability, principle of, 15–16

Grade equivalents, 102, 103

Grade norms, 102

Grade point average (GPA), 32, 364

Graphic summaries, 129

Graphs, 202

Guides, 123, 127

Handbook of Research on Teaching, 74

Handbooks of research, 74

Historical research, 15, 31, 276

data in, 277, 279–281

examples of, 278, 285–289

hypotheses and questions in, 277

nature of, 277–281

organizing for, 290–291

purpose of, 277

topics for, 125, 277

treatment and analysis of data, 281

Holding factors, 116

Holistic perspective, 225–226, 229

Honesty, principle of, 12

Human subjects research approval, 12

Hypotheses, 7–8, 203

examples of, 7–8

null, 57, 58, 66, 104, 106, 109, 121–122, 172, 362

in research proposals, 48, 55, 57, 58, 121–122

retaining a, 109

stating, 117–122

testing, 128, 334

theories versus, 59, 199

types of, 57

working, 115

Hypothetico-inductive analysis, 175

Importance, principle of, 15

Importance of the study, 118–119

Independent variables, 28, 34

Indexes, 77, 80, 123

Indirect costs, 66

Inferential statistics, 179–188

calculating and interpreting, 360–361

Informants, 36, 141, 280

Information. *See* Data; Primary sources; Secondary sources

Information organizers, 2
Ingenta, 80, 81
Ingenta Select, 80, 81
Instructional materials, 49
Instructional methods, 50
Interim analysis, 174
Internal consistency, 150
Internal criticism, 39, 40, 151
Internal validity, 325–326
Interval scales, 160
Intervening variables, 28
Interviews, 38, 154, 279
Introduction, in reports, 62, 115, 130, 198

Journal articles, 205, 208–210
Judgmental sampling, 143

Kendall tau, 302
Kuder-Richardson (KR) reliability, 150–151

Language, simplicity of, 197
Leadership, effective, 51
Legal principles, 10–11
Library
    primary sources in, 76–86
    secondary sources in, 73–76, 123
    skills for locating information in, 72–73, 87–88
Likert scale, 156
Limitations of the study, 66, 118, 119, 199
LISTSERV, 53
Literature, surveying, 66
Literature reviews, 130
    of related topics, 199–200
    writing, 99–100
Logico-inductive analysis, 171, 175
Longitudinal survey, 154–155

Magazine articles, 73, 75
Main question, 119
    Masters' theses. *See also*
        Research report
    format conventions for, 204, 218–220
    sample pages for, 211–217
Mean, 101, 103, 179, 351

Measurement, 39, 127, 140, 160–161
Measures of central tendency, 101, 179, 351–352. *See also* Mean; Median; Mode
Measures of relationship, 180
Measures of variability, 179, 352–355
Measuring devices, 127
Median, 101, 103, 179, 351
Meta-analysis, 36
Method, 62, 115, 130, 201
MINITAB, 183
Mode, 101, 103, 179, 352
Multiple regression, 303
Multistage sampling, 145
Multivariate correlations, 302–303
MYSTAT, 183

Narrowing the topic, 56
National Research Act of 1974, 10
Natural dichotomy, 302
Naturalistic observation, 227
Negative correlation, 107
Network or chain sampling, 144
Newspaper Abstracts, 76, 80
Newspaper articles, 73, 75
Nominal scales, 160
Nondirectional research hypotheses, 57, 58
Nonexperimental research, 29–30
Nonparametric statistics, 350–351
Nonparticipant observer, 226
Nonprobability sampling, 143–146
Normal probability curve, 351, 357–358, 364
    relative standings and, 358–360
Norm-referenced tests, 158–159
Norms, 102
Notation, 37, 126, 152
Note-taking software, 96
Not significant, 109
NSSE Yearbooks, 73–74
Null hypotheses, 57, 58, 66, 104, 106, 109, 121–122, 172, 362

Objects, 36, 38, 140
Office of Human Research Protections (OHRP), 20

Online test locators, 159
Online Writing Lab, 99
Open-ended question, 155, 280
Operating rules of research, 9–19
Opinions, 140
Ordinal scales, 160
Organismic variables, 28
Outline, library search, 122–124

Parameters, 176–177, 350
Parametric statistics, 350–351, 357
Paraphrasing, 99
Parsimony, principle of, 18
Partial correlation, 302–303
Participant observer, 226
Participants, research, 10, 36, 43, 140
Pearson product-moment correlation, 180, 301–302
Percentile rank, 103, 180, 355, 359
Periodical Abstracts, 76, 80
Person, 195–196
Personological variables, 326
Phi correlation, 302
Philosophical principles, 15–16
Plagiarism, avoiding, 99–100
Point-biserial correlation, 302
Populations, 43, 176–177, 349–350
    accessible, 145
    target, 145
Population validity, 326
Positive correlation, 107
Post hoc fallacy, 298–299
Posttest only with nonequivalent groups, 323–324
Practicality, 28–29
Practical significance, 187
Predictions, 5, 312, 356
Predictor variables, 196, 303, 308, 309
Pretest–posttest with nonequivalent groups, 324
Primary data, 35–36
Primary sources, 35–36, 72
    in the library, 76–86
    locating, 79–80
    for professional development, 88–89
    specific directories of, 77

Privileged observer, 226
Probability, 16
Probability levels, 109
Probability sampling, 142–143, 144, 145
Problem, research, 7, 47, 55, 56, 119
Problem statement, 47, 117–122, 165, 199
Procedural principles, 16–19
Procedures, 8, 36, 38, 66, 140
Product-moment correlation, 301–302
Professional development, 88–89
Projects. *See* Research projects
Protection, principle of, 10, 13
Psychological Abstracts, 76, 78, 80, 93
Publication Manual of the American Psychological Association, 100, 130
Public relations, effective, 51
Purposive sampling, 143

Qualitative data, 42, 128
  analysis of, 128, 170–172, 175–176
  validity of, 149
Qualitative research, 29
  planning, 115
  Web site resources for, 241–242
Quantitative data, 42, 128
  analysis of, 128, 170–172, 176–177
  validity of, 149
Quantitative research, 29, 34
  planning, 116
Quasi-experimental designs, 323–325
Quasi-experimental research, 315, 316, 318
  cause and effect in, 319
  fundamentals of, 319–324
  random selection and assignment in, 319
Questioning, 38, 127, 154–157
Questionnaire, 127, 155, 280
Questions
  main, 119
  open-ended, 155, 280

research, 7–8, 26, 30–35, 48, 55, 57, 65, 119, 120, 128, 199, 203
  seeking answers to, 3–4
  semistructured, 155
  stating, 117–122
  structures, 155
  subquestions, 119
Quota sampling, 145
Quoting, 99

Random assignment, 319, 350
Randomization, 116
Random sampling, 15, 126, 142
Range, 102, 179
Rankings
  correlations from, 302, 356
  percentile, 359
Rating scales, 127
Raw numbers, 101
Raw scores, 101, 102, 103
Recording devices, 37, 127
Records, 36, 141
Reference books, 73, 76
Reference sections, 130
Rejecting the null hypothesis, 109
Relationship, measures of, 180
Relationships. *See* Correlations
Relative position, 355
Relative standing, 103, 180, 358–360
Reliability, 39, 40–41
  of data, 150, 229
  in data collection, 148–151
  of non-test data, 151
  relationship to validity, 151
  of test data, 150–151
Relics, 38
Replicability, 16
Reports. *See* Research reports
Research. *See* Educational research
Researchability, principle of, 17–18
Research data. *See* Data
Research design, 116. *See also* Research project; Research reports
Researchers, educators as, 19–21
Research findings. *See* Findings (results)

Research hypotheses. *See* Hypotheses
Research language, fundamentals of, 98
Research methods, 26, 29–30
Research Methods Knowledge Base (Trochim), 42
Research Navigator™, xxv–xxix, 240, 258, 268, 285, 307, 332, 344
Research plan. *See* Educational research
Research problem. *See* Problem, research
Research project. *See also* Research design
  analyzing data for, 168–191
  designing a, 114–135
  example of planning, 131–135
  gathering data for, 137–165
  preparing the report, 193–222
  presenting findings, 188–191
Research proposal, 48, 65–68
Research questions, 7–8, 26, 55, 57, 65, 199, 203, 299
  phrasing, 48
Research reports
  comparisons in, 98, 103–106
  conventions in, 194–198
  correlational, 106–107
  format for, 61–62, 129–131, 194, 198–205
  guidelines for, 130
  organizing with *TakeNote!,* 207
  outline of format conventions, 206–207
  preparing, 193–222
  reading, 93–98
  sample pages, 208–222
  skimming information in, 93–95
  summarizing, 95–98
  title, 195
  understanding, 98
Resources in Education (RIE), 61, 78, 80, 83, 123
Results. *See* Findings
Retaining a hypothesis, 109
Review of Educational Research, 75

Review of Research in Education, 74, 76
Reviews
  of research, 73
  as a secondary source, 77
Rival explanations, principle of, 18–19

Samples, 145, 349, 350
  in correlational research, 310
  necessity for, 141–142
  representative, 15, 36, 142, 176–177, 178
  size of, 146–147
  types and selection of, 141–146.
    See also Sampling
Sampling, 43, 126, 141–146
  cluster, 126, 143
  convenience, 126, 143
  judgmental, 143
  multistage, 145
  network or chain, 144
  nonprobability, 143–146
  probability, 142–143, 144, 145
  purposive, 143
  quota, 145
  random, 15, 126, 142
  snowball, 144–145
  stratified, 126, 142
  systematic, 143
Sampling error, 109, 177, 178
Scholarly books, 73, 75
Scholarly journals, 206
Scientific method, 4, 5–6, 118
  questions concerning, 17
  research and, 6–9
Scientific research, 6
Scores, 140
  converted, 102, 180, 355
  deviation, 352
  raw, 101, 102, 103
Search engines, 52
Secondary data, 35–36
Secondary sources, 35–36, 72
  in the library, 73–76, 123
  locating, 76
Semantic differential scale, 156
Semistructured question, 155
Settings, 36, 140

Significance, 358
  concept of, 108–111
  of correlation, 181, 361
  of difference between means, 181, 361
  of findings, 361, 349
  practical, 187
  statistical, 108, 178, 187
  testing for, 181, 366–368
Single-group pretest-treatment-posttest design, 320–321
Single-participant measurement-treatment-measurement design, 322–323
Single-theme books, 75
Skimming, 93–95
Snowball sampling, 144–145
Social Science Citation Index (SSCI), 79, 80
Sociological Abstracts, 80
Spearman rho, 302
Special Interest Groups (SIGs), 5282
Split-half method, 150
Spread, terms indicating, 101–102
Standard deviation, 102, 103, 180, 353, 357, 358
Standard error, 349, 363–365
Standardized tests, 159, 281
Standard nine, 103
Stanines, 103, 180, 355, 359
StatCrunch, 183–185
Statement of the problem, 118, 119, 199
Statements, 17–22, 140
  tentative versus definitive, 196–197
Statistical analysis, 37, 182
Statistical Analysis System (SAS), 183
Statistical Package for the Social Sciences (SPSS), 183, 353–354
Statistical significance, 108, 187
Statistical tests, 128, 188
Statistics, 177, 348–369
  cautions in using, 187
  concepts and procedures, 348–369
  descriptive, 179–188, 351–357
  inferential, 179–188, 360–361

interpreting, 98–108
  multiple meanings of, 177, 348
  nature and uses of, 348–349
  parametric and nonparametric, 350–351, 357
  uses for, 177–179
  Web site resources for, 182, 183–186
Status, 98
Status reports, 100–103
Stratified sampling, 126, 142
Structured question, 155
Style
  consistency in, 195, 197
  conventions of, 195–198
  writing, 195–198
Style guides, 205–206
Subjects, 140
Subquestions, 57, 119
Summaries. *See also* Abstracts
  graphic, 129
  tabular, 129
Summarizing, 95–98, 99
Sum of squares, 353
Supervision, effective, 50
Surveys, 38, 154
  cross-sectional, 154
  longitudinal, 154–155
Systematic sampling, 143

Table of contents, 205
Tables, 202–203, 205
Tabular summaries, 129
TakeNote!, 207
  using to organize a research report, 371–381
Target populations, 145
Tense, 196
Terminology, 98, 103, 106, 107–108, 369
Testing, 127, 157–160
  for data collection, 127
  reliability of data in, 150–151
  validity of data in, 148
Test locators, online, 159
Test-retest method, 150
Tests
  criterion-referenced, 158
  norm-referenced, 158–159

standardized, 159, 281
statistical, 128, 188
Tetrachoric correlation, 302
Textbooks, 75
Theories, 59
Thesaurus of ERIC Descriptors,
    78, 122
Theses. *See* Research reports
Threats to validity, 325–326
Time calendar, 66
Time schedule, 115, 118
Time series design, 324
Title, 195
Title page, 205
Topics
    for action research, 125
    for administrators, 50
    amorphous, 56
    broad, 55
    for causal-comparative
        research, 125
    clarifying, 56
    for correlational research, 125, 299
    for descriptive research, 125,
        177, 277
    for educators, 51
    for ethnographic research, 125,
        226, 227
    for evaluation research, 125
    for graduate research, 11, 15
    for historical research, 125, 277
    narrowing, 56

preliminary considerations in
    selecting, 51
refining, 47, 54–55, 63–65, 67
regulating the size of, 60–61
rewording, 17
sources for, 52–53
stating, 117–122
for teachers, 49–51
terminology, 55–60
where to find good, 49–51
Tradition, 4
Treatment condition, 318
T scores
t test, 105
Two-group pretest-treatment-
    posttest design, 321
Two-group treatment-posttest-only
    design, 321
Type I errors, 368–369
Type II errors, 368–369

UnCover, 80, 81

Validity, 39, 40–41
    in data collection, 148–151
    ecological, 326
    population, 326
    relationship to reliability, 151
    of test data, 148
    threats to, 325–326
Variables, 26
    confounding, 18–19, 28

continuous, 26–27
correlations among, 297, 349
criterion, 296, 303, 308, 309
dependent, 28, 34
dichotomous, 26–27
discrete, 26–27
in educational research, 26–28
extraneous, 28
independent, 28, 34
intervening, 28
organismic, 28
personological, 326
predictor, 296, 303, 308, 309
Variance, 180
    calculation of, 353
Verbal description, 37
Voice, 195–196

Web citations, within the
    document, 100
Working design, 115
Working hypothesis, 115
Writing style, 99, 195–198
    consistency in, 197

X variable, 303, 318

Y variable, 303, 318

Z, criterion variable, 303
Z scores, 359